PUBLIC HISTORY
AND THE ENVIRONMENT

We dedicate this book to our graduate students, who over the years have challenged, inspired, and pushed us to think about the intersections between public and environmental history.

In memory of my nephew, Christopher Ryan Scarpino, 1976–1995.

PUBLIC HISTORY
AND THE ENVIRONMENT

Edited By

Martin V. Melosi
University of Houston
and
Philip V. Scarpino
Indiana University/Purdue University, Indianapolis

KRIEGER PUBLISHING COMPANY
Malabar, Florida
2004

Original Edition 2004

Printed and Published by
KRIEGER PUBLISHING COMPANY
KRIEGER DRIVE
MALABAR, FLORIDA 32950

Library of Congress Cataloging-in-Publication Data

Public history and the environment / edited by Martin V. Melosi and Philip V. Scarpino.
    p. cm.—(Public history series)
  Includes bibliographical references and index.
    ISBN 1-57524-071-8 (alk. paper)
    1. Environmental sciences—History.   2. Environmental protection—History.
  I. Melosi, Martin V., 1947-   II. Scarpino, Philip V. III. Series.

GE50.P83 2004
333.7′2′09—dc21
                                                                    2003054586

    10   9   8   7   6   5   4   3   2

CONTENTS

ACKNOWLEDGMENTS

This book had a very long period of gestation from concept to finished manuscript, and along the way, we were the beneficiaries of advice and assistance from numerous individuals. The original idea for a book that examined intersections between public history and environmental history came from Martin Melosi. Following his presidential address to the National Council on Public History in 1994, he was approached by Mary Roberts, of Krieger Publishing Company, and the concept that became *Public History and the Environment* grew out of that first meeting. Melosi invited Philip Scarpino to coedit, and we drafted a precis and circulated it widely for comment. Many people made helpful suggestions, but we especially want to thank colleagues who took the time to provide us with significant, detailed critiques of the early drafts, including Craig Colten, Rebecca Conard, Edward Hawes, Christopher Clarke, Lisa Mighetto, Alan Newell, Patrick O'Bannon, Martin Reuss, and Joel Tarr. The final plan for *Public History and the Environment* benefited greatly from the insights that they provided.

We recruited a first-class group of authors, who stuck with us as the book progressed more slowly than we had originally promised. All of them accepted our editorial comments and requests with good humor and professionalism, and they willingly redrafted chapters as we encouraged them to find their own voices with which to tell their stories. Many of the chapters use the first person, as authors acting upon our requests examined the interplay between public and environmental history through the lens of their own professional experiences. We thank each of the authors for their contributions to this volume and for staying with the project.

Krieger Publishing has encouraged and supported this book from the beginning. Barbara Howe and James Gardner served as series editors. Mary Roberts has been a consistent and helpful supporter and backer of *Public History and the Environment*. Elaine Rudd provided significant editorial oversight.

This has been a collaborative venture in the best sense of that term. We learned a great deal from each other and from the diverse group of authors who contributed chapters to the volume. We hope that the work of the authors will encourage readers to think creatively about the issues, problems, possibilities, and challenges that exist at the intersections between environmental history and public history.

INTRODUCTION

Environmental history is one of the most creative and innovative academic fields to appear in many decades. Its main objective is to treat the relationship between humans and their physical environment over time. This breadth and scale compels practitioners to study the past through an understanding of science, environmentalism, and history, and to ask grand questions of its data. However, environmental history as practiced by academics has not yet achieved a strong public voice, despite the fact that several environmental historians have solid records as environmental advocates. In essence, those in the field have not discovered many dependable paths along which to reach laypersons, the policy community, or the environmental movement itself.

The production of good scholarly books and articles alone cannot insure a following among a variety of intended audiences. Nor does it guarantee that policy makers, business leaders, or environmentalists will act upon the "lessons of history." Similarly, the practice of environmental history in the hands of public historians has yet to successfully meld a significant amount of the prevailing academic research with efforts to reach a variety of potential audiences. The merging of the scholarly expertise of the environmental historian and the attention to audience suggests many exciting possibilities yet unrealized.

Public History and the Environment includes original essays written by public and academic historians with working experience on topics relevant to the theme of the book. It describes and analyzes the linkage between public history and the environment, with special attention to the ways in which historical modes and methods are and can be further utilized to deal with current environmental issues and problems; and (2) it treats some of the ways that historians present environmental issues to the public and suggests news ways to do so.

This volume also offers an opportunity to merge the fields of environmental and public history theoretically, thus providing public historians with a broader perspective on their day-to-day research and writing. It also serves to demonstrate the vast opportunities available to environmental historians who choose to practice their craft in the public realm.

Public history and environmental history are relatively new fields of study. Although public historians have been around for decades, it was not until the late 1970s that public history developed into a self-conscious field with a rapidly growing body of literature, graduate and undergraduate training programs, and expanding opportunities for historians outside of the academy. Although the academic job crisis provided early motivation for the expansion of the field, public history has matured far beyond a quest for alternative employment.

Public history is not a discrete field of study; instead, it has become a way of thinking about and practicing the craft that emphasizes the skills that are common to all good history: research, analysis and interpretation, and communication. Public historians do, however, pay a great deal of attention to communication—to the audiences with whom they communicate and the ways that they communicate with those audiences.

Public historians have also proven adept at finding and developing new niches; one of those is in the area of the environment. Some scholars and practitioners go even farther and contend that communication should be two way, opening up the possibility of collaboration between professional historians and the public. The environment of any particular place—farmscapes, suburbs, cities—is a legacy of past attitudes and actions.

People also share the environment in the present, even though their experiences may differ significantly as a result of variables such as ethnicity, occupation, race, class, and gender. Therefore, public history that attempts to involve people in a conversation about the creation of place over time, the meaning of place in the present, and interaction with place in the future, may go a long way toward creating an environmental history that is used and useful.

Environmental history emerged in the 1960s with the birth of the modern ecology movement. It was strongly influenced by the political and social goals of environmental activism, and members of the academic community dismissed it as a "fad." More seriously, some historians charged that environmental history was "advocate history." But historian Donald Worster answered the charge effectively by arguing that "Environmental history was . . . born out of a moral purpose, with strong political commitments behind it, but also became, as it matured, a scholarly enterprise that had neither any simple, nor any single, moral or political agenda to promote."[1]

Early attempts to define environmental history, nonetheless, relied heavily on the outlook of the environmental movement of the late 1960s and early 1970s. Over time, environmental historians have come to depend on an interdisciplinary approach to their research. Environmental history in the broadest sense is about the role and place of the physical environment in the life of humans. And no other field of history, as John Opie stated, "has a legacy from and obligation toward natural science."[2]

Initially, most environmental historians concentrated on "nature" or on the degradation of the natural world as a result of human actions. Recently, as the field has matured, historians are more likely to define nature as a cultural construction and environment in a way that embraces the whole complex, interdependent, and intertwined blend of human and physical elements that makes up our surroundings. This point of view has created some very fertile intellectual ground at the intersection between public and environmental history.

Environmental history in the hands of public history practitioners needs to be viewed not so much as a field of study—such as social history, urban history, or political history—but as a *mode of thinking:* a tool for studying human interaction with the physical environment (natural and built) that emphasizes communication and audience. This requires looking at history in three-dimensional terms, beyond a flat line of chronology where the emphasis on *time* is broadened to incorporate a greater appreciation of *place* (space). Landscapes as well as written documents are essential research tools for the study of environmental history in the public realm.

While the uses of environmental history in the hands of public historians are not as well developed as they could be, environmental issues and problems are providing an ever-increasing volume of work in the areas of cultural resources management, environmental remediation, litigation support, museums and archives, and policy analysis.

"Environmental history is a natural field of interest for public historians." So noted Martin Reuss, Shelley Bookspan, Craig Colten, and Michal McMahon in a 1991 issue of *ASEH (American Society for Environmental History) News*. They based this observation on the notions that (1) "public historians are generally anxious to use history to provide context and insight to discussions on contemporary questions, and hardly any question today generates more interest and activity than the future of the environment"; and (2) "environmental history, properly understood, requires some multidisciplinary knowledge" (which informs much of the work of public historians).[3] These observations suggest a sound basis for linking public history and environmental history.

This current volume includes original essays on a variety of themes at the intersection of environmental history and public history. Rebecca Conard and David Glassberg discuss built and natural landscapes. Lisa Mighetto, Carol Shull and Dwight Pitcaithley, and Hal Rothman examine aspects of cultural resources management, namely researching endangered species, the maturation of the National Park Service, and heritage tourism. Alan Newell and Craig Colten focus on expert witnessing and hazardous waste remediation respectively. Museums, media and historical societies are treated in essays by Christopher Clarke, Philip Scarpino, Char Miller, and Robert Archibald. Martin Reuss and Hugh Groman explore policy analysis. And finally Christopher Foreman, Martin Melosi, and Susan Flader look at environment at the grassroots.

Public History and the Environment is the first book of its kind. It should be a useful addition to the dialogue surrounding the role of public history in a variety of settings. It also should help to broaden the perspective about the practical application of research in environmental history beyond academic walls, and therefore appeal to public and academic historians, history students, environmentalists, social scientists, and those interested in policy making.

NOTES

1. Donald Worster, "Doing Environmental History," in Donald Worster, ed., *The Ends of the Earth* (New York: Cambridge University Press, 1988), pp. 290–91.
2. John Opie, "Environmental History: Pitfalls and Opportunities, "*Environmental Review* 7 (1983):10.
3. "Environmental History and Public Historians, "*ASEH News* 2 (September, 1991): 1.

CONTRIBUTORS

Robert R. Archibald is president of the Missouri Historical Society in St. Louis, Missouri, who regularly serves as a consultant to museums and historical associations. He writes and speaks on pertinent topics in history and on issues regarding the humanities, memory, environmental responsibility, community values, and museum practices. His most recent book is *A Place to Remember: Using History to Build Community* (1999). A collection of his talks and essays was published in 2003.

Christopher Clarke is an independent exhibition developer and consulting historian. He holds M.A. and Ph.D. degrees in history from the University of Rochester and has taught American history at the SUNY College at Buffalo and at Vassar College. From 1990 to 1997, he served as a staff historian at Strong Museum in Rochester, NY. Since he began consulting full time in 1998, Dr. Clarke has created exhibitions and interpretive plans for a diverse group of museums and for sites operated by the National Park Service. He is also the author of several publications on the subject of exhibition development and museum interpretation.

Craig E. Colten is professor and chair of the Department of Geography and Anthropology at Louisiana State University. He spent ten years directing research projects on historical industrial waste management practices for the Illinois Hazardous Waste Research and Information Center. Much of that work is summarized in the co-authored book *Road to Love Canal* (1996). He has been an expert witness or consulting expert in over twenty-five hazardous waste law suits. His research presently focuses on human-environment interactions in New Orleans and it has appeared in *Transforming New Orleans and Its Environs* (2000), *Environmental History,* and the *Journal of Historical Geography.*

Rebecca Conard co-directs the public history graduate program at Middle Tennessee State University, where she also teaches American environmental history. In addition to teaching, she has co-founded two historical consulting firms, PHR Associates (California) and Tallgrass Historians L.C. (Iowa), specializing in historic preservation and cultural resources management services. Conard is the author of *Places of Quiet Beauty: Parks, Preserves, and Environmentalism* (1997) and *Benjamin Shambaugh and the Intellectual Foundations of Public History* (2002). She served as president of the National Council on Public History in 2002–2003.

Susan Flader is professor of history at the University of Missouri-Columbia, where she teaches environmental history and the history of Missouri and the American West. She has published widely on Aldo Leopold, including *Thinking Like a Mountain* (1974/1994) and *The River of the Mother of God* (1991), and edited *The Great Lakes Forest* (1983), *Exploring Missouri's Legacy* (1992), and *Toward Sustainability for Missouri Forests* (2002). She served as president of the American Society for Environmental History and the Missouri Parks Association, and on the boards of other national and state organizations. She has received numerous awards for conservation action.

Christopher H. Foreman is professor of public policy in the School of Public Affairs at the University of Maryland. He previously was senior fellow in the Governmental Studies program at the Brookings Institution. His writings focus on the politics of regulation, public health, and governmental reform, and include *The African American Predicament* (1999), *The Promise and Peril of Environmental Justice* (1998), *Plagues, Products and Politics* (1994), and *Signals from the Hill* (1988), which won the D. B. Hardeman Prize from the Lyndon B. Johnson Library. Foreman chaired the editorial advisory board for *PS: Political Science and Politics* and the American Political Science Association's Committee on the Status of African Americans in the Profession, and is on the board of governors of The Nature Conservancy.

David Glassberg is professor of history at the University of Massachusetts, Amherst, where he teaches courses in public history and American environmental history. Trained as a cultural historian, Glassberg's research explores the ways that a community's perceptions of its history and its environment are intertwined and change over time. Among his publications are *Sense of History: The Place of the Past in American Life* (2001) and *American Historical Pageantry: The Uses of Tradition in the Early 20th Century* (1990).

Hugh Gorman is associate professor of environmental history and policy at Michigan Technological University, where he teaches courses in environmental history and environmental decision making. He is especially interested in the interaction between complex technological systems and the environment. He is the author of *Redefining Efficiency: Pollution Concerns, Regulatory Mechanisms, and Technological Change in the U.S. Petroleum Industry* (2001).

Martin V. Melosi is Distinguished University Professor of History and director of the Institute for Public History at the University of Houston. He also held the Fulbright Chair in American Studies at the University of Southern Denmark (2000–01). He is author and editor of ten books and more than 50 articles and book chapters, including *Effluent America: Cities, Industry, Energy, and the Environment* (2001) and the award-winning *The Sanitary City*. Melosi is past president of the American Society for Environmental History, the National Council on Public History, and the Public Works Historical Society. He is also a partner in History International, LLC and on the board of directors of Historical Research Associates, Inc.

Lisa Mighetto received her Ph.D. from the University of Washington, with a specialty in environmental history. She is director of the History Division at Historical Research Associates, Inc., where her research includes endangered species, changes in habitat conditions, hazardous waste contamination, and Native American treaty rights. Currently she serves on the editorial board of *The Public Historian* and the *Pacific Northwest Quarterly,* and is secretary and newsletter editor of the American Society for Environmental History. Her books include *Muir Among the Animals* (1986), *Wild Animals and American Environmental Ethics* (1991), and *Hard Drive to the Klondike* (2002).

Char Miller is professor and chair of the history department of Trinity University, and director of its Urban Studies program. He is author of *Gifford Pinchot and the Making of Modern Environmentalism* (2001), winner of the 2002 Independent Publisher's Biography award, and of *ForeWord Magazine*'s 2002 Environment Award. Miller is also editor of *On the Border: An Environmental History of San Antonio* (2001), *Fluid Arguments: Five Centuries of Western Water Conflict* (2001), and *Water in the West: A High Country News Reader* (2000).

Alan Newell is a co-founder and principal of two public history firms, Historical Research Associates, Inc. and Litigation Abstract, Inc. He received his graduate training at the University of Montana and, since 1974, has been providing research and analysis services for public agencies and private firms. Much of Newell's work has centered on natural resource issues, including water development, land title, and environmental contamination. For more than 20 years, he has served as an expert witness and has testified in a number of state and federal courts, as well as administrative proceedings. He also served as president of the National Council on Public History from 2000–2001.

Dwight T. Pitcaithley is chief historian of the National Park Service. He began his career with the NPS as a laborer at Carlsbad Caverns National Park and served in Santa Fe, Boston, and Washington, D.C., before becoming chief historian in 1995. He has published in several scholarly and professional journals, contributed numerous book chapters, and wrote *Let the River Be: A History of the Ozark's Buffalo River* (1987). In 2002, Pitcaithley was selected as a Woodrow Wilson Visiting Fellow; in 2000, he was appointed a Distinguished American Scholar, Fulbright New Zealand Board of Directors; and in 1988 he received The James Madison Prize from The Society for History in the Federal Government.

Martin Reuss is a senior historian in the Office of History, Headquarters, U.S. Army Corps of Engineers. He specializes in the history of flood control, navigation, and civil engineering. He is past president of the Society for History in the Federal Government. Widely published in numerous professional journals, he also wrote the monographs *Shaping Environmental Awareness* and *Reshaping National Water Politics,* and has edited *Water Resources Administration in the*

United States and coedited *The Flood Control Challenge*. His most recent book is *Designing the Bayous* (1998). He is presently working with UNESCO on a program dealing with "Historical Perspectives on Global Water Challenges." In 2001–2002, Reuss was a Dibner Senior Fellow at MIT.

Hal Rothman is professor and chair of the history department at the University of Nevada-Las Vegas, where he edited *Environmental History* from 1992 to 2002. He is the author of *Neon Metropolis* (2002), *Devil's Bargains* (1998), which received the Western Writers of America Spur Award for Contemporary Nonfiction, *Saving the Planet* (2000), and numerous other books. He writes for the Bridge News Service and "Writers on the Range" series of the *High Country News,* and is a frequent contributor to the national media. He was featured on A&E's *Las Vegas, Las Vegas Then and Now, The Money and the Power* and more than a dozen network and specialty channel television specials. He also has narrated a German feature film and is a frequent speaker on the lecture circuit.

Carol Shull is Keeper of the National Register of Historic Places and chief of the National Historic Landmarks Survey for the National Park Service. She began her career with the NPS in 1972 and has worked, written, and lectured extensively on historic preservation since that time. Shull has published in a number of professional journals, and authored and edited a variety of National Park Service and other publications. She coedited and wrote the lead article in an edition of the National Park Service's journal, *CRM Cultural Resource Management* (2002). She is also the recipient of the Meritorious Service Award from the U.S. Department of the Interior.

Philip V. Scarpino is associate professor and chair of the department of history at Indiana University/Purdue University, Indianapolis. He ran the statewide Oklahoma Historic Preservation Survey in 1985–86, learning the basics of resource-based historic preservation planning, before joining the faculty at IUPUI. An environmental historian with considerable experience in public history, he has served as a consultant for numerous museum exhibits with environmental themes. He served as a member of the Board of Directors for Conner Prairie Living History Museum, Fishers, Indiana, and past president of the National Council on Public History. Scarpino is the author of *Great River: An Environmental History of the Upper Mississippi, 1890–1950* (1985).

PART I

LANDSCAPE

SPADING COMMON GROUND: RECONCILING THE BUILT AND NATURAL ENVIRONMENTS*

Rebecca Conard

The past becomes a thing made palpable in the monuments, buildings, historical sites, museums, attics, old trunks, relics of a hundred kinds; and in the legends of grandfathers and great-grandfathers; and in the incised marble and granite and weathered wood of graveyards; and in the murmuring of ghosts.[1]

Common ground is hard to spade. Especially when it is crusted with ideological hardpan. Consider the following passage, which comes from a chapter entitled "Exploring the Reserve Concept" in a recent book on Great Plains ecology. Author Daniel Licht writes,"just as important as reestablishing native vegetation is restoring the structural integrity of the prairie landscape—in other words, removing everything that is not prairie, such as buildings, rock piles, old machinery,

---

*The term "built environment" gained currency, in part, to move beyond the limiting connotations of "historic architecture." Even so, "built environment" is an imprecise term. There is consensus that the term encompasses buildings, structures, sites, objects, and artifacts—categories established to distinguish different types of historic "properties" eligible for the National Register of Historic Places. Under this definition, archaeological sites, building ruins, fences, remnants of old roads and highways, windmills, miner's shacks, smokestacks, rock cairns, and hydroelectric dams are as much elements of the "built environment" as are the boyhood homes of presidents, Carnegie libraries, atmospheric theaters of the 1920s, Victorian era "painted ladies," and buildings designed by Frank Lloyd Wright. Others, myself included, extend the term to mean human-made modifications to the physical landscape. This pushes the meaning into a trickier gray area, the humanized landscape, but it also allows one to account for the origins, and evaluate the historical significance, of such things as agricultural field terraces, wagon trail ruts, designed gardens, commemorative (planted) forests, and earthen berms, the latter of which might have been constructed for purposes as diverse as ponding water for erosion control or shielding humans from accidental explosions at military sites. In the past decade, the terms "landscape preservation" and "landscape stewardship" have entered the expanding vocabulary of cultural resources management as a result of worldwide efforts initiated by UNESCO's World Heritage Committee to establish "protected landscapes" for the purpose of maintaining biological and cultural diversity. [For a good summary of this movement and results to date, see *The George Wright Forum*, 17:1 (2000), entire issue.] It is beyond the scope of this essay to address the potential of the landscape preservation movement to stimulate greater appreciation for the intersection of nature and culture, although there are obvious connections between the precepts of this movement and ideas expressed herein. Thanks to Mike Carrier, Andrew Gulliford, Lorne McWatters, Jan Nash, Phil Scarpino, and Lowell Soike for sharing their thoughts while this essay was under construction.

wells, shelterbelts, and other human-made features."[2] In the mode of thinking that flows from the transcendentalists, the ideal wilderness, here applied to grasslands, is devoid of all evidence of human presence on the landscape.

Forget for a moment the obvious: that in the modern world it takes human intervention to construct "wilderness." The banality, if not the brutality, of modern landscapes often encourages retreat to idealized places. "One might go so far as to say," as did William Cronon, "that the replacement of nature by self-conscious artifice is a key defining quality of the modern landscape." When he wrote these words, Cronon had Irvine, California, in mind. "If so, Irvine is a near-perfect example of the genre. Like many planned communities in southern California, it takes its inspiration in part from that amazing planned environment in Anaheim a few miles to the north: Disneyland."[3]

Cronon's theme-park analogy reminds me of a similar reaction I had several years ago when I spent time in Irvine documenting the last vestiges of farm tenant buildings associated with the erstwhile Irvine Ranch, which urban development has now completely replaced. Running errands one evening, I searched nearly in vain for a gas station. During the half-hour that it took me to find one, which, incidentally, was located in nearby Tustin, I noted that Irvine's major thoroughfares also were devoid of convenience stores and other service businesses that we have come to take for granted in urban areas, tacky and unsightly as they might be. In short, this most-planned of all southern California cities was *not* planned for ordinary people living ordinary lives.

The character of this un-ordinary, theme city assumed burlesque attributes the next day when our field crew chanced upon an undocumented Mexican squatter in one of the ramshackle farm houses. He was working in the strawberry fields that were "producing income" until "market forces" transformed the land to its "highest and best use." Once he realized that we were not from the Immigration and Naturalization Service, come to deport him, his hospitality blossomed. He showed off the little garden he had planted and offered us produce from it. Since he did not want to take "no" for an answer, I accepted. I could not purchase a tank of gasoline in Irvine, but a migrant farm worker, living surreptitiously on a pocket of "undeveloped" land, could generously load the trunk of my car with home-grown produce.

A phenomenon of the twentieth century is that we have by and large separated the places where we live from the places we want to be. At one extreme we have constructed "modern landscapes," which can mean anything from cookie-cutter suburban tract housing to strip malls, redeveloped inner cities, interstate highway systems, and, in rural areas, massive livestock-containment facilities. At the other, we have the construct of ideal wilderness, places that show no trace of human activity. Despite the fact that most of us want to experience nature with modern conveniences handy, we are nonetheless compelled to declare some places off-limits to all but the lightest of human use where we ostensibly let nature take its course unimpeded.

Somewhere in the vast territory that lies in-between these extremes, historic preservationists, environmentalists, and land managers work to protect, preserve,

Figure 1-1. Irvine Ranch Agricultural Headquarters/Boyd Tenant House, 1985. Historic American Building Survey, CA-2275B. *Beth Padon, photographer.*

restore, and rehabilitate as much of the past as they can. For the most part, practitioners in all three camps work with their own kind. Even so, there is more and more talk about the need to cooperate. Entrenched ideas about what should be preserved or restored, however, make collaboration arduous. Each camp laces its messages with buzzwords such as "sustainability," "community," "stewardship," and "heritage," but it is difficult to know whether we really speak a common language because we seldom examine our rhetoric together. For instance, among the findings and recommendations of the 45th National Preservation Conference (1991, San Francisco) was that historic preservationists, land conservationists, and environmentalists should join forces. Yet, among the 2000 or so conferees who assembled in San Francisco to "chart a new vision" for the future, there were few representatives of governmental land management agencies or environmental organizations.[4]

The situation has not changed much in the years since 1991. Actually, the situation has not changed much since Aldo Leopold suggested, in 1942, that "a prairie be reestablished as the necessary and logical environment" of the Agency House Historic Site in Portage, Wisconsin. "We have here restored, at great pains," he wrote, "the architecture and furniture of an 1830 household, and then set it in a landscape monopolized by stowaways from Asia. It is only what we don't know about plants that prevents such an incongruity from hurting us."[5] Some agencies and organizations that administer historic sites are now more sensitive to appropriate landscape settings, but all too often the focus remains stuck on image.

Part of the difficulty is that, no matter how much historic preservation visionaries talk about saving historic "environments" and cultural "landscapes," the historic preservation movement as a whole still carries the baggage of high-style architecture and great-name associations. The average local historic preservation commission thinks in terms of design and who lived where, not environment and landscape. Likewise, environmentalists carry their own baggage of idealized wilderness, which, as Cronon notes, "tends to cast any use as *ab*-use, and thereby denies us a middle ground in which responsible use and non-use might attain some kind of balanced, sustainable relationship."[6] And public land managers tend to cast both preservationists and environmentalists as zealots, while preservationists and environmentalists often stereotype land managers as insensitive bureaucrats. Meanwhile, new development continues to eat up more open space and rip up more of the historic fabric that, in many ways, defines the cultures of America. The process of change has become the continuum of our lives, yet we constantly reach out to touch and connect with the past. How do we make the processes of "sustainability" and "stewardship" compatible parts of the continuum?

The dichotomy that persists between protecting the "natural" environment and preserving important elements of the "built" environment is of our own making. Nowhere has this been more apparent than in the national park system. The statutory mandate authorizes the National Park Service (NPS) "to conserve the scenery and the natural and historic objects and the wildlife therein . . . ."[7] From the beginning, however, the resource management focus has been skewed to meet public demand, political necessity, and/or preconceived notions about how a national park should look.

Perceiving the need for widespread public support in order to protect the Park Service from political incursions, the first director, Stephen Mather, focused on building park infrastructure—roads, rail lines, and lodging—to encourage and accommodate tourism. He anticipated, correctly, that tourism would build public support for national parks.[8] At the same time, the National Park Service wanted visitors to see, and visitors wanted to see, uninhabited landscapes where they could gaze into America's past—pristine nature before it was carved up by survey lines, railroads, and fence rows and dotted with farmsteads, villages, and cities. But, as Mark Spence and others have pointed out, "such an idea of wilderness conveniently neglect[ed] the fact that Indians profoundly shaped these landscapes." The strong conceptual hold of the romantic wilderness ideal did not enable either park managers or visitors to "see" that these landscapes were "uninhabited" only because U.S. Indian removal policies either had killed the former inhabitants or had relocated them to reservations.[9] Native American artifacts and sites were subsequently interpreted as part of the pre-European-contact landscape, and Native American culture was thus "naturalized" into the wilderness.[10] That same vision of ideal wilderness led the National Park Service to remove homesteaders' cabins, miners' shacks, and other evidence of previous land use by humans within park boundaries.

People flocked to parks, both national and state, in such numbers that the infrastructure was soon overburdened. The continuing irony of park management is that New Deal programs designed to provide work relief through "conservation" projects produced an incredible volume of new construction in parks at all levels — national, state, and municipal — which both encouraged and accommodated greater recreational use. Harmoniously designed to blend into the "natural" landscape (which more often than we realize was planted and not natural growth at all), the park structures of the 1930s "presented" Nature and made it more accessible to visitors.[11] The park building programs of the 1930s also gave park managers their first real sense of how design could be used to manage *people*. Planners implemented the design concept of "use areas" to group overnight campers away from recreational facilities and built trail systems to guide hikers through nature.

Recreation, not conservation, was clearly the force driving park management in the 1930s and beyond, so much so that by the 1960s wildlife experts were compelled to assert demands for redress. The Advisory Board on Wildlife Management, appointed by Secretary of the Interior Stewart Udall and chaired by A. Starker Leopold, set forth wildlife management principles that influenced a new generation of park managers. "[I]t seems incongruous," the committee wrote, "that there should exist in the national parks mass recreation facilities such as golf courses, ski lifts, motorboat marinas, and other extraneous developments which completely contradict the management goal."[12] In the 1960s, the new science of ecology, not landscape design, began to hold sway in NPS park management policy. "Imbued with a spirit to restore wilderness and funded by new authorities and monies," Melody Webb has observed, "park managers purchased private land, dispossessed the inhabitants, and unceremoniously bulldozed the improvements. Cultivated farmland reverted to forest and brush."[13] These same forces also were at work in state park systems.

It was not until the late 1970s that historical architects within the National Park Service began to challenge the ecology-based mindset and reestablish the value of historic resources in national parks. "One of the more puzzling idiosyncrasies of land management in the United States," notes Robert Melnick, a key player in this reorientation, "has been the forced and often illogical categorization of land and resource types into rigid pigeon holes of natural, historic, wilderness, and recreation . . . . We seem to be mired in a view of isolated resources, not in the sense of ignoring our fundamental ecological understanding of natural systems, but rather in our substantial inability to extend that paradigm to a larger world view which integrates natural and cultural resources."[14]

Lack of professional deference perpetuates a gulf of distrust between historic preservation and natural resource conservation. There are nonetheless instances where distrust has been laid aside to achieve agreed-upon goals. Consider, for instance, two recent news-making crises. In the late 1980s citizen preservationists and environmentalists rallied in a show of combined force to protest the extension of Interstate 710 through South Pasadena, California. At about the same time, on the East Coast, similar groups coalesced and halted the construction of a shopping mall near Manassas Battlefield in Virginia. Edward McMahon and Elizabeth Watson point to these and other instances where preservationists and environmentalists have collaborated, and they rightly note that "wetlands, forests, farmlands, historic buildings, and archeological sites are all being eroded by the same forces . . . . The resources at stake for both preservationists and environmentalists are often irreplaceable. Historic structures and endangered species, once gone, are lost forever."[15] Protesting together, however, is not quite the same as spading common ground to cultivate workable solutions on a daily basis.

There simply are too few professional and institutional arrangements to enable preservationists, environmentalists, and land managers to assemble the building blocks of collaboration. Thus, if we cannot resolve little problems that come along on a routine basis, we cannot develop the lines of communication and trust that are needed to tackle the big issues. Another experience comes to mind. I have spent many summers in the lake-resort community where I grew up. A few years ago, the state natural resources agency constructed a large T-shaped, fishing pier in an area known as the Town Bay. The pier was specifically designed to make the lake more accessible to people with physical disabilities. At the same time, I was preparing a National Register nomination for two stone recreational piers, located on the other side of the bay, that were constructed by Civilian Conservation Corps workers in the 1930s. These piers, even though they sit in state-owned waters, are under the jurisdiction of the city. Preparing the National Register nomination was the first step toward fundraising to restore the piers, which are heavily used in the summertime. A year or so later, the new handicapped-accessible pier partially collapsed. The reason was faulty construction, not overuse, since the new pier was hardly used at all, which gave rise to a few local jokes about the "handicapped" pier. Eventually it was repaired, but it remains lightly used.

In any case, when the fundraising effort began for the historic stone piers, I began taking photographs to illustrate the ways in which people use them and the shoreline park strip that links them. While doing so I discovered that people with physical disabilities were more likely to be found at the stone piers, which, as it turns out, are accessible with a degree of difficulty. When the first grant for restoration came, through the *same agency* that constructed the handicapped-accessible pier, I began to wonder who was more disabled: the wheel-chair fishers or those of us who care for and manage resources. Make no mistake, I respect an agency that takes seriously its mandate to serve *all* the public, but what greater good might have been accomplished had there been well-traveled lines of communication and collaborative planning? For starters, we might have saved money, in this case taxpayer money, had the planning process enabled consideration of adaptive reuse of existing resources. We also might have saved time in arresting the state of deterioration on the historic stone piers.

Nothing in this episode even touches on the big issues and problems of collaboration between historic preservationists, environmentalists, and land managers. That is the point. If we cannot put our heads together on the small stuff, that is, if we cannot "enable" ourselves to think and plan together, we will continue to be "disabled" professionally. And if the resource "experts" are conceptually disabled, then public consensus for greater resource protection becomes a much harder prospect.

Just as there is ample evidence of professional segregation, so too is there evidence that common ground is achievable. Robert Cook, a plant ecologist, recently wrote that "preservation efforts . . . need to move beyond saving single objects of historical or aesthetic significance to the broader *context* of urban or rural planning. This will require full immersion in and better management of the political and economic *processes* that shape change in the built environment." And, Cook continues, "[T]his sounds like a systems approach to preservation, a recognition that cultural relics surviving from the past are just one part of a dynamic, living present."[16] Cook may or may not be aware that the National Trust for Historic Preservation has been actively engaged for some time now in changing "political and economic processes" to be more friendly toward the historic built environment, but it is nonetheless true that such efforts remain largely focused on structures, whether they be individual or clustered.

From the other side, Thomas Woods writes, "When interpreting the history of European settlements along the American frontier, historians and the public often perpetuate the myth that the land had no prior history. Yet human activity has been altering the environment for millennia. . . . Layers of context, both physical and intellectual, create a concrete sense of historic place. Omit a layer and the cohesive web of history unravels; the sense of historic place falters."[17] Likewise, Richard White has argued that America's love affair with "pristine" landscapes is for all intents and purposes a fantasy. Most of what we prefer to view as wilderness has a long and complex history of human habitation and alteration.[18]

Other contributors to this volume address the intersection of public and environmental history specifically as manifest in the recent phenomenon of heritage tourism and the preservation of cultural landscapes. In many respects, heritage tourism and cultural landscape preservation have flowed from the National Trust's Rural Project, launched in 1979 with the lofty mission of combining "historic preservation, conservation, open space protection and farmland retention."[19] One can read these developments as evidence that historic preservationists, environmentalists, and land managers have, indeed, staked out common ground and advanced conceptual frameworks for collaboration. All too often, though, the driving force behind these efforts, especially heritage tourism, becomes economic development based on presenting assemblages of the past without really exploring the educational value of the history they represent. The mission thereby devolves to preserving (or showcasing) *places and things old,* without much regard for the stories that could be told, a point I will return to later.

If halting attempts at professional collaboration often fail to reach their potential for edifying public audiences, it is not for lack of knowledge. Since the late 1970s, the scholarship of environmental history has roused us to consider seriously the sociocultural dimensions of human intervention in the natural environment. Influential works include Donald Worster's Marxist critique of the Dust Bowl on the southern plains in the 1930s, Alfred Runte's cultural interpretation of the national park system, Richard White's study of the relationships between human-induced environmental change and social change on Whidbey and Camano islands in Puget Sound, and William Cronon's analysis of the ways in which both American Indians and European colonists reshaped the ecology of New England.[20] They are among the many works inspired by the nature versus culture debate, the strands of which weave eclectically back through the works of Aldo Leopold, Carl Sauer, Frederick Jackson Turner, Henry David Thoreau, and George Perkins Marsh, among others.[21]

Social and cultural historians likewise began to read the landscape a little more closely, searching for meaning in material culture, i.e., the tangibles of human life, both ordinary and extraordinary. Two vastly different but equally influential works were Leo Marx's critique of industrial technology and the transformation of rural America and John Demos's reexamination of Puritan society through the physical artifacts of daily life as well as legal documents and official records.[22] Their diversity reveals that the intellectual stimulus for material culture studies also has been eclectic, encompassing as it does historical archaeology, folk studies, historical geography, and landscape studies.[23] The interdisciplinary nature of material culture studies has caused most historians to overlook the fact that one of the earliest proponents of integrating material culture analysis into historical methodology was none other than Frederick Jackson Turner, who observed, in 1891, that,

> . . . the materials for [the historian's] work are found in all that remains from the ages gone by—in papers, roads, mounds, customs, languages; in monuments, coins, medals, names, titles, inscriptions, charters; in contemporary annals and chronicles; and, finally, in the secondary sources, or histories in the common acceptance of the term. Wherever there remains a chipped flint, a spearhead, a piece of pottery, a pyramid, a picture, a poem, a coliseum, or a coin, there is history.[24]

Good examples of works that cross the porous boundaries between and among environmental history, social history, urban history, architectural history, material culture studies, and the history of technology, include John Stilgoe's study of how railroads influenced the built environment, in *Metropolitan Corridor: Railroads and the American Scene* (1983); Kenneth Jackson's excursion through the origins and evolution of suburbs, in *Crabgrass Frontier: The Suburbanization of the United States* (1985); and Rhys Isaac's tracing of the paths and secluded meeting places that constituted "an alternative territorial system" created by slaves, in *The Transformation of Virginia, 1740–1790* (1982).

More explicit blueprints for interpreting material culture in historical and environmental contexts have appeared in recent years. Consider, for instance, *Back of the Big House: The Architecture of Plantation Slavery* (1993), in which John Michael Vlach argues that slaves appropriated portions of the plantation landscape, both land and buildings, as a means of creating social solidarity; *Hard Places: Reading the Landscape of America's Historic Mining Districts* (1991), in which Richard Francaviglia shows us that linked to the scarred earth of mining districts there is an important realm of human history; and *The Power of Place: Urban Landscapes as Public History* (1995), based on Dolores Hayden's Los Angeles project of the same name, which seeks to demonstrate that even the built environments of America's most dense urban areas cannot be understood apart from the natural environments in which they grew.

Still, we have not quite figured out how to utilize historic buildings, structures, sites, and objects to communicate effectively the complex processes of cultural layering on the landscape. Those of us who practice in and think about material culture accept David Lowenthal's dictum that "the past is a foreign country," but we have yet to exploit fully the power of history, through place, to connect people with the continuum of the past. A couple of examples, focused on parks and agriculture, demonstrate how close yet how far we are from integrating and applying our knowledge to reach a common, public audience.

Parks are places where cultural and natural history most obviously intersects, and they are therefore places where we could logically begin to spade common ground. One of these parks is in view as I write. It is a state park developed in the 1930s. Like most parks of that era, it contains a handsome complement of native stone buildings and structures, including shelter houses, latrines and drinking fountains, an overlook with trailside benches, entrance portals, and custodial buildings. These tangible resources, along with a string of fish-rearing ponds, no longer used for this purpose, as well as a paved road, provide ample evidence of the Civilian Conservation Corps' role in park development during the 1930s. The National Register of Historic Places (NRHP) registration form explicitly documents the important historical association with the CCC in its statement of significance. It cites NRHP Criterion A, association with broad patterns of history, noting that "[t]he CCC was a national level program which . . . sought to provide recreational opportunities for local communities and conserve the parks' landscapes by utilizing unemployed youths in make-work projects, a move toward social welfare at the national level." It also cites Criterion C, association with an important designer, architectural style, or building type, noting that "[t]he buildings, structures, and objects reflect the effort of [the park rustic] landscape movement to blend park amenities with the natural landscape in their material, design, workmanship, and immediate setting. . . ."[25]

It is a statement that has been written in similar language for literally thousands of municipal, state, and national park structures built under the auspices of one or more New Deal work-relief programs. Collectively, they are cultural riches that document a magnificent enterprise as the nation searched for the keys to restart its economic engine during the 1930s and that fully express the philosophy of a signature park design concept. We value these tangible resources because they are aesthetically pleasing and because they recall a federal program that truly worked to benefit the nation as a whole. We *should* value these historic buildings, structures, and features for these reasons. We should also value these physical resources because, as human constructs, they are part of the historical continuum itself.

There are other stories these physical structures could be utilized to tell, however: complex stories about how these historic buildings, structures, and features
came into being at this particular place, Black Hawk Lake State Park, and stories
about what they represent in terms of the human-driven forces that reshaped the
physical environment in which they are set. Parks do not simply emerge from the
landscape, and, as in this instance, the history of their creation often reflects a pattern of conflict and resolution. The state park is situated adjacent to a town that grew
up along part of the lake shore. There is thus a complicated pattern of land ownership adjacent to the state-owned lake, which, over the decades, has produced a series of jurisdictional conflicts. Many of these conflicts provided opportunities for
the city and the state to negotiate land-use solutions that allow economic development through recreational use and also protect the natural resource base. This is not
to say that such solutions have been wholly acceptable either to those who would
like to maximize the recreational potential of the lake or to those who would like
to minimize such use in order to protect wildlife habitat. Nor has there been a consistent pattern of cooperation. If the terms "stewardship" and "sustainability" have
any substantive meaning, however, it resides in the workable solutions that human
beings sometimes negotiate in order to protect, preserve, and conserve resources.

The history of negotiated land use around Black Hawk Lake began about 1920,
when the newly created Iowa Board of Conservation took steps to assume man-

Figure 1-2. Stone Piers at Black Hawk Lake State Park, Iowa, in their naturalized setting,
c. 1935. Lakeside Park, curving from center front to the left, was created from dredge spoil.
Courtesy of the Iowa Department of Natural Resources.

agement of the state's natural lakes, of which there were approximately seventy. The state-held sovereign ownership of these bodies of water, but effective management necessitated that the state acquire as much surrounding land as possible. This was to be accomplished by working with local communities and private property owners to acquire adjacent land for state park purposes. Portions of the Black Hawk Lake shoreline had already been developed with privately owned summer cottages and an amusement park. According to local newspaper accounts, recreational use was heavy on a seasonal basis; and, even though such accounts probably exaggerated the numbers, a circa 1900 photograph of circus elephants bathing in the lake while hundreds of onlookers crowded along the shore lends credence to growing concern about the nature and extent of land use around the lake.

Only gradual progress toward acquiring adjacent land occurred during the 1920s, in part because private landowners were unwilling to sell. Nonetheless, the local Izaak Walton League chapter served as the lake's unofficial caretaker. The "Ikes" worked with the state to riprap the shoreline and stock the lake with game fish. During the late 1920s, the city donated to the Board of Conservation 150 acres of land containing an abandoned gravel pit. Situated in marshy lands south of the lake, the gravel pit quickly filled with water. The Board designated this parcel as a fish and game reserve, and a local chapter of the Daughters of the American Republic assisted the state by planting a stand of trees along the shore of the new "lake."[26]

Other local residents worked during the 1920s to secure for public access a stretch of shoreline situated within the incorporated city limits. A private landowner initiated efforts in 1920 when he dedicated a 2,153-foot lakeshore strip to the public as part of a subdivision project. This created a public access corridor along the lakeshore in front of a summer cottage development area.[27] The city subsequently assumed management of this public access corridor and purchased additional land to create a lakeside tourist park. Then, in 1924 the city created a park commission and began purchasing residential lots with a view of the lake. By mid-1925, when most of a city block had been acquired, the city began grading the land and working with a landscape architect from Iowa State College (now University) extension service as well as the Board of Conservation to plan and develop the area as a municipal park.[28]

In sum, during the 1920s, local citizens, acting independently and through the town council, approached the prospect of land acquisition and park development from different angles. By the time New Deal work relief and conservation programs began in the 1930s, the vision of resource conservation that initially inspired the Board of Conservation had seeped into the local community. Additionally, the community and the Board had established a working relationship. Thus, in the 1930s, it took relatively little effort for the city, the state, and private landowners to cooperate for the purpose of setting aside and developing additional state park land adjacent to the lake. As a practical result, a reasonably high percentage of lakeshore frontage was preserved as open space and public access, and a portion of the watershed was designated as a fish and wildlife refuge where recreational activity was limited.

The salient episodes of the history that led to construction of the native stone structures that are now icons in the state park do not involve the federal government other than as a vehicle for accomplishing local and/or state goals. Yet, the significance now attached to these historic structures is almost wholly concerned with federal initiatives. The official statement of significance is missing an important component. Undoubtedly, there are similar gaps in the vast majority of National Register nominations. Because preparers are rarely compensated adequately for their efforts, and because documentation standards do not encourage preparers to engage in extensive scholarly or field research to establish significance, there is a strong tendency to avoid integrating local importance into broader regional or national patterns. Yet, local history often is part of the broad patterns of history we seek to discern through the built environment. Equally important, local history has great potential to function as the narrative thread that bonds people to place and to a past in which they can find meaning. It matters not whether we call them resources or icons; the places where there exist tangible evidence of other human activity are the points of contact where historical interpretation can be enriched.

Agriculture is another realm of human activity that integrates the built environment into the natural environment. The typical images of agriculture are farmsteads surrounded by cultivated fields and ranch buildings set in an expanse of grazing land. However, behind these familiar built environments there usually are more subtle manifestations of the humanized landscape: field terraces, gully dams, retention ponds, and fences—and perhaps the rock piles, wells, and shelterbelts that ecologist Daniel Licht would like to see purged from the prairie landscape. Even less obvious, but highly relevant to the agricultural economy, are the farm equipment factories, meatpacking plants, grain elevators, and so forth that are associated with agricultural-based industry and commerce.

An example from the annals of heritage area planning helps me to understand a critical line that distinguishes heritage *education* from heritage *tourism*. In 1991, a small group of citizens in Waterloo, Iowa, pooled their money and launched an effort to revitalize the region's economy by promoting its history and heritage. Rath Meatpacking Plant had recently gone bankrupt, and the City of Waterloo was struggling to recover from the loss of a major employer. One of the initial steps in what was to become a multifaceted program called "Silos and Smokestacks" was to identify, and eventually preserve, historic places that were associated with the agricultural and industrial heritage of the Cedar River Valley.

At this early stage, the mission was to find historically significant places where one could interpret the transformation of tallgrass prairie into cultivated fields and the evolution of agriculture and agriculture-based industry in the surrounding region, in Iowa, and in the Upper Midwest. Accordingly, a preservation planning study identified approximately fifty historic buildings, structures, farmsteads, and districts in a two-county area that were closely associated with prominent themes in the history of agriculture and agriculture-related commerce in the Cedar River Valley: rail transportation; the livestock and dairy industries; other agriculture-related industries, especially poultry, canning, and baking; agricultural mechanization; and even agricultural journalism.[29]

Good ideas evolve, and this one was no exception. By early 1993 Silos and Smokestacks, the nonprofit corporation, had committees working on finance, marketing, and political liaison, in addition to project development, which now had multiple components. Other committees were looking into education, rural projects, and area sites and attractions. The mission also quickly expanded to "recognize, preserve, appreciate, and celebrate *America's* agricultural and industrial heritage *to feed the world*" [emphasis mine].[30] This expansion reflected an early liaison with the Iowa Natural Heritage Foundation, which had acquired the farm where plant pathologist Norman Borlaug had grown up; the foundation was planning to interpret this site to recognize Borlaug's extraordinary achievements in developing super-yielding strains of wheat, for which he won the 1970 Nobel Peace Prize.

The rural projects committee began important work with the Iowa Natural Heritage Foundation and another outside consultant to identify and prioritize rural interpretive sites. The resulting report contained much of interest, particularly in the ways it minimized the value of historic resources and natural areas as places where the expansive history could be interpreted. A list of six recommended priorities included development of a Mesquaki Cultural Center proximate to a Mesquaki-owned and operated casino where visitors could see "authentic reconstructions" (i.e., "small plot plantings in an essentially natural setting") of agricultural practices

Figure 1-3. Rath Meat Packing Plant, Waterloo, Iowa, 1992. The smokestacks, which provided one-half of the Silos and Smokestacks icon, have been razed. *Jan Olive Nash, photographer, Tallgrass Historians L.C.*

among various Great Plains cultures. Another promoted the development of an Amish Cultural Center where the "Golden Age of Agriculture" could be (mis)interpreted through "antique equipment" and "novel clothing" and other cultural expressions of a community that conscientiously limited the use of technology.[31] This report also recommended that "[p]reservation of historic [places] should be encouraged" but, running counter to the direction of the preservation planning study, it cautioned that "Silos and Smokestacks ha[d] little reason to invest resources in most properties eligible for the National Register" and that "[f]unding of preservation efforts . . . should wait until higher priority sites [we]re completed."[32]

The divergence was easy to overlook at the time. Ideas were flying fast and furious; meetings were high-energy affairs full of enthusiasm. An atmosphere of optimism and possibility prevailed: the National Park Service was interested. Indeed, the Department of the Interior Appropriations Act for fiscal year 1994 authorized the NPS to conduct a special resource study of the area, completed in 1995. The *Cedar Valley Special Resource Study* reflected the expanded nature of the project; it now covered seventeen counties in northeast Iowa. It also identified a wide range of both natural and cultural resources in the area and set forth three "conceptual alternatives" for conserving and interpreting agriculture-related resources. One of them, for instance, proposed that natural and cultural resources "directly related to the development of modern agriculture" be emphasized. To develop this concept,

> visitors might be directed to the Norman Borlaug farm . . . to become familiar with the ground-breaking work of this Nobel Peace Prize winner in plant genetics. Visitors also might be directed to a rehabilitated structure at the former Rath Packing Company plant to learn how animal food is prepared for our consumption and how that process has changed over time. Because northeast Iowa's rich soil and landforms are integral to the agricultural heritage of the region, visitors might be directed to the Aldo Leopold Wetland Complex . . . or Hayden Prairie . . . to experience the dramatic and dynamic nature of the land that has sustained a complex network of plant and animal life and has created the opportunity to provide food for people around the world.[33]

The NPS resource study thus integrated various initiatives that had been undertaken by Silos and Smokestacks, Inc. as the latter sought to develop partnerships and stimulate public interest in its project.

Meanwhile, the project kept growing. For instance, Silos and Smokestacks, Inc. contracted with the Institute for Agricultural Biodiversity at Luther College to develop a tourism attraction in Decorah focused on preserving the genetic legacy of agricultural plants. In another instance, the Natural Resources Conservation Service provided Silos and Smokestacks with AmeriCorps workers to study safe travel routes for tourists and to develop a travel guide with accompanying audiocassettes. Public understanding remained low, however, largely because the total concept was hard to grasp and there were no well-defined focal points for interpretation. Dozens of state and local organizations as well as private entities signed on as partners. In the process, Silos and Smokestacks, Inc. began to appear more like the northeast Iowa convention and visitors bureau than a nonprofit organization dedicated to recognizing, preserving, appreciating, and celebrating America's agricultural and industrial heritage. The special resources study diplomatically noted this by stating that Silos and Smokestacks, Inc. had "evolved into a community advocacy program promoting agricultural heritage tourism initiatives across northeast Iowa."[34]

Whatever the pitfalls of partnership-building, such efforts helped to create momentum and attract political support. As a result, Congress officially recognized America's Agricultural Heritage Partnership (AAHP) as a National Heritage Partnership in the Omnibus Parks Act of 1996 (P.L. 104–333). The reformulated goals of AAHP, however, did not mention education or preservation. Rather, Silos and Smokestacks, Inc. continued to focus on "enhancing existing heritage tourism sites . . . developing new 'anchor' facilities or attractions . . . creating a web of linkages—scenic byways, trails, discovery routes, guides, and maps—that tie the heritage tourism story together . . . [and] enhancing the capacity of communities, heritage attractions, and local businesses to become more self-sustaining and stronger partners in a regional effort."[35] The evolutionary process had produced a critical shift in perceptions and priorities: the "heritage tourism story" would now be linked through places, not the history and heritage of agriculture.

Congressional sanction of AAHP is welcome in a state that has few major historic sites or spectacular natural areas to attract visitors. Still, even though there are dozens of historic places and natural areas in northeastern Iowa that could be utilized to provide substantive interpretation of the history and heritage that Silos and Smokestacks initially set out to capture in 1991, few of the historic places have been documented or designated. The potential is great for telling a history that weaves in the value-laden themes of resource protection, agricultural sustainability, cultural diversity, and community identity that liberally sprinkle the pages of planning documents. Whether these worthy goals can be translated into programs and exhibits that communicate a coherent interpretation remains to be seen. The resources, both cultural and natural, are there waiting to be tapped, but the vision is fragmented at best.

The Silos and Smokestacks saga continues to unfold. When Congress officially sanctioned its designation as a national heritage area, Silos and Smokestacks was "partnered" with the U. S. Department of Agriculture, which has no experience or technical support for developing or managing heritage areas. On March 10, 2000, President Clinton signed legislation moved Silos and Smokestacks to the Department of Interior, where it joins all other national heritage areas under National Park Service jurisdiction.[36] This structural change, as well as a change of leadership, opens the door to reconsidering the interpretive framework and fundamental goals.

Many years ago, the great cultural geographer Carl Sauer wrote that "[w]e need to understand better how man has disturbed and displaced more and more of the organic world, has become in more and more regions the ecologic dominant, and has affected the course of organic evolution."[37] Human agency must be considered as part of ecological processes. The scholarship embracing the history of human activity and environmental change has made enormous strides since Sauer wrote these words. Simi-

lar strides have not been made in communicating what it all means to ordinary people. As a result, D. W. Meinig laments, we are in danger of becoming "a people unable to discern, or care about, the difference between a theme park and the real thing—
and ready to turn the real thing into a theme park at the slightest prospect of profit."[38]

Purging the landscape of the tangible evidence of human activity not only de-
prives us of important information as we seek to learn more; such destruction also
hinders our ability to communicate complex, ambiguous, important stories to wider
audiences. "Every tribe or nation creates its own geography," cautions Philip Wagner, and the geography of the United States, "it displays the busiest, most rapid and
extensive remaking of a landscape on a large scale that has ever taken place." Our
own cultural geography "expresses more clearly than ever before the ambiguity of
values inherent in our heritage."[39] This is why it is important for historic preservationists, environmentalists, and land managers to spade common ground. Together
we must find ways to produce messages of meaning for a broad public. It is a challenge made doubly important when one considers that the "ambiguity of values" in
the United States also is a product of our cultural diversity.

Perhaps we could enable a greater degree of cooperation by replacing the idea
of wilderness with the idea of a garden, as Michael Pollen has suggested in *Second Nature*.[40] That is, we should stop romancing nature and put human beings into
the ecological stream of "natural" history. Pollen calls the concept of wilderness
"a profoundly alienating idea, for it drives a large wedge between man and nature."[41]
In a more nuanced historical examination of this dilemma, Max Oelschlaeger
shows that, regardless of which among the many competing wilderness philoso-
phies one examines, all of them posit a boundary between human civilization and
uninhabited, wild nature.[42]

Likewise, we could strip away much of the romanticized imagery that attaches to
historic buildings and structures. Undue focus on the art and form of human creations,
as is the tendency among historic preservationists, drives a wedge between the palpable expressions of human creativity and our ability to understand the environmental and social conditions that helped to create them. This separation fosters a tendency
to use historic resources as if they were stage props for assembling a "heritage tourism
story." It also fosters a tendency to *use up* historic resources as if they were renew-
able. And this, of course, is what makes it difficult to persuade developers that historic preservation, in the guise of recycling the built environment, makes economic
sense. As W. Brown Morton III has noted, "[u]ntil the spirit of usufruct is second nature in the United States, the rule of the bulldozer will continue unabated."[43]

Morton's use of the term "second nature" differs from Pollen's, but both would
agree, I think, that we must construct a common ethic that values both the inge-
nuity of humankind and the natural resources that sustain us.[†] By adhering to

---

[†]Pollen uses the term in its Marxist sense, a concept that William Cronon illustrated so eloquently in
Nature's Metropolis: Chicago and the Great West (1991). At the risk of oversimplifying a complex
idea, the physical materials and commodities of our economy (second nature) are derived from the natural resources of our ecosystem (first nature).

"either/or thinking," Pollen writes, "Americans have done an admirable job of drawing lines around certain sacred areas. . . and a terrible job of managing the rest of our land."[44] The sacred areas Pollen had in mind are "wilderness areas," but one could apply the same observation to many historic places. As long as resource "experts" of every professional stripe perpetuate constructs that compartmentalize resources into "natural" and "built," we shall alienate ourselves from the continuum of the past. We also shall have difficulty cultivating coherent interpretations of, as well as responses to, landscape and history. I leave the final words to Frederick Jackson Turner, because we need to read them again.

"History is all the remains that have come down to us from the past, studied with all the critical and interpretive power that the present can bring to the task."[45]

NOTES

1. Wallace Stegner, *Wolf Willow* (New York: Viking Press, 1962), 29.
2. Daniel S. Licht, *Ecology and Economics of the Great Plains* (Lincoln: University of Nebraska Press, 1997), 143.
3. William Cronon, "Introduction: In Search of Nature," in Cronon, ed. *Uncommon Ground* (New York: W. W. Norton, 1996), 40.
4. Peter H. Brink and H. Grant Dehart, "Findings and Recommendation," in *Past Meets Future: Saving America's Historic Environments*, ed. Antoinette J. Lee (Washington, D. C.: The Preservation Press, 1992), see especially 15, 18.
5. Aldo Leopold, "Prairie: The Forgotten Flora," 1942 manuscript published in Robert F. Sayre, ed., *Recovering the Prairie* (Madison: University of Wisconsin Press, 1999), 161–163.
6. William Cronon, "The Trouble with Wilderness," in Cronon, ed. *Uncommon Ground*, 85–86.
7. U.S. Statutes 39 (1916).
8. Alfred Runte, *National Parks: The American Experience* (Lincoln: University of Nebraska Press, 1979).
9. Mark David Spence, "Crown of the Continent, Backbone of the World: The American Wildnerness Ideal and Blackfeet Exclusion from Glacier National Park," *Environmental History* 1:3 (1996), 30.
10. Derek Bouse, "Culture as Nature: How Native American Cultural Antiquities Become Part of the Natural World," *The Public Historian* 18:4 (1996), esp. 77–78.
11. Linda Flint McCleland, *Building the National Parks: Historic Landscape Design and Construction* (Baltimore and London: Johns Hopkins University Press, 1998), originally published as *Presenting the Past: The Historic Landscape Design of the National Park Service, 1916 to 1942* (Washington, D.C.: U.S. Department of Interior, National Park Service, Cultural Resources, 1993).
12. A. S. Leopold, et al. (Advisory Board on Wildlife Management), *Wildlife Management in the National Parks* (U.S. Department of Interior, National Park Service, 1963), 6.

13. Melody Webb, "Cultural Landscapes in the National Park Service," *The Public Historian* 9:2 (1987), 81–83.
14. Robert Z. Melnick, "Moving Towards the Middle in a World of Extremes: Nature and Culture in Historic Landscapes," *The Geroge Wright Forum* 13:1 (1996), 32.
15. Edward T. McMahon and A. Elizabeth Watson, "In Search of Collaboration: Historic Preservation and the Environmental Movement," *Information, No. 71* (Washington, D.C.: National Trust for Historic Preservation, 1992), 1, 10.
16. Robert E. Cook, "Is Landscape Preservation an Oxymoron?" *The George Wright Forum* 13:1 (1996), 43–53.
17. Thomas A. Woods. "Nature Within History: Using Environmental History to Interpret Historic Sites," *History News* 52:3 (1997), 5–6.
18. Richard White, "The New Western History and the National Parks," *The George Wright Forum* 13:3 (1996), 29–36.
19. Philip Hayward, "Can Rural America be Saved?" *Preservation News* 19 (February 1979), 6–7; see also J. Meredith Neal, "Is There a Historian in the House? The Curious Case of Historic Preservation," *The Public Historian* 2:2 (1980), 30–38.
20. Donald Worster, *Dust Bowl: The Southern Plains in the 1930s* (New York: Oxford University Press, 1979); Runte, *National Parks: The American Experience*; Richard White, *Land Use, Environment, and Social Change: The Shaping of Island County, Washington* (Seattle: University of Washington Press, 1980); William Cronon, *Changes in the Land: Indians, Colonists, and the Ecology of New England* (New York: Hill and Wang, 1983).
21. Cf. often-cited works such as Aldo Leopold, *Sand County Almanac* (1949); Carl Sauer's essays, such as those collected in *Land and Life: A Selection from the Writings of Carl Ortwin Sauer*, ed. J. Leighly (1963); Frederick Jackson Turner, "The Significance of the Frontier in American History" (1893); Thoreau's essays, poems, and journal; and George Perkins Marsh, *Man and Nature, or Physical Geography as Modified by Human Action* (1864).
22. Leo Marx, *The Machine in the Garden: Technology and the Pastoral Ideal in America* (New York: Oxford University Press, 1964); John Demos, *A Little Commonwealth: Family Life in Plymouth Colony* (New York: Oxford University Press, 1970).
23. Cf., for instance, the writings of Fred Kniffen, 1930s-mid 1960s, on folk house types and the material culture of Louisiana; Henry Glassie, *Pattern in the Material Folk Culture of the Eastern United States* (1968); James Deetz, *In Small Things Forgotten: The Archaeology of Early American Life* (1977); John Brinkerhoff Jackson, *Landscapes: Selected Writings of J. B. Jackson*, ed. E. H. Zube (1970), *The Necessity of Ruins and Other Topics* (1980), and other collections of Jackson's essays; D. W. Meinig, *The Interpretation of Ordinary Landscapes* (1979); and Allen G. Noble, *Wood, Brick & Stone: The North American Settlement Landscape*, 2 vols. (1984).
24. Frederick Jackson Turner, "The Significance of History," originally pub-

lished in *Wisconsin Journal of Education* 21 (1891), reprinted in Ray Allen Billington, ed. *Frontier and Section: Selected Essays of Frederick Jackson Turner* (Englewood Cliffs, NJ: Prentice Hall, 1961), 18–19.

25. Joyce McKay, NRHP Nomination, Black Hake State Park, 1 June 1990 (listed 1991).

26. "Lake No Longer Neglected After Izaak Walton League Starts Work," Lake View Resort, 17 July 1924; Minutes, Iowa Board of Conservation, passim 1923–1929. The smaller gravel-pit lake is known as Arrowhead Lake.

27. Crescent Park Subdivision Plat Map, filed 3 February 1920, Sac County, Iowa.

28. Minutes, Lake View City Council, passim March 1924-February 1926; "Filling in of New Park Starts Sept. First,"Lake View Resort, 20 August, 1925; "The Old Stone Mason—A Passing Art,"Lake View Resort, 29 October 1925; "Filling In New Park Completed—Ready for Walks and Landscaping," Lake View Resort, 5 November 1925; "How Lake View's New Park Will Appear When Completed," Lake View Resort, 15 April 1926. In 1933, the municipal park was named for a local physician, E. E. Speaker, who played a key role in spearheading the park acquisition and development effort. Speaker was active in the Izaak Walton League and served on the City Park Commission. He subsequently served on the Iowa Board of Conservation in the mid-1930s, when the park that bears his name was augmented by the development of a companion park on the lakeshore itself. The lakeshore park, which contains the stone piers mentioned earlier, required collaboration between the city and the State Board of Conservation, inasmuch as the work was done by CCC crews then engaged in developing Black Hawk Lake State Park. Speaker undoubtedly played a pivotal role in this effort, but no official records spell out the details.

29. *Silos and Smokestacks: Planning Study for a National Register of Historic Places Multiple Property Document* (Iowa City: Tallgrass Historians L. C. for Waterloo Reinvestment Group), April 1993.

30. *Draft Strategic Plan: Silos & Smokestacks: America's Agricultural/Industrial Heritage Landscape* (Waterloo: Silos and Smokestacks, Inc.), 12 February 1993.

31. Duane Sand and Shan Thomas, "Silos and Smokestacks: Prioritizing Rural Interpretive Sites," Draft Report (Iowa Natural Heritage Foundation with assistance from Silos and Smokestacks Board of Trustees, and Rural Projects Subcommittee), 7 April 1993, n.p.

32. Ibid., n.p.

33. *Special Resource Study: Cedar Valley Iowa* (National Park Service, Denver Service Center, 1995), 31–32.

34. Ibid., 5.

35. *Silos & Smokestacks Partnership Management Plan: America's Agricultural Heritage Partnership of Northeastern Iowa* (Waterloo: Silos & Smokestacks Board of Trustees with assistance from Mary Means & Associates), September 1997, 2.

36. "Heritage Byways," news release, America's Agricultural/Industrial Heritage Landscape Inc., March 2000.
37. Carl O. Sauer, "The Agency of Man on the Earth," 1956, reprinted in *Readings in Cultural Geography*, ed. Philip L. Wagner and Marvin W. Mikesell (Chicago: University of Chicago Press, 1962), 539.
38. D. W. Meinig, "Foreword" to *The Making of the American Landscape*, ed. Michael P. Conzen, 1990 (N.Y. and London: Routledge, 1994), xvi.
39. Philip Wagner, "America Emerging," 1963, reprinted in *Changing Rural Landscapes*, ed. Ervin H. Zube and Margaret J. Zube (Amherst: University of Massachusetts Press, 1977), 16–17, 26.
40. Michael Pollen, Ch. 10, "The Idea of a Garden," *Second Nature* (New York: Dell, 1992), 209–238.
41. Ibid., 214.
42. Max Oelschlaeger, *The Idea of Wilderness: From Prehistory to the Age of Ecology* (New Haven, CT: Yale University Press, 1991), esp. Ch. 9.
43. W. Brown Morton III, "What Do We Preserve and Why?" in Robert Stipe and Antoinette Lee, *The American Mosaic: Preserving a Nation's Heritage, 1987* (Detroit: Wayne State University Press, 1997), 176.
44. Pollen, *Second Nature*, 223.
45. Turner, "The Significance of History," in Billington, *Section and Frontier*, 18.

INTERPRETING LANDSCAPES

David Glassberg

Landscapes are the products of human interaction with the natural environment over time. They contain evidence of how successive generations in a particular place adapted to their natural surroundings, and more often than not remade those surroundings in accordance with their economic goals and cultural ideals. When public historians interpret a landscape, they trace the history of that nature-culture interaction, uncovering not only how past generations shaped the land, but also how they perceived it and gave it meaning. In the process, the historians help the public to give meaning to its contemporary environment.

LANDSCAPES AND ENVIRONMENTAL HISTORY

Any interpretation of a landscape must begin with an analysis of its natural setting. Powerful natural forces shape environments—desert winds blast red rock canyons; rivers slice deep through gorges; slight shifts of rock along a fault line produce dramatic upheavals at the surface. Vegetation and nonhuman animals also modify their surroundings, whether deer grazing a hillside to bare ground, beavers damming a stream to create a pond, or the spread of lichens disintegrating rock into soil. Nevertheless, while taking these nonhuman actions into account, the principal subject of landscape interpretation is the actions of humans on the scene. In the words of J. B. Jackson, "Landscape is history made visible."[1] Evidence of social cultural forces, as well as natural ones, are writ large in the hills, rocks, soil, and plants that humans encountered and rearranged. Environmental historians through careful analysis can find evidence of these forces at work in a particular place over time.

Most powerfully, landscapes bear the imprint of economic forces. Long before Europeans established permanent settlements in the Americas, native peoples had cleared parcels of land in river valleys for farming and burned forests to assist with the hunting of game. The first European colonists reorganized the landscapes that the natives had made, replacing indigenous vegetation with crops that had greater market value abroad, while fencing out native animals and fencing in the domesticated ones they had brought from overseas. The contemporary landscape is replete with evidence from nearly four centuries testifying to Americans' desire to transform the nature they found into products that could more easily be brought to market, from the reduction of hardwood forests into charcoal and potash in colonial New England, the washing away of mountainsides to extract gold in mid-nineteenth century California, to the plowing under of prairie grasses to plant wheat in the Great Plains, which made the soils in that region more vulnerable to the dust storms of the 1930s.[2]

Landscape historians find evidence of the reorganization of nature by economic forces on the water as well as the land. By the end of the nineteenth century, Americans rerouted rivers and dug canals to use water more efficiently for transportation, for powering factories, or especially in the West, for irrigating farms. In the twentieth century they built dams for generating electric power and for controlling floods. And as the population of cities grew larger, the rivers that flowed through them became conduits for human and industrial waste, while nearby ponds and marshes were drained to make more land on which to build housing. Motivated by the desire for economic gain, successive generations of Americans fashioned the water and earth they found into a series of working landscapes.[3]

Figure 2-1. Site of the first public school house, Mormon Island near Sacramento, California, 1953. This landmark was obliterated in 1955 by the Central Valley Water Project and is now beneath Folsom Lake. *Courtesy of the California History Room, California State Library, Sacramento, California.*

Over time, the economic forces that have been the principal determinants of land use in America differentiated landscapes of consumption from those of production. Physically distinct yet socially connected, commercial districts in port cities and rural crossroads marketplaces became specialized landscapes for the exchange of goods. Those same economic forces explain why a suburban shopping mall could emerge in the late twentieth century on the rich soils of what had been a productive farm.[4]

The power of economic forces to shape landscapes has been amplified by new technologies of transportation. By the late nineteenth century, the commuter railroad and streetcar reorganized the spatial characteristics of American cities. No longer restricted to living within walking distance of work, middle class Americans moved to new suburban communities clustered near railroad stations and along streetcar lines. The automobile almost completely remade this linear suburban landscape yet again in the mid-twentieth century, further dispersing population across regions and bringing about the proliferation of gas stations, parking lots, and large street signs directed toward motorists rather than pedestrians.[5]

New technologies transformed natural environments into landscapes of leisure as well as work. By the mid-19th century, railroads and river boats made the experience of visiting Niagara Falls and the White Mountains available to ever more tourists, placing alongside the awe-inspiring natural features elaborate hotels, scenic railways, and viewing platforms. At the same time, technological innovations that increased the amount of leisure time available to the urban middle classes made possible the creation of new "natural" recreational landscapes such as city parks. The "wild" landscape that Frederick Law Olmsted and Calvert Vaux designed for New York City's Central Park in the mid-nineteenth century was every bit as constructed as its urban surroundings. The same technological innovations also made possible the creation of "wilderness" landscapes more remote from the centers of population, such as Yellowstone National Park. Developed by railroad companies so that Americans could temporarily escape from civilization, the western national parks bear strong evidence of the human hand. The landscapes tourists encountered in these parks, seemingly inhabited only by elk and buffalo, would not have existed if the native peoples had not first been defeated and removed to reservations, and the wildlife populations carefully managed to encourage picturesque megafauna and discourage pesky wolves.[6]

Nature could also be remade into sacred landscapes. Native peoples in the West imbued certain natural features, such as the Ship Rock in New Mexico or Devil's Tower in Wyoming, with religious significance. In the early nineteenth century, European-Americans embedded religious values in the "wildness" of the Hudson River Valley, in the landscape of rural cemeteries, or in a vine-covered cottage based on a design from an Andrew Jackson Downing pattern book that symbolized its middle class inhabitants' adherence to ideals of Christian nurture. Elaborate public rituals, such as a Native American ceremony at Devil's Tower or the changing of the guard at the Tomb of Unknown Soldier in Arlington National Cemetery can make these landscapes sacred generation after generation. But landscapes can also become sacred almost overnight through chance association with a popular artistic or literary figure.[7]

Sacred landscapes also come into being on the site of memorable historical events, especially those of violence and tragedy. Battlefields offer the most prominent examples of this, but such landscapes can also emerge in the aftermath of other traumatic events, such as floods, mass murders, or assassinations. Visitors make pilgrimages to Ford's Theater in Washington, D.C., where Lincoln was shot; to the sixth floor of the Texas Book Depository Building in Dallas, where Lee Harvey Oswald took aim at John F. Kennedy; or to "ground zero" in New York City, where the World Trade Center once stood. Sometimes public officials deliberately seek to obliterate these sites of civic loss, only to see the memory of what happened there kept alive through oral tradition. So many tourists came to view the Texas Book Depository Building in the wake of the Kennedy assassination that a museum was established there in 1989.[8]

Landscapes communicate political as well as religious values. The redesign of the Mall in Washington, D.C. at the turn of the twentieth century made tangible the relationship of the three branches of the federal government. At the same time, in Cleveland and San Francisco, new downtown plazas based on Beaux Arts ideals of the City Beautiful movement helped municipal government buildings stand out from their commercial surroundings. Civic monuments and war memorials, such as the Civil War soldier or cannon in a town park, transform the ordinary environments in which they are placed into didactic, political landscapes.[9]

Although all landscapes contain elements that testify to the passage of time, in some those elements have been consciously highlighted to recall a particular historical period. Such "historical" landscapes reveal their creators' attitudes toward the past. In New England at the turn of the twentieth century, village improvement societies refurbished old houses and town commons to emphasize the colonial character of where they lived. By the end of that century, notes historical geographer Richard Francaviglia, no less that six different types of "heritage landscapes" had become popular, each relying for its effect upon progressively more modern fabrication and fewer original elements. At one end of the spectrum are "passively preserved" landscapes, in which a community has maintained its traditional ways of life and the buildings and land use practices that flow from them, and landscapes that have been "actively preserved" to represent a particular historical period. Heritage landscapes also can be "restored," with modern elements that supplement original ones to approximate the look and feel of a period, and "assembled," at newly created outdoor museum villages such as Old Sturbridge Village in Massachusetts and Greenfield Village in Michigan. Taking a cue from Disneyland, at the other end of the spectrum Francaviglia identifies heritage landscapes that have been "imagineered," newly constructed with design details that endow them with historic character in a generic sense without preserving any of the original elements of its particular locale, and heritage landscapes that have been "imagically preserved," through models, dioramas, and other interpretive media rather than on the land itself.[10]

Figure 2-2. Bodie, California, August 2002. This abandoned mining town in the eastern Sierras has been a California State Park since 1962. The historical landscape, with structures dating from the 1850s through the 1930s, is preserved in a state of arrested decay. *Photograph by author.*

Landscapes not only bear the imprint of past economic forces, technologies, and cultural ideals; they also reflect a period's prevailing racial, class, ethnic, and gender relationships. In the words of cultural geographers Denis Cosgrove and Mona Domosh, landscapes are no more than "readings of texts on the part of dominant individuals or groups who inscribe these readings into their transformations of the natural world and then naturalize such readings/writings through their ideological hegemony."[11] The western landscape that concentrated native settlement on reservations displayed a bitter truth about race relations in nineteenth century America. So too were ideologies of racial hierarchy made tangible in the landscape of a southern plantation, from the Greek revival façade of the big house to the slave quarters in the fields; in the landscape of segregated public facilities in the South during the Jim Crow era; and in the landscape of Japanese internment camps in the West during World War II. Interpreting landscapes in terms of the systems of power and authority they embody, historians have discovered inequality writ large in the built environment of a company town, or in the creation of high rise public housing projects in the inner city.[12]

It follows, then, that environmental and public historians ought not to limit their interpretation of landscapes only to physical descriptions of the natural and built environment. Social characteristics not always evident to the eye, such as an area's ethnic and racial composition, or its level of criminal activity, often contribute the most to the distinctive character of a landscape. Whether urban neighborhood, rural village, or affluent suburb, landscapes are characterized not only by the physical arrangement of the land and buildings, but also by the habits of the people who live in them.[13]

In interpreting landscapes, historians investigate not only the convergence of social, economic, and political forces in a particular place, but also the interrelation of places within regions and across the larger society. The social, economic, and cultural forces that most shape a landscape often originate at a great distance. In the colonial era, imperial policies set in London influenced the size of the tobacco crop on a Maryland plantation, the cutting of trees for ship masts in New Hampshire, or the extent of the fur trade on the western frontier. The grid Congress imposed over much of the nation with the Northwest Ordinance of 1785 to facilitate the sale of western lands left a regular pattern still visible from the air. The mansions of Pittsburgh's steel barons were intimately connected to the coal fields of southwestern Pennsylvania and the iron ore mines of Michigan's Upper Peninsula. Across America, landscapes have been shaped indelibly by the railroad, and later, by the automobile. Few forces remade local landscapes more completely over the past fifty years than the development of a national interstate highway system and the growth of chain stores and restaurants that employed a standardized architecture easily recognizable from the roadside. Less obvious, but equally powerful during this same period, landscapes throughout the United States have been shaped by Federal Housing Administration mortgage policies that favored the construction of new single-family homes in spread-out suburbs over the renovation of older ones in more densely settled urban neighborhoods. Analysis of the relationship of landscapes to one another, and to national land use policies and trends, helps historians to situate a local landscape in the larger world.[14]

LANDSCAPES AND ENVIRONMENTAL PERCEPTION

When public historians interpret landscapes, they seek to understand not only how past generations shaped the land, but also how they perceived it and gave it meaning. How land is shaped is a direct consequence of how it is perceived; it makes a difference whether the residents of a community see a field as "vacant" awaiting development or as full of plant and animal life requiring protection; whether they see a block of old buildings downtown as a picturesque historic district or a dangerous slum. Inevitably, when historians interpret landscapes, they recover not only past land uses but also a variety of different past meanings attached to the environment.

In a sense, landscapes are products of the mind's eye, scenes composed through the act of framing disparate elements of the environment together into a coherent whole. We are used to thinking of landscape paintings in this way, or literary memoirs that bring a place to life in the reader's imagination. But any time that we identify a theme for a landscape, such as the California "gold country" or the "dust bowl" of the Great Plains, we are emphasizing one aspect of the land over others, and thus interpreting a landscape in a particular way.[15]

An important aspect of interpreting landscapes, then, is discovering how local residents and outsiders, past and present, have themselves interpreted the land. Evidence of past landscape interpretations exist in maps, paintings, and photographs; in promotional literature aimed at tourists and travelers accounts written by them; in memoirs, newspaper articles, and stories about places handed down in the community. Landscapes are not simply an arrangement of natural features, they are a language through which humans communicate with one another.[16] If landscapes exist in the eye of the beholder, and different observers have different perceptions of the environment, then the task of the landscape historian is to investigate why some views of the land became the prevailing ones in a particular time, and were the ones that gained physical expression through land use legislation, while other views did not. Interpreting landscapes entails reconstructing the different environmental perceptions of the various groups living at a particular time and place, and understanding, when the environmental perceptions came into conflict, whose side won out and why?

Although it is difficult to generalize about the myriad ways that an environment can be perceived (the many different landscapes that can be interpreted in the same space), it is possible to identify some general factors influencing environmental perception. One is the extent of a person's familiarity with the local environment. Long-term residents and tourists tend to value landscapes differently. Tourists are more likely to value distinctive features of the environment, natural and built, that they cannot find back home. Local residents are more likely to value landscape features with which they have had a long personal association. To a tourist, a church's historical significance derives from its distinctive architecture; to a congregant, its significance derives from its having been the scene of important life experiences, one's children were baptized there, or parents buried from there. Differing degrees of sentimental attachments create fundamental differences between what landscape elements are most highly valued in a community.[17]

PUBLIC HISTORY AND THE INTERPRETATION OF LANDSCAPES

Public historians typically engage in landscape interpretation in three professional situations. One situation is when they are asked to analyze the previous land uses on a site. Closely examining the contemporary landscape and the historical record for evidence of past economic activities and cultural ideals, the public historians sometimes testify as experts in conflicts over land use. Such expert testimony is especially important when the landscape still contains physical evidence of past industrial uses in the form of toxic chemicals.[18]

A second professional situation in which public historians frequently interpret landscapes is when they are asked to determine whether or not a landscape is of sufficient historical significance to merit preservation, and if so, to devise and implement an appropriate preservation strategy for it. In recent years both the National Trust for Historic Preservation and the National Park Service have issued guidelines for the nomination and preservation of historical landscapes, and landscape preservation has become among the most exciting, if challenging, areas of contemporary preservation practice.[19]

Preserving landscapes lies at the intersection of environmental and public history. Rather than distinguishing between natural and cultural resources, landscape preservation seeks to preserve the relationship between the two. It is hard to imagine that an agricultural landscape ever existed on a site once a shopping mall and parking lot are built on it, and the surrounding roads are full of traffic. To preserve an agricultural landscape, the natural environment has to be protected along with the built environment, and ways must be found to keep the land economically viable as a farm.

Preserving landscapes is much more complicated than preserving an individual historic structure. While preserving an individual structure is expensive, it is usually possible for a public historical agency to gain title to the property or to make an arrangement with its owner so that its historical significance can be communicated to the public, even if its surroundings have radically changed. By contrast, to preserve a historic landscape means preserving as much of the surroundings as possible, usually far more territory than any one owner possesses or that a single agency can administer. Landscape preservation encompasses the entire look and feel of a place, its views, its sensory environment. To preserve the landscape of George Washington's home at Mount Vernon required curtailing modern development not only on what had been Washington's property, but also on the lands across the Potomac River visible from the site. Moreover, the elements that make a landscape distinctive rarely date from a single period or embody a single interpretive theme. Landscapes are composed of multiple elements dating from different historical periods, and continue to evolve. Preservation strategies for a landscape must consider ways to maintain not only the historical integrity of its component elements, but also their continuing economic viability. What public historians cannot accomplish by outright purchase they try to accomplish with planning tools. Among these tools is the establishment of a local historic district, in which the various private property owners in a neighborhood create a binding legal ordinance specifying that they will maintain the façades of their structures in a certain way. Another planning tool used to protect historic landscapes is the conservation easement, in which a public agency or private organization pays the owner of a property a sum of money (or in the case of government, allows a tax credit) in return for a covenant on the deed to the property specifying that the façade will remain a certain way. In rural areas, the covenant might stipulate that the land must remain in agriculture and cannot be developed for commercial or residential use. A related planning tool, more common in urban areas, is the transfer of development rights, in which the owner of a historic property can sell the right to develop it further to a builder in another part of the city who wants to make his or her project larger.[20]

Since landscapes inevitably change, public historians talk more about the "protection" of landscapes rather than their preservation. In 1972, the United Nations adopted an International Convention for the Protection of the World's Cultural and Natural Heritage. The World Heritage Convention identified three kinds of landscapes needing protection. One is a clearly defined landscape designed and created intentionally by humans, such as a garden or park associated with the work of an important landscape architect such as Frederick Law Olmsted. The second, more difficult to define, is an "organically evolved landscape," one in which a culture has evolved over time in a place and left its mark on it. The World Heritage Convention distinguished between a "relict landscape" in which the impact of a past culture was still visible, but the culture is no longer the prevailing one (many Native American landscapes fit this description), and a "continuing landscape," one in which the landscape reflects the influence of continuing cultural practices (such as an Amish farming community). The third kind of landscape requiring protection is an "associative cultural landscape," one which derives its significance from religious or cultural associations, rather than specific material traces. The traditional homelands of native peoples fall in this category. So would the site of an important historical event, such as the Battle of Gettysburg. While these three categories for landscapes requiring protection offer a framework to help public historians recognize a special place, they do not constitute a specific guide to action.[21]

The third professional situation in which public historians typically engage in landscape interpretation, besides analyzing past land uses and implementing appropriate preservation strategies, is by creating museum exhibits, walking tours, and public programs that interpret landscapes directly to the public. Public programs and exhibits that trace the evolution of a landscape both physically, as it changed over time, and culturally, as perceptions of it changed over time, help to make the contemporary environment more meaningful for tourists and local residents alike.

While public historians usually create programs and exhibits that communicate their own landscape interpretations to the public, they can also develop public programs that explore the diverse environmental perceptions of contemporary local residents, and in essence, create a forum through which local residents can present their diverse environmental perceptions and interpretations to one another. Such programs can reveal what urban planner Randy Hester described as "subconscious landscapes of the heart," the special places in a community rarely noticed by outsiders, or by landscape professionals, but that are highly valued by local residents for the memories of significant life experiences attached to them.[22] Public historians have a unique role to play in promoting public dialogues about the environment, in evoking the multiplicity of memories and meanings attached to landscapes, and incorporating those meanings into their public programs.

Such programs place public historians in dialogue with various members of the community, evoking the many different landscapes that coexist in the same locale. In 1991, in a series of public meetings sponsored by the Massachusetts Foundation for the Humanities, an interdisciplinary team of scholars asked the residents

of three communities in western Massachusetts to discuss what made their home
towns special. One town, Northfield, had the look and feel of a small homogenous
New England village, but its residents exhibited great differences in how they perceived the environment. Long-time residents who lived on farms in the south of
town described a landscape full of associations with family members; one pointed
to a hill on the map as the "aunt hill" because that was where his aunts had lived.
By contrast, those living within the boundaries of the historic district in the town
center described a landscape alive with events from the early history of the town,
but attached relatively few personal or family memories to it. The second town,
Wilbraham, had the look of a sprawled out postwar commuter suburb; the civic institutions customarily located in the town center—public schools, police and fire
departments, post office, town hall—were instead scattered on its periphery. Nevertheless, Wilbraham residents attending a public meeting insisted that their community was as closely knit as any New England town, and they described a landscape of sociability centered around meeting places all but invisible to outsiders,
such as the town dump. The third community, the McKnight historic district of
Springfield, possessed a very coherent physical setting of houses dating from the
Gilded Age. Yet this Victorian landscape loomed larger in the consciousness of
the neighborhood's white residents, who had recently moved in from the suburbs
to restore the homes, than in the minds of the neighborhood's African American
residents, who recalled a landscape of stores and churches dating from the 1950s
and 1960s when their families first began moving into the area. As local residents
participate in public historical programs that encourage them to interpret their local landscape and express their diverse environmental perceptions and values to
one another, they begin to understand the diverse ways that their neighbors, past
and present, might have experienced the same environment, as well as ways to situate that environment in the larger world.[23]

   But it is not enough for public historical programs simply to evoke the multiple
environmental perceptions in a community, how local residents interpret their landscape. Public programs can also address the larger social and economic forces that
shape a landscape. In 1992, the Bostonian Society's Last Tenement exhibit not only
evoked memories of Boston's West End in the 1920s and 1930s, but also critically
examined the public policies that led to the neighborhood's destruction as part of
an urban renewal project in the 1950s. In Los Angeles, Dolores Hayden's "Power
of Place" project of the mid-1980s not only identified and marked landscapes associated with the achievements of local women, non-Anglos, and working class
residents, but also developed public programs that tied them together into a larger
social and political history of the city. Public history programs interpreting landscapes can help local residents to expand their environmental perceptions to include
not only the multiplicity of memories that inhabit a landscape but also the political,
social, and economic relationships that created it.[24] The powerful relationships that
transform landscapes often remain invisible because they originate outside of the
confines of neighborhood or town. Public historians can add a critical sense of location to local residents' sense of emotional attachment, helping them to see what

ordinarily cannot be seen, not only memories attached to the landscape but larger social and economic processes that shaped how it was made.

Through the process of interpreting landscapes, public historians introduce the communities in which they work to the latest research questions in environmental history, identifying the natural, economic, and cultural forces that over time have shaped the contemporary environment. Public historians also bring back to the study of environmental history new research questions developed in the field of public history, such as the importance of understanding how individual and collective memory guides environmental perception, how some interpretations of the landscape gain the force of law through land use legislation while others are dismissed, and how some environmental features become "historical," either through official designation or popular practice. If public historians attempt to involve people in a conversation about the creation of place over time, then landscape interpretation by public historians operates as a critical tool in land use management, helping the residents of contemporary communities to enhance both their sense of place and their sense of location in the larger world.

NOTES

1. Jackson quoted in Helen L. Horowitz, "J. B. Jackson and the Discovery of the American Landscape," in John Brinckerhoff Jackson, *Landscape in Sight: Looking at America* ed. Helen Lefkowitz Horowitz (New Haven, CT: Yale University Press, 1997), x. Jackson offers a concise definition of landscape in "The Word Itself," *Discovering the Vernacular Landscape* (New Haven, CT: Yale, 1984), 1–8.
2. For more on how native peoples and European colonists reshaped the landscape in accordance with their economies, see William Cronon, *Changes in the Land: Indians, Colonists, and the Ecology of New England* (New York: Hill and Wang, 1983). For later periods, see D.W. Meinig, *The Shaping of America,* Volume II: *Continental America, 1800–1867* (New Haven, CT: Yale University Press, 1993) and Donald Worster, *Dust Bowl: The Southern Plains in the 1930s* (New York: Oxford University Press, 1979).
3. For more on economic forces shaping water, see Theodore Steinberg, *Nature Incorporated: Industrialization and the Waters of New England* (New York: Cambridge University Press, 1991) and Donald Worster, *Rivers of Empire: Water, Aridity, and the Growth of the American West* (New York: Pantheon Books, 1985).
4. For more on landscapes of consumption, see the essays in Michael Sorkin, ed. *Variations on a Theme Park: The New American City and the End of Public Space* (New York: Noonday Press, 1992).
5. On shape of suburbs determined by transportation, see Sam Bass Warner, *Streetcar Suburbs: The Process of Growth in Boston, 1870–1900* (Cambridge, MA: Harvard University Press, 1962).
6. On tourist landscapes in the nineteenth century, see John Sears, *Sacred*

Places: American Tourist Attractions in the Nineteenth Century (New York: Oxford University Press, 1989). On the building of Central Park, see David Schuyler, *New Urban Landscape: The Redefinition of City Form in Nineteenth Century America* (Baltimore: Johns Hopkins University Press, 1986). On management of wild nature for tourists in western national parks, see Richard West Sellars, *Preserving Nature in the National Parks* (New Haven, CT: Yale University Press, 1997).

7. See David Chidester and Edward T. Linenthal, "Introduction," in David Chidester and Edward T. Linenthal, eds. *American Sacred Space* (Bloomington: Indiana University Press, 1995). On Native Americans and sacred landscapes, see Donald Hardesty, "Ethnographic Landscapes: Transforming Nature into Culture," in Arnold R. Alanen and Robert Z. Melnick, eds. *Preserving Cultural Landscapes in America* (Baltimore: Johns Hopkins University Press, 2000), pp. 169–85. On the religious connotations of nature for Americans in the early nineteenth century, see David Schuyler, "The Sanctified Landscape: The Hudson River Valley, 1820–50," in George F. Thompson, ed. *Landscape in America* (Austin: University of Texas Press, 1995), pp. 93–109. On the design of rural cottages and Christian nurture, see Clifford E. Clark, Jr., "Domestic Architecture as an Index to Social History: The Romantic Revival and the Cult of Domesticity in America, 1840–70," in Robert Blair St. George, ed. *Material Life in America*, (Boston: Northeastern University Press, 1988), pp. 535–49. Clark's essay originally appeared in the *Journal of Interdisciplinary History* 7 (1976): 33–56.

8. See Kenneth E. Foote, *Shadowed Ground: America's Landscapes of Violence and Tragedy* (Austin: University of Texas Press, 1997) and Edward T. Linenthal, *The Unfinished Bombing: Oklahoma City in American Memory* (New York: Oxford University Press, 2001). On battlefields as sacred ground, see Edward T. Linenthal, *Sacred Ground: Americans and Their Battlefields* (Urbana: University of Illinois Press, 1991) and Reuben M. Rainey, "Hallowed Grounds and Rituals of Remembrance: Union Regimental Monuments at Gettysburg" in Paul Groth and Todd Bressi, eds. *Understanding Ordinary Landscapes*, (New Haven, CT: Yale, 1997), pp. 67–80.

9. On official landscapes at the turn of the century, see Richard Guy Wilson, "Architecture, Landscape, and City Planning," in *The American Renaissance 1876–1917* (New York: Brooklyn Museum, 1979); Thomas Hines, *Burnham of Chicago* (New York: Oxford University Press, 1974); Michele Bogart, *Public Sculpture and Civic Ideal in New York City 1890–1930* (Chicago: University of Chicago Press, 1989); Kirk Savage, *Standing Soldiers, Kneeling Slaves: Race, War, and Monument in Nineteenth Century America* (Princeton, NJ: Princeton University Press, 1997).

10. Richard Francaviglia, "Selling Heritage Landscapes," in Arnold R. Alanen and Robert Z. Melnick, eds. *Preserving Cultural Landscapes in America* (Baltimore: Johns Hopkins Press, 2000), pp. 44–69. On Colonial Revival landscape, see Alan Axelrod, ed. *The Colonial Revival in America* (New

York: WW Norton, 1985), and William Truettner and Roger B. Stein, eds. *Picturing Old New England: Image and Memory* (New Haven, CT., Yale University Press, 1999).

11. Denis Cosgrove and Mona Domosh, "Author and Authority: Writing the New Cultural Geography," in James Duncan and David Ley, eds. *Place/Culture/Representation* (New York: Verso, 1993), p. 25.

12. On the landscape of race relations, see Dell Upton, "Black and White Landscapes in 18th Century Virginia," in Robert Blair St. George, ed. *Material Life in America*, (Boston: Northeastern University Press, 1988), pp. 357–69. Upton's essay originally appeared in *Places* 2 (1985): 59–72. On how social and economic inequality finds expressions in spatial arrangements, see Sharon Zukin, *Landscapes of Power: From Detroit to Disney World* (Berkeley: University of California Press, 1991).

13. On ethnic diversity in landscapes, see Dolores Hayden, "Urban Landscape History: The Sense of Place and the Politics of Space," in Paul Groth and Todd Bressi, eds. *Understanding Ordinary Landscapes* (New Haven, CT: Yale, 1997), pp. 111–33, as well as her book *The Power of Place: Urban Landscapes as Public History* (Cambridge, MA: MIT Press, 1995). See also Gail Lee Dubrow, "Asian American Imprints on the Western Landscape," in *Preserving Cultural Landscapes in America*, pp. 143–68.

14. On the impact of federal mortgage policies on the metropolitan landscape of America, see Kenneth Jackson, T*he Crabgrass Frontier: The Suburbanization of the United States* (New York: Oxford University Press, 1985).

15. See Yi-Fu Tuan, "Thought and Landscape: The Eye and the Mind's Eye," in Donald Meinig, ed. *The Interpretation of Ordinary Landscapes* (New York: Oxford U. Press, 1978): pp. 89–102.

16. On landscapes as media for communication, see Anne Whiston Spirn, *The Language of Landscape* (New Haven, CT: Yale University Press, 1998).

17. Sidney Brower, "Residents and Outsiders Perceptions of the Environment," in *Housing, Culture, and Design* (Philadelphia: University of Pennsylvania Press, 1989), pp. 189–102. On the bonding to place in childhood, see the essays in Irwin Altman and Setha Low, eds. *Place Attachment*, (New York: Plenum, 1992). See also John Stilgoe, "Boyhood Landscape and Repetition," in George F. Thompson, ed. *Landscape in America* (Austin: University of Texas Press, 1995), pp. 183–202.

18. See the other chapters in this volume on historians and environmental impact statements.

19. Among the many useful publications for local communities seeking to document and preserve historically significant cultural landscapes are National Register Bulletin #18 "How to Identify and Evaluate Designed Historical Landscapes"(1987); National Register Bulletin #30 "How to Identify, Evaluate, and Register Rural Historical Landscapes" (1988); and Preservation Brief #36: "Protecting Cultural Landscapes" (1994). An up-to-date list of federal preservation resources is available at www.cr.nps.gov/nr. See also the web-

site maintained by the Institute for Cultural Landscape Studies at the Arnold Arboretum of Harvard University (www.icls.harvard.edu).

20. See Frank B. Gilbert, "Saving Landmarks: The Transfer of Development Rights," *Historic Preservation* 22 (July 1970): 13–17. For an extended discussion of planning tools used to preserve rural landscapes, see Samuel N. Stokes, A. Elizabeth Watson, and Shelley S. Mastran, *Saving America's Countryside: A Guide to Rural Conservation*, 2nd ed. (Baltimore: Johns Hopkins University Press, 1997), as well as the essays in Robert E. Stipe, ed. *New Directions in Rural Preservation* (Washington, D.C.: U.S. Department of the Interior, 1980).

21. See Nora Mitchell and Susan Buggey, "Protected Landscapes and Cultural Landscapes: Taking Advantage of Diverse Approaches," *George Wright Forum* 17 (2000): 35–46. The entire issue of this journal contains useful examples of landscape conservation.

22. Randy Hester, "Subconscious Landscapes of the Heart," *Places* 2 (1985): 10–22.

23. These projects were conducted with the assistance of the Massachusetts Foundation for the Humanities initiative "Knowing Our Place: Humanistic Aspects of Environmental Issues." A more complete description of them appears in David Glassberg, *Sense of History: The Place of the Past in American Life* (Amherst: University of Massachusetts Press, 2001), pp. 131–63.

24. The Last Tenement exhibition ran from October 1992 through March 1994. See the catalogue, Sean M. Fisher and Carolyn Hughes, eds. *The Last Tenement: Confronting Community and Urban Renewal in Boston's West End* (Boston: Bostonian Society, 1992). See also Hayden, *The Power of Place: Urban Landscapes as Public History* (Cambridge, MA: MIT Press, 1995).

PART II

CULTURAL RESOURCES MANAGEMENT

RESEARCHING ENDANGERED SPECIES

Lisa Mighetto

In graduate school I had a professor who scoffed at the potential utility of historical scholarship. "We don't learn anything from history," he was fond of saying, "except that we don't learn anything from history."[1] In his estimation, history did not have to be useful to be worthwhile. Many environmental and public historians would disagree with this sentiment. For them, the intellectual satisfaction that research and writing provide is not enough. Environmental and public historians generally share a common trait: a desire to produce work that will prove useful not only in understanding the past but also in addressing the problems of the present and affecting the future.[2]

Environmental and public history emerged during the 1970s—an era of political activism—and both disciplines encouraged a level of advocacy rarely seen in traditional areas of historical scholarship. Environmental history grew out of the environmental movement, which called for protection of the natural world, while early public history drew similar inspiration from efforts to preserve archaeological and historical resources. As the twentieth century progressed, many environmental and public historians continued to encourage protection of natural and cultural resources, hoping that their work would influence the management decisions—and, in some cases, the policy—of government agencies and private entities charged with regulating these resources.

Public historians were especially quick to recognize the opportunities that legislation like the National Historic Preservation Act presented in terms of their work. Some developed careers in the new field of cultural resources management, helping agencies and companies respond to regulations designed to protect the built environment. By the late twentieth century, natural resource regulations had presented similar opportunities for environmental historians. Historical analysis of fish, wildlife, and plant populations protected under the Endangered Species Act (ESA), for instance, can provide important information to technical experts attempting to save these resources from extinction. Environmental historians have much to offer scientists, engineers, and policy makers, who are faced with questions about early species distribution and habitat conditions, while also grappling with rapidly changing values regarding the natural world and an increasingly complex political arena. The following chapter explains how natural resource issues in general, and endangered and threatened species research in particular, provide a wide variety of opportunities to combine the skills of environmental and public history.

THE IMPACTS OF ESA LISTINGS

Investigating threatened and endangered species requires far more than scientific research. From the outset of its passage in 1973, the ESA generated more political debate than scientific inquiry. Although Congress passed endangered species legislation in 1966 and 1969, these earlier acts were weak and ineffective, while the amended statute of 1973 proved to be one of the nation's strongest environmental measures. The political nature of this legislation became evident during the early 1970s, when the fate of the snail darter—a small perch listed under the ESA—was imperiled by construction of the Tellico Dam on the Little Tennessee River. Although environmentalists ultimately were unable to stop the project, they created a storm of controversy that drew national media attention.[3] The snail darter was more than a tiny fish; it was a symbol of changing environmental values. Moreover, in the ESA environmentalists had discovered a weapon for battling developers—and the legislation became as much a vehicle for fighting projects as a new strategy for management. The ESA thus forced the nation to examine political, economic, and social issues as well as biological questions—and scientists charged with analyzing population distribution and habitat undertook their studies in this context.

During the 1980s, proposals to list the northern spotted owl under the ESA sparked a similar debate. This bird, which makes its home in the old-growth forests of the Pacific Northwest, became a contentious symbol of the nation's conflicting values during that decade, pitting the timber industry against environmentalists. Many biologists felt that they were caught in the crossfire, as they conducted their work in the shadow of the media, and in some cases, threats of physical violence against them.[4] The direction of their research was also affected by litigation, as the courts interpreted the substance behind the owl's symbolism in the late 1980s and early 1990s. It was U.S. District Court Judge William Dwyer, not a biologist, who ruled that the ESA required protection of the ecosystems that the birds needed, mandating development of a conservation strategy on an ecosystem scale. The controversy surrounding these birds thus reflected the emergence of ecosystem management, which marked a major shift in natural resource policy.[5]

By the early 1990s, the marbled murrelet had rivaled the northern spotted owl as the bird of contention in the Pacific Northwest. Although it feeds in marine waters, this elusive, dove-sized seabird flies inland up to fifty miles to breed in old-growth forests. Once again scientists became embroiled in debates directed primarily by environmentalists and timber-industry representatives.[6]

The decade of the 1990s was marked by numerous controversial listings of Pacific salmon populations in California, Oregon, and Washington, which once again revealed the political nature of endangered species issues. Large multipurpose dams had radically altered the Columbia River basin—once the world's premiere habitat for salmon—and declining numbers of these fish prompted the National Marine Fisheries Service (NMFS) to list several species in the early 1990s. This move affected hydroelectric, irrigation, and navigation interests, prompting concern among policy makers about its impact on the region's economy. Under the ESA, it is unlawful to "take" a listed species, which includes causing harm to habitat. "Every man, woman and child in the Northwest," warned Senator Mark Hatfield of Oregon in 1991, "will be shaken as if by an earthquake." By the end of the decade, the NMFS had confirmed that "no one will escape" the effects of the salmon listings.[8]

The consequences of the salmon listings soon became apparent throughout the Pacific Northwest. In the late 1990s, federal agencies studied the radical option of breaching large multipurpose dams on the lower Snake River, allowing the water to flow around the earthen berms and presumably increasing the survival rate of young salmon migrating downstream—an action that sent development interests and policy makers into a near panic. "So what do we get by removing the four Snake River dams?," asked Senator Slade Gorton of Washington in 1999. With characteristic hyperbole, he answered his question as follows: "Shattered lives, displaced families and communities who will have seen their livelihoods destroyed, generations of family farmers penniless, industries forced to drive up consumer costs, air pollution, a desert which once bloomed with agricultural products gone dry," and "a far less competitive Northwest economy."[9] This rhetoric suggests the political climate in which biologists attempted to study the option of breaching the dams.

Additional ESA listings brought further complications. In March 1999 the NMFS, in a bold and sweeping application of the ESA, named nine more species of salmon as threatened or endangered, affecting 72,000 square miles of watersheds in Oregon and Washington—an area that included Portland and Seattle. "It may be the biggest hammer ever brought down in the 26 years of the Endangered Species Act," representatives of the National Audubon Society speculated.[10] This federal action restricted a number of projects, ranging from highway construction to building new housing developments. These listings also curtailed logging, grazing, and farming in salmon habitat. Never before had the ESA resulted in such far-reaching impacts in a heavily urbanized area. "This is simply unprecedented," one U.S. Fish and Wildlife official summarized, while the media in the Pacific Northwest predicted "massive changes ahead."[11] During the late twentieth century, the listing of the ferruginous pygmy owl in southern Arizona similarly threatened to curtail development in Tucson, indicating the complications that occur when endangered species habitat overlaps urban areas. In the 1990s, the number of listings doubled from the previous decade—and if this trend continues, the problem of recovering species in urban areas could become more pronounced in the future.[12]

OPPORTUNITIES FOR ENVIRONMENTAL AND PUBLIC HISTORIANS

These ESA listings created a need for numerous environmental services, including studies of fish populations, biological assessments of development projects, and preparation of habitat conservation plans. For the most part, this work requires the expertise of biologists and engineers. So extensive is the workload that the NMFS, faced with issuing salmon-related permits for development projects, has borrowed biologists from other agencies. "There's no end to it," marveled NMFS branch chief Steve Landino. "It's unbelievable how much work is coming through here." As another scientist remarked in 1999, "there's never been a better time to be a fisheries biologist in my lifetime."[13]

Neither had there been a better time to be an environmental historian. This work presented opportunities to provide not only research, writing, and records management skills but also a historical context for the massive amounts of information gathered. Environmental historians can document early changes in habitat conditions, population distributions, and fisheries management practices, noting the human costs as well as the impacts on the natural environment over time. Natural resource agencies and environmental companies do not always include historians on their staffs, opening opportunities for historians to provide research and writing for them on a contract basis. Historians working on a contract basis offer an "outside" perspective and a degree of independence that allows them to focus on the issues rather than on the internal politics of the agency or company.

Environmental and public historians can offer this expertise in a variety of forums. Researchers in the Seattle area, for example, assist scientists in compiling background information for salmon recovery projects. By gathering historical catch records, hatchery data, and biological surveys, historians help biologists and aquatic ecologists document early population distribution, while historical maps, photographs, and oral histories help provide a picture of early habitat conditions. Scientists incorporate this information into status reports on endangered species.[14]

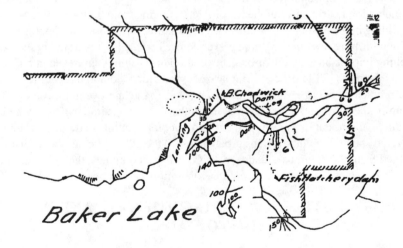

Figure 3-1. General Land Office maps provide the earliest surveys of local waterways, often noting trails, roads, bridges, and structures that could have affected salmon and steelhead habitat. This map, dated 1902, includes a small dam that once sat near a spawning area on Baker Lake in northwestern Washington. *From the author's collection.*

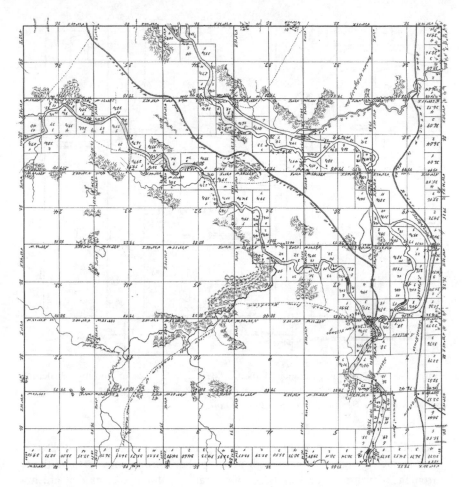

Figure 3-2. This General Land Office map from 1867 notes the presence of an Indian village and early fishing site on the White River, along with early homesteads, trails, and roads south of Seattle. By the late 19th century, engineering projects, road construction, and farming practices had altered this system of waterways considerably. *From the author's collection.*

Litigation is another area that utilizes the skills of environmental and public historians. These professionals can serve as expert witnesses in court cases, outlining land-use practices and harvests of natural resources over time, as well as analyzing the evolution of fish-passage facilities at large dams and the government's intent in establishing regulations and policies affecting natural resources. As an environmental historian, for example, I testified in an insurance coverage action involving a utility that seriously damaged a run of salmon in the early 1960s. In this instance, I researched and reported on the state of knowledge about the effects of hydroelectric projects on salmon among biologists and utility officials during

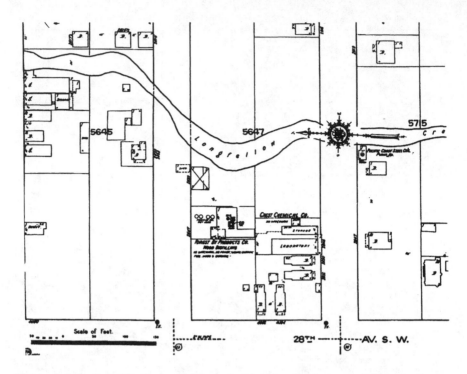

Figure 3-3. Sanborn Fire Insurance Maps provide a detailed look at buildings, structures, and early industrial practices. This map dated 1917, shows development in proximity to a waterway in West Seattle. *From the author's collection.*

the era. For another court case I testified about federal intentions in the 1920s and 1930s regarding construction of high dams in the Pacific Northwest and the requirement of fish-passage facilities for migrating salmon species that are now listed as endangered.

For those historians desiring a wider audience, endangered species research offers an array of opportunities in public outreach and public relations. The National Oceanic and Atmospheric Administration, for example, hired contract historians to research the use of coastal estuaries over time and the development of regulations. The agency then posted this history on its website, attempting to interest the general public and inform viewers about the importance of protecting coastal estuaries. Other agencies have prepared interpretive brochures for public distribution, which include background information on endangered species issues and often incorporate historical images. Historians can contribute research and writing skills to these publications, and can assist graphics personnel in illustrating them. Museum exhibits present another opportunity. Historians knowledgeable about endangered species issues can provide research materials for exhibits, and can write wall texts, chart labels, and interpretive essays.

Some federal agencies, including the USDA Forest Service, National Park Service, and U.S. Army Corps of Engineers, have commissioned book-length environmental histories detailing the development of biological research and fish and wildlife management practices. These agencies distribute the natural resource histories among their staffs, the interested general public, and regional policy makers. The Forest Service, for example, contracted with historians outside the agency to prepare a study of its fish and wildlife management during the late nineteenth and twentieth centuries. This project required research at the National Archives and Federal Records Centers throughout the nation, as well as numerous interviews with Forest Service personnel, including then-Chief Jack Ward Thomas. In addition to examining such topics as the development of ecosystem management, the authors described the agency's efforts—for good and bad—to save endangered and threatened species, including salmon, grizzlies, Mount Graham red squirrels, bald eagles, California condors, marbled murrelets, red-cockaded woodpeckers, and Kirtland's warblers.[15]

Utilities also sometimes hire historians as outside consultants to research historic salmon populations and the evolution of management practices affecting threatened and endangered species. In the late 1990s, Portland General Electric commissioned studies of historic salmon and steelhead runs on the Clackamas and Sandy rivers in Oregon. These histories documented early population distributions and detailed changes to habitat conditions during the last hundred years.[16] Similarly, Puget Sound Energy hired historians to research the Baker River in northwestern Washington. The resulting study provided information on the historic distribution of some little-known salmon stocks that once thrived in tributaries, while outlining early hatchery practices that altered salmon and steelhead populations in the area. General Land Office maps and historical photographs further revealed the early presence of splash dams in the area, indicating changes to habitat. Settlers used these structures to store water in streams, to assist them in transporting logs. The destructive results remain visible to this day, as splash dams scoured streambeds, denuding them of woody debris and clogging salmon spawning areas with silt. The Baker River salmon study also documented the evolution of biological research and the construction of fish-passage facilities at the Baker River Dams, describing the impacts of various salmon management practices on salmon and steelhead populations in the area.[17] The purpose of these "fish histories" is to provide background information for the agencies, companies, tribes, and other entities with an interest in hydroelectric projects and their effects on endangered and threatened species.

Environmental historians are well suited for this work for a number of reasons. First, they can talk to biologists and ecologists, who are themselves accustomed to investigating changes to the natural environment over time. Environmental history is an interdisciplinary field, and most of its practitioners have developed a conversance with the life sciences. Many of them are as comfortable in fisheries and forestry libraries as they are in repositories devoted to the humanities.

This familiarity enables environmental historians to identify and locate a wide assortment of records that might otherwise remain unnoticed. In addition to ex-

Spawning
the Salmon

Figure 3-4. Historical records can provide information on the size and locations of early harvests. *From the author's collection.*

amining sources from other disciplines, some environmental historians are willing to look for primary sources in nontraditional locations. Although much of my research has drawn from university libraries and state and federal archives, for instance, I have also examined federal fish and wildlife records stored in unlikely, unexpected places, including a closet at Bonneville Dam, where the papers of the U.S. Army Corps of Engineers' first biologist on the Columbia River were deposited and then largely forgotten. The most unusual historical records that I have examined included accounts of seal-harvesting activities that were stored in the basement of a tavern in the Pribilof Islands. One advantage of contracting with an agency, tribe, or company is that these entities can grant access to records not otherwise available.

Historical research experience further allows environmental historians to investigate early fish and wildlife records efficiently—and it helps them get the most from the materials that they find. When searching the archives for historical information on endangered bull trout, for example, it is useful to know that before 1978 this species was not considered distinct from Dolly Varden. Environmental historians researching salmon records also become familiar with early vernacular names, many of which changed over time, which helps them to identify sources. Scientists researching kokanee, a land-locked salmon, need to know that these fish sometimes appear as "silver trout" or "little redfish" in historical accounts. Moreover, familiarity with the development of federal and state natural resource agencies—whose names and functions have changed over the years—is essential for locating historical records documenting past management practices.

Environmental historians also offer the ability to manage and synthesize large volumes of diverse records—and most of us find research to be an exciting, stimulating

Figure 3-5. Historical photographs can document changes to salmon habitat. Pictured here is a splash dam in western Washington. These structures were common throughout the region during the late 19th and early 20th centuries. Settlers used them to store water in streams, assisting them in transporting logs. Splash dams scoured streambeds, denuding them of woody debris and clogging salmon spawning areas with silt—and the destructive results remain visible to this day. *From the author's collection.*

activity. One biologist who hired me to assist him once remarked that he felt guilty that I had to spend so many hours in the fisheries library. When questioned about his concern, he explained that "going through those old fish records just seems so—well—*painful*." When I gently suggested that some people might find his work—standing in an icy stream all afternoon looking for salmon—to be painful, he agreed that separate niches for professionals seems advantageous to all parties.

Public history also brings several advantages to this process. First, public historians by definition are willing to look outside the academy for opportunities for research and writing. Like many environmental historians, they might feel more comfortable working with biologists, engineers, and attorneys, than would historians from more traditional fields. Also, many public historians are skilled in presenting information in a manner that engages the public—and they can write clear, concise narratives in terms that the layperson can understand. The ability to tell a good story is very useful in public outreach and interpretive work.

Many public-history consultants are comfortable with initiating contact and introducing their skills and abilities to agencies, municipalities, tribes, companies, and other entities that otherwise might not be aware of the value of historical analysis. Many Requests-for-Proposals for Historic Salmon Distribution Studies call only for qualified fisheries biologists, not for historians. Yet when contracting agencies learn about what environmental history can offer, they are often, in my experience, receptive and even enthusiastic. Environmental historians who wish to work on salmon studies must be willing to cultivate biologists and engineers, and they must be prepared to demonstrate the richness, variety, and relevance of historical records. They also must remain alert to additional opportunities, for the historical methods employed in researching salmon [see below] could be applied to investigations of other endangered species. In the Pacific Northwest, the focus of recovery efforts remains on salmon and steelhead, owing to the cultural and economic significance of these fish and the large number of interested parties advocating their survival. To date, far fewer projects in the region have targeted threatened and endangered amphibians. While frogs and salamanders lack the romantic appeal of salmon—and the funding—efforts to save these animals could benefit from historical research similar to that undertaken on behalf of endangered fish.

DISTINCTIVE METHODS

Much of this research and writing follows a similar process to that completed for traditional fields of historical study. There are a number of distinctions, however, including selection of the general topic itself. As the former editor of *The Public Historian,* Otis L. Graham, Jr. indicated in 1993, one of the defining characteristic of public history is that someone else asks the questions—and in contract histories it is the client who identifies the topic as well as the general objectives of the work. Even so, environmental and public historians can "shape the questions along the way in light of their expertise."[19]

In my experience, natural resource agencies and environmental companies are receptive to suggestions. When the U.S. Army Corps of Engineers asked my company to examine the history of its research on the Columbia River, for instance, agency officials agreed with our recommendation to include the work of other agencies, such as the NMFS and state fish and wildlife commissions. This broadening of the topic was necessary to answer questions about how the Corps related to other agencies and why scientists focused on particular courses of action. Similarly, when clients have presented me with a list of oral-history candidates entirely from their agency or company, most have been receptive to the addition of interviews of "outside" individuals, including officials from environmentalist organizations. Also, most clients I have worked with agree that the topics and outline for the contract history will develop as the research progresses. This process thus involves a degree of consultation and coordination, which distinguishes it from research and writing academic history for traditional fields.

Another potential difference is the number and diversity of reviews. One book-length report I produced was read by more than twenty people, including biologists, engineers, tribal representatives, and historians—all of whom held strong and often conflicting views. Consolidating their comments proved to be a challenge, as did reconciling contradictory information. Ultimately, the decision on what to include must rest with the author, who bears responsibility for the report.

This review process differs considerably from the traditional peer review employed by most academic publishers. To be sure, most reviewers—whether they are academics or readers of contract histories—value accurate information, effective documentation, sound analysis, and clear writing. Yet reviewers of contract histories must also take into consideration the objectives of the report, which, unlike traditional histories, are often established by the contracting agency or company. In addition, reviewers must consider the audience for the contract history, which, again, can be very different from that of a traditional academic study.

The controversial nature of most endangered species work further distinguishes the research and writing from traditional historical inquiries. Agencies and companies contract for this work, ranging from litigation to public outreach, because the issues *are* open to question and more information is needed. Moreover, debates about endangered species evoke high levels of emotion, and researching them is often accompanied by a sense of urgency. Many environmental and public historians do not shrink from investigations with current applications, and they can provide a well-documented historical context that is essential for understanding the contentious issues surrounding the use and management of natural resources.

SCIENCE, POLITICS, AND HISTORY

Few observers of endangered species policy would deny that it is controversial. Yet there is sometimes an expectation that scientists and engineers can somehow study a problem and propose solutions apart from the politics, shedding their personal biases.[20] The debate over transporting juvenile salmon down the Columbia

River, for example, revealed that biologists held diverse opinions, prompting the question "is this science or politics?"—suggesting that the two spheres could be distinct. U.S. District Court Judge Malcolm F. Marsh observed in 1993 that biologists "were losing sight of science and becoming advocates."[21] Similarly, the director of Adopt-A-Stream Foundation in western Washington indicated in 1999 that habitat restoration measures should "reflect science, not politics."[22]

Fisheries biologists who openly refused to separate these two spheres sometimes faced professional repercussions. In March 1999, for example, 206 scientists signed a letter to President Clinton arguing in favor of breaching dams on the lower Snake River, prompting censure from their agencies and employers.[23]

A related problem is the tendency to expect technical experts to provide answers with some degree of certainty, consistency, and permanence. Attempts to save salmon on the Columbia and Snake Rivers demonstrated the difficulty of this task. As one spokesman for the Pacific Coast Federation of Fisherman pointed out, "There will never be absolute, rock-solid science on a system this complex."[24] Senator Gorton similarly argued, "we can talk all we want about sound salmon science, but there isn't one sound salmon science. There's an awful lot that we don't know." Significantly, one fish geneticist in Idaho cautioned against "black-and-white answers" when considering how to save endangered species, comparing the probability of success with salmon to investing successfully in the stock market.[25]

What environmental historians can add to this discussion is a reminder that natural resource policy has seldom, if ever, been based upon "black-and-white answers." As William Cronon has indicated, "Scientific knowledge is rarely so absolute as its devotees sometimes pretend."[26] An examination of the views of biologists and engineers toward fish and wildlife populations over time demonstrates that scientific thought is malleable and that natural resource management practices inevitably change in response to new developments. This point is part of the broad context that environmental historians bring to contemporary debates about how to save species from extinction.

Scientific research does not proceed in a vacuum. In the *Structure of Scientific Revolutions,* first published in 1962, Thomas Kuhn argued that scientists operate within conceptual frameworks that he called "paradigms." He believed that scientists process information according to the dominant paradigm, explaining away the inconsistencies that turn up in their research. When anomalies become too numerous and prominent to fit into the dominate paradigm, some scientists make a mental shift, allowing for the emergence of a new paradigm and prompting a "scientific revolution."[27] Kuhn's book did not invalidate the scientific enterprise. Instead, according to some observers, "it just makes it a little more human."[28] By demonstrating that scientists are influenced by cultural forces, Kuhn's book revealed that scientific inquiry is not an objective pursuit.

This point has implications for environmental history, which can help explain the social, political, and economic forces that have affected the work of biologists and engineers.[29] Pressure from the commercial fishing industry, for example, influenced investigations of fish populations in the nineteenth century, ultimately impacting the nature and extent of harvest regulations. As sport-fishing interests gained prominence in the early twentieth century, fisheries research turned to the maintenance of game species as well. Biologists, then, could be influenced in their choice of study as well as in their conclusions.[30]

Historians can also help explain how changing values and attitudes have resulted in development in management practices. During the early twentieth century, when faith in artificial propagation of salmon remained strong, one celebrated fisheries expert argued that spawning fish should be removed from their streams—an action that was necessary for the operation of hatcheries. Because salmon die after spawning, he argued, natural reproduction left carcasses that clogged waterways, threatening the health of juvenile fish.[31] By the late twentieth century, however, biologists had discovered that other species, including the bald eagle, depended on salmon carcasses—an observation that coincided with a weakening of support for hatcheries and artificial propagation. Accordingly, in some areas, biologists now return the salmon carcasses from hatcheries to their streambeds.

Ideas shift very rapidly, making consistent, cohesive management of natural resources difficult. As late as the 1970s and early 1980s, biologists removed logs and other organic material from streams throughout the West, in an attempt to improve habitat for salmon. By the 1990s, however, many experts had recognized the importance of "large woody debris" for providing cover and nutrients to fish—and some of the same scientists worked to restore it on the very streams that they had cleared earlier.[32]

A more recent example of how shifting values produced changes in management is the listing of various stocks of bull trout under the ESA in the late 1990s. Throughout the early twentieth century, fisheries biologists worked to eradicate this predatory species, in an attempt to increase the numbers of more desirable game fish. For decades, many scientists and anglers considered bull trout—or Dolly Varden—to be "trash" fish, and some states paid bounties on them.[33] In the 1920s, biologists described bull trout in moralistic terms, pronouncing them "the worst enemy" of other fish and deserving of eradication.[34] Their phrasing was similar to the rhetoric used against wolves—another predator that was once condemned but is now valued by some Americans. By the late twentieth century, both wolves and bull trout had become the focus of various recovery efforts.

The recent fate of the kokanee also indicates how changing perceptions have affected management practices. Fisheries agencies once destroyed thousands of these fish in creeks near Seattle, hoping to inhibit their distribution and thus encourage the growth of commercially valuable salmon species. By the late 1990s, some kokanee populations had become threatened, and biologists and policymakers became faced with the new task of recovering them. Fisheries managers and policy makers needed historical background on past management practices to understand how the population became depleted.

Historians, of course, are subject to the same forces that influence scientists. Historical insight, as Cronon has pointed out, will not provide "absolute answers"

to environmental issues. All environmental knowledge—whether derived from
scientific or historical research—is "culturally constructed," and the lesson, according to Cronon, "points us toward humility, tolerance, and self-criticism."[35]

In contrast to this attitude, an aquatic ecologist recently remarked to me that fisheries scientists "didn't know what they were doing" during the early twentieth cen-

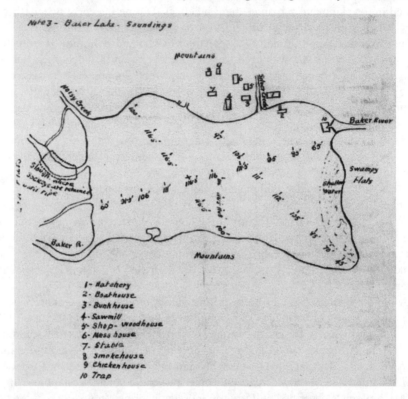

Figure 3-6 & 3-7. During the late 19th and early 20th centuries, early fisheries managers
placed considerable faith in hatcheries—and research of federal and state records reveals
an early reliance of fish culture as a solution to the problem of depleting fisheries. Pictured
here is a diagram of the Baker Lake Hatcher. *From the author's collection.*

tury. When I asked him if we know what we're doing today, he replied—in all seriousness—"yes, we are now correcting the mistakes of the past." Similarly, another fisheries biologist looking back over the last century of salmon management recently remarked, "it's tragic what people didn't know back then."[36] These scientists assumed that current adaptive management practices will provide the flexibility to respond to changing information that was lacking in the past. When I hear such sentiments, however, I wonder how future observers will evaluate our management practices. Attitudes toward the natural world have evolved considerably during the last 150 years, and will likely continue to develop. For decades, many Americans have looked at fish, wildlife, and plant populations as commodities, in terms of the benefits that they provided as food, recreation, and other uses. While the ESA reflects a new approach to the use and management of these resources, we are not certain about the results. Perhaps the most significant contribution that environmental historians can bring to the investigation of endangered species, then, is an awareness of the complexity of the issues and the need to proceed cautiously.

NOTES

1. I also knew a professer who kept a placard on his office door that read, "Those who don't learn from history are doomed to repeat it next semester."
2. William Cronon, "The Uses of Environmental History," *Environmental History Review* 17 (Fall 1993); Mission Statements, National Council on Public History and American Society for Environmental History.
3. Robert Cahn, *Footprints on the Planet: A Search for an Environmental Ethic* (New York: Universe Books, 1978), pp. 3–20.
4. Personal communication, author with Glen Contreras, USDA Forest Service, June 29, 1999.
5. U.S. Senate, Subcommittee on Environmental Protection and Public Works, Conservation of the Northern Spotted Owl, 102nd Congress, 2nd Sess., May 13, 1992.
6. Theodore Catton and Lisa Mighetto, *The Fish and Wildlife Job on the National Forests: A Century of Game and Fish Conservation, Habitat Protection, and Ecosystem Management* (Washington, D.C.: USDA Forest Service, 1998), pp. 199, 263–265.
7. Marla Williams and Jim Simons, "Last Chance for Salmon," *The Seattle Times/Post-Intelligencer*, March 31, 1991.
8. "Snake Dam Report Joins Salmon Debate," *Seattle Daily Journal of Commerce*, December 20, 1999.
9. *Weekly Fish and Wildlife News* (July 19–30, 1999).
10. Bruce Barcott and Keith Kloor, "Saved by Salmon?," *Audubon* (May/June 1999), p. 14.
11. Hal Spencer, "ESA Listing Means Massive Changes Ahead for State," *Seattle Daily Journal of Commerce*, March 9, 1999. Throughout 1999–2001, newspapers in Seattle and Portland provided extensive coverage of the issue.

12. See, for example, "Who's Stopping Sprawl: The Endangered Species Act Goes to Town," *High Country News* (August 30, 1999). The U.S. Fish and Wildlife Service and National Marine Fisheries Service maintain a yearly tally of U.S. species listings.

13. Steve Wilhelm, "Impacts of ESA Listing Are Here," *Puget Sound Business Journal*, May 21–27, 1999, pp. 1 and 85.

14. See, for example, R2 Resource Consultants, Inc. and Historical Research Associates, Inc., *Historic and Current Status of Kokanee in Lake Washington*, September 13, 1999. Prepared for King County Department of Natural Resources, Seattle.

15. Theodore Catton and Lisa Mighetto, *The Fish and Wildlife Job on the National Forests: A Century of Game and Fish Conservation, Habitat Protection, and Ecosystem Management* (Washington, D.C.: USDA Forest Service, 1998).

16. Barbara Taylor, *Salmon and Steelhead Runs and Related Events of the Sandy River Basin—A Historical Perspective* (Portland General Electric, 1999); Barbara Taylor, *Salmon and Steelhead Runs and Related Events of the Sandy River Basin—A Historical Perspective* (Portland General Electric, 1998).

17. Historical Research Associates, Inc., *Salmon on the Baker River* (Puget Sound Energy, 1999).

18. See, for example, Alfred W. Crosby, "The Past and Present of Environmental History," *The American Historical Review* 100 (October 1995), and John Opie, "Environmental History: Pitfalls and Opportunities," *Environmental Review*, 7 (Spring 1983).

19. Otis L. Graham, Jr., "Editor's Corner," *The Public Historian* 15 (Winter 1993), pp. 6–7.

20. Matthew W. Klingle, "Plying Atomic Waters: Lauren Donaldson and the 'Fern Lake Concept' of Fisheries Management," *Journal of the History of Biology* 31 (Spring 1998), pp. 1–32, provides an excellent case study of the reliance on science to correct natural-resource problems by separating them from their social context.

21. Dug Dugger, "Science or Politics?," *Nor'Wester* 14 (June 1993), p. 7.

22. Jon Savelle, "Salmon Listing Will Bring More Work to Consultants," *Seattle Daily Journal of Commerce*, March 9, 1999.

23. Lynda V. Mapes and Danny Westneat, "Breaching Dams May Save More Fish," *Seattle Times*, April 14, 1999.

24. Ibid.

25. *Weekly Fish and Wildlife News* (May 31- June 11, 1999).

26. William Cronon, "The Uses of Environmental History," p. 15.

27. Thomas Kuhn, *The Structure of Scientific Revolutions* (Chicago: University of Chicago Press, 1962). See also James L. Penick, Jr., Carroll W. Pursell, Jr., Morgan B. Sherwood, and Donald C. Swain, editors, *The Politics of American Science*, 1939 to the Present (Cambridge, MA: MIT Press, 1965; revised 1972).

28. Joyce Appleby, Lynn Hunt, and Margaret Jacob, *Telling the Truth About History* (New York: W.W. Norton, 1994), p. 165.
29. For a discussion of the pitfalls of this approach, see Richard White, "American Environmental History: The Development of a New Historical Field," *Pacific Historical Review* 54 (August 1985), especially pp. 315–317.
30. See, for example, Larry A. Nielsen, "The Evolution of Fisheries Management Philosophy," *Marine Fisheries Review* 38 (December 1976), pp. 15–23. See also Joseph E. Taylor, *Making Salmon: An Environmental History of the Northwest Fishery Crisis* (Seattle: University of Washington Press, 1999).
31. John N. Cobb, *Pacific Salmon Fisheries* (Washington: Government Printing Office, 1917), p. 94.
32. Personal communication, author with James Shevock, USDA Forest Service, February 20, 1996; Personal communication, author with Glen Contreras, USDA Forest Service, June 29, 1999.
33. W. B. Scott and E. J. Crossman, *Freshwater Fishes of Canada* (Oakville, Ontario, Canada: Galt House Publications), 1998.
34. State of Washington, *Biological Survey of Washington Waters*, July 6, 1921, Washington State Archives, Olympia, Accession No. 84–6-664, Box A, Fisheries—Misc. Studies.
35. William Cronon, "The Uses of Environmental History," pp. 15–17.
36. The Seminar Group, Continuing Legal Education Seminar, "Salmon in the Northwest," Seattle, Washington, October 19, 2000.

MELDING THE ENVIRONMENT AND PUBLIC HISTORY: THE EVOLUTION AND MATURATION OF THE NATIONAL PARK SERVICE

Carol Shull and Dwight T. Pitcaithley

A common adage is that history is rewritten every generation. A corollary to that adage is that each generation preserves and commemorates what is important to its image of itself. A second corollary might be that governmental agencies evolve in line with both. They move and sway in the short term according to the power of the dominant political party, and they change over the long term in response to more subtle, yet powerful, shifts in the culture at large. The National Park Service has changed profoundly since its creation by Congress in 1916, as its mission has evolved to face the challenges of melding the environment and public history.

The culture of federal agencies is created in great part by their enabling legislation, which assigns them specific duties or mandates as defined by Congress and the President. These parameters set the general tone and direction for the agency. Within those limits, however, the political and bureaucratic environment of the agency is shaped by its leadership and the interpretation of its mandate over time. One need only reflect upon the Federal Bureau of Investigation and its first director, J. Edgar Hoover, to understand the effect leadership can have upon a single agency and the cultural environment that is created as a result. Society also exerts changes upon agencies as its perception of the military prompted the Department of War to become the Department of Defense during the 1940s.

Although not originally understood as such, national parks are very complicated places. While originally seen as pleasuring grounds and classrooms where one could learn about the nature of nature, today they are seen in those lights as well as many more. They are at once repositories of cultural traditions and human history, cultural constructs, and preserves of bio-diversity. At one time, the National Park Service believed it could cleanly segregate parks into three categories: natural, historical, and recreational. These classifications lasted only a short while as the Service came to realize that many, if not most, parks embody all of these values. American Indian use of many of the largest natural parks is well documented. Natural resources are often valued for their cultural significance. Battlefields and encampment sites, such as Valley Forge and Morristown, consist of large forests and fields that are managed from a cultural perspective, yet they remain natural resources. National Parks (natural parks) are increasingly viewed less as vignettes of a "primitive America" and more as extensions of our own collective identity. As the Yellowstone handbook reminds us, "Yellowstone is a conduit of wisdom from deep, mysterious places to living people . . . It reminds us . . . that human beings are part of the universal interplay of change and continuance that the ancients called 'fate.' It reminds us that Yellowstone's story is also our story."[1]

Even the term *environment* is now defined in cultural as well as natural terms. Both the National Historic Preservation Act (NHPA) of 1966 and the Wilderness Act of 1964, as amended, embrace this view of the environment, and in so doing, have powerfully shaped the development of the National Park Services's management of the natural and humanized environment. The NHPA institutionalized an important shift in the understanding and practice of historic preservation by affirming preservation of a broad spectrum of properties that illustrate the diversity of the humanized, cultural environment. Indeed, the NHPA encourages preservation of properties, including designed and vernacular landscapes, as a part of living communities. Embracing a similar theme, the Wilderness Act recognized that remnants of human occupation were not antithetical to the idea of wilderness or wildness. But intellectual and managerial clarity in these matters takes time, and the sense of a public legacy of parks and the broader role of the National Park Service in environmental history and historic preservation took many decades to evolve.

The National Park Service began its existence on the eve of the country's entry into World War I during the administration of Woodrow Wilson. Stephen T. Mather, who lobbied hard for the agency's creation, became its first director. Mather's vision for the collection of parks entrusted to the Service was progressive and expansive. He saw them as extensions of local parks, places where the American public could and should go to recharge their batteries, places where they should expect to find hotels and roads and other amenities that would accommodate their visit without too much hardship. Mather did not, indeed could not, envision the use of national parks by backpackers who would spend days and weeks alone in the wildness of these places. Neither did Mather envision a role for the National Park Service working with partners to preserve much of this country's cultural history. Certainly, the Service managed the odd cultural property, Casa Grande, for example, but the primary mission of the agency was in the preservation and development of natural parks. The Civil War battlefields established by Congress during the 1890s and the Anasazi Indian sites established under the 1906 Antiquities Act were largely managed until the 1930s by the War Department and the Forest Service in the Department of Agriculture.

Mather's Service was, by virtue of the times, male, quasi-militaristic, and focused on "selling" the American public and its representatives in Congress on the wonders of the, largely western, parks and the ease with which travel to and between them could be realized. Mather and his society could not have imagined a National Park Service as a national leader in historic preservation; could not have imagined a National Historic Preservation Act or, for that matter, a National Register of Historic Places (more about that later); and certainly could not have imagined even the need for a Wilderness Act, an Endangered Species Act, an Environmental Protection Act or, for that matter, a Civil Rights Act or Voting Rights Act. The 1910s and 1920s were different and the National Park Service reflected those times.

Mather's successor and protégé, Horace Albright, began changing the mission of the National Park Service and moving it into the realm of public environmental history almost from the moment he became Director in 1929. Harboring a long interest in American history, Albright convinced Franklin D. Roosevelt to transfer the 56 parks and monuments then administered by the departments of War and Agriculture, and the Office of Public Buildings and Public Parks of the National Capital, to the National Park Service. With the stroke of an executive order (actually two executive orders, Nos. 6166 and 6228), Roosevelt reshaped the Service preparing the ground for the Historic Sites Act of 1935 and the cornerstone of the historic preservation movement today, the National Historic Preservation Act of 1966.

The National Historic Preservation Act gave the Secretary of the Interior the authority to expand and maintain a National Register of Historic Places of districts, sites, buildings, structures and objects significant in American history, architecture, archeology, engineering and culture. Since 1966, when the National Park Service broadened its mission by assuming the responsibility for its administration, the National Register has played a major and continually expanding role in involving a wide range of government agencies, organizations and individuals in public history. Research to identify, document, and evaluate an ever-growing variety of historic places that reflect human interaction with both the natural and built environment and their recognition by the National Register have helped make environmental history relevant far beyond academic institutions.

The Act encourages broad-based participation by providing for nominations to the National Register by states, federal agencies for places under federal ownership or control, and Indian tribes for tribal lands, and requiring that federal agencies identify and consider places eligible for or listed in the National Register in the planning for federal projects. Cultural resource surveys are carried out at every level of government, sometimes assisted by matching grants from the Historic Preservation Fund authorized under the Act. Government agencies have their own staffs but hire consultants to do much of this research. Preservation organizations, volunteer groups, and academic institutions are also involved. A large number of historians, architectural historians, archeologists, and professionals in related disciples are employed in doing environmental history with the places themselves the primary documents of study. Anyone can do National Register nominations. National Register criteria for evaluation and the guidelines for documentation and evaluation in a series of widely available National Register bulletins provide the basis for deciding which places have historic significance.

Given its mandate, it is not surprising that at the beginning of 2003, after more than 35 years, the National Register includes some 76,000 listings. Because 14 percent of listings are historic districts with large numbers of cultural resources, more than 1.2 million buildings, sites, structures an objects are actually registered. The Register recognizes historic and cultural units of the National Park System, over 2300 National Historic Landmarks designated by the Secretary of the Interior for their national significance, and important places in communities throughout the nation nominated by states, federal agencies and Indian tribes. Well over 90 percent of the listings are of state and local significance and about 74 percent are privately owned. A third are part of multiple property nominations, which include groups of properties related by theme or historic context.[2] The studies submitted on the National Register's multiple property documentation form trace the history of communities or topics, such as the iron and steel industry, agriculture, or the work of the Civilian Conservation Corps, as reflected in the built environment and recorded on the landscape.[3]

The existence of a National Register has altered the National Park Service and American perceptions about the relationship between history and the environment in ways that could not have been imagined even in 1966. National Register recognition has assisted in preserving a wide range of historic places. Listing or a determination of eligibility assures that historic values are considered in the planning of federally assisted projects, and listing is the threshold to qualify historic properties for federal tax benefits and grants, as well as for a number of state and local financial incentives for preservation. By 2002, the federal tax incentives alone that have been in place since 1976 to encourage the rehabilitation of registered historic buildings have been used in nearly 30,000 projects. These projects have resulted in nearly 25.5 billion dollars in private investment for preservation of the historic built environment in communities throughout the nation.[4] Many more registered historic properties have been preserved as living parts of communities as Americans have become more cognizant of the values of historic places.

The National Register's files have become a valuable source of information for research, interpretation, preservation planning and public education. Records on each listing include descriptions, statements of significance, bibliographies, maps, photographs and sometimes other useful documents. The NPS has a computerized index to listings, the National Register Information System (NRIS), with forty-five data elements that allows researchers to find historic places by location, resource type, dates, areas of significance, ethnic associations, architect/builder, significant persons, functions and so on.

The National Register makes documentation on historic places available to the public on request and uses it for public education by publishing classroom-ready lesson plans for teachers and students as part of its Teaching with Historic Places program, and a series of travel itineraries to encourage heritage tourism. Developed in partnership with communities and organizations throughout the nation, these "Discover Our Shared Heritage" itineraries describe, map, and link registered historic places to help travelers plan their trips. The National Register Information System, lesson plans, travel itineraries, National Register bulletins and other features are accessible on the National Park Service Web site at www.cr.nps.gov/nr, which reaches millions of people each year with information from the National Register on environmental history. As the value of this rich archive becomes better known, the NPS is getting large numbers of requests for copies of National Register documentation, and has responded by beginning to digitize the information in National Register files to make it available via the Web. Books based on National Register documentation are being published, and popular travel guides and the press frequently identify which sites are listed in the National Register. Even novelists like John Grisham, Barbara Kingsolver, and Jane Smiley refer to the National Register in their books, another way environmental history is becoming part of popular culture.[5] While National Register criteria for evaluation have remained the same throughout the history of the program, with the passage of time, new scholarship, the growing diversity of participants, and changes in peoples' perceptions about heritage, the National Register is evolving as new resource types are identified.[6] The range of National Register bulletins reflects the variety of historic places now being studied and added to the National Register as the public's interest in environmental history grows. Recent bulletins providing technical assistance on documentation and evaluation include those for rural and designed historic landscapes, traditional cultural places, vessels and shipwrecks, aids to navigation, historic archeological sites and districts, battlefields, mining, cemeteries and burial places, post offices, suburbs, and aviation. Researchers of historic places have been pioneers in practicing the "new American history," studying places associated with local history, gender, ethnic and minority groups, and common, everyday life in the past. Public historians working in the preservation field have drawn from other disciplines such as anthropology, ethnography, and geography to make the study of environmental history an increasingly interdisciplinary pursuit. Professor Bernard L. Herman of the University of Delaware in his article, "The 'New' Architectural History" says, "The National Register as a research strategy places buildings at the center of historical inquiry, and raises their significance from association with an individual, event, or style to their active role in signifying changing human relationships defined through interpretive categories such a class, ethnicity, occupation, environment, technology, and landscape. This is architectural history with a large agenda."[7]

While the National Register has been expanding in response to evolving public perceptions about the meaning of place, the National Park Service has been changing in other ways. Most notably, the collection of places directly managed by the National Park Service began to change, building upon the new direction set by Roosevelt and Albright.

During the nineteenth century as the historic preservation movement began to define itself, the preservation of biographical sites dominated the field. The homes of George Washington, Thomas Jefferson, and Andrew Jackson became popular focal points. At the turn of the century, the preservation of Civil War battlefields and precontact archeological sites added other dimensions to the effort. The 1920s and 1930s witnessed the re-creation of historic structures with Colonial Williamsburg setting a standard to which the remainder of the preservation world would aspire for decades. By 1949, while an astonishingly large number of places were being preserved, they all fit comfortably within the national framework of self-identity presided over by the homes of important men, battlefields, and forts. Over the next two decades, during the height of the Cold War, additional patriotic places were identified and preserved, not the least of which were sites from the Revolutionary era in Concord and Lexington and Boston. Beginning in the 1970s, the landscape of preservation, and that of the National Park Service, changed as did society's sense of itself. As historical scholarship began to expand and become more inclusive, historic sites became more representational of the national story. Historic places associated with the history of women and African Americans and artists and writers became more commonplace. Many of them had been nominated and listed in the National Register and designated National Historic Landmarks by the Secretary of the Interior. In addition, the Service's National Historic Landmarks Survey has completed theme studies on such topics as the Underground Railroad and the racial desegregation of public education in the United States.

Over the last decade, this expansion of the historic preservation movement has matured to the point where Congress added to the National Park System places such as the Monroe School in Topeka, Kansas; Manzanar National Historic Site, a Japanese internment camp during World War II; and Central High School in Little Rock, Arkansas—places that remind us how much the words "freedom" and "equality" are central to our cultural heritage and how our society has struggled to ensure that they apply universally to all Americans. These sites, combined with Washita Battlefield, Sand Creek Massacre, and Selma to Montgomery National Historic Trail, have altered the National Park Service's sense of mission. These special places remind us of our past, cultural as well as natural, and serve as strategic reference points as we think about where we want to go, what values we desire and imagine for our children and our grandchildren.

Challenged thus by Congress, the National Park Service over the past decade has rethought and redesigned its approach to interpreting all of the places entrusted to its care. The most notable of these changes is evidenced in the manner in which the Service conceptualizes its self identity. Prior to the early 1990s, "preservation" was the watchword that defined NPS activities and philosophy. But as the management of the Service became more introspective, it realized that preservation for its own sake had no relevance to contemporary society; simply preserving places tended to limit rather than expand the mission horizons of the agency. Within the last several years the Service has realized that societies preserve places because they have meaning to that society; they embody the hopes and dreams and sometimes failures of that society, and they manifest the collected stories of past generations. And it is, the storytelling aspect, the educational aspect, of places important to the country's cultural past form the context within which the Service now frames its mission. (In retrospect, it would appear that the National Park Service has come full circle for when the founders of the agency spoke of an NPS mission, they spoke of preservation and education.)

The addition of Selma, Manzanar, and Little Rock to the national collection of places managed by the National Park Service forced those who interpret these places to become better students of the past, to think at once more deeply and more broadly about these places in the sweep of American history. One cannot address, much less present to the visiting public, the sad story of Central High School without a sophisticated understanding of black/white relations in the country not only in the twentieth century, but also in the nineteenth as well.

A related change in the management practices of the Service is the belief that publicly funded bureaucracies not only could, but should interpret contentious and sensitive issues in American history. Historical topics that are controversial in contemporary society are so because issues remain unresolved and they will be resolved, or at least closer to resolution, if they are discussed and debated in public forums. In *A Place to Remember: Using History to Build Community,* Robert Archibald argues that "controversial topics are controversial precisely because they are markers for what is important in our world."[8] In an effort to prepare interpretive rangers to work with contested issues, the interpretive training program throughout the Service has been realigned. Interpreters are now encouraged to discuss with the American public, after properly immersing themselves in the subject, park related issues such as clean air and water, environmental sustainability, human and civil rights, and even the causes of the American Civil War. Indeed, it is this last subject, seemingly so innocuous, that perhaps best represents the Service's new appreciation of its education imperative.[9] For the past sixty years, the National Park Service's interpretive programs at Civil War battlefield parks consisted of detailed descriptions of troop movements, of battles, of casualties. One looked in vain for any explanation of why the men on those sacred fields wanted to kill each other, for any explanation of why the country could not solve its problems at the midpoint of the nineteenth century short of war, for any explanation of what those problems might be. The closest the National Park Service came to explaining to the eleven million visitors who annually toured its Civil War battlefield parks was in a passing phrase in Fort Sumter's park brochure, "after decades of sectional conflict." Nowhere in any of the almost thirty battlefield parks could one find an explanation for secession.

Beginning in 1998, at the insistence of the battlefield superintendents themselves, the National Park Service began revising brochures, exhibits, films, and attitudes. Working with Civil War scholars from around the country, the managers of these important places developed a plan for offering the visiting public increased opportunities to explore the meaning of the Civil War in contemporary America. Through training programs, expanded offerings in park book stores, discussions with academic historians, and public workshops the Service finally confronted the essence of the meaning of the Civil War. Over the next decade, managers, interpreters, interpretive planners, and historians intend to make the drama and the consequences of the Civil War more meaningful to the visiting public. At the onset of the Sesquicentennial of the Civil War in 2011, visitors to battlefield parks managed by the National Park Service will not only learn about the military actions that define the sacred places it manages, but also understand the causes of the war and the implication of the war's results to contemporary society. For Civil

War buffs, historians, and interpreters the changes within the agency are nowhere more pronounced.

While the National Park Service has evolved steadily over the last eighty-five years, the past decade has witnessed profound changes in its management and its approaches to environmental history. In a sense, one can argue that the historical scholarship that has burgeoned since the late 1960s, combined with the fairly recent awareness of and concern for the fragility of the planet, have placed added responsibilities on the Service. As a result, the agency is far less insular than it has been in recent memory. It seeks the assistance and advice from a number of affiliated organizations and individuals through a wide variety of partnerships. The park science program, under the direction of Dr. Michael Soukup, Associate Director for Natural Resources, has inaugurated a Canon Scholarship program that funds dissertations annually on some aspect of science in national parks. At the same time, Dr. Soukup instituted a system of Cooperative Education Study Units (CESUs) at colleges and universities across the country to assist the NPS in research and monitoring projects that is now being broadened to the study of environmental history.

New directions and emphases are also evident in other ways in the cultural programs that reach beyond park boundaries in addition to the increasing breadth of the National Register of Historic Places. In response to the changing needs of a more preservation minded public, the Service, at the insistence of Congress, reconceptualized its thematic framework for history. The original framework adopted in 1936 had reflected the historical scholarship of the times and, accordingly, focused principally on the achievements of military and political figures and on historical eras. It was conceived in terms of the "stages of American progress." Although it had been "revised" in 1970 and 1987, the framework continued to relate more to historical concepts of the 1930s than the 1980s or 1990s. The 1993 revision, a joint effort of the Organization of American Historians, American Historical Association, the National Coordinating Committee for the Promotion of History, and the National Park Service, created a structure for assessing the significance of potential National Historic Landmarks and park units, as well as for designing and enhancing park interpretive programs. As noted in the Introduction, "The framework draws upon the work of scholars across disciplines to provide a structure for capturing the complexity and meaning of human experience and for understanding that past in coherent, integrated ways."[10] More to our purpose here, the framework recognized that "environment" is more than nature, it is "where people live, the place that supports and sustains life."[11]

The 1993 revision explicitly added a theme called Transforming the Environment to *The National Park Service's Thematic Framework*. The framework states that "this theme examines the variable and changing relationships between people and their environment, which continually interact . . . While conservation represents a portion of this theme, the focus here is on recognizing the interplay between human activity and the environment as reflected in particular places, such as Hoover Dam, a National Historic Landmark."[12] The addition of this theme veri-

fies how the field of environmental history has matured to embrace the interdependent relationship between nature and human beings and gives direction to the
National Park Service to recognize, and interpret places that illustrate the overlapping roles of public and environmental history.

With the new framework, came a new and expanded view of park interpretive
programs. The historical scholarship of the past three decades required that the
interpretation of specific places be less omniscient in nature and more inclusive
of voices ignored or omitted by the consensus view of history that dominated historical scholarship prior to the 1960s. An early impetus for this change came from
Congress, which in 1991 changed the name of Custer Battlefield National Monument to Little Bighorn Battlefield National Monument. Explicit in the legislation was the expectation that the National Park Service would replace the wor-
shipful interpretation of George Armstrong Custer with a balanced story that
would also present the plight of the Sioux, Arapaho, and Cheyenne, as settlers
and gold-seekers pushed into their traditional lands after the Civil War. (A possible apocryphal story from earlier days, has the Service placing exhibit text in
the park's small museum that read, "There were no survivors!") To make the will
of Congress more emphatic, the legislation also directed the Service to erect an
appropriate monument to the Indians who fell that July day in 1876.

Coming on the heels of the Little Bighorn legislation, was the publication of the
results and recommendations of the Servicewide conference that commemorated
the seventy-fifth anniversary of the National Park Service. *National Parks for the
21st Century: The Vail Agenda* (1992) contained a long list of recommendations designed to strengthen the Service's abilities to manage and preserve the country's
natural and cultural heritage. The report recommended that the Service "should re-
vise its philosophy, policy, and management approaches to reflect the legitimate
role the agency has as a national public education system." In light of this and other
suggestions of *The Vail Agenda* and the Service's acceptance of the New American History, interpreters and interpretive planners began designing programs that
presented park stories using multiple points of view. Fur trapping and trading sites,
for example, no longer relied on a single narrative, but on several. This rich historical drama now could be viewed through multiple lenses: from the perspective of
the trapper, from the perspective of the Indian, and no less important, from the perspective of the beaver for its near extinction had repercussions for the environmental history of the country. Women, African Americans, laborers, and ethnic
groups began to appear in park stories where a decade earlier those voices had been
nonexistent. Within this expanded interpretive framework, the National Park Service also ventured into the realm of social conflict. During the 1990s, Congress assigned places to the care and management of the National Park Service that were
different in the stories they had to tell, the values they held for all Americans. These
"sites of shame" required that the Service deal with stories that were not of the up-
lifting sort generally associated with national park sites. The story of Manzanar, a
camp where the United States relocated and interned Japanese civilians during
World War II; or Central High School in Little Rock, Arkansas, site of the 1957

school desegregation confrontation; or the Edmund Pettus Bridge where voting rights demonstrators were attacked in 1965 by the Alabama State Police are all stories that must be told in detail and within the context of their times for the visiting public to understand the power of the place. As Congress was debating the inclusion of several of these places with conflicted histories, the historian Robin Winks provided encouragement and a reason to include in the National Park System places that challenge our socially progressive sense of ourselves. "Education is best done with examples," he wrote. "These examples must include that which we regret, that which is to be avoided, as well as that for which we strive. No effective system of education can be based on unqualified praise, for all education instructs people of the difference between moral and wanton acts and how to distinguish between the desirable and the undesirable. If this premise is correct, we cannot omit the negative lessons of history."[13]

The maturation of the National Park Service was further in evidence with the publication in 1998 of a book highly critical of the Service's management of its natural resources. *Preserving Nature in the National Parks: A History* by Richard West Sellars presented a sophisticated and well argued critique of the Service's emphasis on scenery management over ecosystem management.[14] Using detailed archival evidence, Sellars explored the degree to which the Service had slighted its science research and monitoring program over the years while promoting and encouraging its park planners and landscape architects to "develop" the parks with roads, parking lots, and other visitor amenities. The response of the Service to this devastating criticism was one that could not have been envisioned fifteen years earlier. Instead of absorbing the report with silence, or promising all kinds of remedies that were not forthcoming, the Service established a working group of scientists and managers to analyze the institutional problems identified by Sellars and design solutions for a long-term fix. The result was the Natural Resource Challenge, a five-year plan which, with the strong support of Congress, pumped tens of millions of dollars in research, monitoring, and management programs for natural resources into the National Park System. The Service's bureaucratic environment of the 1990s encouraged, even insisted upon, creative, if painful, introspection.

The evolving social and political milieu within which the Service today carries out its mission is further characterized by the complexity of determining the very definition of historical significance. Since its inception, the Keeper of the National Register has routinely been called upon to adjudicate eligibility for the National Register where there are conflicting opinions on the significance of human interactions with the physical environment and competing uses for the same resources. Just one of the more complex and nuanced evaluation issues that the Register staff is required to address is the historical significance of natural landscapes and other places that possess cultural meaning to Native Americans, who are speaking up more often about these traditional cultural places, particularly when they are threatened by development. Two examples illustrate the complexities of environmental history and interpretations of cultural significance as they relate to nature.

The Zuni Salt Lake and Sanctuary in New Mexico is a 182,406 acre site sacred to six tribes, the Zuni, Western Pueblos (Acoma, Laguna, Hopi), Apache and Navaho. Its heart is the Zuni Salt Lake, a historically important source of salt and home to Salt Mother, a deity sanctified by all of the tribes. The lake also is associated with the war gods of the Western Pueblos, who have a shrine in a small volcanic cone within the main crater of the lake. The Sanctuary, or neutral zone, which encompasses most of the acreage, is a sacred place, inextricably linked with the Zuni Salt Lake, where Native Americans pay homage to Salt Mother by keeping a reverent attitude and avoiding any type of hunting or violence. Each tribe makes pilgrimages to Salt Lake and maintains and uses shrines in the Sanctuary zone defined by the natural topography of the area as viewed from the crater containing Salt Lake. The lake and sanctuary have a long history of significance based in traditional practice extending from time immemorial to the present and an ongoing role in the retention and transmission of the cultures of the tribes who maintain their traditional use of the site for religious pilgrimages, collecting and processing salt and medicinal herbs, and for therapeutic healing. Five trails through the Sanctuary to the lake, most of which were not visible to the naked eye, were relocated and mapped as a result of the aerial survey. The National Register nomination was sponsored by the Indians who were concerned about a coal mining project's effects on the sacred landscape. Most of the land is administered by the federal government, but some of it is privately owned. The nomination was hotly disputed in New Mexico, and while the state's historic preservation review board

Figure 4-1. Zuni, Salt Lake, New Mexico. *Photo by Beth Boland, National Register of Historic Places, National Park Service.*

supported its eligibility, the State Historic Preservation Officer did not support the nomination of such a large natural landscape. Neither did the mining company, local officials or the private owners who questioned the cultural significance of the site and were concerned that a determination that it was eligible for the National Register would interfere with its use for mining and ranching. The National Register determined that this large site was eligible for listing.

Where nature itself is culturally significant, changes to the environment have an impact on whether the landscape can physically convey significant cultural associations. To be eligible for the National Register according to the criteria for evaluation, historic properties must have integrity of location, design, setting, workmanship, feeling and association. Sometimes groups continue to value a place even though it has been destroyed or drastically altered. Such was the case when the Federal Energy Regulatory Commission (FERC) requested a determination of eligibility for the North Fork Skokomish Traditional Property District in Washington State. The agency was considering an application for a new license for the Cushman Hydroelectric Project on the Olympic Peninsula that serves the City of Takoma. The traditional territory associated with the Skokomish Indians occupied a substantial area encompassing the natural drainages of the North and South Forks of the Skokomish River as they drained out of the Olympic Mountain range into Puget Sound, a distance of approximately thirty river miles. The district as proposed, consisted of the traditional use areas and focused on various historic fishing and hunting locations within the river drainage, along with scattered historic village and ceremonial sites along the original shorelines of the river. Also included was a loosely bounded mountainous area to the north of the North Fork valley said to be associated with important Skokomish ceremonial use and traditional stories. The river areas below the two twentieth-century Cushman hydroelectric dams are now dry as a result of the dam projects, while much of the upper river area lies submerged beneath the dam's reservoirs and impoundments.

Both the Skokomish Tribe and the Washington State Historic Preservation Officer believed the district was eligible for the National Register, while FERC had concluded that many traditional cultural sites in the proposed North Fork district have been severely disturbed and therefore lacked integrity of condition and relationship to warrant eligibility either as a district or as individual sites. The nominations for the Cushman No.1 and No. 2 hydroelectric dams, listed in the National Register in 1988, documented the severe damage to salmon and steelhead trout populations, which had flourished prior to the construction of the dams. Besides destroying most of the historic fish runs on the Skokomish, the dam projects had a devastating impact on the Tribe's economy and opportunities for tribal members to earn a living and obtain food for their families because the project was sited on top of fishing sites in use since ancient times. In addition, wildlife resources that tribal members used for subsistence had been displaced and greatly reduced by the project. The Cushman Dams also symbolize the condemnation of their tribal lands and water resources for the benefit of a public utility located over sixty miles from the reservation. The Skokomish have been fighting the issuing of the license by

FERC. The documentation provided ample evidence of the continuing importance of the area to the tribe, which believes that both the inundated areas above the dams and the down-stream sections without water are only temporary conditions that are partially or completely reversible. Much of the traditional use area in the proposed district, including some of the most important ethnographically identified sites, lie under the waters created by the dams. Long stretches of the river had been dewatered. The dramatic changes brought to the landscape of the North Fork area by the dams and logging significantly altered the integrity of setting and the natural features that defined the cultural landscape necessary for traditional Skokomish use within the area removing the important link between the cultural use aspects of the district and the biological and natural features on which these uses were based. The location of some of the sites identified in the ethnographic literature was not known with any certainty, and documentation was vague and contradictory since the Skokomish had been unable to use these sites after construction of the dams in the mid-1920s and 1930s.

The National Register staff ultimately determined that because the project had so altered the landscape, the North Fork Traditional Property District as a whole was not eligible for listing. However, the National Register's opinion letter suggested that both the area that has been physically modified by the Cushman project and some of the individual sites were potentially eligible for listing for their importance to the Skokomish if the water levels were adjusted and if fish and wildlife returned and the sites and their traditional uses were restored. One individual site at the Little Falls was determined eligible. Even though the Little Falls is currently dry, the general location of the falls appears to retain its essential natural character and campsites, fishing camps located atop the bluff, the trails down into and out of the gorge, the falls location and the traditional gathering, preparation and socializing areas identified in the vicinity of the falls remain. While the Cushman project was devastating to the traditional native use area, the dams themselves are historically significant as engineering feats, a demonstration of the complexity of human interactions with the natural environment and how changes overtime can destroy the ability of the landscape to convey one type of cultural significance and replace it with another.[15]

As the National Park Service continues to evolve in response to the mandates of Congress, the demands of a growing and vocal public, and the advice of innumerable scientific and historical constituent organizations, it must continue to strengthen its new-found introspective nature. In the short term, it is receiving assistance in this respect from the National Park System Advisory Board, an independent body of scholars and park supporters appointed by the Secretary of the Interior.

The most recent Board, chaired by the distinguished historian John Hope Franklin, produced a report that likens the Service to a sleeping giant "beloved and respected, yes; but perhaps too cautious, too resistant to change, too reluctant to engage the challenges that must be addressed in the 21st century." *Rethinking the National Parks for the 21st Century*[16] serves as a reminder that as the population grows and changes, the demands upon, and the responsibilities of, the National Park Service grow and change accordingly. Park management is not and should never be considered a static ideal. Based upon a series of seven recommendations, *Rethinking the National Parks for the 21st Century* presents a vision for the future. The report is expansive in its assessment of need and direct in its articulation of the problem. "We are a species whose influence on natural systems is profound, yet the consequences of this influence remain only dimly understood. Our increased numbers have altered terrestrial and marine systems, strained resources and caused extinction rates never before seen. As developed landscapes press against or surround many parks, pollutants in both the air and water impact park resources. Our growing numbers encourage a drifting away from knowledge about nature and our own history as a nation and a people." In its belief that the Service should be a major voice in "confronting" those issues, the Board envisions a National Park Service that will embrace its mission as educator, encourage a broad and inclusive study of the American past, adopt the conservation of biodiversity as a core principle, advance the principles of sustainability, actively acknowledge the connections between native cultures and the parks (natural as well as cultural), encourage collaboration among park and recreation systems at every level, and improve the Service's institutional capacity by developing new organizational talents and abilities and a workforce that reflects America's diversity. These are weighty challenges. The vision, if realized, will constitute yet another step in the evolution of the National Park Service. Constructed as an "attempt to look afresh at the Park Service; the social, cultural, and political environment within which it operates, and the ways it can serve the American public more effectively," the report anticipates and encourages the development of a new cultural ethic within the agency.

Whether the Service is capable of sustaining the remarkable changes it has experienced over the past decade and expanding them to address the expectations of the Board remains to be seen. What is clear, is that the National Park Service of today is fundamentally a different agency from the one Stephen Mather created in 1916. As we write, the National Park System has grown to 385 individual units and consists of natural and cultural parks that constitute a rich public legacy. The management of these places and their interpretation to the visiting public place the Service at the intersection of public history and environmental history. Our collective sense of how humans relate to the environment and how the environment shapes human activities and beliefs is fundamental to the responsible management of these places. It is not by accident that the wilderness areas in many of the large western national parks are indeed more "wild" today than they were in the 1920s and 1930s. The reintroduction of the wolf into the greater Yellowstone ecosystem is a recognition by our society that our collective physical and psychic health is linked directly to the health of our natural environment. By the same token, the expansion of the National Register of Historic Places and the number of "heritage areas" formally established by Congress reflect the growing sense that the preservation of our built or otherwise historically significant environment is equally important to the health of our society.

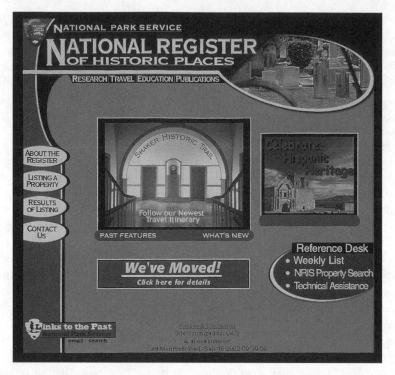

Figure 4-2. The National Register of Historic Places' website (www.cr.nps.gov/nr) is visited by millions of people each year and provides the public with information including a database of listed sites (NRIS), electronic versions of National Register Publications, and a series of lesson plans and travel itineraries highlighting listed places.

As the National Park Service approaches the centennial of its establishment in 2016, its role in the spheres of public and environmental history will only increase. At the same time it will continue to define and redefine itself in the future based on the agency's internal management, the will of Congress and the president, and society's sense of itself and its vision for its natural and cultural heritage.

NOTES

1. David Rains Wallace, *Yellowstone: A Natural and Human History.* (Washington, DC: U.S. Department of the Interior, 1999).
2. The statistics on the National Register of Historic Places are current as of the middle of 2002.
3. The National Register section of the National Park Service Web site includes a list of multiple property submissions and copies of multiple property documentation. See www.cr.nps.gov/nr.

4. National Park Service, *Federal Tax Incentives for Rehabilitating Historic Buildings, Statistical Report Analysis for Fiscal Year 2001.*
5. See Jane Smiley's *Moo*, John Grisham's *A Time to Kill*, and Barbara Kingsolver's *Pigs in Heaven.*
6. The National Criteria for Evaluation and guidance for applying them are found in the National Register bulletin, *How to Apply the National Register Criteria for Evaluation*, National Park Service, 1997.
7. Bernard Herman, "The 'New' Architectural History," CRM 17, No. 2 (1994): 6–7.
8. Robert R. Archibald, *A Place to Remember: Using History to Build Community*. (Walnut Creek, California: AltaMira Press, 1999), 94.
9. While implicit in the 1916 enabling legislation for the National Park Service, Secretary of the Interior Franklin K. Lane made the educational mandate explicit in his letter of instruction to Stephen T. Mather the following year. "The educational, as well as the recreational, use of the national parks," he wrote, "should be encouraged in every practicable way." See Lary M. Dilsaver, ed., *America's National Park System: The Critical Documents*. (Lanham, Maryland: Rowman & Littlefield Publishers, 1994), p. 50.
10. National Park Service, *History in the National Park Service: Themes & Concepts,* 1994.
11. Ibid.
12. Ibid.
13. Robin Winks, "Sites of Shame," *National Parks*, (March/April 1994), 22–23.
14. Richard West Sellars, *Preserving Nature in the National Parks: A History*. (New Haven, CT: Yale University Press, 1998).
15. Documentation on both Zuni Salt Lake and Sanctuary and the North Fork Skokomish Traditional Property District from which these examples are taken is found in the National Register determination of eligibility files maintained by the National Park Service.
16. National Park System Advisory Board, *Rethinking the National Parks for the 21st Century,* 2001.

CULTURAL TOURISM AND A CHANGING SOCIETY

Hal K. Rothman

In the summer of 1999, I led the American Orient Express train tour of the national parks. At $5000 a berth, this was a specialty experience that took travelers on a ten-day trip that began in Denver. It continued to Salt Lake City, down through the Utah parks, out to Death Valley, and around to the Grand Canyon. From El Tovar, we rode the train to Acoma, the Sky City, and finally finished in Santa Fe. The train was a refurbished 1940s luxury train, with small berths and shared showers in a style long gone from American society. Glorious five-course meals in the beautiful dining car and entertainment in the club cars and observation car transcended limited personal space. The train offered both past and present, a luxury tour reminiscent of an earlier America, a cultural experience really, as well as a combined train and bus tour through the national parks of today. It gave its travelers an image of the past in the train and showed them the spectacular national parks, an affirmation of American culture in themselves, as they were wined and dined with the best that postmodern America has to offer.

First and foremost, the American Orient Express offers a deluxe experience. The needs of the passengers—what they sought, what they wanted, and what they expected—were paramount. They'd chosen a mode of travel with powerful cultural overtones, but they had not in any way agreed to shed the trappings of class, context, and position. The train took them back in time, but provided them the soft edges of an experience with the rough corners thoroughly planned. A sleeping car porter turned down the beds; he left water in the ubiquitous plastic bottle. This wasn't the 1940s at all; it was the 1990s in 1940s costume, which was better than the old days ever could have been. It might even have been better than real.

The train was filled with people in their sixties and seventies, people who could very well have traveled on such a train in its heyday. They were of a different America than I, people who could remember a nation of small towns and farms, who knew of places like Bucklin, Kansas, and Pesotum, Illinois. That lonesome whistle meant freedom and adventure to them as did the automobile to their children. Once, it spelled out the names of places they'd never seen, experiences they only dreamed of. Now it brought back memories.

They moved comfortably on the train, part of a culture that was raised with the shared space of club cars and dining cars. Within one day of boarding the train, I understood the need for manners in a society that shared space; after more than forty years of living, I'd finally found a reason to be polite! In postmodern America, where we insult each other in traffic and think of it as communication, the older virtues that made a world where people stood, walked, sat, and chatted in common space have fallen by the wayside. On the train, where everyone lived in a 10 by 7 compartment, the ability to negotiate public space was critical. Everyone had to be able to deal with people they didn't necessarily like; they had to abide by a code that allowed people to disagree without disagreeing, to deflect unwanted conversation or attention without giving offense. It was a skillful dance, where disapproval was established by a turn of the head or a reorienting of the shoulders, certainly not with words, mild or harsh. Here was a lesson to younger America, a vision of a past where interactive skills were essential to the persistence of community in a world in which only the wealthiest could separate from the rest. Space and privacy in that world conveyed status; in ours, only time allows that distinction.

The most overwhelming feature of the train was service. The entire ethos of the train stemmed from a world where labor was cheap. In part because of the price and equally because of the age of the travelers, the train staff spent most of its time performing little tasks that made the trip not only special but memorable. This attention was the personification of enlightened self-interest; I learned only later that the staff depended on tips as a crucial part of their income. Besides train staff, waiters, porters, and cooks among them, the train company hired not only lecturers like me, but also tour guides who transferred people from the train to buses and other conveyances, arranged for hotel rooms and meals on the nights we were not on the train, and otherwise handled the day-to-day arrangements. Like the tours Japanese companies provide their countrymen in the United States, nearly every aspect of the train travelers' experience filtered through one or another of the service people.

Here was a form of cultural tourism, a package of events and experiences in a setting that was made comfortable for its audience. Travelers could experience culture and many of them were able to relive an earlier time in their life through the mechanism of the train. One man told me that he traveled home on a similar train with his severance pay from the military at the end of World War II. Another couple told how they'd honeymooned on such a train in 1947. Clearly culture and personal history—some might say nostalgia—melded. This was a trip in the present and the past simultaneously.

This intersection has a lot to show, for the American Orient Express is a harbinger of the future, a window into the complexities of cultural tourism. Cultural tourism has come to mean a great deal more than most scholars envision, education about the past. It has become an industry that brings together a combination of history, nostalgia, myth, and entertainment, in the guise of teaching about American culture. It also includes status markers such as labor-intensive luxury experience, memory, and a definition of what's important that stems from an ideal of high- and low-brow cultures, of knowledge worth having. It has also become a cash cow, a way to sustain communities and regions when other economic strategies fail. The train fused the elements that make cultural tourism an integral part of the future not only of tourism, but of the restructuring of the economy of much of the nation. It mirrored a process long evident throughout the Southwest and spreading more and more across the nation, a story that combined imagery, accouterments, and experience in an effort to persuade the public that in fact what they'd experienced was different from the norms of daily life. The combination of age, wealth, service, and cultural symbolism of the train portend a future with plenty of possibilities and equally many challenges. The train carried us through more than the Southwest. It illustrated many of the essential challenges of promoting culture in a changing age.

In the past decade, tourism has become one of the major buzzes in American society. It became important quickly, coming from nowhere as the nation went through the first stages of an excruciating shift from an industrial to postindustrial economy. The combination of Vietnam War era inflation and the OPEC oil embargo brought postwar prosperity to a screeching halt and unmasked the aging of American industrial infrastructure. Industrial America was forced to compete against newer facilities and cheaper labor overseas, and the result was disastrous. Between 1974 and 1997, the real value of American wages declined every year for twenty-three successive years. The nation even lost entire industries. Once the United States made televisions. The last place in the nation to assemble them was the Zenith plant in Springfield, Missouri. By 1998, the same building housed the mail order inventory for Bass Pro Shops, a recreational tourist entity that catered to the tastes of blue-collar America. As electronics and others disappeared, communities and regions sought a panacea, something to replace the lost jobs in the figurative widget factory, the ones that paid the bills for families and filled tax coffers, the dollars that hired new teachers and repaved torn-up roads. In many places, there were few alternatives—stories of retraining programs for forty-five-year-old steel workers who'd been in the mill since they turned eighteen and in the words of Bruce Springsteen, "got a union card and a wedding coat" abounded—and as county commissioners and city officials scratched their heads, they cast about for a way to sustain their communities and themselves. Tourism seemed a ready-made panacea; it rarely required tax abatements or give-backs and it seemed to provide jobs and opportunities. Even better, people got paid for being themselves.

When the rest of the nation looked for models of how cultural tourism worked, they looked to the Southwest and the Civil War battlefields. The Civil War had become the creation story of the second American Republic, the one that resculpted a Liberty Bell without the fissure of slavery. Its birth happened in blood, the most dramatic sequence of events in American history. The mythical Southwest was its byproduct, the panoramic dreamscape of the nation. In the West, the nation reinvented itself after the Civil War; there the galvanized Yankees went, the retread, the unreconstructed southerners, and the mass of immigrants who in mythology yearned to be free. The weird and spectacular scenery and divergent cultures of the Southwest, from the petrified forests of Arizona and the festive Mexicano nature of San Antonio to the solitary cliffs of the Colorado Plateau and the Navajo Nation, the Southwest promised difference and in that difference authentic experience. You could be yourself in the Southwest, Americans wholeheartedly believed; you could become whoever you wanted to be and in the process you could feel the past of the nation, could see the American pageant before you. You could be part of the past, free of the indignities of the oppressive present. When others looked at models for tourism, especially cultural tourism, as an economic engine, no region had done it better than the Southwest. From Santa Fe to Santa Barbara, from San Antonio to Las Vegas, the Southwest has been a landscape for visitors, a place where people can see the past as they wanted it to be, take a piece of it with them, and feel their distance from the norms of the mainstream. Here's a landscape that works—because it isn't what it claims to be; it's a softer, manipulated, more valued version of the realities of the region.

This particular look at the Southwest skewed its evolution, transposed a past awkwardly on the present. The region had been in transformation since the end of World War II. Tourism had long been the shadow industry in the region, seemingly ephemeral to states that traditionally made their living in timber, ranging, agriculture, and mineral extraction. In the quarter-century that followed the end of World War II, a combination of economic innovation, access, and technology brought millions to visit the region and almost as many to live there. All of a sudden, tourism catapulted to enormous significance; the long history of visitation turned into a torrent of cars, backpackers, opera-goers, skiers, mountain-bikers and history buffs. Even states such as California, the core area for the West, began cultural tourism initiatives. California has the twelfth largest economy in the world. Its interest in cultural tourism affirmed this new importance and at the same time, made it the subject of scrutiny as a model for similar endeavors.

Tourism grew in importance as the seeds of a new, connected future were taking shape. The catalyst of this transformation came from a minuscule piece of silicon called the microchip. This little chunk of information processing material caused the radical, inexorable, fundamental, and overnight transformation of the basis of the world economy; it created a transformation every bit as great as the Industrial Revolution, a divide across which people peered with great trepidation. The Microchip Revolution, the constellation of changes associated with the rise of this funny little piece of equipment, changed life as we knew it. Microchips created the so-called Information Age, in which knowledge and the ability to manipulate it genuinely became power, and it dramatically increased the range and significance of the service economy.

Without the microchip, all the revolutions of the past twenty years, in everything from manufacturing and banking, to health technologies and elite job choice simply could not have taken place. This transformation created large amounts of wealth and equal amounts of consequences. Cyber transactions now move capital around the globe, creating what the noted cultural critic Christopher Lasch recognized as a transnational class of monied individuals who are essentially stateless in their sense of national obligations. This boundary-free wealth has few obligations to people and places and its incredible mobility may even constitute a threat to the stability of individual places and national economies. The tremendous exporting of manufacturing to developing countries, from the *maquiladora* corridor in Mexico to the Far East where Michael Jordan inspected Nike factories and Kathie Lee Gifford got in so much trouble, are only two poignant examples of a trend that has profound implications for anyone dependent on a paycheck. The result has been that some skills—especially white-collar information-based skills—have gained in value, while others have seen their skills deprived of value. "Foreman says these jobs are going boys," sang Springsteen, the bard of the dispossessed, in the early 1980s, "and they ain't coming back," and right he was. What replaced them was a dispossession of the old American working class, the lunch bucket and hard hat brigade who voted Democratic and sent their children to college to eventually turn into Republicans.

Like all its predecessors, this new revolution picks winners and losers. Some sectors of the economy fare marvelously. The educated, the highly skilled upper end of the service sector—everyone from attorneys to consultants of all stripes—find opportunities galore at fees that reward their choice of career. The technically proficient—and here skilled health care professionals stand out, along with the denizens of Silicon Valley—also benefit greatly. They are their skill; they sell their knowledge, and it is transferable from the equipment of one employer to another. These two groups lead the pack. Wage workers of all kinds, agricultural workers, and the semiskilled and unskilled bear the economic brunt of this change. Their skills have simply lost value and many have been consigned to the scrapheap of economic history. Stocking bottles in a 7–11 never had the upward mobility of industrial work, not to mention the job security, wages, or benefits.

In the end, this revolution has changed the way life progresses in the United States. We don't work as we did even fifteen years ago; PCs and the Internet created access and information transfer in ways that seemed like science fiction in the 1970s. We no longer rely on the sources of capital that once drove the American economy. The junk bonds of the 1970s, themselves an innovation, have become the derivatives, a computer-generated sort of splitting and matching, of the 1990s. We don't do the same tasks in the same ways, and we barely experience the constraints that once placed limits on the way business was done.

The transformation has been powerful and comprehensive. It has diminished not only the market value of American resources but a significant piece of the national mythology as well. The United States was built on two premises: cheap labor, often provided by immigrants and family members, and cheap natural resources. Labor hasn't been cheap in the United States since before World War II and the formerly cheap natural resources are both more expensive and less necessary in a global economy. Although it may be premature to declare the end of the natural resources-based world economy, it is clear that ways in which resources are organized, used, and the purposes to which they are put have dramatically changed—especially in the First World. The changing economy and a changing culture put a premium on experience—precisely the entity that tourism and travel could provide—that was new in its scope and scale. In a society charged with questions of race and ethnicity, the Southwest became a canvas for the nation, a place to visit in anticipation of working out the complex tensions at the core of a diversifying nation. No better landscape, no better demography existed on which to paint American dreams. Nowhere did the United States offer a clearer image of a multiracial past; nowhere did that image draw Americans more completely into a mythic past. The nation had treated the Southwest as a dreamscape for more than a century, psychically taming the landscape and its people in a way that the public culture of tourism, the set of signs and symbols that the tourist landscape gives off like radiation, wholly embraced. The result was a script for change without change, a cultural tourism that genuflects to a mythic past as a way to minimize and finally erase tension.

In this new world of individual expression, experiences became currency and entertainment, replacing conventional culture. This equation had enormous ramifications for the country, but especially for the Southwest. On the canvas made of American dreams of expansion and the creation of order, the rise of culture as commodity sent hundreds of thousands streaming to the Southwest, the most mythic region of the nation and the destination of the greatest number of tourists. Not only did visitors seek to find themselves and to solve their qualms about a changing society both then and now, they also sought to possess the amorphous culture of the self. The Old Southwest promised self-realization in a world of inauthentic and fabricated experience. Even you, Greg Brady of *The Brady Bunch,* could befriend an Indian boy of the same age and with your family be adopted into his tribe. Only here could you see mythic Indian people making the crafts that gave you credibility. Only here did Spanish seem like an indigenous language, not an overlay as in *West Side Story.* Against the backdrop of the American Indian and Hispano past, cultural tourism attained great cachet.

And no wonder. Much of the physical landscape of the region, its public symbolism, the construction of its roads, trails, and even cities reflected a process that took cultural history, planed off its rough edges and placed it in a neat little wrapper that was intelligible to the traveling classes. Even 100 years ago, Americans saw in the reflected mirror of a constructed Southwest a canvas on which to paint their social tensions. New Mexico excelled at that process, often at the expense of its natives; California obliterated a past but kept its symbolic vestiges in names, roads, and trail, and entire industries devoted to the creation of "authentic" goods—souvenirs really—and the assigning of status to them developed with a flourish. The poverty of the region, its difference from humid-clime America, its browns and golds instead of green, made a persuasive setting for a nation in love with its self-designated mission that needed precisely the space, close in but illustratively far away, in which allow cultural dissent. The presence of seekers from Charles Lummis through Mary Austin and Mabel Dodge Lujan and on to Georgia O'Keefe confirmed that here was space that was different, but not so different that the ways of American life, the assertions to high culture, to literary publishers, to art museums, did not hold sway.

Cities such as San Antonio embraced this new conception of a manufactured past, recognized in it a future that they could not find in any other activity. Without industry, with low wages and masses of unskilled and semiskilled workers, San Antonio sought a package for its attributes. Along with Santa Barbara and Santa Fe, San Antonio became one of the earliest cities to package an exotic but smoothed past for the consumption of a public who seemed likely to pay for little else from it. Tourist cities morphed from there. Las Vegas became the first city in the world entirely devoted to tourism. Even vaunted California joined the game in the 1990s with its cultural tourism initiative that left smaller cities complaining of the dominance of Los Angeles, San Francisco, and San Diego. A full generation before much of the rest of the nation recognized anything but conventions as having an impact on regional economies, Southwestern cities understood the value of tourism and catered to it with a subtle determination to make it pay.

By the time of the Microchip Revolution, this construct was set in stone in the Southwest. Tourism and the soft corners of culture described the place of the Southwest in American iconography and generations of southwesterners, Native, Latino, and Anglo, were accustomed to the dance of tourism. The serving of outsiders at the expense of locals had gone from sacrifice to custom to way of life. People complained about it, but they recognized it as essential to their existence. If the tourists weren't going to mail in the checks and just stay home, the Southwest would have to deal with them, their needs, their litter, their mythic misconceptions of the places they visited. Tourism offered an embrace, a close hug, that sometimes squeezed the air out of the Southwest.

The future of tourism in some ways looks very bright. In the Southwest especially, the changes in American culture and demography speak to a future full if not inundated with tourists. In a world where trees are more valuable as scenery than as timber, places with long histories of providing experience on surface stand to do very well. In states like Nevada, Hawaii, and New Mexico, long histories in tourism speak to the potential of the industry.

A new world is dawning, one that will change cultural tourism and especially the places that depend on it. The Baby Boomers, the largest birth cohort in American history, are reaching the onset of retirement. These are the wealthiest group of people in human history, in no small part because of the run-up in the stock market of the 1990s, who will also be the recipients of the biggest cross-generational transfer of wealth in human history as they inherit from their parents. The nation will have an older, more affluent population in far better health than any people of its age in human history. As the new century dawns, they are hitting precisely the stage of life where cultural tourism, the reach for a past not necessarily their own, will become important to them. They'll travel in ever-growing numbers to see the places they associate with their own personal history as well as those important to their construction of their nation and its heritage. They'll need not only gasoline and meals, but rooms and tour guides, IMAX theaters and medical care. They'll demand amenities; this is the most self-indulgent cohort yet to travel through American life. And more than anything, they'll require parking lots for their recreational vehicles. From now until about 2040, when the last of the baby boomers reach the logical end of their traveling years, all cultural tourism providers have to do is figuratively build parking lots—provide more and better amenities to the ever increasing number of retirees who search for the past as recreational and enlightenment. It's a dream for museum professionals and park rangers, people who deal with the visitor populations of today.

If only it were this easy. There's a flip side, far more difficult to negotiate. A quick look around American society shows a culture without continuity. There's a fault line in American culture that I call the MTV line. If you came to maturity before 1982, when MTV came on the air, you're part of one culture with a widely shared set of signs and symbols. You're likely to know who Abraham Lincoln was, that the Civil War was in the nineteenth century, and that presidents before John Kennedy weren't necessarily telegenic. If you're a little older, you're likely to have traveled somewhere by train and if you're male, to have been conscripted and fought in a war. If you crossed that line after 1982, you come from a different world, visual and post-literate. It's a spectator culture, one where you watch and change channels if you're dissatisfied with what you see, where you put a value on your ability to choose and to experience without effort.

This is what John Seabrook of the *New Yorker* has called "Nobrow," a culture of neither high nor low, when all comes together in a manifestation of the self. Nothing's better any more and maybe that's a good thing; the glassware at Target is as good as that from the best houses, the knock-offs are better than the real watches. It's a world where, as Seabrook tartly puts its, "culture and marketing are as cozy as Mickey and Minnie." Everything had become mainstream, creating independent sets of signs and symbols to describe culture.

For the young this was particularly telling. Coming from a spectator youth culture, they understood the world in different terms, genuflected at different statues, and generally understood a parallel set of cues to the world. What these young people—and all who subscribe to their culture—know and how they learn it is different from the world of "culture" with a capital C. Spoon-fed from an "I'm OK, You're OK" motif they crave experience, not in the authentic terms of Livingston or Stanley, not in the quest for knowledge of Humboldt, but in the self-indulgent, "experience is a mirror for my desire" terms of postindustrialism. In this frame, it is experience, culture with a video camera that makes the self important, that gives meaning to existence. It is the process, the act of doing, not the knowledge acquired, that is the grail here.

Culture has become a script that places the visitor at the center. Riding around Las Vegas, backpacking in the wilds of Chaco Canyon or Southern Utah, and sitting in the IMAX have come to have the same meaning. Its not that the people on the other side of the MTV line don't know the difference between inauthentic and authentic; it's very simply a problem of communication: the denizens of the old have not given sufficiently good reasons for their definition of authenticity. From the signs and symbols around them, they've shaped their own view of culture and it follows their dictates, not those based in the historical and cultural past. It's a new culture and its adherents regard their symbols as their guidelines; in it Dr. Dre is more important than Abraham Lincoln, Thomas Jefferson's possible liaison with Sally Hemings more significant than the Declaration of Independence and his lifelong struggle with the institution of slavery.

For cultural tourism, this is a whole new world, one in which the Rock 'n Roll Hall of Fame in Cleveland is more important than the Civil War battlefields that dot the eastern half of the nation. Cultural tourism as it is currently practiced sells learning, reverence and dismay at the past, immersion in the values of society. Unlike its counterparts, recreational and entertainment tourism, both wrapped up with the self in different ways, cultural tourism is about more than individuals and their needs. It affirms culture . . . but what culture and under what circumstances?

This distinction turns out to be as hard for the Baby Boomers as for the MTV generation. It reflects more than the transformation of culture; it is also the transformation of what culture means. Cultural tourism is supposed to do more than reflect the self; that is its promise and its value. In a "me, me, me, now, now, now" culture, its audience is necessarily the smallest. Even those in midlife, most likely to inquire about the context of the world around them, most likely to see themselves in a quest for enlightenment—not about the self, but about society—the persuasiveness of self-indulgence persists. Like the MTVers, the Baby Boomers pull away from a culture of sacrifice—hey, we're on vacation after all!—and toward messages that affirm the self even under the guise of learning.

The American Southwest has long experienced these issues and the transformations they embody. One of the first loci of the power politics of identity, one of the first regions of the country whose objects became commodities of authenticity, a place that turned itself over to tourism while industrialism still ground forward, giving it cities as different as San Antonio and Las Vegas devoted to tourism in different forms, a part of the country where daily life and mythology melded, often to the disadvantage of daily life, the Southwest experienced the cataclysmic transformation at the root of the tourist economy before the rest of the nation. Its cultural tourism and the issues that still swirl around it instruct a nation increasingly consumed with visiting itself in the figurative mirror of affirmation.

In this respect, the Southwest serves as a model for the rest of the nation. History is important to Americans, but not the history that academics produce. The public loves narrative history, particularly when it is coded with a message of the affirmation of the viewer. This is not significantly different from a century ago, when Americans came to the Grand Canyon to view its splendor as a reflection and indeed affirmation of their culture. Now there are so many more cultures to consider, so many subgroups that claim a place at the table of American history. The older notions—of progress toward a more perfect society, largely white, small town, and Protestant, have disappeared as we've become a different nation. In that process, history has not reached the new publics—through no fault of academics, who have incorporated a diverse range of perspectives in their scholarship and teaching. Instead, it seems that visitors to many places are the same people who visited them thirty and even fifty years ago—much like the people on the American Orient Express I traveled with—only older, bringing their children and grandchildren in tow. A trip to the Grand Canyon will still yield a diverse audience, people from the Far East and Europe galore, but mostly white Americans. Disney, a new way of belonging in our society, draws more Latinos, participating in the new meaning of American society as consumerism, the possession of goods and experience.

For conventional cultural tourism, inclusiveness is a challenge. Historians must prove again the value of the places we choose to think historical, this time in a No-brow society that refuses to make qualitative distinctions. For cultural tourism to be more than edutainment, practitioners must reconceive their relationship with their audiences. We must create the ears to hear our new messages, not only in the suburbs but in the cities as well, not only at private high schools, but where people sit on piers and fish. In a mass media society that transmits it message through public communication, cultural tourism must compete with a range of factors for the attention of the public. That is the challenge of the twenty-first century.

PART III

LITIGATION SUPPORT AND ENVIRONMENTAL REMEDIATION

ENVIRONMENTAL HISTORIAN AS EXPERT WITNESS: A PRACTICAL EVIL?

Alan S. Newell

Professor George Pinder arrived at the courtroom prepared to instruct the court on the intricacies of hydrogeology. Dressed in a blue blazer, brown pants and argyle socks, the professor had clearly ignored his attorney's advice that the court preferred conservative dark suits. Nonetheless, as the preeminent authority in the field, plaintiff's counsel believed that this noted expert would make a favorable impression on the judge. Only on cross-examination, did the lack of understanding of the legal forum first exhibited by the witness in his careless and casual dress begin to show how ill prepared he was for his current role. In subsequent days, an able and experienced defense counsel succeeded in convincing the witness that every conclusion that he had reached should be limited and qualified. An attorney's worst nightmare ended the examination when the judge remarked to both counsel that "I'm beginning to get the impression that this fellow has either got a very loose grasp of the language, or he will say anything that comes into his head."[1]

The "fellow" actually had a very good grasp of the technical language of his field and he was methodical and precise in his analysis. What he didn't have was an ability to convey his knowledge in the legal forum. While few such experiences rise to the dramatic level detailed in Jonathan Harr's 1995 account of the environmental lawsuit against W. R. Grace Company in Woburn, Massachusetts, *A Civil Action,* the fate of George Pinder haunts the academic expert witness and the attorneys who rely on him. What Pinder failed to realize and what his inexperienced trial attorney failed to inform him of is that being an expert is not the same thing as being an expert witness. The expert is an authority in a field who conducts analyses and offers interpretation of data. The expert witness, by contrast, has the privilege under the procedural rules of the court to offer opinions, based on his expertise, on the ultimate questions before the court. Being the foremost authority in a particular subject is valuable but may not persuade a court unless those expert opinions are delivered in a logical, succinct and credible way. Having a working knowledge of courtroom procedure can help the witness establish that credibility and relieve the inevitable anxiety produced by the adversarial legal process. This is particularly true when historians testify in environmental cases.

Historians have an added burden when they serve as expert witnesses in that, by training, they are more comfortable offering interpretations than they are rendering conclusive opinions. The discipline of history does not lend itself to the presumed clarity of the physical and biological sciences. Because they operate in a relatively new field, environmental historians may also have an inclination to employ untested theories. Although professional historians understand that some historical interpretations are more credible than others based upon documentation and analysis, we are still uncomfortable dismissing what may he a novel and insightful thesis for more accepted and, perhaps, pedestrian arguments. This problem may be a particular concern for the environmental historian who is excessively theoretical, formalistic and short on concrete facts.[2]

Historical witnesses also confront a prevalent belief held by attorneys and courts that, as Carl Becker opined in 1932, everyone can be "his own historian." In his famous essay Becker was, of course, seeking to broaden the historian's perspective and sense of history by suggesting that everyday actions involve some aspect of the historian's craft.[3] The attorney or judge with no graduate training in history might readily agree with Becker's observation and take it a step further by concluding that, since historical interest is commonplace, valid historical interpretation is similarly accessible to all, regardless of formal training. Although few judges would be so brazen as to contend that professional historical testimony is not useful to the court, there is little doubt that the historian's interpretation or opinion, however well-founded, often does not present much of an impediment to a court that sees itself equally capable of comprehending what it considers to be facts.[4]

As others have noted, the public historian who specializes in environmental history is well positioned to work in the area of public policy and the law.[5] The opportunities for historians to work in litigation are expanding as states and the federal government file increasing numbers of lawsuits seeking compensation for damages to natural resources. Concurrently, these entities also face claims for compensation for alleged infringements on private use of those same resources. Environmental historians can play a valuable role in these cases by identifying, gathering, and synthesizing both scientific and cultural data. The historian who undertakes the role as a litigation support specialist is held to a high standard for thoroughness and accuracy. It is unlikely that he will ever face the grammatical scrutiny that confronted George Pinder in *A Civil Action*. But, as the environmental historian moves beyond the role of researcher and synthesizer and becomes the expert witness, offering opinions to the court about the condition of the environment, he will face situations for which he may be ill prepared.

Litigation is adversarial and it presumes that for each party who seeks to employ expert testimony, there are others who are obligated to diminish its value. The expert's obligation is to preserve the integrity of his testimony against the attacks of those who would undermine it. The challenge for the historian as expert witness is to present an opinion as succinctly and with as few qualifications as possible, while maintaining the nuance and uncertainty inherent in historical inquiry. This chapter seeks to explore how the historian can strike this balance, participate in the growing need for historical analysis in environmental cases, and demonstrate to the legal community the value of environmental history.

LITIGATION SUPPORT OPPORTUNITIES FOR ENVIRONMENTAL HISTORIANS

The appearance of professional historians is not a common occurrence in the courtroom, despite the increasing number of examples of expert historical testimony in scholarly literature.[6] A recent practice handbook on expert witnesses published by the American Bar Association lists more than a dozen typical experts, including those who work in the area of environmental litigation. Historians are conspicuously absent from the list. Although environmental historians have clearly established themselves in a recognized field of history over the past two decades, recent experience suggests that attorneys still view the introduction of a historian into an environmental action as a novelty.[7]

The absence of historians in the legal arena may be a function of the types of cases that historically have employed social scientists and humanists. Beginning in the 1950s, when many Native American tribes sought compensation for past land takings by the United States, attorneys representing those tribes looked first to the social sciences and to anthropologists/ethnologists. These academicians could point to half a century of work documenting the Indian diaspora and were ready and willing to aid tribes in the recovery of their lost estate. The Indian Claims Commission, established by Congress in 1946 to hear claims for compensation for the taking of aboriginal lands by the United States, found anthropologists eager to offer expert testimony on the nature of those claims. Historians, while not absent from those proceedings, played a smaller role. It is not surprising then that it was the anthropologist working with historical documents in claims litigation who spawned the new field of "ethnohistory."[8]

Anthropologists continued to dominate the expert arena of history well into the 1980s, even though many of the questions facing the federal courts no longer concerned land claims. In the area of treaty interpretation, anthropologists and archaeologists successfully made the leap between ethnography and documentary analysis by crossing the bridge of ethnohistory. Far-reaching decisions in *United States v. Washington* and *United States v. Michigan* turned on the testimony of anthropologists who hoped to glean an Indian understanding of treaty negotiations from the written historical record.[9]

Gradually, the expertise of historians, and increasingly those with a specialty in environmental history, has been more fully recognized in the Indian law arena, as well as in litigation involving water and public land policy in the West. Historians are sought as consultants and expert witnesses by the federal government, states and private parties engaged in litigation over historic water use in most of the jurisdictions governed by the doctrine of "prior appropriation." This interest in historical testimony has been prompted by efforts to reach comprehensive, basin-wide water rights determinations in western states beginning in the 1970s, as well as by pivotal decisions in the United States Supreme Court that made it imperative that the United States defend its title to water.[10]

Figure 6-1. Indian dipnet fishery, Cellio Falls, Columbia River. The Dalles Dam inundated this site in 1956. *U.S. v. Washington* addressed fishing rights and Cellio Falls was the most important site on the Columbia River. *K. Ross Toole Archives, The University of Montana, Missoula.*

Opportunities for environmental and other historians also have arisen in the fields of public land policy, governmental jurisdiction and civil rights, where questions of legislative and administrative history are at issue.[11] The rash of actual and potential litigation since passage of the Comprehensive Environmental Response, Compensation and Liability Act (CERCLA) in 1980 and the Superfund Amendments and Reauthorization Act (SARA) in 1986 has vastly expanded opportunities for historians. Serving as researchers, litigation consultants and expert witnesses, historians and their related academic siblings have found challenging venues in which to practice their craft and to address new audiences.[12]

Figure 6-2. Indian dipnet fishery, Cellio Falls, Columbia River. The Dalles Dam inundated this site in 1956. *U.S. v. Washington* addressed fishing rights and Cellio Falls was the most important site on the Columbia River. *K. Ross Toole Archives, The University of Montana-Missoula.*

Much of the environmental research undertaken by historians pursuant to CERCLA and SARA during the past two decades has focused on identifying the ownership and historic use of contaminated sites in support or defense of a "potentially responsible party" (PRP). CERCLA's definition of a "PRP" is sufficiently expansive to warrant an investigation of a wide array of companies, both existing and defunct, that have been owners or operators of a site. The Environmental Protection Agency's interpretation of its statutory authority convinced program managers in the 1980s to concentrate their initial research efforts on identifying the full range of PRPs. Historians working under contract to the agency or for potential defendants spent countless hours developing detailed chains of title for hundreds of acres of potential superfund sites.[13] PRP liability can, by law, touch many identities, even those that have limited involvement with a site. Companies have found it virtually impossible to avoid liability once they have been implicated in the chain of ownership. Consequently, much of the early corporate title work undertaken by historians has not led to courtroom testimony.

Questions of ownership that often were foundational issues in environmental enforcement actions no longer define the role that historians play in PRP research. Increasingly, the EPA and defendant companies are recognizing the particular skills and methodological approaches that historians bring to uncovering and narrating corporate history. Understanding why and how a company located and de-

Figure 6-3. Train load of ore from Washoe Smelter, Butte, Montana, ca 1908. *K. Ross Toole Archives, Mansfield Library, The University of Montana-Missoula.*

veloped a site over time, exploring the interlocking relationships of firms associated with a site through use, ownership or operation, and tracing the changing technology employed at the facility have driven litigants into the waiting arms of environmental historians.[14] This was the case in 1993 when the State of Montana retained my firm (Historical Research Associates, Inc) to research the history of gold and silver mining in Silver Bow County, Montana. That research involved assessments of not only what kinds of mineral extraction and refinement occurred over a wide geographical area, but also how those activities altered the environment over a hundred-year period. Extensive "live" testimony was necessary to make the appropriate impression on the court.

These same skills are requisite in the emerging field of "natural resource damage" (NRD) litigation. NRD litigation is an outgrowth of CERCLA actions, although it has ancient legal roots in public trust doctrine. This landmark 1980 legislation provided the first specific legal authority for holding a party responsible not just for restoring a damaged environment, but also for loss to the public of use of that resource. CERCLA also, for the first time, gave a federal, state, or tribal trustee the authority to seek monetary recovery for the environmental damage and mandated that regulations be developed to assess that damage. As a result of CERCLA, its 1986 amendments (SARA) and the 1990 Oil Pollution Act, various states and the United States have filed multimillion dollar NRD actions.[15]

The most noteworthy NRD case occurred in the aftermath of the grounding of the oil tanker *Exxon Valdez* in 1989. The litigation and eventual settlement between the United States and Exxon over this environmental disaster totaled more than one billion dollars and remains, today, one of the largest monetary awards in an NRD lawsuit. Since *Exxon Valdez,* Department of Justice attorneys have filed a number of NRD actions and the department currently has more than twenty such cases pending in federal courts. Some of these actions, such as the one against Montrose Chemical Corporation for the disposal of DDT off Palos Verdes Peninsula in California, approach the magnitude of the Alaska case. Comparably large NRD litigation also involves General Electric plants on the Hudson River in New York and stream and river contamination from mine tailings in northern Idaho and western Montana. Other smaller cases focus on bays and estuaries, such as Commencement Bay at Tacoma, Washington, and Bayou Bonfuca in Louisiana.[16]

The vast majority of NRD cases, similar to the federal case against Exxon, settle prior to trial. By this time, however, the necessary historical and scientific research has been completed. Thus, historians find themselves an integral part of the litigation team—subject more often to deposition during the discovery process than to actual trial testimony.

CERCLA, SARA and, more recently, NRD litigation has generated most of the work for environmental historians in the last fifteen years. As these opportunities for historians increase, so too do the anxieties of historians who find themselves engaged in what can best be described as controlled conflict. Although most academic historians are not immune to controversy either within their departments or with their peers, the formal adversarial relationships in the courtroom necessitate that the historian acquire professional skills that are not learned in college history classes or graduate seminars.

NAVIGATING THE LEGAL PROCESS

Historians have only recently begun to explore the dynamics of "expert witnessing." By contrast, physicians and psychologists, who not only have a long tradition of serving as experts, but also have a clinical interest in understanding the legal arena, have authored most "professional witness handbooks."[17] It is not unexpected that the historical profession's exploration into this employment sector has coincided with the rise of the public history movement. Although a brief perusal of the literature on this issue suggests that most experts who have publicly discussed their trial experiences do not necessarily consider themselves public historians, it has been an interest in using history publicly that has provided them a forum for their ideas.[18]

The few historians who have spoken on the topic of historical testimony raise common complaints. J. Morgan Kousser admitted to being initially shocked when challenged that his research might be inherently biased by his ideological beliefs or by the fact that he was being paid for his testimony. Katherine Jellison, in relating the historical testimony in a gender discrimination case involving Sears, Roebuck and Co., recounted the extended controversy among her peers that surrounded the kind of testimony and evidence that historians should offer to the court. Garnering the most comments from testifying historians is the issue of whether or not the historian is explicitly or implicitly purchased by a litigant.[19]

These observations of testifying historians can generally be categorized as (1) revealing a lack of understanding of the role of the testifying historian and a perceived misunderstanding by the court of the interpretive nature of history; (2) an ignorance of the evidentiary constraints faced by experts; and (3) unnecessarily vexing ethical concerns about the distinct roles of history and advocacy in the legal forum. The environmental historian has the burden of confronting all of these issues in their fullest form given the nature of his discipline and the technical parameters of civil litigation.

THE HISTORIAN IN THE COURTROOM

The distinguished lawyer and legal scholar Learned Hand, writing in the *Harvard Law Review* in 1901, observed that expert witnesses occupy an anomalous position in the judicial system. A plaintiff or a defendant calls on the expert to offer not simply facts, but opinion as to the meaning of those facts based upon a specialized knowledge. The judge or jury can accept or reject those opinions. But, in doing either, they insert the expert into the role of furnishing "general propositions which it is ordinarily their function and theirs only to furnish to the conclusion which constitutes the verdict." Hand was uncertain whether or not this process worked "any practical evil" on the judicial system. But he did conclude that juries and often judges were ill equipped to discern the validity of an individual expert's opinions.[20]

The essential purpose of expert testimony has not changed since Learned Hand's time. Historians who qualify as experts, unlike fact or percipient witnesses, are able to offer their opinions on the ultimate questions before the court. They do so under Federal Rules of Evidence 702 and 703, or their state counterparts. Under these rules, any witness who by "knowledge, skill, experience, training, or education" can assist the trier of fact with specialized knowledge can be qualified as an expert. An expert need not possess all of the qualifications under Rule 702 to be deemed an expert and the trial judge has great latitude in determining whether or not an expert can testify.[21]

Although the definition and purpose of expert testimony remain intact after nearly a hundred years, the bases on which expert historians and others can testify have been greatly liberalized. Changes at the federal level in 1975 now permit an expert to offer opinions about knowledge of facts not in evidence in a specific trial. If the facts are the type that the expert's peers generally rely upon in their analysis, then those facts can be discussed and presented as the basis for conclusions about unrelated cases.[22] The ruling in *Daubert v. Merrell Dow Pharmaceutics, Inc.* in 1993, further expanded the admissibility of expert testimony by allowing unproven theories and reasonable, but not necessarily conclusive, evidence into the record.

Daubert concerned the numerous instances of birth defects allegedly caused by the antinausea drug bendictin. The plaintiff's case rested solely on the testimony of eight experts that the drug bendictin caused birth defects in laboratory tests. The trial judge did not admit the plaintiff's testimony because his finding indicated that the expert's opinions were not based on established scientific principles. Although the Ninth Circuit Court of Appeals upheld this ruling, the Supreme Court reversed the decision in 1993, claiming that federal rules contemplated a more relaxed standard. The Supreme Court said that the trial judge had broad discretion in admitting expert testimony, but cautioned that the decision should depend on whether or not there was a general acceptance of the theory within the field of the testifying expert.[23] The 1999 U.S. Supreme Court ruling in *Kumho Tire Co., Ltd., et al. v. Carmichael et al.* affirmed the *Daubert* standard and clearly stated that it applies "to all expert testimony."[24]

The rulings in *Daubert* and *Kumho* are instructive for environmental historians. Environmental historians have one of the closest relationships with the natural sciences of any field of history. John Opie and William Cronon have noted that one of the defining characteristics of environmental historians is their willingness to enter into a dialogue with the sciences. Cronon argues that environmental historians have "demonstrated [an] ability to draw on the insights of radically different fields—ecology, geography, economics, anthropology, and many others—in [their] attempts to construct a more fully integrated synthesis."[25] John Opie speaks of the need for a "dual literacy" that will allow the historian to apply the language and theories of the natural sciences to the interaction with human cultural values in order to help us better understand environmental change.[26] The nexus between environmental history and the sciences suggests the prominent role that historians can play in natural resource litigation under guidance articulated by the court in *Daubert* and *Kumho*. If these cases can be interpreted to give latitude to testimony that, while theoretical, is generally accepted within the profession, then the continued efforts by the historical community to explore the interactions between human decision making and the environment may find a receptive ear in the courtroom.

Historical testimony will be most useful, however, if the historian can clearly explicate the connection between human activity and environmental change. Environmental and public historians speak to a broad array of audiences—academics, policy makers, and the general public. Each of those audiences approaches history with particular perspectives and expectations. When environmental historians explore the topic of wilderness, for example, they can profoundly impact how legislators and the public shape land management policies. Similarly, the notion of wilderness being constructed by and, perhaps, constrained by historical events has a certain appeal to the scholarly community. Yet, this cerebral approach to our understanding of the appeal of wilderness areas may not resonate with a court that must decide the intent of Congress in designating a specific wilderness area. Of far greater importance to the judge hearing such a case are pivotal political and legislative events leading to passage of such legislation as the 1964 Wilderness Act or the particular forces that compelled Congress to create a specific wilderness area. To be given the credence required of a testifying expert, the environmental historian must be attuned to the limitations of the court's receptivity to theory.[27]

Even where historians are testifying about well-established historical interpretations, they face the problem of being "second guessed" by a trial judge or, more rarely, by jurors, who have their own notion of history. Although they may not be aware of Carl Becker's "Everyman" analogy, judges have often used and misused history to correct a perceived inequity or to further a political agenda. Constitutional historian Alfred H. Kelly traced the evolution of the Supreme Court's application of historical interpretation and concluded that the Anglo-American tradition of judicial precedent inevitably has led judges to play "the role of historian."[28] According to Kelly, it was Justice John Marshall who first served the court as a "walking historical primary source" in the early nineteenth century and proclaimed his interpretation of the Constitution by "judicial fiat" and "authoritative revelation." Later justices, such as Roger Taney in the *Dred Scott* case, of necessity resorted to a more distant perspective and used history as a "precedent-breaking instrument"—in Taney's case by arguing that the Constitution was a "white man's document."[29] Kelly recognized a resurgence in what he called "law-office" history at work in the courts during the 1960s. He noticed this historical variant at work in the activist courts that selected "data favorable to the position being advanced without regard to or concern for contradictory data or proper evaluation of the relevance of the data proffered."[30]

The tendency for judges to employ "law-office history" is not confined to the U.S. Supreme Court. Historians testifying in civil cases, most of which are "bench trials" or trials with only a judge presiding, often face an uphill battle in overcoming rather simplistic historical interpretations. One prominent case in the late 1970s focusing on Native American hunting and fishing rights included testimony from half a dozen anthropologists and historians. The resulting record was voluminous, with hundreds of archival documents addressing Indian relations with the United States in the Old Northwest during the 1830s and 1840s. Federal District Judge Noel Fox, while acknowledging the extensive record of primary sources, chose to rely on overly broad secondary works in rendering his opinion in *United States v. State of Michigan*. For instance, the *American Heritage Pictorial History of the Presidents* became the underlying support for judicial opinions of Andrew Jackson's influence over his Secretary of War, Lewis Cass. Similarly, Fox cited *The Oxford History of American People* for broad characterizations of the federal treaty-making process with native tribes. Samuel Eliot Morison may have a justifiable reputation for his ability to narrate the broad sweep of American history, but he could hardly be considered a leading authority on the nuances of more than 370 federal treaties with Native Americans. In the *Michigan* case, Judge Fox blended his views of history with those offered by experts without critically evaluating either and rendered a decision that can only be characterized as "law-office history."[31]

Sometimes, the court's interest in history works to the advantage of the testifying historian. In one environmental case addressing questions of land and mineral disposal, opposing counsel sought the exclusion of my testimony on the basis of relevancy to the ultimate conclusion required by the court. In that case, the court not only allowed the testimony but also admonished the plaintiff's counsel that he should be aware of the court's strong interest in history. In a later case in which I offered testimony on historic environmental degradation, a federal judge interrupted my direct testimony to query both plaintiff and defense counsel if there was really any disagreement with what the judge believed was the well-established history to which the expert was testifying. In both of these cases, the trier of fact clearly entered the courtroom with a body of historical knowledge that affected how he heard and interpreted the historical testimony.[32]

The question could be posed as to how the environmental historian can overcome initial judicial bias, particularly where the historical interpretation may be new to the court. The simple answer is that it is unlikely that any expert's testimony can substantially alter a trial judge's proclivity to interpret facts in a certain way, if those biases are well formed. There are a number of ways, however, for the historian to influence the record of the case, and thereby preserve issues for appellate review: (1) predicate your testimony on documentary evidence, rather than generalized theory; (2) consider and address in the direct testimony what might be viewed as contradictory evidence; and (3) strive for synthesis and avoid to the extent possible the exceptions and qualifications that are inevitable components of historical epistemology.

The above suggestions may seem obvious elements of the historian's craft, but the rigor with which the historian must adhere to these canons is far greater in the courtroom than in the classroom. In 1982, historian Carl M. Becker, [not the 1931 American Historical Association president] recounted an embarrassment, feared by all experts, of being contradicted under cross-examination by a source that he has used in his direct testimony. In this particular case, Becker admitted to failing to read the entire source and had to acknowledge the contradiction, although subsequent testimony apparently did not undermine the validity of his conclusions. As Becker recalled, "There was enough egg on my face to make an omelette for the Chicago Bears' training table."[33]

Becker's predicament underscores the attention to detail required of testifying historians. Unlike the seminar process in which historians hope to respond to constructive criticism, the purpose of cross-examination is not designed to strengthen the historian's research and interpretation. Opposing counsel endeavor to either cast doubt on the credibility of the expert's opinion or to show the court how that opinion supports a different conclusion. Displaying apparent weaknesses in research or analysis, however inconsequential, is an obvious way to begin to mold the witness to counsel's needs. This was the trap that caught Professor Pinder in *A Civil Action*. The expert's resume and credentials will not overcome perceived inadequacies on the stand. The only way for the historian to resist an attorney's efforts to twist testimony to an unintended purpose is to have complete command of the primary documentary evidence and to be able fluidly to place it in broader historical context.[34]

Acknowledging evidence that may contradict the historian's opinion during the presentation of the direct testimony can confirm the historian's role in the courtroom. Showing that the expert is aware of the full nature of the documentary record and that he did not ignore evidence, however antithetical it maybe to his argument, enhances credibility. This approach to the direct testimony, if not over used, also can anticipate and potentially blunt efforts of opposing counsel to characterize evidence in a particular way during cross-examination. But the real benefit of offering both supportive and apparently unsupportive documentation is to alert the court to the full range of historical interpretation, while lending support to the validity of your argument.

The nuances of historical interpretation, however, present a separate problem. Although historians are peculiarly comfortable with and adept at weaving exceptions into the historical fabric, it is often because there are no immediate winners and losers. Courts, on the other hand, must issue opinions that are, in fact, decisions. In most cases, the prevailing and losing parties are immediately obvious. As one environmental historian with experience in testifying has observed, "The courtroom testimony of a historian is a communication process with the potential to vastly influence important proceedings."[35] The historians' role in the courtroom is to employ all of the skepticism and analytical skills that their craft makes available to them—but to do so in a way that offers some assurance to the court that his view of what happened is not only possible, but probable. The ability of the historian to offer a clear and succinct narrative of the past, free from excessive qualification and ambiguity, can make it more difficult for a trial judge to ignore accepted professional opinion in favor of a more simplistic rendition of history.

EVIDENTIARY CONSTRAINTS

Few historians are likely to have a copy of the *Federal Rules of Civil Procedure* in their office library. Fewer still would feel that it is incumbent upon them to understand how their testimony could be offered into or excluded from the trial record. Most undoubtedly would consider this technical procedure to be the sole domain of their attorney. But the reality is that a small fraction of practicing attorneys are accomplished in courtroom procedure and experience suggests that most lawyers appreciate testifying experts who understand how to operate in a courtroom.[36]

An example from my trial experience may be instructive. In 1984, I was asked by attorneys for the State of Montana to assist them in researching the ownership and historic use of a large parcel of land ceded by the Crow Tribe of Montana to the United States in 1904. The testimony offered in that case involved the legislative and administrative history of various federal acts that affected the land cession. Opposing counsel sought to exclude the historical testimony based on the difference between legislative *history* and legislative *intent,* arguing that the former may be interesting to historians but irrelevant to the judge, who must decide the later. This may seem to be a "makeweight" argument to historians who routinely gather legislative documents with the goal of undertanding a bill's intent. But, opposing counsel raised a valid objection when one considers the broad reach of the historian and the more circumscribed approach of the court. Historians have an interest in a wide range of sources when seeking to understand the purposes and effects of legislation. Earlier attempts to pass the legislation, influential thinkers, political interests groups, and contemporary historical events all provide ample context for the historian's interpretation. In court, however, the relevant legislative history is far more restrictive. In the case in point, what preserved my testimony was a reliance on the specific hearings, committee reports, draft bills and legislative debates that related directly to passage of the legislation in question. Knowing the specific evidence that would be accepted by the court and that I hoped would be used in rendering its decision on legislative intent was an integral part of my job as a testifying historian.[37]

This caution should not prompt would-be historical experts to rush to their nearest law library for a copy of Sunderland on statutory construction. It does suggest, however, that testifying experts should be aware of the evidentiary procedures in the courtroom and should query their attorneys on how they would like the expert opinions to be presented. They also should seek the advice of their attorney on possible evidentiary limitations and potential procedural objections to their testimony.

The environmental historian can gain a working knowledge of the use of evidence and expert opinion through trial experience. Of more importance to the novice testifying expert is a willingness and ability to understand relevant case law. The foundation of our legal system is precedent, and the record established in earlier cases often defines the evidentiary boundaries of present litigation. In 1983, I was retained to work on a case that had been decided a number of years prior to my involvement on the basis of an extensive documentary record, but no direct expert testimony. A federal court of appeals reversed the district judge's initial ruling on several key points and remanded the case to the lower court on very limited grounds. At this point, the attorneys who retained me wanted to correct the tactical error in the initial litigation by having me address some of the same issues that had been heard years earlier. Although this testimony might have been helpful to the trier of fact, the court was nonetheless constrained by the "law of the case" from hearing this testimony. My understanding of the previous decisions and ability to work within the limits of the legal framework was integral to providing testimony and evidence that would be accepted by the court.[38]

ETHICS AND ADVOCACY

Environmental history is provocative. Historians often are drawn to environmental topics that have contemporary importance. Indeed, a central premise of the field is that humans and the environment have interacted to produce change, much of which has tended to diminish the quality of life. Because or as a result of this focus, many environmental historians come to the field initially with a commitment to advocacy. Although there is little doubt that the field has diverged and become increasing complex and multidimensional in the last two decades, it is also true that many environmental historians still view themselves as environmentalists.[39] This orientation of environmental historians makes their appearance in the courtroom paradoxical. For, while they are brought to the bar ostensibly for the purpose of informing the trier of facts of specialized knowledge that will assist in understanding how the law applies to facts, they also may have strong opinions as to the moral and equitable outcome of the trial.

This conflict is not confined solely to environmental historians. Other historians who have written on the subject of testimony invariably discuss the problem of bias. Most recognize that the question of bias is inherently entwined with the historical profession's concern for objectivity and the dynamics of working on contemporary problems that are resolved in an adversarial process. The judicial process relies on opposing attorneys advocating the position of their client. Although legal ethics prohibit an attorney from knowingly presenting false or misleading evidence to the court, few attorneys would voice much concern if their view of the facts was the only view heard by the court. Having the court hear the best and most reliable historical interpretation of a factual matter at issue is not of particular concern to an aggressive legal advocate—that is unless that interpretation is beneficial to his client.

Public historians, whether working on environmental topics or not, are in the center of this ethical vortex. There are those who claim that the very nature of public history is different from "academic scholarship" and that it cannot fail to be influenced by the public process in which it is conducted and by the money that sponsors it. Public history, one historian contends, cannot be disinterested and "Fairness [can only be maintained] by the rules of procedure, which provide for testing of claims by advocates of opposing interests."[40] Other historians in applying this perspective to expert testimony believe that they inevitably identify with their "side" and rate their professional stature according to who prevails in the litigation. At least one experienced historical witness baldly asserts that "Expert witnesses do not merely give opinions; they join a company."[41] Historical objectivity, whether or not it exists in an epistemological sense, cannot survive the rigors of an adversarial judicial process. Aggressive cross-examination by a skilled attorney will invariably reveal an expert's bias, whether it is apparent to the testifying historian or not. Only by acknowledging one's interpretive slant and addressing the implications of that perspective under direct examination from your counsel can the expert historian mitigate potential damage to his opinions on cross-examination.

Of course, we know from contemporary historical interest in the question of objectivity, that it is neither possible nor, perhaps, desirable.[42] Practicing historians readily admit that the instant they select a topic, they have betrayed a bias. The knowledge, experience, and interest that we bring to a subject cannot help but affect how we initially frame our research questions. This is true whether we are choosing a thesis or dissertation topic or whether a nonacademic third party has brought a problem to us. Similarly, the funding that underwrites a project, whether in academia or in the private sector, cannot be ignored. If this source of monetary support has a politicizing effect on the resultant scholarship, then it is not a problem faced solely by historians working in the public sector. Rather it affects all professionals both in and outside of the academy.

The difficulty for historians testifying as experts however, is that, while they can accept the limitations of the discipline, the court may not. As noted earlier, a judge or jury looks for degrees of certainty of fact, not interpretation. Indeed, the common perception of most participants in the judicial process is that history *is* a series of facts. They may look to the historian to arrange those facts in a meaningful pattern. But, the ultimate significance of that pattern often seems to be as easily discerned by layman as by the practicing historian. The most visible evidence of the importance of facts is the final decision of the court, which arranges the Findings of Fact as a predicate to the Conclusions of Law.

Given its genesis in the environmental movement of the 1960s, environmental history entering the legal arena through public historians may naturally be more suspect of bias than other fields of history.[43] Add to this the requisite dual literacy in humanities and science noted by John Opie and the potential for novel theoretical constructions and environmental historians might struggle to convince the court that they meet the threshold for relevancy.

As suggested in this chapter, the principal way that environmental history can influence judicial decisions is for historians to understand their legal audience and their role in the adjudication. They can do so by first knowing their formal role as advisor and explainer, not advocate, and by understanding how their testimony can and cannot be used as evidence. By actively participating in the legal process as a professional, the environmental historian also has the opportunity to inform counsel, the judge, and jury of a view of history that may be unfamiliar to them. Presenting history as interpretation inevitably skewed by our cultural, social, and political bias is a perspective that can help defuse a charge of environmental advocacy. So too can a proper foundation of the basic principles of historical scholarship (e.g., addressing contradictory evidence) that underlies historical interpretation and allows historians to reach conclusions that can assist the court. Finally, environmental historians are in a unique position to aid the court in understanding the legacy left by our interaction with the physical world. Had George

Pinder a better understanding of what the judge and jury needed from him and how he could present it most effectively, perhaps his expertise would have been more useful to his client.

Advocacy and ethical constraints become less of an issue as well when the environmental historian understands his role in litigation. Historians have an obligation to undertake as thorough and informed an analysis as possible. Since their profession demands it and their credibility depends upon it, historians should make comprehensiveness a requisite part of the engagement with his client. But the historian and the client attorney can only interact on this level if both parties understand the parameters of each profession. Experience suggests that the burden of establishing the appropriate level of discourse in this relationship lies not with the attorney but with the historian.

Concerns about advocacy need not present a dilemma for testifying historians. Accepting the premise that controversy surrounds most historical analysis at some level frees expert witnesses to acknowledge their underlying interest in a topic (whether political or pure curiosity) and to address it appropriately in the research, analysis and, if required, testimony. It is not unusual that historians, as part of the litigation team, will eventually develop a conviction for the correctness of their counsels' position. This is especially true if the working relationship is grounded on mutual professional respect. But, such an intellectual bonding is no different in litigation than it is in any scholarly endeavor that has been intense and dynamic. The environmental historian should not shrink from such an engagement but should embrace it. The testifying historian should be an advocate for his position and should remember that the attorney is the advocate for the client.

CONCLUSION

Public historians working in the evolving field of environmental history have a substantial contribution to make to the legal community. Environmental history has at its core an interest in giving a voice to the human interactions with the physical world and articulating the legacy of that multifaceted dialogue. By integrating a cultural and philosophical view of our relationship to the environment with the science of ecology, environmental historians are poised to introduce a unique perspective into the judicial process. To make this contribution, the expert historian must join the legal team as an equal intellectual partner.

Historians can accomplish this professional merger by first acknowledging the need to add a "third literacy" to their vocabulary. Knowing the procedural rules that govern the use of expert testimony and accepting the evidentiary constraints placed on a particular case injects a commonality into the conversation between attorney and expert witness and frees both of them to concentrate on the substantive aspects of the case. Historians, especially environmental historians, can participate in the judicial process and avoid ethical qualms by acknowledging how personal interests invariably affect all historical work. By distinguishing individual and voluntary advocacy from the institutional advocacy required by our system of jurisprudence, historians have the potential for being extremely credible and valuable witnesses in natural resource litigation.

It is incumbent on the public environmental historian to make the effort to engage in the legal process. Trial attorneys are accustomed to employing experts from a variety of disciplines and have developed tools for molding what they learn from an expert to their client's interest. On first impression, attorneys may not feel as comfortable working with history as they do with other, more established courtroom disciplines. But, environmental historians have important stories to tell the legal community about our environment and are uniquely qualified to offer that narrative. If historians choose to enter the legal arena center stage, they may find a surprisingly attentive audience.

NOTES

1. Jonathan Harr, *A Civil Action* (New York: Random House, 1995), p. 331.
2. Richard White commented on this problem faced by environmental historians in his commentary on Donald Worster's sweeping notions of agroecology. White observed that "Environmental historians assert amazing interactions, but there is a certain sketchiness of detail as to how they all work. There is not much reason for a skeptic to believe the larger claims." Richard White, "Environmental History, Ecology, and Meaning," *Journal of American History* 76 (March 1990): 1114.
3. Carl Becker, "Everyman His Own Historian," *The American Historical Review* 37 (January 1932): 221–236.
4. The format for presenting a judicial decision is to first present the "Findings of Fact" and then to apply the law to an interpretation of those "facts." This format gives the court wide latitude to practice history. See Alfred H. Kelley, "Clio And The Court: An Illicit Love Affair," *Supreme Court Review* (1965): 119–158.
5. See "Environmental History and Public Historians," *ASEH News* 2 (September 1991): 1.
6. *The Public Historian* has probably published more articles on historians who work in some aspect of litigation than any other scholarly journal. Many of these articles, such as Leland R. Johnson's "Public Historian For The Defendant," *The Public Historian* 5 (Summer 1983); J. Morgan Kousser's "Are Expert Witnesses Whores? Reflections On Objectivity In Scholarship And Expert Witnessing," in Theodore J. Karamanski's *Ethics and Public History: An Anthology* (Malabar, FL: Kreiger, 1990), and William K. Klingaman's "Historians and the Law," *The Public Historian* 3 (Summer 1981) appeared early in the journal's history and reflect a certain degree of naivete about the practice of expert witnessing. More recent contributions to *The Public Historian* reflect maturation in the field of public history, particularly with respect to the role of environmental historians in litigation. For example, see Hal K. Rothman's, "Historian v. Historian: Interpreting the Past in the Courtroom." *The*

Public Historian 15 (Spring, 1993): 39–53 and Craig E. Colten's "Ground-water and the Law: Records and Recollections," *The Public Historian* 20 (Spring 1998): 25–44.

7. See for example Faust F. Rossi, *Expert Witnesses,* Section of Litigation, American Bar Association (Chicago: 1991). Recent conversations with a federal attorney and a private, corporate attorney indicate that historians are not routinely solicited for environmental research for which they are obviously suited. Interview with Tom Clark, Assistant Deputy, Environment and Natural Resources Division, United States Department of Justice, Washington, D.C. (January 27, 1999).

8. James Axtell, "Ethnohistory: An Historian's Viewpoint," *Ethnohistory* 26 (Winter 1979): 1–13.

9. *United States et al. v. State of Michigan, et al.* Vol. 471, *Federal Supplement* (1979), pp. 192–281; *United States et al. v. State of Washington,* Vol. 384, *Federal Supplement,* (1974) p. 350. For an interesting analysis of how anthropologists testified using historical materials in one of these cases, see Robert Doherty, *Disputed Waters: Native Americans & the Great Lakes Fishery* (Lexington: University of Kentucky Press, 1990), pp. 88–95.

10. Since the mid-1970s, the federal government's "trust responsibility" has required it to become a party to state efforts to recognize and to quantify water rights throughout the West in what are known as "general streamwide adjudications." As an advocate for Indian tribes, the United States Department of Justice has recently been engaged in as many as 48 ongoing water disputes in 12 western states, most of these involving litigation. Virtually all of these cases require the United States to both assert the reserved water right of the tribe or tribes involved in the adjudication and to review critically and, if necessary, to challenge the rights of nonfederal water users. Lloyd Burton, *American Indian Water Rights And The Limits Of Law* (Lawrence: University of Kansas Press, 1991), pp. 50–57.

11. Johnson, "Public Historian For The Defendant"; Katherine Jellison, "History In The Courtroom: The Sears Case In Perspective," *The Public Historian* 9 (Fall 1987).

12. Martin V. Melosi commented on these phenomena in his presidential address to the National Council on Public History in 1993. Melosi identified private historical consulting firms, including my own, as examples of public historians who have succeeded in practicing environmental history outside of the academy. He also noted public historians in other private or public agencies who regularly work in the field. Martin V. Melosi, "Public History and the Environment," *The Public Historian* 15 (Fall 1993): 15–18.

13. Interview with Tom Clark, January 27, 1999. My firm, Historical Research Associates, Inc., contracted for title work with a variety of firms working for the EPA beginning in 1983. Much of this research later proved of little use in actual litigation against responsible parties.

14. Melosi, "Public History and the Environment," pp. 15–16.

15. William D. Brightman and David F. Askman, "The Role of Government Trustees in Recovering Compensation for Injury to Natural Resources," in Restoring *Our Natural Resources: What Will It Cost? Exploring Natural Resource Damage Under CERCLA And Other Federal Laws,* 20th Annual Public Land Law Conference, March 4 and 5, 1999, University of Montana School of Law, pp. 179–185.

16. See *Seattle Times,* February 12, 1998; *Los Angeles Times,* January 18, 1997; Interview with Tom Clark, January 27, 1999. Recent administrative changes giving the Departments of Interior and Agriculture authority to initiate litigation without the involvement of EPA may lead to a dramatic increase in the number of NRDs.

17. For example, see Stanley L. Brodsky's *Testifying In Court: Guidelines and Maxims For The Expert Witness,* (Washington, D.C.: American Psychological Association, 1991). There also is a monthly newsletter published for expert witnesses entitled *The Testifying Expert* (Horsham, PA: LRP Publications). It is apparent to even the casual reader of this newsletter that the medical and mental health areas of expert testimony seem to dominate the "how to" literature.

18. For example, see Carl M. Becker, "Professor for the Plaintiff: Classroom to Courtroom," *The Public Historian* 4 (Summer 1982): 69–77; S. Charles Bolton, "The Historian As Expert Witness: Creationism in Arkansas" *The Public Historian* 4 (Summer 1982): 59–67.

19. Kousser, "Are Expert Witnesses Whores? Reflections on Objectivity in Scholarship And Expert Witnessing," p. 36; Katherine Jellison, "History in the Courtroom: The Sears Case In Perspective," *The Public Historian* 9 (Fall 1987): 11–16.

20. Learned Hand, "Historical and Practical Considerations Regarding Expert Testimony," *Harvard Law Review* 15 (May, 1901): 52.

21. "Rule 702. Testimony of Experts," "Rule 703. Bases of Opinion Testimony by Experts," *Federal Rules of Evidence* (St. Paul: West Publishing Co., 1996), pp. 373–373. See also Rossi, *Expert Witnesses,* pp. 7–8.

22. "Rule 703. Bases of Opinion Testimony by Experts"; Rossi, *Expert Witnesses,* p. 45.

23. *Daubert v. Merrell Dow Pharmaceuticals, Inc.* 509 U.S. 579 (1993). Michael E. Sacks, "An Overview of the Law: A Guide For Testifying and Consulting Experts," (Horsham, PA: LRP Publications, 1995), pp. 30–32.

24. *Kumho Tire Co., Ltd., et al. v. Carmichael et al.* 526 US 137 (1999). Wendie Ellen Schneider explores the relevancy of Daubert and Kumho Tire to historical testimony in "Past Imperfect," *Yale Law Journal* 110 (June 2001): 1531–1545. Using a British court's decision in a libel suit involving Holocaust denier David Irving, Schneider argues for a *Daubert* standard of "conscientious historian". Such a standard would avoid the pitfalls of arguing for "objective history" and would offer the court guidance for evaluating a historian's methodological rigor, rather than his or her conclusions.

25. William Cronon, "The Uses of Environmental History," *Environmental History Review* 17 (Fall, 1993): 4.
26. John Opie," Environmental History: Pitfalls and Opportunities," *Environmental Review* 7 (Spring, 1983): 13.
27. William Cronon explores the reasons why we have created wilderness in "The Trouble with Wilderness or, Getting Back to the Wrong Nature." In a reply to this essay, "Comment: The Trouble with Bill Cronon's Wilderness," Samuel P. Hays demonstrates how he participated in an effort to convince the Forest Service and Congress that specific provisions of the 1964 Wilderness Act applied to cut-over areas of the East. Hays argues that wilderness groups have not resorted to quoting the "major thinkers" on wilderness when seeking support for wilderness designation. Rather, they rely on their intimate knowledge of the area to justify its designation. Both articles appear in *Environmental History* 1 (January, 1996): 7–32. Cronon correctly acknowledges, however, that the views of both Hays and Roderick Nash have had a significant impact on public opinion over the past three decades. See Cronon, "The Uses of Environmental History," pp. 2–3.
28. Kelley, "Clio And The Court: An Illicit Love Affair," p. 21.
29. Ibid., pp. 122–125.
30. Ibid., pp. 122.
31. *United States et al. v. State of Michigan, et al.* 471 Federal Supplement 192, pp. 228–230. Robert Doherty explains how Judge Fox got this testimony into the record by having the defendant's expert read from these sources at trial. This tactic also demonstrated the judge's opinion of the defense's expert testimony. Doherty, *Disputed Waters,* pp. 98–99.
32. The land and mineral case was heard in federal district court in Billings, Montana, in 1984—*Crow Tribe v. United States, Federal Supplement,* Vol. 657 p. 573 (1985). The second case involved a state claim against a multinational energy conglomerate for natural resource damages resulting from more than 100 years of mining and smelting activity in south-central Montana—*State of Montana v. Atlantic Richfield Co.* No. CV-83–317-HLN-TGH.
33. Carl M. Becker, "Professor for the Plaintiff: Classroom to Courtroom," p. 75.
34. Based on my experience at trial, it is dangerous for the expert historian to assume that he has a better command of the documents in evidence than the attorney. Competent trial attorneys spend considerable time with the primary source material and usually have their own experts to consult with them. What the attorney often lacks, both by training and inclination, is the ability to interrelate disparate fragments of the record into a broader historical context.
35. Rothman, "Historian v. Historian: Interpreting the Past in the Courtroom," p. 39.
36. I once asked a seasoned federal attorney whether he would prefer a witness who was the acknowledged expert in a field, but who had no experience to a competent expert who had experience as a witness. This was an attorney who regularly used historians and anthropologists in his work. He responded with-

out hesitation that the witness who had testified successfully on more than one occasion was preferable to an untried expert.

37. For a short, practical review of the use by courts of legislative history see Gwendolyn B. Folsom, *Legislative History: Research for the Interpretation of Laws* (Charlottesville: University Press of Virginia,) Part I, pp. 1–19.

38. The case that I participated in was but a portion of a much larger lawsuit involving various Chippewa bands of Wisconsin and the State of Wisconsin. The decision in my portion of the case is reported as *LacCourte Oreille v. Wisconsin, Federal Supplement,* Vol. 653, p. (1987).

39. John Opie, William Cronon, Donald Worster and others have commented on the interest in environmentalism that contributed, at least in part, to the emergence of the field of environmental history. As Cronon recently noted, his ties to environmental causes, such as wilderness propagation, have been an integral part of his personal and professional life. See William Cronon, " The Trouble with Wilderness: A Response," *Environmental History* 1 (January, 1996): 47–48. See also Cronon, "The Uses of Environmental History," p. 5–7; Opie, "Environmental History: Pitfalls and Opportunities", p. 10–11; Donald Worster, "Doing Environmental History," *The Ends of the Earth* (Cambridge: Cambridge University Press, 1988), p. 290.

40. Ronald C. Tobey, "The Public Historian As Advocate: Is Special Attention To Professional Ethics Necessary?" in *Ethics and Public History,* p. 21.

41. Kousser, "Are Expert Witnesses Whores?" p. 41. See also Becker: "Professor For The Plaintiff," pp. 73, 76.

42. See for example, Peter Novick, *That Noble Dream: The "Objectivity Question" and the American Historical Profession* (Cambridge: Cambridge University Press, 1988); Joyce Appleby, Lynn Hunt, and Margaret Jacob, *Telling The Truth About History* (New York: W.W. Norton, 1994): Richard J. Evans, *In Defense of History* (New York: W.W. Norton, 1999). For the application of "objectivity to the courtroom" see Daniel A. Farber's "Adjudication of Things Past: Reflection on History as Evidence," *Hastings Law Journal* 49 (April 1998): 1009–1038.

43. In an essay written early in the public history movement, John Opie suggested that public history "could become an outlet for environmental advocacy in an appropriate historical perspective." See "Environmental History: Pitfalls and Opportunities," p. 14.

HAZARDOUS WASTES AND ENVIRONMENTAL REMEDIATION

Craig E. Colten

INTRODUCTION

Hazardous wastes did not exist before 1976, at least as defined by federal statute. Yet, the production and disposal of substances that fit the definition long predated the legislation that "created" hazardous wastes. Consequently, the industrial activity, waste management practices, and cleanup efforts associated with hazardous materials constitute a nearly limitless realm of research possibilities for historical investigators. Unfortunately, engineers and geoscientists have narrated much of this dimension of our industrial past and often their presentations are not what historians might expect as quality reporting.

The process of remediating, or cleaning up, hazardous waste sites requires a series of technical reports that detail the degree and extent of contamination and offer remedies. Each contains a "site history." Typically, the history consists of a page or two that presents the barest description of facility ownership, a chronology of operations, and a thumbnail sketch of waste management practices. The authors seldom, if ever, cite their sources and they commonly borrow the history section from a previous report with few modifications and no attribution. By contrast, when the same consulting firms carry out field sampling or laboratory analysis, investigators follow formalized procedures, they document each step, and clearly cite sources. There is a vast gap between the technical and historical protocol due largely to the training and background of those preparing the reports and the procedural requirements in those fields. This lapse of rigor in historical documentation has gone on largely unnoticed by the engineering and geotechnical firms that prepare the reports on hazardous waste sites. On the bright side, this offers excellent opportunities for skilled practitioners to repair the job done by professionals with high skill levels, albeit in other disciplines.

This chapter will analyze the evolution of the term "hazardous waste" as a backdrop to current discussions on the subject. It will examine how social scientists employing historical analysis can contribute to our understanding of hazardous waste contamination and site remediation. Finally, it will discuss the public arena in which public historians can participate.

DEFINING HAZARDOUS WASTES

Congress passed legislation in 1976 that called for procedures to track and safely dispose of hazardous wastes (Resource Conservation and Recovery Act or RCRA).[1] In order to determine which substances fell under federal jurisdiction, the act authorized the Environmental Protection Agency (EPA) to define hazardous wastes. Over the course of several years, the EPA defined hazardous wastes as substances that can cause or contribute to an increase in mortality or an increase in serious illness, or materials that "pose a substantial present or potential hazard to human health or the environment" if improperly managed. Although the EPA has produced a legally defined group of hazardous wastes, Congress, the chemical industry, and trade organizations had used the term for years.[2]

An analysis of the historic use of the term "hazardous waste" is important in the context of current litigation. As a participant in environmental cases, I have frequently encountered the argument that in the absence of legally defined "hazardous wastes," manufacturers were unaware that some by-products were hazardous and could be discarded as if they were office trash. Although the chemical industry and legislators have refined the definition over time, waste management professionals recognized several basic qualities as hazardous since the 1940s.

In 1948 the National Safety Council identified thirty general industry types that "sometimes produce nuisance or *hazardous waste* [emphasis added]." Its waste management booklet discussed "corrosive and poisonous chemicals, explosives, and unstable compounds" as materials that had caused serious injuries. It also pointed out the persistence of radioactive wastes and noted acidic and caustic substances were hazardous as well.[3]

A standard reference book prepared for chemical plant managers, continued the discussion in 1954. It advised that a corporate "research program should be extended to cover waste products, their *hazards* [emphasis added], and the best methods for disposal." Among the dangers of wastes, the manual recognized "fire hazard, health or life hazard, injury to or death of animals, damage to property, injury to vegetation and crops, and pollution of streams or water supplies."[4] It also cited Sax's *Handbook of Dangerous Chemicals* (1951) which as the author stated "covers hazardous materials in common industrial use" and noted that it included information on toxicity and fire and explosion hazards.[5] Additionally, chemical data sheets prepared by trade associations presented the hazardous properties of both products and wastes.[6] Those engaged in chemical production during the 1950s acknowledged that wastes had hazardous characteristics. Among those they recognized were wastes with toxic, explosive or flammable, and acidic or caustic properties.

In 1961 the Manufacturing Chemists' Association issued a publication on "hazardous wastes." Their brief safety guide called the industry's attention to "hazards involved in the disposal of certain types of material and to the legal difficulties and poor public relations which may result if proper disposal of these materials is not carefully planned and regularly carried out."[7] It did not itemize all hazardous chemicals, but cited Sax's volumes on "dangerous materials" as a source that described "hazardous properties" of hundreds of chemicals.[8] The guide explicitly mentioned flammable, toxic, corrosive, and reactive properties as hazardous qualities to be concerned with. The American Petroleum Institute's (API) 1963 manual on solid refinery wastes also pointed out that toxic, corrosive, or chemically active wastes required special handling.[9] By the early 1960s, industry trade groups and standard reference works used by manufacturers had acknowledged the hazardous properties of both chemicals in the workplace and wastes outside the production lines.

Of fundamental importance is that the makers and users of chemicals were fully cognizant that some products and by-products presented hazards to humans and to the environment. Discussions of "hazardous wastes" in the pre-1970 period typically were general, although there were manuals that provided more detailed information on hazardous traits of chemicals. The term "hazardous waste" was not foreign to chemical makers and they recognized that materials in that category required special care and handling. In the absence of detailed legal requirements, which were not part of the 1940s-1960s legislative approach, public authorities held manufacturers accountable for safe use and disposal of the materials that issued from their plants.

By 1970, the public had come to expect a more intrusive federal role in chemical waste disposal and Congress called on the EPA to develop a comprehensive report and plan for the disposal of "hazardous wastes." The Resource Recovery Act of 1970, mandated that the EPA address "radioactive, toxic chemical, biological, and other wastes which may endanger public health or welfare." In its report, the EPA identified an array of wastes that fell under its rubric of hazardous waste. They included toxic metals, toxic chemicals (organic and inorganic), explosives, radioactive, biological—including pathogenic and biological warfare agents.[10] The 1974 report provided a compelling case for more effective control of hazardous wastes and provided a basis for the Resource Conservation and Recovery Act (RCRA). Most characteristics that came to be defined as hazardous under RCRA had been discussed since the 1940s—poisonous (toxic), corrosive (acidic and caustic), combustible and explosive, and reactive substances were a concern by the 1960s. Although RCRA called for a more formal definition of hazardous wastes, it did not address the question of remediation.

Shortly after RCRA's passage, media exposure of notorious sites such as Love Canal, the Valley of the Drums in rural Kentucky, and Times Beach outside St. Louis, Missouri, shocked the public into widespread recognition of the hazardous waste problem. Love Canal, a disposal site in Niagara Falls, New York, became a high-profile example of waste mismanagement in the late 1970s. Hooker Chemical Company had dumped tons of chemical wastes in an abandoned excavation during the 1940s and early 1950s. They sold the property to the local school board and the filled dump became the playground for an elementary school. Public exposure to the wastes in the 1970s heightened concern in the neighborhood and ultimately caught the nation's attention. As soon as Love Canal hit the airwaves, other abandoned waste sites gained notoriety and hazardous wastes became a household term. We cannot associate the public's recognition of "hazardous wastes" with the origin of the term, however. Hooker Chemical itself acknowledged that its wastes had hazardous properties by the time it sold the property. The legacy of the term illustrates that the public was introduced to the concept somewhat belatedly.

Figure 7-1. Love Canal site, Niagara Falls, New York in 1990. Former Hooker Chemical Company waste disposal site hardly resembles site in the 1940s when it was used as a repository for more than 20,000 tons of hazardous wastes. When a chemical brew surfaced in the school yard in the late 1970s, the site prompted a massive neighborhood evacuation. Now largely cleaned up, the site was the single greatest impetus behind the passage of the federal Superfund Act. *Photo by author.*

Congress, although it had dealt with hazardous wastes, was caught off guard by the discovery sites like Love Canal that lay outside the reach of RCRA, forcing it to consider how to address relict dumps.[11] In large measure, the legislative response was the Comprehensive Environmental Response, Compensation, and Liability Act (1980), also known as Superfund. The act provided a means to remediate or clean up the abandoned dumps scattered across the country.

The concept underlying the Superfund liability provisions was that the polluter should pay and the courts have found that the act imposes "strict, joint and several," and retroactive liabilities. Strict liability means that responsible parties can be held liable without being negligent, or even if they followed common practice at the time that they discarded the wastes.[12] Joint and several liability applies to multiple parties involved at a site. In essence, any single party can inherit full liability or all parties who contributed can be held equally liable. Finally, and perhaps most important to historians, there is no statute of limitations for activity resulting in damages; therefore, the liability is retroactive, even to events that occurred before the law's passage. These elements have created a clear historical dimension to site evaluation and the legal efforts associated with remediation. From this liability framework opportunities for historical research have emerged.

HISTORIANS' CONTRIBUTION AS PRELUDE TO REMEDIATION

The initial call to investigate the history of hazardous wastes stemmed from lawsuit-inspired research, largely associated with single sites. The stirring account of the Woburn, Massachusetts, case recounted by Jonathan Harr in his book *A Civil Action,* and then made into a Hollywood movie, reflects the efforts of lawyers and environmental agencies to document the history of waste disposal.[13] Contamination of public wells in Woburn prompted a landmark lawsuit to force the manufacturers to compensate families who suspected cancer and other aliments resulted from drinking the tainted water supply. In preparing for a class-action suit against manufacturers who discarded industrial solvents found in the local drinking water, the law firm and its consultants did pioneering work to reconstruct past waste management practices. They relied heavily on interviews with eyewitnesses and government inspectors along with public agency records. This historical information was critical in establishing which parties contributed to the site contamination.

Since the Woburn case, government agencies and private companies have undertaken massive efforts to trace the parties and their actions that created hazardous waste sites. Some of the early efforts, such as the case against Hooker Chemical Company Inc. for its role in creating Love Canal scoured records back into the 1940s.[14] In the Love Canal case, aerial photographs along with nearly every scrap of documentary evidence, ranging from city council and school board minutes, to newspaper reports, to land transaction records, to eyewitness accounts became part of the evidentiary record. In my first participation with the Love Canal litigation, I assisted the State of New York by researching past standards for landfill operations. In particular, I traced Illinois landfill policy and practices to assist the former state sanitary engineer review his efforts to control land disposal activities during the 1940s and 1950s. Through an analysis of the historical record, we demonstrated that there were no major industrial waste dumps under school grounds and that state agencies conducted geological analysis of potential landfill sites since at least time of the Love Canal operation. Furthermore, Illinois had taken legal action against groundwater polluters in the past.

This historical information was vital to the testimony of the witnesses. With it, attorneys for the State of New York sought to establish that public health officials and industrial waste disposers shared a professional concern with the potential for environmental damage stemming from municipal refuse in the 1940s and 1950s. We hoped this would convince the judge that dumping tons of waste in the midst of a residential neighborhood was reckless at the time. The judge ultimately ruled that Hooker's conduct, while negligent, did not warrant punitive damages.

From litigation-based research, states began to take proactive steps in the 1980s. Various agencies began to compile computerized inventories of businesses as a way to identify sites requiring remediation[15] In addition, analyses of historical industries revealed several prominent contributors to the hazardous waste landscape. Notably, agencies found that creosote operations, gas works, and primary metal operations, among other industries, had hazardous legacies pushing back into the nineteenth century. Seeking to incorporate older industrial facilities and the sites where they sent wastes into computer data bases, states have developed geographic information system coverages of business depicted on fire-insurance maps and also closed landfills.[16] The procedures for identifying historical sources have become more formalized and the list of past waste generators more lengthy. Identification and inventory is an essential precursor to remediation.

Beyond site-specific studies and statewide inventories, scholars have offered more conceptual discussions of past hazardous waste management practices. Joel Tarr developed a chronological framework for waste management activities that depicted a gradual shift from land disposal sites in the nineteenth century, to water sites in the early twentieth century, followed by a return to land disposal in the second half of the twentieth century.[17] The sequence for industrial wastes is not quite so clear cut. Industries variously used water, land, and air sinks during most of the past century. There have been attempts to divert their wastes from one sink to another, such as the use of vaporization of phenolic wastes in the Ohio River valley after states pressured industry to divert them from the Ohio River.[18] Nonetheless, many industries continued to use rivers even after 1945.[19] With efforts to restrict surface water pollution, industries have sought land disposal options since the 1930s.[20.] As with municipal wastes, Tarr described the diversion of solid industrial wastes from water to land sinks—in some cases comingling with general municipal refuse. This, of course, increased the need for remediation at landfill sites in addition to manufacturing properties.

Considering several Illinois industrial districts, I developed a geographic model of past waste management that complements Tarr's chronological model. My investigations revealed an outward shift of industrial waste disposal in response to transportation, regulatory, and economic concerns. By the second half of the twentieth century, the encroachment of industrial waste disposal activity on rural areas, reliant on groundwater supplies, contributed to the increased public concern with hazardous wastes.[21] This geographic model has utility in addressing current concerns with derelict industrial facilities, waste site inventories, and brownfields (real property complicated by the presence or potential presence of hazardous substances, pollutants and/or 146 other contaminants).[22] It also illustrated that there is historical regularity in the geography of industrial waste disposal and this aids in identifying sites needing remediation.[23]

Remediation of contaminated properties demands the identification of the responsible parties, and with no statute of limitations under Superfund, the liability extends back through the full history of hazards-related activity at a site. Potentially Responsible Party (PRP) searches involve the identification of owners and operators and their corporate predecessors and successors. The challenge faced in this endeavor is much the same as that encountered by a historian tracing details of a business, although with a sharp focus on a single site. This procedure requires investigative skills to identify not only past owner/operators of a site, but to identify the types of chemicals they employed, and their waste management practices. Since contaminants can move through the soil, PRP investigations must consider activity at surrounding properties as well.[24]

Hazardous waste researchers have established the basic temporal and geographic contexts that framed waste management practices. Yet, much remains to be done. One of the most critical challenges that faces the site-specific compilers of PRP information and those engaged in generalizing about past hazardous waste-related activity is merging the two bodies of information. Although public historians have compiled massive amounts of data for private-sector clients, they are hampered by what they can share, what can be made available for the generalizers. For example, I have seen internal corporate documents from numerous chem-

Figure 7-2. Petro Processors Superfund site near Baton Rouge, Louisiana. The complex of roads and tanks in the lower center of the picture is the groundwater pumping operation and waste treatment facility of a site used for chemical waste disposal in the 1960s and 1970s. A spill from one of the Petro Processors lagoons in 1970 damaged a neighbor's property and led to a law suit well before the public discovery of the Love Canal. *Photo by author.*

ical companies. These reveal specific knowledge about the hazards of chemical wastes, the corporate decision-making process, the relationship of waste generator to waste disposer, and role of trade associations in disseminating information about waste management practices. This type of internal documentation would greatly augment the public record, gleaned from government documents, annual reports, and other generally accessible information. It would go a long way toward shoring up the historical and geographic models of waste management practices, yet tragically it seldom becomes part of the public record.

Furthermore, infusion of general discussions with company-specific information would support the bases for drawing universal conclusions. More precise historical periods and geographic patterns would undoubtedly emerge from systematic analysis of corporate documents. I have found that despite national concern with and training about trade wastes, the adoption of particular practices was not done with great synchronization or geographic consistency. Traditional manufacturing states such as Michigan and Illinois, for example, dealt with industrial wastes differently from some of the states that experienced rapid industrialization during and after World War II. Further, enactment of laws and their enforcement illustrate additional areas for idiosyncratic behavior. The generalizations, thus, must be used with regional peculiarities in mind.

HISTORIANS AND REMEDIATION

As with the legal term "hazardous waste," a formalized concept of "remediation" is arguably a recent construct. This position, however, must be built on an analysis of how manufacturers, waste management, and real estate professionals viewed deposits of hazardous industrial wastes in the pre-Superfund era. Not infrequently, I encounter testimony of experienced waste management professionals who claim that there was no expectation that waste disposers would have to clean up their messes long after they created them. I agree that in the 1950s manufacturers could not and did not foresee the passage of CERCLA and the remediation requirements it has imposed, but I suggest testifying experts need to examine, not current federal laws, but the historical record before making assertions about past expectations concerning what should be done with damaged property.

An analysis of four related areas of historical information indicates that notions about remediation were in place before 1980. First, the War Assets Administration produced a manual that spelled out procedures for selling contaminated industrial properties after World War II. Conditions for releasing properties containing either hazardous chemicals or explosives called for qualified purchasers to decontaminate the sites.[25] Second, the National Safety Council's guidebook on chemical waste management called for waste disposers to keep good records of where and what types of waste were discarded to help prevent inappropriate development of sites containing troublesome wastes.[26] Although it did not advocate remediation, its advice reflected the understanding that some wastes had persistent qualities in the environment and that dump sites were virtually permanent fixtures that required special care. At least one manufacturer prepared maps showing an old "toxic dump," a reflection of this guidance.[27] Third, an American chemical company reported on efforts it took to remediate its own contaminated property. Koppers pumped oil from the ground beneath a New Jersey plant in the early 1950s to "decontaminate" the soil and groundwater.[28] Finally, in a 1967 real estate text, William Kinnard discussed concerns of those acquiring industrial property. His checklist for industrial brokers called for an examination of "subsoil and topsoil conditions," "nature of industry in the area; its effect on the subject property," "waste disposal: source of service, capacities; special disposal equipment," and water supply.[29] As a reflection of its concern with inherited site defects, the leading industrial real estate organization published a booklet on how to rehabilitate "problem" industrial property.[30] Government and private sector participants in industrial property management understood that relict wastes could pose hazards for subsequent occupants of industrial property. The literature advised taking steps to avoid inadvertent contact with dumps or remediation as procedures minimize future problems.

Legal liability for contamination also had a pre-Superfund legal precedent. Under common law, a property owner could be held liable for harmful conditions created by a previous owner or tenant. According to the *Restatement of Torts,*

Figure 7-3. Tex-Tin site in Texas City, Texas. Although tin and copper smelting operations took place at this site in the 1940s, it eluded Superfund designation until the 1990s. Remediation was underway in the early years of the new millennium. *Photo by author.*

a vendee . . . of land upon which a harmful physical condition exists may
be liable under the rule here stated for failing to abate it after he takes possession, even though it was created by his vendor, lessor, or other person
and even though he had not part in its creation.[31]

Thus even before the passage of Superfund, the common law included a concept that a property owner should abate a harmful condition inherited from a previous owner.

CERCLA did not create the concept that polluters pay, nor did it invent the legal principle that a seller could be held accountable for passing on damaged goods
to a buyer. Historical exploration of the fundamental real estate concept of due
diligence and site remediation presents important research opportunities. In buying an industrial property, what burden lay with the buyer to ascertain that there
were no hazards lurking or that the property was not damaged? One might examine historical property transactions and contracts. It was typical for buyers to purchase all assets, but none of the liabilities. What bearing does this have on site contamination? What were the contractual arrangements when one chemical company
took over another? Did the buyer insist on a site inspection to detect any flaws with
the equipment or the site housekeeping? Did the buyer seek to insert clauses that
would limit its exposure to product liability suits, pending nuisance claims, or
other possible costs associated with the acquisition? There could be revealing case
law on undetected property damage. Certainly the concept *caveat emptor* (buyer
beware) has been a cornerstone of real estate dealings in this country. But did manufacturers expect all parts of an industrial property to be working properly or did
they buy with all warts and blemishes? The efforts of the War Assets Administration suggest that the federal government felt beholden to notify factory purchasers
of the hazards associated with past practices. Even Hooker Chemical Company insisted that the deed transferring Love Canal indicate that the site had been a chemical dump while also providing legal protection from any future law suits stemming from problems at the site. Although this type of contractual arrangement did
not call for remediation, it underscored recognition of long-terms hazards and liabilities. What were the expectations that sellers should clean up property when
turning over the title to a new owner?

Beyond the role of remediation as an industrial practice, implementation of the
Superfund policy bears historical scrutiny. Imposed on an anti-environmental
Ronald Reagan administration, the Superfund program got off to a rough start.[32]
The lack of funding for enforcement efforts, the political shenanigans of President
Reagan appointees, and the evolution of procedures all contributed to a rocky history of Superfund's first decade. Yet, this is a fascinating story that remains to be
told by an historian. How did the unwillingness of administrators to push the remediation agenda forward shape the process? Certainly, the pace of site clean ups
was abysmally slow, with fewer than fifty sites (out of over 3,000) cleaned up after a decade.[33] By the end of 1997, the Clinton administration had reinvigorated
the remediation process and touted over 500 completed clean ups. Furthermore,
what impact will the delisting of over 20,000 potential CERCLA sites have on re-

mediation? There is a critical need for public historians to be involved in both the administrative history of the EPA, and the development and implementation of state environmental programs. As key acts and agencies near landmark anniversaries, historical researchers should alert agency directors to these important dates and offer to prepare histories of developments during the first twenty or twenty-five years.

Additionally, the initial intent of the EPA was to compile a list of NPL sites that were distributed somewhat evenly among the states. The first list had 100 sites, with at least one from each state.[34] Yet, the states did not have comparable industrial histories, manufacturing complexes, or populations at risk.[35] As the Superfund process evolved, the distribution of remediated sites came to reflect the actual distribution of industrial waste disposal and population density. The mechanisms that sought a national "equity" gave way to what was perhaps a more appropriate distribution of Superfund dollars in terms of population density and risk. There remains a need for a good telling of how and where CERCLA dollars have been spent. At the national level this would involve an assessment of the total expenditures by state in relation to their populations and industrial bases. From a political sense, have districts with delegations that supported environmental protection been able to direct more dollars to their districts or have the opponents of Superfund secured the lion's share of funding? Such accounts would find value among the agencies themselves, the general public, environmental watchdog groups, and legislative bodies.

Another component of hazardous waste site remediation involves the many government sites where contamination has occurred. Military bases are prime examples of sites where government personnel handled and discarded hazardous substances. SARA, the 1986 amendments to CERCLA, directly addressed the issue of Department of Defense and Department of Energy sites. It provided for evaluation of sites, following the basic Superfund procedures, and called for remediation agreements between the EPA and the agency responsible for the site. There is a separate fund for Department of Defense (DOD) restoration (the DOD term for remediation).

Also, government-operated manufacturing facilities are the subject of much litigation and provide an intersection between Superfund and other programs aimed at remediating government properties. Private companies, who have been named as responsible parties at Superfund sites, are able to win assistance for remediation costs from the federal government if they can demonstrate that the government was an "owner or operator" during the time that contamination occurred. Suits against the government address "Government Owned/Company Operated" facilities that produced World War II materiel.[36] Also subject to litigation are sites where private plants produced goods for the military. In both types of suits, extensive analysis of wartime contracts, production agreements, and other forms of government involvement become central to determining the government's role and share of financial responsibility. Although the time frame of such cases typically has pushed research back into the 1940s, some cases make the argument that contamination stems from the government's involvement in WPA programs or World War I, and even Spanish-American War activities. The objective of most suits seeking government responsibility is to attach a portion of the joint and several liability to the government and thereby distribute a share of the costs to another deep pocket.

THE PUBLIC DISCUSSION

Who is the public that historical research should address in the discussion of hazardous wastes and environmental remediation? The audience is amazingly broad and diverse. This makes it essential to communicate through outlets normally used by nonhistorians. At the most fundamental level, historians must be prepared to carry their discussion across disciplinary boundaries.

I struggled to interest the historic preservation and industrial archeology communities in historical hazards for nearly a decade, almost to no avail.[37] I felt the industrial archeology professionals had much to add to the analysis of past waste generation and disposal. Yet, they were oriented to preservation of historic structures and not environmental dimensions of hazardous waste. The role of government agencies devoted to environmental protection is to clean up all evidence of contamination—or to destroy the landscape of contamination. These two professional objectives are fundamentally at odds with each other. Plus, there was a basic reaction on the part of preservationists, as there is among members of the public, to cringe at the alphabet soup of environmental regulation—RCRA, CERCLA, SARA and RTK to name a few. Environmental concerns, some thought, were best left to others, there was ample challenge within the core of historic preservation to keep these professionals busy without learning a new language and set of regulations.

Nonetheless, as historic property managers and preservation organizations began to encounter more and more problems associated with hazardous wastes and the complexities of remediation, they became reluctantly interested in the subject.[38] One state historic preservation officer lamented, "We don't want to know about hazardous wastes, but we have to." The current interest in "brownfields," derelict industrial districts with potentially burdensome environmental liabilities, has created a forum for discussion across professional boundaries—preservationists, planners, developers, and environmental agencies.[39] One environmental consultant in New Jersey used to joke that Newark had the largest number of national register sites that were also Superfund sites—underscoring the overlap of contamination and preservation. The court decision authorizing the EPA to proceed with remediation without conducting normal Sec. 106 cultural resources evaluation was another intersection between environmental and preservation concerns.[40] These points of contact open up a forum for an essential discussion. Preservation officials and those involved in historic interpretation must be aware both of the potential hazards found on remediated properties, but also of the historical significance of the Superfund program.

One exceptional example of the merging of preservation and remediation concerns took place in Montana. The mining and processing of copper and other metals in and around Butte created extensive zones of contamination.[41] As part of the cleanup effort, the historic preservation community became involved and secured funding to include an interpretation of the industrial activity that created environmental damage. Their interpretation went beyond the technological and social history of a mining community. It also included an innovative effort to interpret contamination and remediation efforts. Among the historic resources included in the interpretive plan are early twentieth-century ponds used to trap heavy metals and neutralize acid waters and the Colorado Tailings, a waste heap that has been cleaned up but remains part of the historical narrative. Certainly, since the closure of the mines, environmental remediation has been the biggest economic boost to the community and deserves to be part of the story.[42] Indeed, the interpretive plan seeks to make known the reclamation and pollution abatement program.

Planners of the Rocky Mountain Arsenal interpretive program, now converted to a U.S. Wildlife Refuge, grappled with how to present the story of the site's transformation from one of the most contaminated properties in the country to a sanctuary for bald eagles and other wildlife that chose the site as a permanent or seasonal habitat. With strong support from a local community group, the National Park Service recommended including interpretative elements that discussed both the story of chemical warfare agent production and site cleanup under Superfund.[43] Although the Fish and Wildlife Service opted to minimize the hazardous waste history of the site for its interpretive program, the discussion introduced a broad array of professionals to the topic. There are other refuges, such as Crab Orchard Lake in southern Illinois, where investigators have discovered contamination. Including the degradation chapter of human-environment story is a valid part of the site's history.

There will also come a day when the sites that gave rise to the Superfund act will be nominated as national register sites or national landmarks. Already the notorious trio of Love Canal, New York, Times Beach, Missouri, and Valley of the Drums, Kentucky, have been remediated. New York operated a public information office at the Love Canal site as an educational service to visiting officials and school groups, with an emphasis on the remediation process and public safety. There remains an obvious need to interpret the fenced off compound as a key site in the nation's environmental history. After being fenced off for more than a decade, Times Beach, Missouri, is the site of a new state park. It received national attention as the site where dioxin-laden oil was spread on unpaved streets to control dust. This prompted a complete evacuation of the community and a protracted remediation process. Now that cleanup efforts are completed, state officials have chosen to develop an interpretation around Route 66, the historic highway which runs near the property, rather than focus on the site's more infamous historic role. Valley of the Drums has been remediated and delisted from the National Priorities List (the national register of Superfund sites). It sits as an idle, fenced off property that is still under observation by environmental agencies. With thousands of other Superfund sites across the country, it is time to think about how to interpret these sites and the appropriate ways to reuse them if they contain other historically significant elements. The environmental movement has been a significant issue in the last third of the twentieth century and Superfund sites have been among the places where this struggle has been played out. As Gettysburg is to Civil War history and Hetch Hetchy to wilderness preservation, the major Superfund sites deserve designation as important sites for the history-hungry public. Admittedly, this may be a hard sell, but it is essential to place these sites in proper historical context and not neglect this element of the late-twentieth-century landscape.

The litigious nature of remediation-spawned research often inhibits widespread circulation and discussion of one's findings. Reports prepared for private-sector clients cannot be republished in public forums. Confidentiality restrictions may prohibit use of material and ideas developed during a contract project. At best, a consulting historian may author a portion of a technical report that finds its way into the limited distribution world of the grey literature. There are, however, opportunities to reach a broader audience even under the legitimate restrictions of consulting. Certainly lawyers and judges are one critical, but typically attentive, audience. Demonstrating the value of historical scholarship to this group will open doors for additional research on other topics. By doing work for one law firm in an environmental case, I was later called on to investigate the history of a particular place name in a trademark dispute. This illustrates how spin-off opportunities can come from work in environmental litigation.

Another outlet is the professional newsletters that readily accept brief descriptions of project work. By targeting several newsletters beyond normal historical outlets, historians can broaden their impact. As long as they present their findings in general terms, historians can discuss their work without betraying client confidentiality. Environmental and legal organizations should be prime targets. Archivists and small history organizations need to be clued in to the world of environmental conflict as well. It is all too common that small archives or history societies are invaded by teams of paralegals in search of obscure documents. Such encounters leave the small organizations reeling. They need assistance to cope with such intrusions and guidance on how to respond. Indeed, they should look at the invasion of the paralegals as opportunities to let high-stakes litigation help with organizing and cataloging their own collections. Communicating with these professionals is important. Furthermore, with the advent of internet discussion groups, lively exchanges on topics of interest to consultants can disseminate information about the value of historical research.

Finally, where the opportunity exists to draw on nonprivileged materials, consulting historians have an obligation to share their findings with their peers. Forums such as the *Public Historian, Environmental Practice,* and *Environmental Management* permit discussions about the results of investigations and the issues facing practitioners. Publications targeted to preservation and archival professional, as well as lawyers and public policy makers should also be considered. Publishing in such outlets provides the important peer-review process that can add to a consultant's credibility, and more important, it allows a broader discussion to build on one's work.

CONCLUSIONS

Hazardous wastes have been a common output of our industrial society for more than a century. How we chose to deal with them has been a socially defined process that has changed over time. In recent years, more rigorous and formalized procedures for managing wastes and for cleaning up relict waste sites has opened the door for solid historical research. Historians, although excluded from the crafting of the Superfund law, have been challenged to participate. The law that has no statute of limitations demands the input of historians. The identification of past actions that contributed to contamination, the allocation of responsibility, and the determination of remedial procedures all hinge on historical documentation.

As the remediation process winds down, which it is, the role of historians or others employing historical methods will actually expand. We must provide a suitable assessment of the environmental era of the late twentieth century for environmental agencies and policy makers. Furthermore, we must work with preservation organizations and museums to ensure some landscape legacy of the Superfund process survives and is presented in an informative way to the public.

NOTES

1. For a good discussion of the establishment of hazardous waste programs see M. R. Greenberg and R. F. Anderson, *Hazardous Waste Sites: The Credibility Gap* (New Brunswick, NJ: Center for Urban Policy Research, 1989).
2. For a discussion of hazardous wastes in their historical legal context see, Martin V. Melosi, "Hazardous Wastes and Environmental Liability: An Historical Perspective," *Houston Law Review* 25 (1988): 741–79.
3. National Safety Council, *Industrial Waste Disposal* (Chicago: National Safety Council, Industrial Safety Series No. Chem-7, 1948), 1.
4. Henry Anderson, "Insurance and Loss Prevention," in J. H. Perry, ed. *Chemical Business Handbook,* (New York: McGraw-Hill, 1954), 18–42.
5. N. Irving Sax, *Handbook of Dangerous Materials* (New York: Reinhold, 1951).
6. For a listing of the National Safety Council data sheets, see, National Safety Council, *Historical Index to the Occupational and Safety and Health Data Sheets* (Chicago: National Safety Council, 1994). This index contains over 700 citations, some very recent, but many dating from the 1950s.
7. Manufacturing Chemists' Association, *Disposal of Hazardous Waste* (Washington, D. C: Manufacturing Chemists' Association, Safety Guide SG-9, 1961), 1.
8. Sax, *Handbook of Dangerous Materials,* and *Dangerous Properties of Industrial Materials* (New York: Reinhold, 1963).
9. American Petroleum Institute, *Manual on Disposal of Refinery Wastes: V. VI, Solid Wastes* (New York: American Petroleum Institute, 1963), 35.
10. U.S. Environmental Protection Agency, *Report to Congress: Disposal of*

Hazardous Wastes (Washington, D.C: U.S. Environmental Protection Agency, Office of Solid Waste Management, SW-115, 1974), 3–7.

11. New York State Department of Health, *Love Canal: A Special Report to the Governor and Legislature* (Albany: New York Department of Health, 1981).

12. Robert T. Lee, "Comprehensive Environmental Response, Compensation and Liability Act," in T.F.P. Sullivan, ed., *Environmental Law Handbook* (Rockville, MD: Government Institutes, 1997), 430–80.

13. Jonathan Harr, *A Civil Action* (New York: Random House, 1995). A movie by same name appeared in late 1998. See also, *Anderson v. W. R. Grace & Co.*, 628 F Supp 1219 [1986]).

14. William Glaberson, "Love Canal Suit Focuses on Records from 1940s," *New York Times* (October 22, 1990): B1. See also, Craig E. Colten and Peter N. Skinner, *The Road to Love Canal: Managing Industrial Wastes before EPA* (Austin: University of Texas Press, 1996).

15. Washington Department of Ecology, *Site Discovery Project* (Olympia: Prepared by HDR Infrastructure, 1987) and S.C. Schock, et al., *Enhancement of HWRIC Database: Year 2* (Savoy: Illinois Department of Natural Resources, Hazardous Waste Research and Information Center, 1988).

16. Craig E. Colten, "The Historical Hazards GIS," *Mapnotes* 11 (Summer 1993): 48–49. This Illinois data base contains over 33,000 sites from Sanborn Fire Insurance Maps. Sites were included if they were businesses that typically handled hazardous substances at the time mapped. The Texas Natural Resource Conservation Commission developed a GIS coverage of more than 4,100 closed landfills in the state.

17. Joel A. Tarr, "The Search for the Ultimate Sink: Urban Air, Land, and Water Pollution in Historical Perspective," *Records of the Columbia Historical Society* 51 (1984): 1–29.

18. Joel A. Tarr, "Searching for a 'Sink' for an Industrial Waste: Iron-Making Fuels and the Environment," *Environmental History Review* 18 (1994): 9–34.

19. See the extensive listing contained in U.S. Department of Health, Education and Welfare, *Municipal and Industrial Waste Facilities: 1957* (Washington, D.C: U.S. Department of Health, Education and Welfare, Public Health Service, 1958).

20. Joel A. Tarr, "Historical Perspectives on Hazardous Wastes in the United States," *Waste Management and Research* 3 (1985): 95–102.

21. C. E. Colten, "Historical Hazards: The Geography of Relict Industrial Wastes," *Professional Geographer* 42 (1990): 143-56.

22. C. E. Colten, "Chicago's Waste Lands: Refuse Disposal and Urban Growth," *Journal of Historical Geography* 19 (1994): 124–42.

23. For an English example see K.L. Walwork, *Derelict Land: Origins and Prospect of a Land Use Problem* (London: David and Charles, 1974).

24. Shelley Bookspan, "Potentially Responsible Party Searches: Finding the Cause of Urban Grime," *Public Historian* 13 (1991): 25–34, and USEPA, *Po-*

tentially Responsible Party Search (Washington, D.C: USEPA, OSWER Directive 9834.6, 1987).

25. War Assets Administration, *The Disposal of Contaminated Chemical Explosives Plants* (Washington, D.C: War Assets Administration, 1947).
26. National Safety Council, *Industrial Waste Disposal,* 1948.
27. Monsanto Chemical Company, General Plant Map (Monsanto, Illinois, April 1, 1942) Illinois State Water Survey, Groundwater Section, Monsanto Chemical Company Files, Champaign, Illinois.
28. Charles Koons, "The Prevention of Pollution by Oil," *American Gas Association Proceedings,* Atlantic City, NJ, 1952, 667–77.
29. William Kinnard, *Industrial Real Estate* (Washington, D.C: Society of Industrial Realtors, 1967), 206–207.
30. Frank G. Binswanger, *Techniques in the Rehabilitation and Marketing of Problem Properties* (Washington, D.C: Society of Industrial Realtors, 1964).
31. *Restatement (Second) of Torts* (1979), sec. 839, quoted in *State of New York v. Shore Realty Corp.,* 759 F 2d 1032 (1985).
32. See Joel A. Mintz, *Enforcement at the EPA* (Austin: University of Texas Press, 1995).
33. Roger Downer, "Hazardous Waste," in P. R. Portney, ed. *Public Policies for Environmental Protection,* (Washington, D.C: Resources for the Future, 1990), 151–99.
34. M.R. Greenberg and R.F. Anderson, *Hazardous Waste Sites* (New Brunswick, NJ: Center for Urban Policy Research, 1984), 74.
35. John Hird, *Superfund: The Political Economy of Environmental Risk* (Baltimore: Johns Hopkins University Press, 1994), esp. chapter 5, 117–39.
36. Important court decisions on the topic of government involvement include *FMC Corp. v. U.S. Department of Commerce,* 786 F.Supp. 471 (1992) and *Clark, et al. v. U.S.A,* 660 F. Supp. 1164 (1987).
37. C. E. Colten, "Industrial Middens in Illinois: The Search for Hazardous Wastes, 1870–1980," *IA: The Journal for Industrial Archeology* 14 (1988): 51–61.
38. C. E. Colten, "Environmental Liabilities," *Building Renovation* (January February 1993): 13–16.
39. Charles Bartsch and Elizabeth Collaton, *Brownfields: Cleaning and Reusing Contaminated Properties* (Westport, CT: Praeger, 1997).
40. See "Boarhead Decision Affirmed on Appeal," *Preservation Law Reporter* 10 (January 1991): 1001–1003. The case was heard in the 3rd Circuit of the U.S. Court of Appeals, *Boarhead Corp. v. Erikson,* No. 90–1040 (1991).
41. Advisory Council on Historic Preservation, *Report to the President and Congress* (Washington, D.C: Advisory Council on Historic Preservation, 1990), 59–64 and Dan Baum and Margaret Knox, "We Want People Who Have a Problem with Mine Wastes to Think of Butte," *Smithsonian* 23:8 (November 1992): 46–56.
42. Regional Historic Preservation Plan Joint Committee, *Regional Historic*

Preservation Plan (Butte, MT: Regional Historic Preservation Plan Joint Committee, 1993).

43. Division of Interpretation, National Park Service, *The Plan for Interpretation of the Rocky Mountain Arsenal National Wildlife Refuge* (Denver, CO: National Park Service, 1995). The Urban Design Forum, a Denver organization, organized a conference on reuse of the RMA facility and encouraged consideration of all aspects of the site's history, even the less desirable topic of contamination and remediation. Participants from government, business, academe, and the community were involved.

PART IV

MUSEUMS, MEDIA, AND HISTORICAL SOCIETIES

MUSEUMS, THE ENVIRONMENT, AND PUBLIC HISTORY

Christopher Clarke

Museums are public institutions. They draw their vitality and their purpose from the public audiences who walk through their doors. Because communication and dialogue with the public is now (or is quickly becoming) deeply ingrained in the mission of most American museums, they constitute one of the most promising places of connection between the American public and public history. Over the past twenty-five years, American history museums and the field of public history have discovered broad and complementary areas of common interest, including the environment. Like other pressing questions of the day, the environment is a subject on the minds of many museum visitors and a prism through which an increasing number of Americans have begun to view their own experiences and to observe and assess the world around them.

American museums have an important contribution to make to public discussion of the environment and to the public's nascent but growing understanding of environmental history. Museums collect, preserve, and document material evidence about the past and the present. These important resources have the potential to help us explain how our behavior has influenced and shaped our surroundings and our attitudes toward the phenomenon we call "nature." These same resources can help us sort out the many different meanings we assign to "nature," whether we define it as the nonhuman world that surrounds us, the imaginary forest in which Bambi and Thumper reside, or the many real places and spaces that humans have created through interaction with the environment.[1]

Through exhibition and interpretation of the evidence they preserve, museums provide an important public forum for exploration and critical discussion of human behavior and its environmental consequences. The advent of environmental history as a component of public history interpretation offers museums the opportunity to incorporate this important new subject into their ongoing dialogue with public audiences. Increasingly sophisticated methods of material culture analysis enable us to analyze and interpret the objects in museum collections as historical evidence about our relationship to the environment, much as we read the volumes in a library or examine primary documents in an archive.

Objects carry two important kinds of meaning that are relevant to this inquiry. First, they frequently embody or represent time-specific attitudes toward nature. The meaning of a nineteenth-century child's dinner plate adorned with an image of nautical hunters clubbing seals, or of an early twentieth-century inkwell made from the preserved foot of a rhinoceros, is quite accessible to even the casual observer. Second, "man-made" objects embody specific relationships to the environment because each one has its own unique combination of environmental consequences arising from its creation, use, and, disposal. The individual who owns or uses any such object is inextricably connected through the object itself to a complex web of environmental interactions.

American museums have sought since their earliest days to explore and explain the world around us, especially through the study and classification of the natural world. Even before museums embraced American history as a separate and fit subject for interpretation, they attempted to document and to preserve America's natural history. The subject of natural history occupied the interests of the pioneers of American museums such as Charles Wilson Peale, whose Philadelphia Museum, founded in 1786, documented the natural world through the display of minerals, insects, fossils, and all manner of natural specimens. The museum, Peale declared, would be a "Great School of Nature."[2] Likewise, Joseph Henry, first Secretary of the Smithsonian Institution, and his Assistant Secretary, Spencer Fullerton Baird, both assumed that the Smithsonian's United States National Museum (later the National Museum of Natural History) would use its considerable collection of natural history materials to document the larger story of scientific and historical progress into which they believed American history fit. Later, extensive displays of the Smithsonian's natural history collections became staples of national celebrations of progress like Buffalo's 1901 Pan-American Exposition and the St. Louis World's Fair in 1904.[3]

The professionalization of historical study and its ultimate institutional separation from natural history and from museums helped to reinforce the divide between histories of people and histories of nature.[4] The master narrative that emerged from late-nineteenth and early-twentieth-century historiography, which focused in part on the triumphal subjugation of nature to the larger needs and aims of the American nation, left little room for consideration of the reciprocal connections that we now think of as essential to understanding environmental history. This fundamental divide dominated the work of most twentieth-century museums of history and natural history. Exhibitions about natural history tended to depict or explain nature as a spectacle to be observed and understood by humans who stand on the outside. Exhibitions about American history frequently discussed natural history and the environment as a brief preamble to (European) human settlement and to the transformation of the North American landscape. Once people appeared in the story, however, the environment tended to disappear from the narrative, returning to its subordinate role as the object of human activity and the source of food, shelter, and economic benefits to its human inhabitants.

Since the emergence of environmental awareness that began in the later 1960s, however, American museums have begun to think more critically about what their exhibits say, or could say, about the environment. Publications that circulate among museum professionals, such as the American Association of Museums' *Museum News*, *History News* from the American Association for State and Local

History, and the Canadian Museums Association's *MUSE* have within the last decade devoted full issues to a discussion of "museums and the environment."[5] World-class natural history museums, such as the American Museum of National History in New York, and The Smithsonian Institution's National Museum of Natural History, have featured path-breaking exhibitions on environmental topics such as global warming and ocean ecology.[6] "Global Warming: Understanding the Forecast," opened at the American Museum of Natural History in 1992 and traveled around the country for several years. This high-tech exhibition featured complex simulations of future global warming scenarios and explanations of the role of greenhouse gases and some of the potential long-term effects of human activity on the biosphere. Ocean Planet, on view at the National Museum of Natural History from April 1995 to January 1996, also traveled extensively and made much of its content available on its own web site. Like Global Warming, Ocean Planet presented scientific analysis of a major environmental issue, but the latter also explored political and cultural dimensions of our contemporary connections to the oceans as a global resource.

Proliferating museum web pages and other sources linked to web indexes list a rapidly growing body of museum programs, exhibitions, and publications that explore a huge variety of topics related to the environment. Funding agencies like the National Endowment for the Humanities (NEH) have responded to this groundswell of interest by supporting a variety of museum projects that embrace environmental topics and themes. On the other hand, the subject of environmental *history,* which tends to place humans inside nature by focusing on dynamic, time- and place-specific relationships between people and their surroundings, has been directly addressed in only a handful of exhibitions in history museums. Most museum visitors would probably still agree that the environment is a subject best suited for science or natural history museums. Environmental history awaits its breakthrough into the mainstream interpretive vocabulary of most American history museums.

The time-lag between the emergence of environmental history as an exciting new dimension of historical inquiry in the academy and its appearance as the subject of museum exhibitions should not surprise us. The academic revolution in social history began nearly forty years ago, but museum exhibitions incorporating these new perspectives have become widely visible only within the past fifteen years. However, a major change in the historical profession since the appearance of the new social history in the 1960s—namely the emergence of public history as, among other things, a conduit for quickly delivering new academic ideas into the public domain—may mean that this time around Americans will not have to wait quite so long to encounter this new historical thinking in public exhibitions. Public historians have an important role to play in bringing the subject of environmental history to the attention of the museum community as well as to the public at large.

This need is especially critical because by the end of the twentieth century the environment had become a *cause célèbre*. The environmental movement gener-

ated an enormous body of writing about our contemporary effects on and relationships with the natural world, much of it uninformed by historical perspective
or sound critical thinking. Environmental history needs to become visible in the
public eye not merely for the purposes of information but to serve the larger purpose of damage control. Knowledge of environmental history encourages citizens
and policy makers to be suspicious of quick fixes and simple nostrums about "saving the environment." This knowledge also provides an essential, if sobering, perspective on the limits of personal choice to produce a measurable impact on the
overall state of our relationship to the nonhuman world we inhabit. The more we
learn about environmental history, the better we understand both the possibilities
and the limitations we face in trying to define what is good for the environment
and how we might achieve it.

   Despite the potential advantages museums possess as public forums for critical
conversations about the environment, the fact that their interpretive methodology
rests in significant measure on the interpretation of material culture also poses significant challenges. Over the past few decades, many history museums have set
out to broaden their interpretation of the past by incorporating the history of (work-
ing-and lower-middle-class) women, African Americans, ethnic identity groups,
and so forth only to discover that they had no materials in their collections on
which to base such an interpretive effort. Facing up to this reality has led to several outcomes: a mad scramble to find something (anything) that represents these
largely undocumented histories; artifact-poor exhibits that depend on visuals, in-
teractives, and text to carry the interpretive argument, or, in some cases, the abandonment of efforts to document these important stories altogether.

   Fortunately for the field of environmental history, museums do not face a similar shortage of artifactual materials that can be used to explore the subject of humans' relationships with their surroundings. In fact, any museum possessing even
the most mundane American material culture collection has in its storage areas a
broad array of evidence that can serve this interpretive function very effectively.
Advances in the methodology of material culture study mentioned above have
opened the way to using familiar objects from most any museum collection to interpret environmental history. Museum exhibitions and programs can ask what
types of ideas everyday objects convey about nature and about the relationship between people and the environment. They can also probe more deeply into object
meaning by exploring the actual environmental relationships that objects embody
and the patterns of lived experience to which they attest. Both of these avenues of
interpretation are grounded in critical thinking about everyday objects.[7] These critical questions served as the foundation for an NEH-funded exhibition called "Un-
Earthing the Secret Life of Stuff: Americans and the Environment" which opened
in 1994 at Strong Museum in Rochester, New York. To date it is one of only a
handful of history museum exhibitions that have systematically explored environmental history through material culture, but others will surely follow as an understanding of how to use object collections in this way penetrates further into the
museum field.

As material evidence about past ideas and behavior, museum collections have a great deal to say about our changing relationship to our surroundings. The preoccupations of traditional material culture study with the creation and use of objects speak directly to environmental history themes such as resource use and the environmental demands of rising consumption, especially in the hands of creatively thoughtful scholars whose interests transcend the formal structure of object study.

Consider the work of Henry Petroski, a professor of engineering who has made wonderful contributions to the literature of object study through books like *The Pencil,* and *The Evolution of Useful Things.* Petroski's discussion of everyday objects is laced with potential connections to environmental history. Museum curators and historians will find any number of interesting story lines in Petroski's work that could become fascinating exhibitions that use objects already present in their artifact collections but are not being used in the expansive way Petroski's scholarship suggests. For example, Petroski ventures into territory highly compatible with environmental history when he suggests that objects have unintended consequences that are for the most part unforeseen by their creators. How many museums explore these unintended consequences in the analysis of their object collections? Public historians have a responsibility to encourage the institutions with which they work to explore the implications of Petroski's admonition that "each artifact introduced into the universe of people and things alters the behavior of both."[8]

Another example of recently published work of interest to museum curators and historians explores the present-day environmental consequences of making, using, and getting rid of everyday objects. *Stuff: The Secret Lives of Everyday Things,* published in 1997 by John C. Ryan, Alan Durning, and their colleagues at Northwest Environment Watch in Seattle, examines the environmental implications of creating, consuming, and disposing of t-shirts, shoes, computers, hamburgers, automobiles, and other familiar items we depend on in our daily lives.[9] An appendix even documents the environmental impact of developing, printing, and distributing the book itself. Unfortunately, *Stuff* lacks the historical perspective that makes Henry Petroski's work so valuable, and the book's origins in the work of an environmental advocacy group require the reader to sort carefully through the politics of its presentation. Nevertheless, *Stuff* suggests a number of stimulating interpretive ideas that could work their way into museum exhibitions about environmental history that are organized around contemporary objects from our material culture.

Highly publicized recent trends in "consumer archeology" demonstrate the potential environmental interpretive content that adheres even to the trash we throw away. Archaeologists have used the buried and abandoned detritus of human existence as the basis for recreating entire civilizations from the distant past. William Rathje's *Rubbish* (1992) and his related path-breaking work in the field of "garbology" has shown that the stuff we get rid of can tell as much about our cultural values and behaviors as the objects we place on mantelpieces or pass down as revered family treasures.[10] In fact, the decisions we make about what to consume and when and how we throw it away constitute daily reiterations of our relationship to the environment. Here again a novel interpretive approach beckons museum interpretation to follow. What is trash? How do we define it? How do we get rid of it? Do we throw away the same things today that we did 50 or 100 years ago? Why do we save some "old" things, but throw others away? These are questions that museums of any size could pose to their audiences in any number of creative ways.[11]

Recent developments in material culture scholarship that focus on the ideological content of objects further intersect with environmental history concerns about social constructions of nature and the evolution of our sense of place within and outside the natural world. A growing body of work has examined the symbolic meanings that attach to goods in Western consumer culture. Grant McCracken's *Culture and Consumption* is an excellent starting point to pursue this thread in contemporary scholarship.[12] McCracken explores the myriad ways that cultural significance and meaning attach to objects in the marketplace, exposing the possibility that the meaning of goods in consumer culture bears no relationship to the thing itself or the circumstances of its creation. The echoes of McCracken's argument that consumption shapes the cultural meaning of objects (including what they tell us about "nature") reverberate, albeit in a distinctly minor key, through the writings of other scholars as diverse as cultural historian Neil Harris, cultural geographer Robert Sack, environmental historian William Cronon, and the late intellectual historian Christopher Lasch.[13]

Some American museums are particularly well suited by subject and mission to interpreting environmental history. For example, the Adirondack Museum in upstate New York documents and explores the history of both the Adirondack region in general and more specifically the Adirondack Park, a state-protected "wilderness preserve" established in 1892. When the Adirondack Museum gathered a group of scholars in 1993 to undertake an NEH-funded self study, members of the group returned repeatedly to the new interpretive questions raised by environmental history as the basis for their recommendations on future interpretive directions that the museum's future exhibitions might pursue. Subsequent scholarly input into the Adirondack Museum's exhibition program has continued to emphasize this interpretive focus.[14]

The legislation establishing the Adirondack Park declares that the land within its boundaries will be kept "forever wild," a phrase that is often quoted but seldom subjected to critical analysis. By the mid-nineteenth-century, the Adirondacks had already been stripped of much of their natural wealth—timber, minerals, iron ore—by extractive industries seeking commercial gain. The coalition of interests who later supported the creation of the Adirondack Park—nature lovers, outdoor enthusiasts, urban elites seeking to restore their connection to the natural world, and even representatives of some of the same commercial interests that had originally denuded the landscape in the first place—had to overlook the historical record of resource harvesting that makes their commitment to "preservation" more

than a bit ironic. Seen from the perspective of recent environmental history scholarship, a phrase like "forever wild" cries out for explication. Documenting for a
public audience the process of social construction—in this case the ways that
Americans have invented and recreated "nature"—is a daunting task in part because the notion itself is abstract. But in the case of the Adirondack Park we have
concrete, tangible evidence of how and why this occurred.

Another irony that attaches to this region offers the Adirondack museum a
wealth of interpretive potential for environmental history. Wild or not, the Adirondacks have suffered serious consequences from acid rain since the mid-twentieth
century. The well-documented source of this environmental scourge is the nation's
industrial heartland further to the west. The inability of Americans in the Northeast to halt or reverse the corrosive effects of acid rain on the Adirondacks mocks
the hubris of the late-nineteenth-century Americans who believed that they could
by fiat create and preserve a piece of nature through their own (considerable) political power.

Public historians know that their work transcends the traditional boundaries of
"scholarship" as defined by the academy. But the work of public historians has the
potential to contribute to and even redefine areas of more traditional scholarship.
For example, museum scholars and historians working with material culture have
it within their collective power to help reshape a part of the field of early American history by examining the connections between environmental history and the
ideological implications of early American material life. Since the mid-1960s
scholars have argued with one another about the origins of consumerism as a cultural ethos and as the undisputed engine that drives our national economy. Material culture researchers who read the literature of environmental history will discover surprising connections between the history of the objects American have
consumed over the past 200 years and the history of our attitudes toward nature.

Recent work on the history of consumerism by material culture scholars like
Ann Smart Martin, when read together with the work of environmental historians like Donald Worster and Richard White, suggests important connections between consumer behavior and American attitudes toward nature that predate the
rise of mass production. Although the ascension of consumerism to a position of
undisputed dominance in American life would await the later nineteenth-century
explosion of the nation's mass production capability, Martin (and other scholars) trace the *introduction* of consumer goods into our culture to the mid- to late-
eighteenth century. This coincides closely with the time that, according to Donald Worster, American attitudes toward nature, especially among the
self-reflective elite, became fixed on instrumentality. It is therefore conceivable
that the origins of our cultural illusions about the meaning of consumer goods
may be traced to the very birth of American culture and society. If, as Richard
White argues, the American connection to nature was from the beginning medi-
ated through its transformation into commodities, then our vision of American
nature as the Garden of Eden may have helped shape a cultural universe in which
consumer goods derived from nature were simply an extension of our initial im-

pulse to discover and consume whatever commodities we could extract from the environment.[15] Does this challenging line of argument also have a place in programs or exhibitions destined for public audiences? Why not? Most American are only too familiar with the tension between consumption and preservation, and the issue of how and when Americans came to see the environment predominantly as a source of personal material wealth has important public policy implications that communities across the nation continue to confront.

Although new insights about the history of Americans' relationship with their surroundings at the national level are bound to emerge from the incorporation of environmental history insights into the work of public history, many of the most important impacts of this new scholarship will be local in scope, and will be rooted in the behavior of communities of people linked to specific places. As Hal Rothman has observed, "environmental history is as grounded in the bedrock of local context as any historical field can be."[16] The majority of successful future museum exhibitions about environmental history will revolve around human relationships to the environment in specific places like the Adirondack Park, or the City of St.Louis, or the Mississippi River watershed, or any one of the hundreds of thousands of small communities in America whose agricultural past is written indelibly on the landscape, however much the ink is now beginning to fade.[17] For example, nearly every local museum tells the story of how one or more local industries contributed to the community's economic growth and development. Yet the story of those industries' impact on the local environment seldom if ever appears, despite its practical value as well as its historical interest to the communities in question.

Once the novelty of simply encountering environmental history in a museum setting wears off, the most interesting interpretive questions are likely to arise from the *differences* between the relationships with the environment that Americans have experienced (and constructed) in the forests of New England, on the prairies of Iowa, in the deserts of Arizona, or in the mountains of Colorado. Our lives as intensive consumers of material goods may link us across the landscape at one level of the environmental web, but the monumental variations in our connection to water, landscape, geography, and built environment that are determined principally by our place on the ground will ultimately set us apart as distinctively as the differences in ethnicity, gender, and class that have become so visible in the scholarship of the last two generations.[18]

How then can museums large and small begin to seize a toehold in this remarkable new area of historical inquiry? Some of the responsibility rests with museums themselves, and some rests with the public history community. Public historians will need to carry an awareness of environmental history issues to the institutions in which and through which they do their work. But the public's need to become conversant with environmental history (the "damage control" issue to which I referred earlier) is acute, and should not have to wait for the slow tide of gradual institutional change to carry it along. Public historians can work as advocates for public awareness of the issues this new field confronts (especially one with such obvious relevance to contemporary debate) without crossing the line be-tween scholarship and political agitation. They can add environmental history to the ready list of disciplinary approaches that they carry with them into any inter-action with public institutions, and employ the critical language of environmental history where appropriate, just as they now do with social history, cultural history, and other important fields that have now become accepted as part of public his-torical discourse.[19] To do this effectively public historians must become conver-sant with basic environmental history scholarship in its current academic and pub-lic history applications.

Museums have a responsibility to reassess their understanding of the role of place, surroundings, and landscape on the human history the attempt to document and interpret. Their curators and historians need to become familiar with the is-sues that animate environmental history scholarship. Museums where this occurs will soon begin collecting materials that support environmental history themes. But even more important and more immediate, museum interpreters who become knowledgeable about environmental history will begin to think differently about the collections they already possess. This much they can do in a way that is virtu-ally cost free to their home institutions, because it requires no expenditure on new acquisitions or, for that matter, on new exhibitions (however attractive a prospect that might be). Incorporating environmental history into museum interpretation re-quires that we change the way we think about the objects in our collections, the things we say and write about them, and the way we discuss them with the public. This is the time-honored process of renewing our understanding of what histori-cal evidence tells us about the past and about who we are as people. It is no dif-ferent from changing the way we read an important text, or the way we understand the meaning of an important document, or the way we interpret the significance of an important event in the past.

Museums that begin to employ the insights of environmental history into their essential interpretive fabric will find that their perspective on the importance of place and region will evolve beyond political and judicial boundaries to include the natural and/or geographical position they occupy on the landscape. Imagine the impact on local history that might arise from shifting our reference beyond the "county" (a politically significant but otherwise arbitrary boundary) that is a nat-ural consequence of the dependence of local history on the county historical soci-ety for its institutional support. The same impact on a broader scale might signif-icantly alter some aspects of the focus at "state" historical institutions.

Perhaps even more challenging to our current way of doing business in the mu-seum world is the potential to forge new partnerships with institutions that are of-ten seen to exist outside our perceived communities of interest, yet which have a keen interest in environmental issues—for example, business and government. Environmental history could provide the foundation for new or enhanced com-munity relationships that create new linkages between public history institutions, the local and regional business community, and local and regional government. Obviously such relationships exist in many communities already. The difference here is that environmental history offers the potential for partnerships constructed around new areas of mutual and community self-interest.

These goals make up an ambitious and far-reaching agenda for the future. They may sound like far-flung hopes, divorced from much of present-day reality. But imagine how unlikely it seemed in 1965 that explorations of African American life would become a staple of the interpretation at Colonial Williamsburg, or that the Yorktown Battlefield would focus on the lives of ordinary soldiers, or that a major Washington D.C. museum would be dedicated to the Holocaust, or that a National Park Service site would be devoted to the women who wrote the Declaration of Sentiments in 1848. These remarkable changes in the public presentation of American history, changes that have taken place during the lifetimes of most of the adults who read this chapter, should encourage us to imagine just how broadly environmental history will some day affect the way American museums represent our past—after we have begun to do the work that lies ahead of us.

NOTES

1. Donald Worster, "Doing Environmental History," in Donald Worster, ed., *The Ends of the Earth: Perspectives on Modern Environmental History* (New York: Cambridge University Press, 1988), pp. 289–307; Ralph H. Lutts, "The Trouble with Bambi: Walt Disney's Bambi and the American Vision of Nature," *Forest And Conservation History* 36 (October 1992): 160–171.
2. Quoted in Gary Kulik, "Designing the Past: History-Museum Exhibitions from Peale to the Present," in Warren Leon and Roy Rosenzweig, eds., *History Museums in the United States: A Critical Assessment* (Urbana: University of Illinois Press, 1989), p. 4.
3. Robert Rydell, *All the World's a Fair: Visions of Empire at American International Expositions, 1876–1916* (Chicago: University of Chicago Press, 1984).
4. On the professionalization of history, see Peter Novick, *That Noble Dream: The "Objectivity Question" and the American Historical Profession* (Cambridge: Cambridge University Press, 1988); and John Higham, *History: Professional Scholarship in America* (Baltimore: Johns Hopkins University Press, 1965). For an extended discussion of the relationship between museums and the academy in the early 20th century, see Steven Conn, *Museums and American Intellectual Life, 1876–1926* (Chicago: University of Chicago Press, 1998).
5. *Museum News,* March/April 1992; *History News,* November/December 1993; *MUSE,* Winter 1991.
6. For publications related to these two exhibitions, see Andrew Revkin, *Global Warming: Understanding the Forecast* (New York: Abbeville Press, Inc., 1992); and Peter Benchley and Judith Gradwohl, eds., *Ocean Planet: Writings and Images of the Sea* (Washington, D.C.: Harry N. Abrams and *Times Mirror* Magazines, in association with the Smithsonian Institution, 1995).

7. These questions are explored in more detail in Christopher Clarke-Hazlett, "Interpreting Environmental History Through Material Culture," *Material History Review* (Ottawa: National Museum of Science and Technology) 46 (Fall, 1997): 5–16.

8. Henry Petroski, *The Pencil: A History of Design and Circumstance* (New York: Alfred A. Knopf, 1990); Petroski *The Evolution of Useful Things* (New York: Alfred P. Knopf, 1992).

9. John C. Ryan and Alan Thein Durning, *Stuff: The Secret Lives of Everyday Things* (Seattle, WA: Northwest Environment Watch, 1997). (Despite the similarity in titles, this book has no connection to the Strong Museum exhibition referred to in this chapter.)

10. William Rathje and Cullen Murphy, *Rubbish!: The Archaeology of Garbage* (New York: HarperCollins, 1992).

11. One such exhibition appeared at the New York Public Library from November 12, 1994, to February 25, 1995. For the exhibit catalog, see Elizabeth Fee and Stephen H. Corey, *Garbage! The History and Politics of Trash in New York City* (New York: New York Public Library, 1994).

12. Grant McCracken, *Culture and Consumption: New Approaches to the Symbolic Character of Consumer Goods and Activities* (Bloomington: Indiana University Press, 1988).

13. Neil Harris, "The Drama of Consumer Desire," in *Cultural Excursions: Marketing Appetites and Cultural Tastes in Modern America* (Chicago: University of Chicago Press, 1990), 174–97; Robert Sack, "The Realm of Meaning: The Inadequacy of Human-Nature Theory and the View of Mass Consumption," in B.L. Turner, et al., eds., *The Earth as Transformed by Human Action: Global and Regional Changes in the Biosphere over the Past 300 Years* (Cambridge: Cambridge University Press, 1990), 659–71, William Cronon, *Nature's Metropolis: Chicago and the Great West* (New York: W. W. Norton and Co., 1991), 340; Christopher Lasch, *The Minimal Self: Psychic Survival in Troubled Times* (New York: W.W. Norton and Co., 1984) 27–31.

14. The author was a member of the visiting scholars group that conducted the review. "Adirondack Museum NEH Self-Study Final Report: December 1, 1993," in possession of the author. Copies of all consultants' reports are located in the Adirondack Museum archives.

15. Ann Smart Martin, "Makers, Buyers, Users: Consumerism as a Material Culture Framework," *Winterthur Portfolio 28:2/3, 141–57;* Donald Worster, *The Wealth of Nature: Environmental History and the Ecological Imagination* (New York: Oxford University Press, 1993), 8–11; Richard White, "Discovering Nature in North America," *Journal of American History* 79 (December 1992), 874–91.

16. Hal Rothman, "Environmental History and Local History," *History News,* November/December 1993, 8–9.

17. The Missouri Historical Society has published an excellent volume on the environmental history of St. Louis: Andrew Hurley, ed., *Common Fields: An*

Environmental History of St. Louis (St. Louis: Missouri Historical Society Press, 1997).

18. Alan Taylor, "Unnatural Inequalities: Social and Environmental Histories," *Environmental History* 1:4 (October 1996): 6–19; Nancy Shoemaker, "Regions as Categories of Analysis," *AHA Perspectives* (November 1996): 7–10.

19. The author was involved in reworking a major interpretive exhibition project at one of the National Park Service's battlefield sites. A lengthy critique of the previous exhibition plan prepared by senior staff at the NPS site roundly criticized that plan for the absence of diverse cultural perspectives, and for its failure to incorporate social history interpretation into the exhibition narrative. The absence of environmental history interpretation, on the other hand, passed without significant comment.

THE CREATION OF PLACE OVER TIME: INTERPRETING ENVIRONMENTAL THEMES IN EXHIBIT FORMAT

Philip V. Scarpino

Upon first glance, environmental history and public history seem like natural allies in a common quest to understand and explain the historical relationship between people and their surroundings. Both grew out of significant social and professional changes in the last third of the twentieth century; both share a dedication to research, analysis and interpretation, and communication; and both embrace a commitment to illuminating the complex historical processes whereby human beings make and remake the places they inhabit and the cultural meaning of those places over time. Despite apparent similarities, public and environmental history have evolved on roughly parallel tracks with surprisingly little intentional overlap. Generally speaking, environmental history occupies an academic niche. Practitioners add to knowledge through their contributions to a significant and growing body of refereed literature, which they target largely at their peers. Public historians have contributed to a body of literature that describes and analyzes the content of their field, but they put their emphasis on communication of public scholarship to a wide variety of audiences. Museums that develop and mount historical exhibits with environmental themes almost by definition work at the interface between public and environmental history. The trick becomes finding ways to communicate across the subdisciplinary barriers and boundaries that litter the potential common ground between the two fields.

Although the contemporary media pay a great deal of attention to environmental issues, much of it is crisis driven and largely devoid of context and history. Problems seem to bubble up out of nowhere—without a past—only to subside and be replaced by something else. Oil and chemical spills, ground water contamination, landfills, land-use planning and urban sprawl, mineral and energy development, parks and refuges, appear and disappear from the headlines. Perhaps the overriding challenge for exhibits with environmental themes is to show that past, present, and future are not separate domains. The intertwined and interdependent natural and cultural environments that we occupy in the present have important historical dimensions. Past actions have not only shaped the present but also create momentum that influences the future. At their best, museums explain and educate, challenge and inspire, and provide spaces for reflection and conversation that influences the content of individual and collective memories. In so doing, museums are both interpreters of the past and participants in a constantly unfolding story that takes place at the moving fault line between past and present. From this perspective, environmental history and environmental exhibits become a study of the journey we have taken to arrive at the present—an examination of the creation of place over time.

On-the-job challenges consulting for a number of museums that were developing exhibits with environmental themes forced me to think about the intersections between environmental history and public history—between an academic subdiscipline and a way of practicing the craft that emphasizes communication of appropriately tailored public scholarship to a variety of audiences. My doctoral training was in environmental history. One of my first jobs was Director of the Oklahoma Historic Preservation Survey, headquartered in the Department of History at Oklahoma State University, where among other things I got a crash course in developing resource-based historic preservation planning. By 1986, I had "backed into" the directorship of a graduate program in public history, at Indiana University/Purdue University at Indianapolis (IUPUI), by trading on experience and expertise in historic preservation. IUPUI's advertisement for the public history position also stated that they wanted someone with a field in environmental history. At the time, I am not sure that either the department or I understood the potential for connections between the two fields.

Over the past fifteen years, I have served as a consultant for a number of exhibit development projects, many of which were peer-reviewed and funded by the National Endowment for the Humanities (NEH) and state humanities councils. Both NEH and state councils insist that the projects paid for by the grants that they award be staffed by appropriate subject-area experts. In my case, a book on the Mississippi River brought me to the attention of several museums that were planning exhibits with river-related themes.[1] The first call came from the Illinois State Museum with a request that I consult on a barge-mounted exhibit, "Harvesting the River," which would be towed down the Illinois and the Mississippi Rivers to St. Louis. NEH funding added the imprimatur of peer review to a bold and successful exhibit. Next came "Always a River," another barge-mounted exhibit, inspired by "Harvesting the River," that interpreted the history and culture of the Ohio River and its valley at ports of call from Pittsburgh to Cairo. "Always A River," brought together funding from several sources, including NEH and humanities councils of states bordering the Ohio River. The River Museum, located in Dubuque, Iowa, has asked me to work on four projects funded by NEH that ranged from self-study, to planning, to implementation. Stepping back from rivers, I have had the opportunity to participate in the development of exhibits with more general environmental themes at institutions such as the Adirondack Museum and the Strong Museum, in upstate New York, the Missouri Historical Society, in St. Louis, and the Canal Museum, in Easton, Pennsylvania.

The key for me became developing strategies for combining the scholarship of environmental history with the emphasis on audience that was at the heart of public history in ways that would meet the needs of interpreting environmental themes in exhibit format. Building upon the familiar and comfortable emphasis that history museums put on interpreting material culture offered a means to that end. What I would like to do is sketch out an approach to interpreting environmental themes in exhibit format. What I have in mind is more of a strategy than a model—an interpretive framework that draws on the familiar language of the humanities and of artifacts and material culture. One of the things that I quickly discovered when I started working on museum exhibits with environmental themes is that there are few links between the fields of environmental history and material culture and museum interpretation. What follows is an attempt to build some bridges.

During 1994/95, I had the opportunity to work as a consultant on an NEH planning grant awarded to the Mississippi River Museum in Dubuque, Iowa. Part of our assignment was to develop a plan for making the environmental history of the Mississippi River and its valley central to the interpretive program of the museum. As often happens with projects such as this, the director of the museum created opportunities for the outside consultants to meet with the officers and Board of Directors of the museum. At one such gathering, I found myself talking to a member of the Board about the environmental history of the upper Mississippi. During a conversation about historical changes in the river, he told me that while the river had indeed been heavily modified along Dubuque's waterfront, just a short distance downstream one could still encounter the upper Mississippi as it had existed "since time immemorial." He then went on to expound on the wonders of this unaltered river, including its quiet backwaters and secluded sandy beaches accessible only by boat.

Figure 9-1. The Boatyard at Eagle Point, Dubuque, Iowa, 1889.

Figure 9-2. Lake Peosta, Mississippi River, Dubuque, Iowa, 1889.

Figure 9-3. Campers on the Mississippi, Dubuque, Iowa, 1907.
Figure 9-1, 9-2, & 9-3. Historical photographs help document ways in which people have imagined, used, and shaped the upper Mississippi River. *National Mississippi River Museum and Aquarium, Debuque, Iowa.*

Although not an uncommon point of view, his description of the river nonetheless overlooked the profound transformation the upper Mississippi has undergone since the mid-nineteenth century. Although attempts to tame and discipline the great Father of Waters have met with mixed results, in both form and function the present-day upper Mississippi is the end product of a long process of human use and development. In the last third of the nineteenth century, silt from cut over pineries and expanding agriculture, stimulated first by the steamboat and later by the railroad, washed into the upper river. There, in the river, silt mixed with the untreated sewage and industrial wastes from rapidly growing cities and towns from Minneapolis/St. Paul to St. Louis and began a long-term process that physically, biologically, and aesthetically remade the river. Navigational improvements that began with snag removal and that progressed through programs intended to maintain a four-foot channel and then a six-foot channel altered the face and hydrology of the river. The golden age of the steamboats ended before the Civil War, and railroads spanned and paralleled the river and eventually would integrate barge traffic into a national and international transportation system. Drainage of wetlands and agricultural levees changed both habitat and flood cycles, and by the mid-1920s, provided the issue that sparked broad-based public support for congressional approval of the Upper Mississippi River Wildlife and Fish Refuge. In the late 1920s and 1930s, the upper Mississippi was reengineered from a free-flowing river to a chain of slack-water navigation pools, as the result of the construction of a series of locks and dams.[2] In all likelihood, even the sandy beaches this man so loved had a human origin: dredge spoil dumped by the Army Corps of Engineers as it worked to maintain the navigation channel for commercial barge traffic.

What this story did for me was to highlight some of the challenges faced by museums and other institutions that want to present environmental history to public audiences. How do you interpret something that is literally as big as all outdoors? How do you approach the subject? What do you want visitors to know about the history of the interaction between people and their surroundings? How do you work with, build upon, and incorporate into the exhibit process what visitors know, as well as their memories of particular places? How do you put modern environmental issues or the present-day physical environment or contemporary attitudes toward nature or recent scientific knowledge into historical perspective? When the River Museum began planning for updated and expanded interpretation and new physical facilities, it did so in the context of a significant, ongoing reassessment of the role of rivers in American life. At the same time, the River Museum faced physical challenges directly associated with past attitudes and actions toward the river. Easy access to the Mississippi from downtown Dubuque was limited by railroad tracks and highway interchanges. Dubuque, like many other American cities, such as Louisville, Kentucky; Hartford, Connecticut; and Kansas City, Missouri, had literally and figuratively turned its back on the river that once had been central to its economic and cultural life. Reinvigorated interest in the Mississippi (and the Ohio, Connecticut, Missouri, and other American rivers) followed on the heels of the environmental movement and improvements in water quality due to federal and state pollution control laws. By the early twenty-first century, the River Museum's plans for new interpretive exhibits and a new building had become incorporated into a larger multimillion dollar renovation of Dubuque's waterfront. The transformation of the waterfront offers a physical expression of a major shift in attitudes towards the river. It also reflects and continues an ongoing process of human interaction with the Mississippi in which the

Figure 9-4. "Harbor at Dubuque, Iowa, with hull of *Windom*," taken in 1896 by Henry Bosse, shows a humanized landscape in which the railroad had pushed aside the steamboat, but the city and the river remained tightly bound together.

river has been imagined and reimagined, shaped and reshaped over time. The museum is both the "author" of, and a "character" in, a continually unfolding story.

In his presidential address to the Organization of American Historians in 1980, Carl Degler pointed out that historians make and remake history. Degler talked to his audience about why historians interpret and reinterpret the past in ways that have continuing value for students of history nearly a quarter of a century later. Degler admitted that sometimes reinterpretations grow out of the discovery of new information. But, he added, the most common reason for making and remaking history rests in the fact that historians, like most other human beings, make sense of the past through the prism of their culture. While historians subscribe to rules of evidence and interpretive honesty, their analytical emphasis changes as the culture of which they are a part evolves. They examine new subjects, reexamine old ones, pose different questions, and revisit sources worked by earlier generations of scholars.[3]

Environmental history, which emerged as field in the late 1960s and 1970s, grew out of the passion and broad, popular interest in the environment that became such an important part of American society at that time. Not all of the first generation of self-proclaimed environmental historians were environmentalists, but they were certainly influenced by contemporary interest in the environment to ask questions about the historical relationship between people and nature. It is not surprising to discover that most environmental historians who helped to create and shape the field turned to ecology and ecosystem theory as a model for analysis.[4] Not only had ecology emerged as central to the work of scientists and resources managers, but also, thanks to important books by writers such as Rachael Carson and Aldo Leopold, a popularized version of ecology formed the intellectual and philosophical foundation for the modern environmental movement.[5] The ecological underpinning of the environmental movement distinguishes it from conservation, which dominated the first half of the twentieth century. Ecology represents one of two great intellectual watersheds in understanding and explaining the relationship between people that their environment; the other being Charles Darwin's theory of natural selection.

Much as historians make and remake history, human beings make and remake nature in two important and intertwined ways: First, as society changes over time, so too does the way that people define nature and their understanding of their relationship with the natural world. While there certainly is a physical reality to nature, for all practical purposes nature is what people think it is. Second, acting upon the values and attitudes embedded in our cultures and using the technologies and energy at our disposal, we literally change and transform nature—either deliberately to meet our needs or as the result of the unintended or unanticipated consequences of our actions. Indeed, in modern industrial nations like the United States and Canada, it is possible to interpret nature as a human artifact—as an example of human material culture. This is the point at which environmental history, material culture, and museum interpretation really come together.

The way that people understand nature powerfully influences how they interact with and use the natural world. English colonists who came to the New World carried with them memories of the English countryside, a mélange of what they had seen at home and in pictures by British painters, such as Aelbert Cuyp and John Constable, who depicted settled, ordered, and productive landscapes.[6] After the Revolution, Americans continued to embrace attitudes toward nature that crossed the Atlantic with Europeans. They viewed land and other resources as property, and considered nature and the products of nature (fish, lumber, furs, minerals, crops) as commodities that had a cash value in a market. Other important and related attitudes included the belief that God created nature to serve people; that progress was measured by improving nature; that improvement required that na-

ture be conquered and controlled; and that nature could be divided into good and
bad, useful and useless, flowers and weeds, game and varmints. All of this rested
on a nearly universal, bedrock belief in the unlimited abundance of nature. Alle-
giance to the triumvirate of property, commodity, and market, along with corollary attitudes, opened a wide and almost unbridgeable gulf between the settlers and
the Native Americans—two groups that sometimes occupied the same environment. Acting on these attitudes produced a significant reshaping of the visual landscape and of biological communities. Mid-nineteenth century American artists,
such as Edward Hicks, Thomas Chambers, and George Inness, painted landscapes
that captured how successfully and dramatically transplanted English memories of
a "civilized" and productive countryside had been recreated in the United States.[7]

The way that people define nature also has a historical dimension; it has
evolved over time, often in response to the unintended or unanticipated consequences of their own actions. For example, when considering a subject like pollution, it is worth remembering that values have changed a great deal in the last
fifty years or so. In the late-nineteenth and early-twentieth centuries, many people saw factory smoke as a symbol of progress. "Birds-eye" maps of American
cities from the last third of the nineteenth century, often depicted smoke pouring
from the chimneys of factories—a proud statement of the perceived link between
smoke and progress. It was only in the last decade of the nineteenth century that
attitudes began to change to any significant degree. They changed largely in response to the consequences of unregulated spewing of smoke into the air—consequences centering around public health, quality of life, wasteful use of energy
through inefficient combustion, and other social and economic costs. In the case
of rivers, in the early twentieth century, conservationists tended to think in term
of wise use, efficient management, and prevention of waste. From that perspective, conserving a river meant developing its potential to serve human society
with navigation improvements, hydroelectric dams, flood control works,
drainage of wetlands, and so on. By the late 1950s and 1960s, people caught up
in the post-WWII environmental movement saw nature and rivers through the
lens of ecology. Environmentalists prized the qualities represented by free-flowing rivers, and for them dams became symbols of the destruction of these increasingly endangered and valuable attributes of American rivers. This shift in
attitudes set up a series of intense confrontations between conservationists and
environmentalists over the best use of rivers.

Analysis and interpretation of people's past interaction with the environment really focuses on a series of questions:

1. What did people think that nature was?
2. How did they understand their relationship with nature?
3. How did they act on their definitions of nature and their understanding of
   their relationship with nature?
4. What was the outcome of their actions?

5. How did the unintended or unanticipated results of their actions reshape their definitions of nature and their understanding of their relationship with nature?

This kind of emphasis on nature as a cultural construction is solidly grounded in the humanities, which distinguishes it from other approaches to environmental exhibits based on science or natural history or technology. It uses values, beliefs, and attitudes as the starting point for the analysis and interpretation, and it argues that the key variable in shaping the interplay between people and the environment is culture. It is not enough just to have the ability to do something; people have to want to do it as well. Our values, beliefs, and attitudes shape the way that we define and use nature. They have a major impact on the ways that we imagine and depict nature in literature, art, and folklore; they influence the kinds of technologies that we develop and the ways that we use those technologies and available energy; they have a powerful impact on the work of scientists and the application of their results; and they play a role in shaping policy at the local, state, and federal levels. One of the best studies of changing attitudes towards the natural world is Thomas Dunlap's *Saving America's Wildlife,* which examines the dramatic evolution of attitudes and actions towards wolves, coyotes, and other "varmints" in the period between 1850 and 1990.[8]

The landscape that Europeans and Americans created had little room for predators, which they viewed as dangerous, as symbols of uncivilized and uncontrolled nature, and as competitors for domestic livestock and useful wild species like deer. By the early twentieth century, the U.S. Bureau of Biological survey had teamed with stock raisers and declared war on coyotes in western sheep and cattle country. Coyotes proved hard to vanquish, but hunting reinforced by government policies dramatically reduced the numbers of large carnivores, including wolves, bears, and mountain lions. Their destruction represented both an actual and a symbolic taming of the wilderness; their removal as predators had a dramatic impact on animal communities; and their absence changed the "feel" of forest and wilderness experiences. After World War II, a combination of new scientific knowledge, the ecology-based environmental movement, and the animal rights movement, prompted a rethinking of the role of predators and varmints. Recent, often controversial, attempts to restore wolves and grizzly bears not only reflected a scientific interest in reconstructing past ecosystems but a profound attitudinal change toward the value of these animals in the natural world and to human society.

I do not mean to imply that everyone has agreed on what nature is or what the relationship between people and nature should be. That is contested terrain—a point that interpretations of environmental history should not lose sight of. It is also important to keep in mind that not everyone has shared the same environmental experiences. In America's cities and suburbs, for example, environmental experiences have been highly correlated class, race, and ethnicity. And, so long as many women worked at home and most men traveled to work, there were differences by gender as well. During the course of the twentieth century, suburbs have been the primary environmental experience for millions of Americans. Kenneth

Jackson's *Crabgrass Frontier* does an excellent job of explaining the historical processes that resulted in the physical and cultural evolution of American suburbs and segregation of population between suburbs and cities based largely upon race and class. In describing the characteristics of post-WWII suburbs, Jackson asserts that perhaps the "most important characteristic of the postwar suburb was economic and racial homogeneity."[9]

There is a second important way that people make and remake nature: by acting upon the attitudes and values in their cultures and employing technology and energy, they actually transform their surroundings. It is at this point that museums' interpretation of material culture intersects with environmental history. The best definition of material culture is the one coined by archaeologist James Deetz and used often by Thomas Schlereth: "that segment of man's physical environment which is purposely shaped by him according to culturally dictated plans."[10] If you think about this definition and let it roll over and over in your mind, the degree to which human beings have made and remade their surroundings should begin to take shape. The more I study past human interaction with the environment, the more I see the environment in terms of Deetz's neat little definition of material culture. Deetz's emphasis on purposely shaping the physical environment "according to culturally dictated plans," draws together the making and remaking of nature as a cultural construction with the physical making and remaking of the environment that comes from acting on the attitudes and values embedded in culture.

Deetz's definition highlights the fact that most of what we call nature is part of our material cultural legacy; it helps us to see the that the purview of environmental history and environmental exhibits is much more than "nature." There are plenty of things that human beings did not create and cannot control. Even so, the environment that we inhabit from cities to suburbs to farm fields is largely a human artifact. It is a cultural mosaic that reflects the changing and often conflicting values of those who imposed their own visions of order on the face of the land. As such, our surrounding environment is subject to the same kinds of material culture-based interpretation that museums are accustomed to doing. Alfred Crosby's *Ecological Imperialism: The Biological Expansion of Europe, 900–1900* does a remarkable job of analyzing the ways in which European migration contributed to a worldwide exchange of disease organisms, plants, and animals, that has had a profound (and continuing) impact on human society and on the making and remaking of the humanized environment.[11]

Even wilderness areas are human artifacts, preserved, protected, and managed by people who value those surviving fragments of our natural heritage. In many ways, wilderness areas are like environmental museums where we preserve, care for, display, and, interpret protected fragments of our natural heritage. So too are many state parks. In the early 1980s, I participated in a revegetation work trip, sponsored by the Sierra Club on land managed by the United States Forest Service in what was then the Willowa Primitive Area in northeastern Oregon. Much as a historic preservationist would sensitively replace damaged fabric with appropriate materials, our work consisted of carefully transplanting just the right vegetation from a similar elevation contour to restore ground cover trampled by hikers and campers around a high country lake. I would like to think that some twenty years later hikers pass that spot and imagine that the lake shore looks wild and unspoiled, much as it would have when only Native Americans knew those mountains. Adirondack State Park, in upstate New York, proclaims itself "forever wild." Yet, the "wilderness" qualities that many now enjoy are the result of decades of managed and natural reforestation. Careful inspection often reveals the decaying or deteriorating material remnants of former, large-scale harvesting of timber.

Thinking of environment in terms of material culture also challenges us to understand that nature is part of our environment, but so too are cities and suburbs and towns; transportation and communications and utility networks; electricity and air conditioning; factories and parking lots; grocery stores and shopping centers; farm fields and clear cuts; strip mines and sanitary landfills; antibiotics and pesticides. In many ways, the interconnected and interdependent life support system that is our present-day environment is like a cyborg. It has natural and artificial parts: Both of which are essential to its functioning, and both of which need to be a part of our analysis when we examine the history of human interaction with the environment. In an insightful and thoughtful volume on the Columbia River, historian, Richard White, has referred to the highly humanized environment as an "organic machine."[12] When I was in high school, I enjoyed reading science fiction. In some of that literature, the authors wrote about people traveling into space in order to "terra form" alien worlds and make them suitable human habitats. In fact, that is exactly what people have done here on earth. And, the rate of transformation has accelerated dramatically in the last hundred years or so. Along with that has come increased pressure on resources, such as rivers, to satisfy multiple, diverse, and frequently conflicting needs. Without minimizing the benefits that most of us derive from our heavily humanized surroundings, they nonetheless mask vital links between people and the natural world and create the illusion that we have achieved control over nature. Among other things, this interpretive strategy makes it possible to lift the mask and set our continuing and absolute dependence on natural processes in historical context.

Characterization of the environment as a human artifact is an important first step in interpreting environmental themes in exhibit format. It makes it possible to draw upon the literature of environmental history and related disciplines, but to use it in a way that is consistent with what museums already do. From this perspective, the environment itself becomes the material culture base that forms the interpretive foundation of the exhibit. The artifacts and other materials used inside the museum build upon that base. For example, the consultants urged the staff of the Mississippi River Museum, in Dubuque, to consider the Mississippi and its valley as the primary artifact upon which to base their exhibits on the river and its valley. We argued that the interpretive strategy should begin with the river and its valley as they are in the present and pose the question: How did they get that way? The advantage of doing this is that it starts with the familiar, connects past to present, and invites examination of the creation of place over time.

Even though I eagerly proselytize for this kind of an approach to environmental exhibits, I also want to point out two pitfalls that lie side-by-side along this path for both visitors and staff. Because visitors are not simply passive, spongelike recipients of information, it is important to design exhibits with environmental themes in a way that allows and encourages them to draw on their knowledge and experience without slipping into these traps. One pitfall is the tendency for exhibits to explicitly or implicitly encourage the impression that "bad" or "wrongheaded" people in the past messed up the environment or that the general theme in environmental history is one of degradation and destruction. Certainly, there were people in the past who deliberately set out to do destructive things, but more generally, people saw their actions in positive terms—promoting progress or economic growth or some other social benefit, as they understood those things in their own time.

Frequently, problems manifested themselves in the form of unintended or unanticipated consequences. Indeed, understanding past human interaction with the environment requires paying as much attention to the unintended and unanticipated consequences as it does to what people deliberately set out to accomplish. In the late nineteenth and early twentieth centuries, for example, lumber companies like Weyerhaeuser engaged in logging off the vast pineries of the Great Lakes states of Michigan, Wisconsin, and Minnesota. This logging was done in the context of faith in the unlimited abundance of the American forests and in the belief that the highest use of land was for agriculture. Cutting the forests would produce two good things: lumber and farms. It turned out that the climate and soil of much of the formerly forested areas did not support profitable agriculture, and the speed and wasteful practices associated with the logging helped to persuade millions of Americans that the nation's resources were not without limits. In the end, the lumber industry moved on to the Far West and left behind a cut over and impoverished landscape. The rapid and destructive logging of the Great Lakes forests was one of several factors that stimulated a shift in attitudes that gave rise to the Progressive Era conservation movement.[13]

It is equally important to guard against judging past human interaction with the environment against modern values and knowledge and then concluding that people in the past were evil or stupid. Whether or not we consider ourselves environmentalists, for most of us our interpretive angle of vision is influenced by the interrelated concepts of environment and ecology. These are terms that were not even in popular use before the early 1960s. Embedded in those words is a value system and a way of understanding the place of human beings in nature. Those values and that understanding influence the way that we define our research problems; the questions that we ask; and the ways that we reconstruct and interpret past relations with the natural world. Problems arise when we judge people's actions in the past against this perspective. Although it is important to point out the consequences that we see from our angle of vision, and although we don't have to like or admire everything that our ancestors did, it is historically appropriate to analyze their actions in the context of their society, their value system, and their knowledge of their surroundings. What did the people at the time know? What did they think was the appropriate relationship between people and nature? What did they want to accomplish? What was the outcome? How did they react or respond? Were there conflicting points of view? What were the long-term ramifications of their attitudes and actions?

Despite the potential pitfalls, the interpretive possibilities are nonetheless very broad. No matter where a museum or historical society is located, from the inner city to the suburbs to the most remote rural area, it is possible to interpret the evolution of your place over time from an environmental history perspective. In the modern world, it is hard to overemphasize the degree to which the environment is a human artifact, a product of historical interaction between natural and human processes. Several years ago, the Toronto *Globe and Mail,* in an unusually insightful piece of journalism, captured and explained the degree to which Lake Ontario had been modified by human action:

> The road leading to the Glenora fisheries research station on the north shore of Lake Ontario carries a lesson on its shoulder. First there is a front-yard display of plastic cows. Then, as the road curves to meet the lake, there is a house sided with panels of fake stonework.
>
> And then there is the lake, seemingly a refuge from all that is artificial. On the land side is an environment shaped by human hands, while in the depths, human impact is minimal. But that assumption is deceiving.
>
> Just like the false stonework and fake cows, Lake Ontario's ecosystem is contrived by humans. . . .[14]

This article in the *Globe and Mail* then went on to explain how human actions had remade the environment of Lake Ontario so that its aquatic ecosystem was a much a product of human actions as the obviously modified terrestrial environment that surrounds the lake. Lake Ontario emerges not as a place unchanged since time immemorial, but an environment shaped by human action, an example of human material culture that can be employed to interpret the creation of place over time.

The approach that I have suggested is portable; it can be used for interpreting nearby or distant environments, as well as present and past human interaction with the environment. At the same time, it offers some real possibilities for looking at local surroundings—to include incorporating the environment itself into the exhibit. As David Glassberg suggests in his chapter, it is possible to draw into the exhibit process local people who have different memories of the place in which they live. It is also possible to figuratively open the windows and doors of a museum and carry the interpretation outside with signs, walking and driving tours, field trips, and so on. At the Mississippi River Museum, for example, the consultants urged the staff to incorporate waterfront area surrounding the museum into its interpretive strategy—a cultural landscape that includes the river, a flood wall, an artificial harbor, a historic bridge, parallel transportation systems in the form of railroads and highways, and fill land that was formerly used for industrial and boat-building purposes and that more recently served as parking lots and land-based support for river boat gambling. Understanding the Mississippi River, or any part of the environment, as a work in progress, as a material manifestation of the creation of place over time, as "that segment of man's physical environment which is purposely shaped by him according to culturally dictated plans," integrates environmental history and the public scholarship of museum exhibits. Museums can draw upon the rich and sophisticated literature of environmental history but apply it within a public historical framework that interprets the environment in familiar material cultural terms.

NOTES

1. Philip V. Scarpino, *Great River: An Environmental History of the Upper Mississippi River, 1890–1950* (Columbia: University of Missouri Press, 1985). For a recent, but different, examination of interpreting environmental history in museums, see: Jeffrey K. Stine, "Placing Environmental History on Display," *Environmental History* 7 (October 2002): 566–588.
2. Scarpino, *Great River*. See also: John O. Anfinson, *The River We Have Wrought: A History of the Upper Mississippi* (Minneapolis: University of Minnesota Press, 2003). For an excellent, recent examination of human modification of a river and its valley, see: John Thompson, *Wetlands Drainage, River Modification, and Sectoral Conflict in the Lower Illinois Valley, 1890–1930* (Carbondale: Southern Illinois University Press, 2002).
3. Carl N. Degler, "Remaking American History," *The Journal of American History* (June 1980): 7–25.
4. For environmental histories that employ an ecosystem model, see: William Cronon, *Changes in the Land: Indians, Colonists, and the Ecology of New England* (New York: Hill and Wang, 1983); and, Susan L. Flader, *Thinking Like a Mountain: Aldo Leopold and the Evolution of an Ecological Attitude Toward Deer, Wolves, and Forests* (Columbia: University of Missouri Press, 1974). The standard work on the history of ecology and of ecological thinking is Donald Worster, *Nature's Economy: A History of Ecological Ideas* (New York: Cambridge University Press, 1985, 1977).
5. Aldo Leopold, *A Sand County Almanac and Sketches Here and There* (New York: Oxford University Press, 1949); Rachel L. Carson, *Silent Spring* (Boston: Houghton Mifflin, 1962).
6. Alebert Cuyp (1620–1691), "River Landscape with Horseman and Peasants," "Pasture with Cows and Herdsmen," 1641/43, "Horsemen and Herdsmen with Cattle," 1655/60; John Constable (1776–1837), "Wivenhoe Park, 1816.
7. Edward Hicks (1780–1849), "The Cornell Farm" 1848; Thomas Chambers (1808-c1866), "The Connecticut Valley," mid-19th century; George Inness (1825–1894), "The Lackawanna Valley," c1856; Albert Bierstadt (1830–1902), "Lake Lucerne,"1858; Charles C. Hofmann (c1820–1882), "View of Benjamin Reber's Farm," 1872.

8. Thomas R. Dunlap, *Saving America's Wildlife: Ecology and the American Mind, 1850–1990* (Princeton, NJ: Princeton University Press, 1988).
9. Kenneth T. Jackson, *Crabgrass Frontier: The Suburbanization of the United States* (New York: Oxford University Press, 1985). Quoted on page 241.
10. Thomas J. Schlereth, "History Museums and Material Culture," in Warren Leon and Roy Rosenzweig, eds., *History Museums in the United States: A Critical Assessment* (Urbana: University of Illinois Press, 1989), Chapter 12, Dietz is quoted on p. 294. Chapter 1, by Gary Kulik, offers an overview of the development of exhibitions in history museums, which considers the overlap between history and natural history, especially in the nineteenth century. For an older, but useful volume, see: Ian M. G. Quimby, ed., *Material Culture and the Study of American Life* (New York: W.W. Norton and Company, 1978). For a volume that takes the long view on the shaping and reshaping of American forests, see: Michael Williams, *Americans and Their Forests: A Historical Geography* (New York: Cambridge University Press, 1989). For a related and applied examination of assigning value to historic, rural landscapes, see: Linda Flint McClelland, et al, *Guidelines for Evaluating and Documenting Rural Historic Landscapes* (Washington DC: National Park Service Bulletin Series, 1989, revised 1999).
11. Alfred W. Crosby, *Ecological Imperialism: The Biological Expansion of Europe, 900–1900* (New York: Cambridge University Press, 1986).
12. Richard White, *The Organic Machine: The Remaking of the Columbia River* (New York: Hill and Wang, 1995).
13. Charles E. Twining, *Downriver: Orrin H. Ingram and the Empire Lumber Company* (Madison: State Historical Society of Wisconsin, 1975); Susan L. Flader, ed., *The Great Lakes Forest: An Environmental and Social History* (Minneapolis: University of Minnesota Press, 1983). On the Progressive Era Conservation Movement, see Samuel P. Hays, *Conservation and the Gospel of Efficiency: The Progressive Era Conservation Movement, 1890–1920* (New York: Atheneum, 1974).
14. Toronto *Globe and Mail,* July 15, 1995, page D8.

GREEN SCREEN: PROJECTIONS OF AMERICAN ENVIRONMENTAL CULTURE

Char Miller

The setting was sublime. With the majestic Half Dome dominating the horizon, Vernal and Nevada Falls plummeting down into the vast floor of the Yosemite valley, and pine trees jutting up from craggy rockfaces, producer Larry Hott and his crew from Florentine Films had no trouble finding stunning footage for a then-forthcoming documentary on that most riveting moment in the history of this national park—the early-twentieth century fight over a dam that would inundate a portion of the Yosemite known as the Hetch Hetchy valley. But their attention to their work wavered occasionally: as Hott and the others crisscrossed this corner of the Sierran landscape, they kept seeing large crowds "pointing at people climbing on the rocks." Finally, their curiosity piqued, they stopped to see what all the fuss was about, only to discover that they had come upon the filming of a scene for *Star Trek 5: The Final Frontier* (1989). When they arrived, Mr. Spock, Captain Kirk, and Lieutenant Uhura were busily scaling a rock formation that looked unlike any other the Florentine crew had seen while exploring the valley's rugged terrain. There was a reason why this was so—the Star Trek rocks were fake. The Hollywood film crew had constructed this massive set in the national park to make the Yosemite backdrop seem real, Hott observed, "and it made me think that perhaps in the future all we would have was a memory of the way the wilderness actually looked. [Then] we will have to reconstruct it," just as the Trekkies had done.[1]

This anxious speculation about the future of nature, and our place within an increasingly "artificial" environment, is part of a larger cultural debate that, since World War II, has helped define the subject and thrust of documentary films about the American landscape. Also implicit in this debate, as it is in Hott's commentary, is that nonfiction films or documentaries—in contrast to movie-industry blockbusters—are more genuine in their approach, more true to their subject, more persuasive because they are more "real." This distinction depends on an important assumption—that documentarists' representations of nature are more reliable because they are wedded to the historical record; using archival and contemporary imagery, as well as human memory, they apparently more accurately convey the rich texture of a complex past. Their cameras, focused on an authentic space—not on some manufactured prop—do not lie.

Or, more accurately, the scenes they are designed to capture fall within what critic William Stott has called the "genre of actuality"; its essence is "the communication, not of imagined things, but of real things only." Yet how those "real things" are conveyed through images, dialog, and music, and which of their viewers' emotions they tap, and thus what responses they engender, complicate our embrace of the neat dichotomies between fiction- and fact-based filmmaking. This is a point of some contention. British film producer Jerry Kuehl, for one, disputes the notion that there is any blurring between the two forms, that each can instruct equally well: fictionalized versions of events and people in the past deflect us from the "understanding of motives," he argues, and instead lead us "not to the historical figures [themselves], but to the writers who wrote the lines, the actors who spoke them, and the directors who orchestrated their performances." Traditional documentaries, by contrast, revolve around what he calls "truth claims," assertions that are based "on argument and evidence." They make therefore more reliable guides to human intention and motive.[2]

Such claims for reliability, other observers argue, are themselves a kind of fiction. As film critic Philip Rosen puts it, movie industry narratives and low-budget documentaries are linked by the very structure each employs to tell their stories. Both centralize meaning through what he describes as "internal sequenciation"— one scene builds on another to extend a particular theme or argument or narrative; each subsequent scene is legitimized by reference to the preceding ones—a methodology that structures the audience's perceptions. This narrative format indeed makes the *viewer* "a terrain to be organized," a manipulative approach that clouds the capacity to assert "truth claims," regardless of the kind of filmmaking involved. "All films," another critic concludes, "whether they are labeled fiction, documentary, or art . . . are structured articulations of the filmmaker and not authentic truthful objective records."[3]

It is no less true, then, that audiences have been differently organized over time; the images presented within documentaries, and the reactions they have evoked, have assumed certain patterns that identify shifting modes of cultural expression. Changes in culture also have influenced how we experience documentaries shot in another era. Those from the 1930s, for instance, may not be speak to us as powerfully as those crafted out of the materials of the age within which we live. I have been regularly reminded of this whenever I screen films for an undergraduate seminar in environmental history. My students, for example, are considerably more disengaged from and critical of the imagery and argument embedded within Pare Lorentz's *The Plow that Broke the Plains* (1936) than they are of *The Wilderness Idea* (1989), the film Larry Hott was shooting in Yosemite when he encountered the Star Trek crew. Explaining why this is so, why we may be more readily persuaded by one set of rhetorical claims than another depends on a recognition of the intricate interplay between audience, filmmaker, and historical context.

This interplay should be of particular importance to environmental and public historians interested in the production and use of those nonfiction films concerned with environmental issues, for it allows us to explore three related questions: how these films and their subjects have evolved since their origins in the 1920s; what role historians and historiography have played in the crafting of this subject matter; and how as a result we might best understand the evolving relationship between these environmental documentary productions and their widening audience.

Figure 10-1. John Muir (right) is shown here with President Theodore Roosevelt at Glacier Point in Yosemite National Park. Muir, a friend and advisor to Roosevelt, was the founder and first president of the Sierra Club. His role as an early conservationist is documented in the film *The Wilderness Idea: John Muir, Gifford Pinchot, and the First Great Battle for the Wilderness,* by producers Larry Hott and Dianne Garey. *Library of Congress, Prints and Photographs Division [reproduction number, LC-USZ62-110212]*

TAKE ONE

At the heart of the evolution of environmental documentaries is a narrative tension that shaped their early history. Film scholars generally locate the origins of the genre in the contrasting work of American Robert Flaherty and John Grierson of Great Britain. *Nanook of the North* (1922), *Moana* (1926), and *Man of Aran* (1934)—Flaherty's first films—offered close observations of humans living within nature. In these features, he sought to capture the Eskimo, Samoan, and Irish struggle for survival, and recapitulate (and, when necessary, even *recreate*) their often vanishing cultural mores, all with an anthropological eye. He was not an anthropologist, however, and many of that profession would roundly criticize him for what he did not observe about the people and places he filmed. But his partner (and wife), Frances Flaherty, would later insist that their work was anthropologically oriented in the sense that it was focused on "discovery and revelation," an observational emphasis that Grierson picked up on in his 1926 review of Flaherty's *Moana*: "being a visual account of events in daily life of a Polynesian youth and his family, [it] has documentary value." Film historians believe this to be the first time the word "documentary" had been used in relation to film, and its use nicely linked the two figures who are acknowledged as the first to define the character of this form of filmmaking.[4]

But Grierson would also be the first to critique his friend Flaherty's work, precisely because of its reflective emphasis. "His metaphor for the contrast between Flaherty's way and his own was that Flaherty used film as a mirror while he was more interested in using it as a hammer," observes critic Jack Ellis; for Grierson, film was a tool that if properly wielded could reconstruct contemporary perceptions and behaviors. To do so, he focused on collective endeavors, in contrast to Flaherty's tales of the strivings of lone individuals or single families. Take his first film, *Drifters* (1929), a study of the British herring fleet. It recreates a day in the life of these fishermen, from their leaving port, through their storm-tossed trawling along the North Sea banks, to the final auction of the catch. The significance of *Drifter*, in Ellis words, is its unique attempt to locate labor "within the context of economic actualities" and its portrayal of the working class "with dignity rather than as comic relief." His goal was not to make these men exotic—and therefore distinct from the viewer—but to bind together subject and audience, a goal of some political importance in a society as class-conscious and—riven as the early twentieth century Britain.[5]

Grierson used film to expose contemporary social structures and enlighten about their consequences, and believed that filmmakers must interpret and shape the world around them, just as they must edit the film itself to achieve the desired effect. This vision and methodology clashed with Flaherty's renunciation of the cutting room and his editorial assumption that the pre-industrial past and peoples had a greater intrinsic value than the then-modernizing societies in which he lived. As thoroughly as Grierson embraced the "chaotic present," as fully Flaherty spurned its materialistic temper, yet their friendship endured. As Grierson later noted: "In the profoundest kind of way we live and prosper, each of us, by denouncing the other."[6]

The differences in the two men's aesthetic choices and political orientation have been woven throughout the subsequent development of documentary filmmaking. Grierson, for instance, had a profound impact on the "social" documentaries that flourished during the Great Depression. Among those who pursued this genre was American Pare Lorentz. Although he disliked Grierson's pedantic approach to film, he nonetheless produced *The Plow that Broke the Plains* (1936) and *The River* (1937) under the aegis of the Resettlement Administration (later folded into the Farm Security Administration). This governmental sanction brought with it social and political ends: the films were to inform and persuade their audiences that the nation, through an engaged citizenry and via federal planning and regulation, could resolve some of the environmental problems that had devastated the American landscape during the 1930s; among the most pressing were the Dust Bowl and Mississippi River Valley flooding. Integrating clips from contemporary newsreels and feature-length films, with work from some of the finest cinematographers of the day, and accentuating the films' narrative structure with scores from Virgil Thompson that were a deft blend of folk tunes and modern rhythms, Lorentz probed the historical antecedents of the then-current dilemmas, decried contemporary inaction, and proposed governmental and grassroots remedies.

In *The Plow,* the rapacious energies let loose via westward migration and a capitalist economy had stripped the land of its topsoil and its regenerative capacity; over time, the farming communities that had been dependent on the land became the victims of their inefficiencies and greed. Only the intervention of a benevolent, outside force—Franklin D. Roosevelt's New Deal—would turn this tragedy around; salvation would come with the construction of greenbelt communities, the introduction of new methods of soil conservation, and the practice of a more conservative form of agriculture.

The River is similarly framed—the unchecked surge of floodwaters that routinely churned up the Mississippi's vast watershed, sweeping away land and life, was a direct consequence of human error, compounded over many decades. The destructive clear-cutting of the nation's forested estate, abusive cotton farming, and industrial exploitation of the landscape unleashed the deadly torrents that undercut the ability of Americans to live along the rivulets and creeks, brooks, rills, and streams that flowed into the Father of Waters. Having destroyed the land, it was no wonder that the people themselves were impoverished. The cure? Through the ministrations of the Tennessee Valley Authority, and the good work of the Farm Security Administration, floods would be brought under control, the hilly, if eroded, terrain would be restored, and the human inhabitants would be redeemed.

The link between Lorentz's portrayal of an activist and compassionate government and the Roosevelt political agenda was unmistakable, and the subject of considerable contemporary controversy. Inside the Resettlement Administration, staff was split between those who praised the intense dynamics and political overlay of *The Plow* especially, and others—including a vocal delegation of agency workers in Texas—who objected strongly to its exaggerated depiction of the environmental disaster then engulfing the southern plains. They concluded, in a memo that listed a large number of its errors of fact and interpretation, that agency head Rexford Tugwell should not show the film in The Lone Star State, for it "would arouse . . . rather bitter criticism of the Resettlement Agency."[7]

That these films were, in scholar Richard MacCann's words, "propaganda for the New Deal, for specific government agencies, for a certain view of history, and a certain way of looking at public affairs" is not, in retrospect, the only set of issues they raise. They also were embedded with pre-ecological cultural values about the human relationship to nature: our dominion could be established and sanctioned through rational planning and scientific management. The easy assumption that the federal government stood as ultimate protector of the physical and human environment, and the implication that this was an outgrowth of the second Roosevelt's idealism, ignored the political capital the earlier Roosevelt— Theodore—had expended to advance similar ends. Moreover, by framing the issue in this manner, the films masked just how contentious the assertion of federal sovereignty was in the 1930s, a point that is particularly significant because the strong public response to *The Plow* and *The River*.[8]

That response was so potent because Lorentz's work perfectly embodied what Stott calls the documentary "doctrine." Effective because it treated "unimagined experience of individuals belonging to a group generally of low economic and social standing in the society (lower than the audience for whom the report is made)," these films then revealed this "experience in such way as to try to render it vivid, 'human,' and-most often-poignant to the audience." Through moral suasion and emotion appeal, the films bound viewer and viewed. To build on this powerful, affective connection, the Department of Agriculture established the United States Film Service to expand the range of its documentary investigation, and tapped Lorentz as its first director. Congress had other ideas: it initiated hearings into "the propriety and politics of the project," slashed the service's budget, leading to the outright dismantling of the new agency. Henceforth, government-sponsored nonfiction filmmaking would be more tightly controlled, ideologically and financially.[9]

One consequence of the assertion of this control was that succeeding generations of nature filmmakers, seeking to avoid overt political pressures, would pursue private funding sources. After World War II a crucial source of that capital were the new television production companies and the fledgling TV networks themselves. Their money, when combined with the vast audiences that this new medium would create, and the resultant innovative filmmaking technology that has emerged over the past fifty years, led to an explosion of films and videos designed to throw wide-open our window onto nature. These alterations enabled the audience to "see" nature in greater detail and thus in unique, more intimate ways. These new-found insights altered Americans perceived relationship with what they think of as the natural world—a wild place separate and apart from human civilization. This veritable outpouring of images of wildness have done "a lot of good," writes journalist-critic Bill McKibben, by which he means political good. Whether in still or moving form, whether originating in a TV-sitcom such as "Flipper" or the cinematography of Jacques Cousteau, these images have "helped change how we see the wild." Indeed, he concludes that it is "no great exaggeration to say that dolphin-safe tuna flows directly from the barrel of a Canon, that without Kodak there'd be no Endangered Species Act."[10]

Actually, McKibben *is* exaggerating, but the effect of photography on our understanding of the postwar world nonetheless has been pronounced. That said, the modern story that those Kodak-shooting Canons have captured is really an old tale—it draws heavily on Robert Flaherty's elegiac vision and evocative landscapes and on a Griersonian critique of the human assault on nature.

It was Flaherty, after all, who gave rise to a form of cinematic narration that included travelogues such as Merian Cooper's and Ernest Schoedsack's *Grass* (1925), a study of the animal and human migratory patterns of central Iran. Building on this tradition were Martin and Osa Johnson, who spun out a large number of what critic Alexander Wilson has tagged as "photosafari" films, among them *Simba, the "King of Beasts* (1928), *Wonders of the Congo* (1931), *Baboonia* (1935), the very titles of which give a sense of their "exotic" content, reason enough for their great appeal. As Wilson observes, the Johnsons, who had financial backing from George Eastman and the sponsorship from the American Museum of Natural History, were convinced that they were "filming 'the world as it once was,'" "but in retrospect their work seems an "embarrassing amalgam of bad anthropology, natural history, and adventure—a formula that meant 'box office' right up to *Raiders of the Lost Ark*.[11]

The heirs to this tradition have been the televised "nature" shows that emerged in the early 1950s and since have become a staple of contemporary broadcasting, whether on PBS or its many competitors on cable. These programs, often underwritten by the National Geographic Society and its ilk, and entitled so as to titillate—*Wild Kingdom, New Wilderness, Wild, Wild World of Animals*—have offered safe excursions to far-distant worlds filled with strange floral and fauna. These exotic landscapes have been translated to western eyes and ears by men *of* science (they were not necessarily scientists) who, like Jacques Cousteau or Marlin Perkins, Lorne Greene or Richard Attenborough, have helped us comprehend the incomprehensible.

But it is how we are instructed to comprehend these outlandish places or peculiar behaviors we witness from afar that is so crucial to the evolution of environmental documentaries. Consciously or otherwise, many of these films have depended heavily upon a perception of a humanity that is directly at odds with nature, is in sharp conflict with its design. The relevant filmmakers may not explicitly cite Aldo Leopold, John Muir, or Henry David Thoreau, but they have absorbed these writers' conceptions of a contested relationship, and in doing so have used these environmentalists' ideas to organize and frame their film narratives. So as Cousteau dove into tropical waters to reveal the abundance of marine life in sun-kissed seas that otherwise we would never have seen, as intrepid *National Geographic* photographers have snapped shots of primitive people or primeval landscapes much removed from our living rooms, always there was the presumption that these places and societies—at once like us, and not—were not long for this world. The moment civilization descended on these pristine environments and naive human communities, they would be forever lost, a point the very presence of the looming film crews foreshadowed; the whir of the video camcorder announced the end was at hand.

Such worries, Alexander Wilson argues, were perhaps first inserted in the nature films that Walt Disney produced, and in his studio's educational series, *Film-*

ing Nature's Mysteries (1956). It was the Bard of Anaheim who pressed nature's case with "new urgency," who believed it was necessary to "get wildlife on film before civilization could wipe them out."[12]

His concern was perfectly attuned to a key alteration in mid-century American culture. Beginning with the depression, there was a massive surge of population out of rural, agrarian cultures and into urban, industrialized economies. Poor whites and African Americans moved from Appalachian valleys and river deltas north to Detroit and Chicago; sharecroppers victimized in the Dust Bowl, who once had been the subjects of Pare Lorenz's film studies of the Plains states, fled to the Pacific coast. This pattern of displacement and migration widened during the economic boom of the war years, so much so that that is when Texas, long the locus of the legendary, frontier-roaming American cowboy, officially became an urban state.

What happened, however, when ranch hands became factory workers or aircraft assemblers, when they dug not fence post holes but drilled oil wells? The impact of these significant alterations in daily life were particularly manifest in the changes in the relationship between humans and the animals with whom they once had shared a more rural environment. Wilson and other scholars contend that urbanization over the past two centuries, which certainly intensified in the United States following World War II, led to the excision of animals "from the everyday lives of most Westerners, an excision recorded in the subsequent proliferation of zoos and animal toys and animal movies." We have created these institutions and material representations to maintain a record of "lost species," and, simultaneously, to reintroduce "the idea of nature" into our lives. Reflected in this effort is a poignant human urge: wildlife films, Wilson observes, "reveal a deep desire simply to be in the world, a world "beyond our skins if not beyond our culture." This quest becomes all the more complicated as we become an even more intensely urbanized people, leading, ironically, to a further proliferation of this genre of film.[13]

TAKE TWO

The cultural significance of environmental documentaries is compounded by a crucial shift in how late-twentieth-century Americans obtain information about the world around them. As film historian Alan Rosenthal notes about documentaries in general: they have "become a major—possibly the most important—means for learning about the past. In an age when reading is in decline, the documentary— much more than the theater, newspapers, or feature films—may well be the only serious access people have to history once they have left school." This trend has accelerated with the "growth of cable and satellite-based television since the mid-1980s," historian Robert Brent Toplin has confirmed. These new forms of telecommunication have "created a multichannel universe that permitted greater attention to audience niches. A proliferation of channels enabled TV producers to direct attention to much smaller clusters of audience interests than NBC, ABC, and CBS could handle in the days of their shared monopoly over commercial entertainment." Environmental filmmakers are among those documentarists who have taken good advantage of these developments, and whose work regularly has appeared on The History Channel, A & E, and, on PBS, *The American Experience*. That being so, it becomes vitally important to think through how these "visual" narrations are constructed for these new audiences, as well as who and what lies behind their construction. Doing so leads to a much-debated question of who is best qualified to be a film's author, a query that drives the heated exchange between historian Donald Watt, and producer Jerry Kuehl.[14]

The distinctions they draw about who is the most appropriate author revolves around who controls a film's central narrative thrust. For Watt, it is "self evident that the making of a nonfiction film or television program on a historical theme is as much an exercise in historiography as is the composition of a learned monograph . . . . " But it is no less obvious, he remarks, that a "historical statement made audiovisually is different from one made in writing. The tempo is different, there can be no recall, no flipping of the page, no elaboration of parallel themes by footnotes or parentheses." These profound distinctions are then magnified if the filmmakers and historians are insensitive to one another's professional foci. At its worst, their relationship can devolve into a bitter dispute over film content and audience expectations, the two being parts of a whole; as Watt acerbically notes: "the biggest problem" has to do with the "state of mind of those who direct the media, who cannot believe that waiting in front of their sets is an educated, interested, mass audience . . . " Unbelieving producers, in short, dumb down historical content to appeal to the lowest common denominator, a tactic that undercuts historians' contributions. The best that can be hoped for is to develop a relationship that is more of a partnership, one that shades into "symbiosis, where each understands, even if he cannot practice, the craft of the other," making "audiovisual historiography" a kind of "bimedial art, like ballet and opera."[15]

Such a harmonic convergence is rare. Only at England's chronically underfunded Open University has it been "most closely approximated," Watt observes; there, budgets allowing, film producers collaborate with historians, who write the script and select "the material they wish to see incorporated into the film." The pronoun—"they"—is revealing of a shift in the control of production. Historians, in Watt's scenario, are the creative forces that drive a documentary's development from idea to film; their assumptions dominate the text's construction and the context in which the final product should be viewed (and interpreted).[16]

It is precisely this claim of preeminence that Kuehl believes has so troubled relations between "academic historians and producers of television documentaries," and made their collaboration so "uneasy." While he acknowledges that misapprehension of one another's roles is usually what undercut successful joint ventures, he is not ready to relinquish to historians the control that Watt believes is their due. He resists because he does not believe scholars understand the special requirements of television filmmaking. Consider that most "integral part of every documentary," the commentary: "who should write it, how should it relate to the film,

to whom should it be addressed, and above all, what should it contain?" The answer to these critical queries is shaped not by a historian's professional compe-
tence but by the amount of time usually allotted to this form of documentary—
most have but fifty minutes to tell their tale. That being the case, he estimates that
"a commentary of between one thousand and fifteen hundred words is quite long
enough—any more, and the film . . . will appear to viewers as dense, over stuffed.
They will be repelled, not informed," an observation Kuehl hopes is "quite sobering to an academician." Film writers only have enough time to give the equivalent
of a "*fifteen-minute* lecture," and that lecture must conform to this reality: "because
of their brevity, they cannot be in any real sense exhaustive or comprehensive."
More evocative than coherent, the commentary is neither an "independent literary
form" nor a means by which to narrate "complicated narrative histories"; it is,
moreover, "quite hopeless at portraying abstract ideas." For this work, historians
need not apply.[17]

What professionals of the past should do instead, he concluded, is to stick with
the academic terrain they knew best: rather than "trying to replace mass television
history of our day with their own mandarin versions, they should concentrate on
doing their jobs as historians as well as they can, so that the history they write will
be as good as it can be, so that popular accounts which we can provide will be as
true as they can be." Note Kuehl's pronoun of choice—"we"—which signals, as
if the rest of his conclusion did not, that documentaries are, and should remain, the
domain of filmmakers who better understand how to engage mass audiences.[18]

Another who identifies this point as the source of creative conflict is Richard
White, an environmental historian who has "worked as an adviser or been a talking head for a half-dozen or more documentary film projects." He believes there
"are always moments when the historian confronts the limits of television, filmmakers, and the television audience." Their limitations are many: the documen-
tarist demand for "iconic" stories that streamline the films' narratives but which
forsake historical complexity; producers' fondness for a "binary cast of charac-
ters" whose conflict moves the storyline along and thereby maintains audience attention; and the "cavalier" use of evocative photographs, however out of context
their use might be. Filmmakers "want pictures that will carry the idea," he asserts,
and given "the choice between a somewhat deceptive photograph and a talking
head, the photograph wins almost every time."[19]

My relatively limited experience working on several environmental documentaries confirms many of White's insights. That said, the collaboration between
filmmakers and historians is not always antagonistic. On three projects for Florentine Films—*The Wilderness Idea: John Muir, Gifford Pinchot and the First
Great Battle for Wilderness* (1989), *Wild by Law* (1991), and *Divided Highways*
(1997)—-I joined a host of scholars to offer insights into the struggle over Hetch
Hetchy, the intellectual and political antecedents to the Wilderness Act of 1964,
and the profound impact of the interstate highway system on the human and physical landscape of the United States. We were extensively interviewed off-camera
on the relevant topics, and our commentary served as one basis for a lengthy

"script" whose various iterations we then read and critiqued. This was a fascinating perspective from which to observe the narrative unfold, watch the voice-over commentary be refined, and track shifts in the placement of some of the set images. Much of these initial efforts would be modified, more or less extensively, once the interviews took place before the cameras, of course. But it was evident that the questions the producers asked us during the taping also had been defined in good part by historical research and subsequent conversations with the filmmakers. The resultant films were a fruitful outcome of this intense interaction between filmmakers and historians, suggesting that is possible to construct environmental documentaries that engage and educate television audiences, and remain faithful to both crafts.

TAKE THREE

Yet it was also clear that in these instances the control of the final product lay very much in the hands of the films' producers. Proof of this lies in White's quip about the ability of a photograph to trump a talking head, and in my ready resort, after viewing the films in which I (briefly) appeared, to this Hollywoodian wail: they left my best lines on the cutting room floor! That there is a cutting room is a critical reminder of how essentially different modern documentaries are from those Robert Flaherty once produced; he eschewed editing (though was not above doctoring scripts and coaching his subjects). That modern documentaries are thoroughly, self-consciously edited reminds as well of the care their viewers must take when watching them, especially those as emotionally charged and politically driven as environmental documentaries can be. We have to learn to read films with all the subtlety we apply to literary analysis.

In practical terms this requires historians—public and otherwise—to assess the archival resources that were consulted, what experts were interviewed, which eyewitnesses spoke on screen, and how those interviews were framed. Knowing this helps identify the film's larger argument and organizing structure; for the same reason it is important to clarify who sponsored and paid for the film.

Gaining clarity on a documentary's point-of-view is just as crucial. It "must tell a story that will hold the viewer's interest," James G. Lewis has observed, and "it must do so in a clear, concise manner so that the subject matter is accessible to as many people as possible." Because accessibility determines content, it is all the more important that the intended audience recognize the formulaic quality of the documentaries it watches on PBS or cable; only by doing so can it develop a more detached examination of a film's interpretative agenda.[20]

One of the hardest elements to detach from is the omniscient narrator—-he or she, after all, is the guide who unifies the audience's reading of a film. It is for this reason that the use of such a voice has become so controversial. Many critics decry the insertion of a consistent, authoritative narrator, believing that this "Voice of God" serves as a divine intermediary between subject and audience; this "didactic reductionism" dominates the viewers' aural experience. Surely this situation is compounded when a celebrity stands in for a historical character. In *Rachel Carson's Silent Spring* (1993), Meryl Streep speaks for the embattled author, a choice that confounds—-are we persuaded of Carson's heroics because of her incisive mind and enduring legacy, or because her accomplishments (and identity) are now intertwined on film with the vocal persona of one of the late-twentieth century's greatest actresses?[21]

A different form of spin revolves around the selection of background music to emphasize mood, sensibility, and moral standing. In *Battle for Wilderness,* which pits the dam's chief opponent, John Muir, against one of its proponents, Gifford Pinchot, the musical score becomes a box score. For Muir the key is minor, a tragic tone that befits his valiant, if failed, attempt to thwart the drowning of his beloved valley; the triumphant Pinchot, in stark contrast, is enveloped in a giddy waltz-like air, an insubstantial a piece of music as his victory apparently was unconscionable.

Establishing such critical distance, and the knowledge on which its development depends, should not remain cloistered on the campus. Environmental and public historians have an obligation to carry their insights into the civic arena, because it is there that national conversations about the meaning of contested pasts are debated. A recent, nonenvironmental, yet prototypical example of public historians "teaching" films in public venues to insure a more critical understanding of documentaries and the history they are designed to convey is the project entitled *From Rosie to Roosevelt.* Across the country scholars screened films in community libraries about the American experience during World War II, and then led discussions exploring the relationship between visual and written evidence. On a smaller scale, but with similar intent, those involved in the making of *The Wilderness Idea*—including producer Larry Hott and many of the consulting historians—staged public showings of the film. I participated in four such evenings, in Massachusetts, Oregon, Washington, and Texas, and each time when the house lights came back on, discussion erupted. In the Pacific Northwest, then at the height of the spotted owl controversy, the film spoke vividly to a citizenry at loggerheads over clearcutting of public forested lands. But there, and in other regions not buffeted by such contentious environmental issues, debate also swirled around how that film shaped its arguments; even those who applauded the Muirite vision that informed *The Wilderness Idea* could be critical of its intellectual bias.[22]

These experiences—and others subsequent to them—taught me a valuable lesson: being aware of a film's many manipulative devices only increases its heuristic value. That seems paradoxical, but only if we assume that "truth" is the single best teacher. Blatant falsehoods, historical inaccuracies, overly dramatized reenactments, subtle intercuts: all are vehicles by which to explain authorial intent. How producers argue their points, after all, tells us a great deal about their take on the relationship between humanity and the landscape in which we are enmeshed, knowledge that allows for a more sustained analysis of the central environmental dilemmas that lie before us.

NOTES

1. Larry Hott to Char Miller, June 14, 1998. Hott was co-producer of *The Wilderness Idea,* which originally aired on PBS in 1989.
2. William Stott, *Documentary Expression and Thirties America,* (New York: Oxford University Press, 1973), 5–17; Jerry Kuehl, "Truth Claims," in Alan Rosenthal, *New Challenges for Documentary,* (Berkeley: University of California Press, 1988), 103–09; this tension is repeatedly discussed in "Reel History," a special issue of *AHA Perspectives,* April 1999. See Robert Brent Toplin, "Film and History: State of the Union," 1, 8–9; Richard White, "History, the Rugrats, and World Championship Wrestling," 12–13; and Simon Schama, "Shooting Britannia," 21–22, 24.
3. Philip Rosen, "Document and Documentary: On the Persistence of Historical Concepts," in Michael Renov, ed., *Theorizing Documentary,* (New York: Routledge, 1993), 75–77; Jay Rubin quoted in Richard M. Barsam, *Nonfiction Film: A Critical History,* (Bloomington: Indiana University Press, 1992), p. 376.
4. Jack C. Ellis, *The Documentary Idea: A Critical History of English-Language Documentary Film and Video,* (Englewood Cliffs, NJ: Prentice Hall, 1989), 15–28; Stott, *Documentary Expression*, p. 9.
5. Ellis, *The Documentary Idea,* 64–5; for additional analysis of the differences in Flaherty's and Greierson's films, see Barsam, 46–55, 89–94; Stott, *Documentary Expression,* 9–12.
6. Grierson quoted in Ellis, *The Documentary Idea,* p. 73.
7. Richard Dyer MacCann, *The People's Films: A Political History of U.S. Government Motion Pictures,* (New York: Hastings House Publishers, 1973), 79–85.
8. Ibid, 79–80; in response to the political charges leveled against *The Plow,* the last minutes were removed from many of the copies of the controversial film shown in theaters.
9. Stott, *Documentary Expression,* p. 62; MacCann, *The People's Films,* 79–85; Barsam, *Nonfiction Film,* 151–57.
10. Bill McKibben, "Curbing Nature's Paparazzi," reprinted in *Harper's Magazine,* November 1997, 19–21, 24.
11. Ellis, *The Documentary Idea,* 26–27; Barsam, *Nonfiction Film,* p. 43; Alexander Wilson, *The Culture of Nature: North American Landscape from Disney to the Exxon Valdez,* (Cambridge, MA: Blackwell, 1992), 124–25.
12. Wilson, *The Culture of Nature,* p. 125.
13. Ibid., 126–8; David Guss, *The Language of the Birds: Tales, Texts and Poems of Interspecies Communication,* (Berkeley, CA: North Point Press, 1985).
14. Rosenthal, ed., *New Challenges for Documentary,* p. 426.
15. Donald Watt, "History on the Public Screen: I," in Rosenthal, *New Challenges for Documentary,* 436, 442.

16. Ibid; an American counterpart of the Open University is the Center for History in the Media, at George Washington University; for a discussion of some of its work, and the comparable tensions that have emerged, see James G. Lewis, "History, Lies, and Videotape: Historical Documentaries in the Classroom," *OAH Council of Chairs Newsletter*. (April and June 1997): 1–5; Toplin, "Film and History," p. 9 makes mention of similar ventures.

17. Jerry Kuehl, "History on the Public Screen: II," in Rosenthal, *New Challenges for Documentary*, 444–446; Richard White, after extensive work on the documentary *The West*, concluded that the tension between filmmakers and historians had much to do with the differences in the mediums in which they presented their work: "Documentaries are primarily a visual medium, and, secondarily, an oral medium. Academic history is primarily a print medium." This striking difference led White to propose to Geoff Ward, lead writer of *The West*, that the kind of writing that worked best in documentaries was "topic sentences." No, Ward countered, "there are no topic sentences. The pictures are the topic sentences." White, "History," *AHA Perspectives*, p. 12.

18. Kuehl, "History on the Public Screen: II," p. 453.

19. White, "History, the Rugrats and World Championship Wrestling," 11–12.

20. Lewis, "History, Lies, and Videotape," *OAH Council of Chairs Newsletter*, p. 2.

21. Authoritative omniscience may backfire, of course, leading viewers to be suspicious of that which it "asserts most fervently." The documentary form itself may have changed in reaction to challenges to its narrative voice. As one critic has noted, the "emergence of so many recent documentaries built around strings of interviews" may be a "strategic response to the recognition that neither can events speak for themselves nor can a single voice speak with ultimate authority. For a discussion of these and related issues, see Bill Nichols, "The Voice of Documentary," in Rosenthal, *New Challenges for Documentary*, 54–55; they are also covered in James Roy MacBean, "Two Laws from Australia, One White, One Black," in Rosenthal, *New Challenges for Documentary*, 210–226.

22. Toplin, "Film and History," p. 8.

HISTORY TRIP: HISTORICAL SOCIETIES AND A SENSE OF PLACE

Robert R. Archibald

Along the slow rise of the Missouri River on the run from St. Louis to Kansas City, Amtrak's "Missouri Mule" hits seventy-nine miles per hour. Small towns once dependent upon railroads whiz past, no longer train stops and now absolutely dependent upon cars and highways. The Missouri River runs alongside to the north. Once the river bore the country's trade but trade moved to the rails and then the river's work was further diminished by trucks and cars, and now it floats only a trickle of its former flood of commerce. Older railroad grades are still visible, arcing bulwarks between our tracks and the river, abandoned for higher ground in a scramble to get above unpredictable spring floodwaters, despite the best efforts of engineers to channel the Missouri. It's a history trip. Two vintage passenger cars, a dome car and an observation car, are coupled to the end. The refurbished passenger cars are luxurious. Wood paneling, brass hardware, upholstered chairs, end tables with flowers in vases, an attentive waiter with chocolate chip cookies and apple juice compensate for the erratic swaying of old suspension systems.

What passes beyond the old-fashioned wood-framed window is evidence of change—proofs through time of changes mostly caused by human endeavor and in the last one hundred and fifty years changes at an escalating rate. While shifts and turns and permutations are intrinsic to our entire universe, the acceleration in the speed of change precipitates disconnection, discontinuity, isolation, and a preoccupation with the present that threatens the future of human communities and perhaps even democracy itself. My work with historical change in communities has convinced me that although change is inevitable, change that is too rapid is destructive of human relationship and community life. My work in an expanding historical society has helped me determine that one role of a public historian is to advocate a more reasonable rate of change, a pace that will allow time for consideration of consequences and permit new forms and relationships to evolve in place of those mangled by change. How else will we fulfill our obligations to each other and to our places on this earth, when the world so quickly becomes "virtual," impersonal, homogenized?

I don't know my fellow passengers very well. Cheryl, a middle-aged woman, sits near me. Now living in suburban St. Louis, she was raised, one of sixteen children, on a southern Illinois farm. Her parents still live there. She talks about them back then.

168

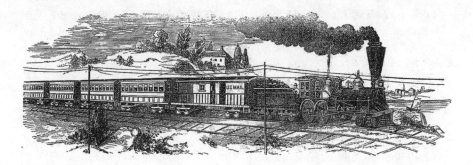

Figure 11-1. Shifts and turns and permutations, but a place that allows for community and human relationships. *Courtesy Missouri Historical Society, St. Louis.*

"When Mom was pregnant, she would take solitary walks in the woods, and Dad worried." "Go find your mother," he would say. "No," Cheryl told him, "she is doing what she needs to do."

"Mom had two miscarriages," Cheryl continues. "She took the three-month-old fetuses, one and then later another, and buried them, and a part of herself, in the ground. Later Dad decided to plow and plant this part of the land. Mom reminded him, and Dad let the plot alone. Dad is a good farmer," she says. "He judges soil fertility by eye and feel, his corn is always the tallest, and he and Mom still go for walks in the woods. And now near the end of his life he will not give up farming." Cheryl muses now, wondering why, with decent health and a good income, her parents do not travel like other people for whom life's final horizons loom close.

While few of us can claim a linkage to place as intimate and indivisible as Cheryl's mom's, all of us and all of our histories are attached to place. This need for the physical to remember and to confirm memories is very basic in all of us. It is the underlying premise of historic preservation and of public history. If too many of these places are destroyed too quickly, our memories and hence our identities are sundered with the removal of those physical symbols, those confirming referents.

My neighbor John is on the train. We sit at the small table and watch Missouri landscape roll past. John lives in an old house built about the same time as my own. We are discussing roof maintenance, bathroom remodeling, and wood stripping—comparing notes on the tribulations and joys of century-old houses. "You know, I feel like a custodian. I don't feel that Grace and I really own the house." I nod, knowing exactly what he feels. "The house," he says, "has been there for a long time, and I expect that it will be there long after Grace and I are gone. We have even discussed moving to a condominium in one of the old gracious apartment buildings in the neighborhood, but Grace says she cannot live without the porch. No apartments we have seen have anything like our porch. We sit there on a warm summer evening, and with the ceiling fan whirling away it is really comfortable."

I don't mention it in our conversation, but I am thinking about the trek I made to Bellefontaine Cemetery last weekend looking for the graves of Thomas and Hildegard McKittrick, the people who built my house in 1897. Bellefontaine is a nineteenth-century cemetery park, a place of peace and beauty where the living and the dead can interact. There are no flat headstones for the convenience of lawn-mowers in this place: here architects designed mausoleums of red granite, obelisks of stone, elaborate tombstones with carved angels and elegant epitaphs in curving tree-shaded lanes—a city of the dead. I looked for Mr. McKittrick with the help of the sexton. "Before or after 1900?" he asked and then pulled out the three-by-five card with the block and lot number.

Next to Thomas is an infant son. (His wife Hildegard died later and was not buried in St. Louis.) I surmise he died in one of the second floor bedrooms in my house, perhaps the little one next to what must have been Hildegard McKittrick's bedroom. McKittrick's wake was held at his sister's, in the house two doors west of mine.

The Pettus lot is just a cemetery block east. Eugene and Marguerite Pettus lived in our house for fifty-two years after the McKittricks. I remember the label in the third floor cedar closet: "Mr. Pettus's suits." I think of the drawer in the attic still labeled, "Thomas McKittrick's junk drawer." I write this chapter in my office on the second floor of the house in the room I am certain was first Thomas McKittrick's and then Eugene Pettus's bedroom. Their floor-to-ceiling clothes closets are three feet to my left.

Nostalgia is now a suspect word, a sentimental marker of time passages, a sadness at aging, and an idealization and romanticizing of the past. Yet longing for the way things used to be is an attribute of humans; and nostalgia can provide connection to the past, implicitly a connection to time beyond our own and an admonition that we are trustees of our places, not owners in any real way, a reminder that we are not the first to have come this way nor the last. I do not want to live in Thomas McKittrick's time for uncounted reasons, but I do not dismiss all of the values of the late nineteenth century. If nothing worthwhile could be discovered in the past, it would not be worth remembering; it would be only a supercilious confirmation of our own superiority and unerring progress. While we must avoid infatuation with the idea of a paradise lost in the past, nostalgia that is not self-indulgent is an antidote to the fallacy that what is new is always an improvement. Change is not necessarily progress, and history is not just an examination of the way we have come. History is a form of self-analysis upon which we can base judgments about what has worked and what has failed and what has simply just been change. History is the basis for action, and public history organizations facilitate public discussion of the burdens and legacies of the past as a prelude to decision making.

As the train winds around another curve, I talk with Pattie. She is thirty-six, the mother of three young girls. She is also the mayor of one of St. Louis's still affluent nineteenth-century rail line suburbs. Her tenure has been rewarding but not easy; she survived a very unpleasant recall election. We talk about democracy in

late-twentieth-century America. Gradually our conversation turns to the importance of place. We discuss St. Louis's grand nineteenth-century City Hall with its
imposing architecture, magnificent rotunda, and its placement in relationship to
the civic opera house, the classical central library, and the Soldiers' Memorial
building. We contrast this with newer suburbs and their strip-mall city halls. Pattie suggests that the difference has something to do with a diminishment of civic
life: less focus on the importance of "us" as a community and more on the "me"
individualism and self-gratification. I have spoken casually with this woman on
several occasions, but never until now seriously enough to sense the passion, dedication, and commitment to community building that clearly animates her.

Our discussion turns to neighborhood planning. We compare and contrast the
merits and the defects of suburban cul-de-sacs and streets on grid patterns, and the
way the structuring of space influences human relationships, and the extent to
which modern street layouts often reflect the same sense of planning as sewer systems or natural gas distribution networks. We agree that these street systems adapt
the same design principles to the collecting and distribution of automobiles from
garage door and driveway to street to arterial to highway. Pattie and I both lean
over the table toward each other as the intensity of our conversation rises. "Perhaps," she says, "poor design and planning have something to do with decreasing
levels of civic involvement. Only forty-nine percent of Americans who are eligible to vote even register." I think about this. The day before I gave a talk to a Ro-
tary Club whose ranks dwindled by half since I last spoke to them just two years
ago. We discuss the characteristics of spaces that facilitate informal relationships
between people, the bonds of civil society. I ask Pattie whether she thinks that
technology is inherently isolating. "My daughters think that we are crazy because
we refuse to air condition our house," she replies. "But it's fine for them to know
that when it is hot, people sweat. It creates a palpable sense of the passage of sea-
sons, and people survived here long before air conditioning was invented. I remember when people first bought air conditioners," she continues. "You could immediately tell who had them. At first only a few people were inside with their doors
closed in the evenings and on weekends instead of sitting on porches and steps,
walking along the street, informally gathering in the public outside space where it
was coolest. After a few years," Pattie muses, " nobody was outside anymore." I
know that in the midst of a sweltering St. Louis summer I will not trash my air con-
ditioner. However, with hindsight I wonder whether we would be so eager to adopt
new inventions and new gadgets from automobiles to air conditioning and television if we completely understood the consequences. Perhaps if we were more critical of new technology and made provision to ameliorate the worst consequences
at the outset, we could ensure that we gain more than we lose. If we fail in this, we
and our successors will continue to be victims of our own scientific and technological prowess.

Pattie and I also discuss books: Dan Kemmis's wonderful *The Good City and
the Good Life: Renewing the Sense of Community;* Ray Oldenburg's insightful *The
Great Good Place: Cafes, Coffee Shops, Community Centers, Beauty Parlors,*

General Stores, Bars, Hangouts and How They Get You Through the Day; and James Howard Kunstler's *The Geography of Nowhere: The Rise and Decline of America's Man-Made Landscape.* Although very different in perspective, the three authors agree that quality of space has an important impact on civic life, informal associations between people, and human happiness. Oldenburg makes the connection between place and relationships especially vivid:

> In using *nearby* facilities, in visiting them afoot and regularly, the residents of an area effectively create a casual social environment and reap its benefits. The pedestrian mode of transportation invites human contact that automobile transportation precludes. People get to know their merchants and their neighbors; from the many, the compatible few are able to discover one another. Neighborhoods, like small towns have never been "big happy families." Rather, the key to their amenities is that they facilitate the discovery and easy association of people destined to become special to one another . . . From among the many, a contingent of casual friends emerges. For some there will be the great gift—a deep and abiding friendship in the form of one who also lives close by and is *available*. For all, there is a control valve. One can have as much engagement and involvement with the neighborhood as one wishes. Those who prefer none may have it just that way.[1]

Much of the work of the Missouri Historical Society examines the interrelationship of people, place, and technology. Our Urban Forum series is a public program that investigates the idea of neighborhood, the influences of architecture upon human relationships, the environmental impacts of varied living arrangements, the effects of transportation choices, and the social and environmental consequences of land use decisions. Our "Exploring the Hood" program involves students in investigation and evaluation of the causes and consequences of neighborhood change, changes driven by values, made possible by wealth and technology and profoundly effecting both the environment and potential relationships. Whether we look at the sidewalk, streetcars, or formal civic spaces, we see that our community like most others has lost much of the space that once facilitated familiarity between strangers and stimulated a sense of civic spirit and those sets of voluntarily assumed reciprocal obligations that are the bedrock of democracy. Public discussion of these issues is the business of public history. No other discipline or organization is better equipped to discuss the consequences of historical change or support and realize the possibility that we can control the future through the power inherent in voluntary association and vigorous democratic action.

The train arrives in Jefferson City, Missouri's Capital. This is our destination today; we are not going all the way to Kansas City on the "Mule." Instead, we eighty representatives of Citizens for Modern Transit are here to meet our legislators and tell them once again about the importance of mass transit. I chaired this citizens' advocacy group for several years; I am involved in light rail and transit advocacy because I know what dramatic consequences transportation decisions have had in our region. My goal during my tenure as chair of this very effective organization was to broaden community understanding of the relationships among transportation decisions, land use policy, infrastructure costs, clean air, rates of resource consumption, urban abandonment, suburban sprawl, historic preservation, and most importantly livable neighborhoods. Transportation decisions and other choices have profoundly changed the relationships between neighbors and even the meanings of neighbor, neighborhood, town, and city, so this kind of community involvement is central, not peripheral, to the work of public history. We must not just study the past, preserve stuff, mount exhibits, publish books, and conduct programs. If there are implications to our work, we must act upon those implications in concert with our communities. It is our business to discuss the interrelated consequences of decisions made in the past. In *The Next American Metropolis: Ecology, Community and the American Dream,* Peter Calthorpe puts it this way:

> Today the public world is shrunken and fractured. Parks, schools, libraries, post offices, town halls, and civic centers are dispersed, underutilized, and underfunded. Yet these civic elements determine the quality of our shared world and express the value we assign to community. The traditional Commons, which once centered our communities with convivial gathering and meeting places, is increasingly displaced by an exaggerated private domain: shopping malls, private clubs, and gated communities. Our basic public space, the street, is given over to the car and its accommodation, while our private world becomes more and more isolated behind garage doors and walled compounds. Our public space lacks identity and is largely anonymous, while our private space strains toward a narcissistic autonomy. Our communities are zoned black and white, private or public, my space or nobody's.[2]

My city, St. Louis, is unfortunately an extreme example that proves the point. Between 1950 and 1990 the population of the St. Louis region grew slowly by only 35 percent, but during that same forty-year-period the acreage of developed land increased by 355 percent. Dismally, the City of St. Louis lost more than half of its population and nearly half of the inner suburbs were also losing population.[3]

Predictably, St. Louis ranks high on indexes of urban sprawl, poor environmental quality, extreme racial and economic disparity.[4] This is what I have come to call the great sorting out, and it afflicts most of our nation to varying degrees. Fed by racism, lubricated by automobiles and highways, and encouraged by unimaginative developers and planners, we have hyper-segregated ourselves by income in developments with homogenous real estate values. In many communities like St. Louis with an African American population disproportionately poor, this results in de facto racial segregation as well. An African American friend made a pungent observation in the midst of a conversation about the causes of urban sprawl in St. Louis. Fed up with obfuscation, she looked around at the predominantly white group and said, "Nonsense: this happened because people like you left the city to get away from people like me."

There are two sides to this process, abandonment is one and the other is dispersal. We disperse into the fringes, where absolutely automobile dependent subdivisions go up instantly, each one comprised of stick-built houses in the same price range and on lots that range from a half acre to three acres. Houses are zoned for single family, set back uniformly from the street, without alleys, generally without usable front porches, homogenous, strung along curvilinear streets that end in cul-de-sacs, often without sidewalks. Driveways and garage doors are prominent. Each of these new developments generates demands for new roads, bridges, schools, libraries, sewers, water mains, government services, police and fire protection. These necessary amenities are only fractionally paid for by the developer and property owners and largely become a part of the tax bill shared by the whole region. Obviously enormous quantities of finite resources are consumed in both the house construction and in the building of the infrastructure to sustain them. Meanwhile farmlands, wetlands, and other lands are consumed at prodigious rates.

These edge cities are further segregated by function. Zoning ordinances separate residential development from retail, commercial, and industrial places. Many of the communities are devoid of civic spaces: there are no grand civic malls and in some instances government offices are unobtrusively located in strip shopping developments. Schools are very large, and size combined with location requires most students to ride buses. There are few neighborhood parks although there are regional parks that also require travel by automobile. Indeed, every trip requires the insertion of a key into an ignition and the consumption of scarce fuel accompanied by emission of pollutants from combustion. Most often people who work in restaurants, stores, hospitals, and other service businesses cannot afford to live near the people they serve. Ironically, even the police and fire personnel upon whom people depend for their very lives often must live elsewhere. Civic life is diminished and people are isolated, especially the elderly and the young.

Architecture, the very design and arrangement and materials, in these places is impoverished because builders and buyers do not insist that anything be built to last. I contrast that architecture with my own century-old home in the City of St. Louis. Now, after one hundred years, the copper valleys on the slate roof need replacement. The slate itself is still in good shape. I appreciate the mindset of Thomas McKittrick who built the house knowing that it would endure. He constructed, perhaps consciously, a message from the past, a message of aesthetics and values and of confidence in a future beyond his lifetime. It is a mixture of hubris and humility, a desire on the one hand to build something enduring as a monument to his achievement, but on the other an implicit acknowledgment that his house would last long after his body and bones rested in Bellefontaine Cemetery. McKittrick also acknowledged societal obligations in his undertaking, an understanding that buildings built by a man with the means to do so must be built to endure. This was how things were to be done.

These new barren and impoverished developments have more serious complications than their transient nature. The ties of community in these places are tenuous because these places are without stories that bind, experiences that build trust, an understanding of common interest upon which civic life and democracy depend. These places lack narrative. Communities are built with narrative, built upon shared memory, a sense of the common good as opposed to individual interests, a commitment to the distinctive qualities of a place. Narrative implies a recognition of a shared past, a sense of history, a mutual understanding that your place is assuredly not interchangeable with countless other places. But the structure of these exurban developments is not conducive to the informal association between residents that fosters community and hence community does not emerge. People encased in automobiles fan out from their subdivisions to shop in a faraway mall, attend church or temple and visit friends, and they rarely mingle with those whose houses are nearby. In most cases the prior history of the place where their houses are has been obliterated with the new development, and no one is left to tell the tales. Further, their physical arrangement ensures that community cannot develop. The nature of the new place is not suitable for the creation of new stories, of narratives that give meaning to the place, shared identities to the people, and common purpose to civic life.

The rootlessness of contemporary life is reinforced in these places with uniform residential real estate values. If income goes up, if the family grows, or if a larger and more expensive house is desired, the family moves out to another place that boasts higher real estate values. Likewise if income decreases or other family circumstances change, people must move out of the place to find what they need. Because most people view residences as merely temporary, they do not build to last and they have powerful incentives to avoid deep attachments. Such places are not environmentally sustainable and they undermine civic life and democracy, because they have no history, no bonds of common interest, few shared stories, little sense of identity.

Yet those of us who have chosen to live in such places made rational decisions. These places are for the most part new, clean, uncrowded, secure, with good schools, lots of green space, and stable real estate values. And these places are in many ways more suited to our contemporary peripatetic world in which economics is global, information moves at the speed of light, and our "place" is transitory and interchangeable. Although these places were built in response to deteriorating and overcrowded cities, and were made possible by prosperity and an automobile culture, they have had unintended but dramatic impacts upon social relationships and the functions of democracy.

But these are not just big city problems. As I drive through small towns all over America, I see the civic and commercial life dissipated in downtowns, with an attempted reincarnation in the guise of fast food joints and chain discount stores adjacent to the nearest highway. Downtown grocery stores, lumber yards, movie theaters, hardware and clothing stores are scarce, replaced with antique malls, boutiques, and vacant store fronts. Pedestrian traffic on sidewalks is greatly diminished. I see older residential areas disintegrating as people even in small towns opt for new houses developed on suburban models built on the outskirts. I see locally owned businesses decimated as people are seduced by the low prices and huge selections in the square-boxed, asphalt-surrounded, automobile-convenient chain stores on the highway. Meanwhile what was the town square shrivels, locally owned stores whither, and what was once civic space where people informally met is abandoned. The brownstone building on the corner with retail shops at sidewalk level and offices or residences above is vacant, the last movie theater on Main Street closes, and the people go to the miracle market just off the interstate and the multiplex cinema ten miles away. This is no way to build community and nurture civic life and buttress democracy. This is no way to strengthen ties that bind.

Although generally ignored, a definite causal relationship exists between exurban explosion and urban abandonment. A telling and forlorn column by journalist Gregory Freeman called "Scattered Neighbors Find Solace in Reunions" appeared in the *St. Louis Post-Dispatch* in the fall of 1996.[5] Freeman described two "ghost reunions" of former residents of neighborhoods now gone, one decimated by the construction of an interstate highway that plowed through it and the other demolished to make way for a hospital parking lot. In both instances there is a sense of irreplaceable loss, some of it nostalgia but much of it an acknowledgment of real loss of community that could not be replicated elsewhere. "Neighborhood was very important to us in those days," said Delores Abernathy Dickens. African Americans lived in this area as did those with Polish, Italian, and German backgrounds. "We all got along," said Dickens who is black. "This was before the schools were integrated but we all played together. We went to our schools and they went to their schools, but we all got along." The neighborhood was mixed both by income and race. "But we were safe," Delores noted. "You didn't have to have locks and burglar alarms and things like you do now. If you went away, somebody would keep an eye out for you, and if they went somewhere, you'd do the same for them."

Gladys Cofield, a resident of the second neighborhood, observed that "We just thought there'd be a few people at first, and then it just grew and grew," she said. More than a hundred people signed up to see former neighbors. Like Dickens, Cofield says that her neighbors were all very close. "Today, I don't know who my neighbors are except those who live in the next couple of houses," she said. "In those days, we knew everyone on the block and we cared for everyone on the block." Ties to this place and its people were so close that Cofield says that next to her parents dying, "my greatest fear was that one day we would all grow up and not be as close. Of course that happened," she said. "But it will be nice to bring everyone back together again—if only for a few hours."

It would be reassuring if these comments could be dismissed as aberrant romantic nostalgia. But they cannot. I recently chaired a panel discussion that included all of the living former mayors of the City of St. Louis at a conference sponsored by the St. Louis Association of Community Organizations. Several other staff of the Missouri Historical Society presented talks and moderated discussions about neighborhood change. Hundreds of concerned citizens attended. All attendees shared a profound concern for neighborhood preservation. They understood the loss described by Greg Freeman's informants and were determined not to wind up as attendees at "ghost reunions." While discussions were practical, they were not only focused on real estate values; most important, they embraced the preservation of those relationships that create neighbors and support neighborhood. Anecdotally I know that attendance at such meetings is on the rise. I read this as a hopeful barometer of community concern and a shift in community values. This reinvigoration of grass roots community life is also revitalization of democracy at its most fundamental level: people who share a space assuming responsibility for the terms of their own lives and the health of the places where they live. While I have not quantified the contributions of my colleagues at the Missouri Historical Society to this process, I do know that we are very much involved in the process in a myriad of ways and that our contribution is significant.

St. Louis is a city of brick. High quality clay was deposited by the Mississippi and Missouri Rivers as they meandered through the valley over eons, slowly precipitating their burdens of fine earth over wide swaths of land. Pressed and baked in rectangular bricks, this earth became the building blocks of the nineteenth-century city. Now the city is being demolished. Now I drive through nineteenth-century streets, and I see again and again neat pallets of brick. The pallets are not at construction sites, but instead they are piled next to demolition projects. The bricks are salvage. They will become the decorative fireplaces and backyard patios in a suburban development, while the compact neighborhoods those bricks had built, neighborhoods that contained housing for multiple income levels and permitted mixed residential, retail, and commercial development erupt in piles of dust and debris. I am appalled by what is happening here. Neighborhoods where people once walked to stores, church, school, and parks and shared an informal life on streets and sidewalks are pockmarked with vacant lots, garbage, rubble, and often characterized by violence as they are abandoned to those who cannot escape, despite the best efforts of people involved in organizations such as the St. Louis Association of Community Organizations and the Missouri Historical Society.

However, the destruction is not just physical oblivion. It is an even more ominous kind of oblivion. It is a desecration of the terrible sort that would have occurred if Cheryl's father had plowed up the ground where his wife buried her unborn children. What is happening in cities and towns all over this land is a forgetting, a truncation of narratives that attached people to each other and to their places and gave them a sense of lives lived before their own and lives that will be lived later. This is the real destruction, for in this process something singular, intangible, and irreplaceable is gone, never to be recovered except in commemorated form at "ghost reunions." Places are produced in that wonderful interaction of people, place, narrative, and time. When the people desert these places, narratives are forgotten, ties break, and the place is unmade. What is forgotten in abandonment cannot be re-remembered in transient automobile suburbs with too few places for shared experience and story making.

Some narratives are even more expansive than those that establish individual identities. Some ripple beyond into the neighborhood and immediate community.

Figure 11-2. Abandoned buildings: This is no way to build a community and nurture civic life. *Courtesy Missouri Historical Society, St. Louis.*

Late nineteenth-and early twentieth-century St. Louis civic narratives are symbolized in public architecture. Dearly held ideals are reflected in public hospitals, grand parks, public fountains and public art, the extensive public library system, the network of public bathhouses, the memorial built to honor veterans of the First World War, courthouses, boulevards, a civic auditorium. These impressive public works embody the idea of the public welfare, the common good, and the certainty that the civic enterprise transcends the individual. Such edifices were meant to uplift, entertain, inspire, and civilize.

Rarely are such places built now. Our single-minded focus on the individual and the bottom line preclude such extravagant expenditures that neither directly benefit the individual nor produce profits. In *History Without a Subject: The Postmodern Condition,* David Ashley examines the idea that in our age everything is commodified and that which cannot be commodified is devalued, including value systems that are not economic. Unfortunately the civic ideal is one of these systems and it is now debased.[6]

St. Louis's Municipal Auditorium opened on April 14, 1934, paid for with the proceeds of a bond issue passed in 1923. The front facade of limestone and Corinthian columns faces the civic mall, and the vista extends past the Soldiers

Memorial to the central Public Library. There are inscriptions on the front of the auditorium: "Erected by the People of St. Louis, A Temple Whose Altar is Ever Glowing, the Flame at Which Patriotism May Be Rekindled." These words of Carl Schurz are on the east facade: "Democratic Government will be the more successful the more public opinion is enlightened and inspired by full and thorough discussion." When the auditorium opened, then-Mayor Bernard Dickman observed, "Two panels by a young St. Louis sculptor, Robert Cronback, typify the activities to which the auditorium is dedicated: 'Discussion' and 'Recreation.'" It was to be a place for citizens to celebrate their city and each other. This was to be a center for civic life, a center that both reflected and enhanced the community's sense of itself.

The auditorium closed in 1991. Three weeks ago I sat on the edge of the gargantuan stage, looking out into hazy dim light over the forlorn opera house that could seat 3,500. It looked like the symbolic deterioration of civic life, a demeaning of the intent of those who ordered Schurz's words inscribed at its entrance. Once this stage backed up to a moveable wall. Behind the wall was an auditorium with more than ten thousand seats. Open the wall, and the stage could serve in two directions. The auditorium part was demolished for the construction of a professional hockey arena with very expensive seats.

This building symbolizes civic values certainly, but it is also a repository of communal memory. Columnist Greg Freeman wrote about this building in the *St. Louis Post-Dispatch:* "It's a special place," he wrote, "that holds a spot in the hearts of many. Mikhail Baryshnikov danced there. Peter, Paul, and Mary sang 'Puff the Magic Dragon' there. Diana Ross and the Supremes urged St. Louisans to 'Stop in the Name of Love' there. Countless high school students held their graduation ceremonies there. Until 1968, the St. Louis Symphony Orchestra performed there."[7]

To this list, I would add, war bond rallies, the first National Folk Festival, grand opera, youth conventions, evangelical crusades, presidential appearances. "For many of us," Freeman concluded, "the opera house remains a special place." Not only a symbol of the civic ideal, this civic edifice is a repository of community memory. And the dusty stage, the whole disheveled state of the Municipal Auditorium is a communal form memory loss, a civic forgetting of what we are and can aspire to be together.

Yet, even if the people and their narratives could be transplanted to a new place where new stories could be made, the damage is still horrendous. For abandonment is not only a physical and human disaster; it is also an environmental debacle. For these places were built at enormous cost of resources and energy. Houses, civic structures, retail and commercial buildings, and public facilities such as schools and libraries are carted off to landfills. Infrastructure such as sewers, streets, sidewalks, water mains, utilities, street lights, and gas lines capable of sustaining a much larger population are now dramatically underutilized but must be maintained for those who remain. Yet the tax base shrinks. So we destroy the buildings, abandon the infrastructure, and replicate it all on the fringes. In doing

Figure 11-3. Municipal Auditorium: St. Louis Municipal Auditorium, a place for citizens to celebrate their city. *Courtesy Missouri Historical Society, St. Louis.*

this we lay a heavy mortgage upon this planet, a debt to be paid in the future and by tomorrow's children. This is reckless and shortsighted. It reeks of the selfish "I," of the isolated "me," and it incarcerates us in a chilly here and now, absent of connections to past and future and, deplorably, even to each other.

In this process of destruction and abandonment we may be destroying our most important future economic asset. What we are destroying is what gives our places identity. Those places that retain distinctive architectural, historical, and cultural attributes will attract economic activity. In a transient nation increasingly characterized by sameness and interchangability, our capacity to attract those on the edge of the new economy will partially depend upon our ability to maintain some cultural distinction and physical individuality, an identity to distinguish our place from any other.

Destruction of places, environmental degradation, poor aesthetics and design, uncritical use of technology, increasing taxation, rigid zoning, population dispersal, segregation by race and class, concentration of poverty, homogenization of culture, human isolation, the decline of civic life—all these elements are interrelated. At the core these unfortunate consequences are both causes and effects of the disappearance of sustaining and embracing narratives. And narrative is at the very core of public history.

All public history organizations collect and preserve narratives. Our collections— the artifacts, documents, maps, paintings, photographs, prints and engravings, the archeological evidence, films, oral histories and audiotapes, books, and buildings are only symbols and connections. Symbols because they represent values, aesthetics, thoughts, actions, and culture of those who were once alive and who built our places. Connections because they are tangible evidence that others once lived in our places. The narratives symbolized by our collections relieve us from permanent confinement in a momentary present, and they allow us to transmit knowledge from all generations, thus permitting experience and information to accumulate and disseminate rather than disappear with death. We are the living link in a continuum of our species that began in an indeterminate past and extends through an unknowable future.

What we make of the symbols we collect is an interpretation, a mental map, a facsimile of our world that is regularly updated. What we do is a core characteristic of our species. We do not tell everything as we compose our narratives. Much of what happened in the past is forever lost, buried with ancestors, forgotten, destroyed, or discarded. Further, a narrative, a history if you want, that told everything would have little meaning. Our readers, listeners, or visitors would insist that we identify what is most important and that we point out causal relationships, construct a narrative, ascribe meaning, tell a story with a beginning, a middle, and an end. Narratives, histories, are for the living, not for the dead. They explain the world to us in meaningful ways. They are updated and revised to inform present circumstances and are expressive of future aspirations.

A group of African American St. Louisans recently got together with staff of the Missouri Historical Society. They were looking at a painting called *The Last Slave Sale*. In the painting the slaves are standing on the top steps of the Old Court House, which is still there on Fourth Street in downtown St. Louis. The auctioneer is ready, and a number of white people have gathered in the street below the steps. We ask the audience to write their reactions to the painting. Then the curator fills in some details. "The man who painted this picture," she says, "was an ex-soldier, a Confederate who, after the Civil War, bitterly concluded that he had fought on the side of wrong. He spent the balance of his life painting scenes like this one depicting the abomination of slavery. The event portrayed in this painting occurred in 1861, although he did the painting seven years later. There is," she continues, " an unverifiable civic tradition that on that day, the white audience refused to participate, effectively canceling the sale. This was," she concludes, "not a slave sale but rather a public protest against the sale of slaves in St. Louis."

The man seated next to me leaned toward me. "If you exhibit the painting," he urged, "you must tell the story." I agree. This story suggests that citizens in the past have rallied to oppose gross injustices against their fellow human beings of African descent, and it is an accessible and valuable narrative for now. Whether the protest story is true or not cannot be fully determined. But it does not matter. For truth is conveyed in the telling and retelling of the story, calling upon and also revealing the better sides of our natures. This narrative is valuable for our city in the present, usable despite its lack of irrefutable evidence.

Figure 11-4. The story of the Last Slave Sale is a usable narrative; its verification less important than the connection it makes between people and their place. *Courtesy Missouri Historical Society, St. Louis.*

We are advocates for usable narratives. We know that narratives connect people and place. We know that in our work we make choices about which narratives to preserve and tell. We also know that we live in a time when civic narratives are devalued, that we are more detached from our places and from each other, that we are trying to build communities where places for the construction of narratives are scarce.

What sorts of narratives should we advocate? We must strive to facilitate creations of narratives like Cheryl's that connect her parents and their place in an intimate relationship; and like Mayor Dickman's dream for St. Louis's Municipal Auditorium; and like the tradition of protest that stopped the last sale of slaves; and the sense of trusteeship that John and I attach to our old houses. Not just any narratives will suffice. The stories we promote must speak to enduring concerns in their present manifestations. What is a good place? What obligations do we owe to those with whom we share a place? What inspires the best of what we are capable? What do we owe to those not yet born who will occupy our place after us?

I am convinced that history has implications. It is not simply a good story, nor a set of materials for self-congratulation, nor a rosy look in a rear view mirror — and not a museum. History must lead to changed beliefs about what is right and good and those beliefs must lead to action. And yet history is conservative for it seeks to preserve what is good; and it takes the long view. History must guide us to narratives that connect generations, that attach us to place, that elevate concern for the common good and excoriate behaviors that denigrate or even destroy people and their places. History must underscore our ties to our places and our planet and our obligation to leave both better than we found them. History must insist on the creation of places that, by the relationships they facilitate and the values they incorporate, promote and enhance the making and preservation of such stories.

History is a process engaged in by the living, a process of facilitating creation of narratives shared broadly enough to inform civic decision making. It is a discussion of what we have done well, what we have done poorly, and how we can do better. And it's about perspective, too . . .

The "Mule" picks us up for the return trip in early evening. The night is luminescent and chilly. The train is a good place. The camaraderie is apparent. Dozens of people mingle, chatting, recapitulating the day's events. Strangers become friends and share stories. I think of Cheryl's story, John's house, Grace's porch, Pattie's experience as mayor, and of Thomas McKittrick's house, now my house — a day of narratives shared in a place conducive to their telling; a good place. The last car on the train has an observation platform outside the rear door. I walk out. The train's rush through the night leaves a pocket of eerily still air on the platform. I stare into the night, astounded at a revelation of reverse perspective. As I look at where the train has just been, I see tracks, ties, roadbed, trees, and sky coming together and then disappearing in the distance. If I was in the engineer's cab in the front of the train, I would peer into the future. Here, on this platform I look into the past. I see where we have been. Future and past conjoin right here on this train at this instant. This, I think, is an apt analogy for history. Past and future are separated by only an infinitesimal present. The dividing line is tiny. The difference is a matter of perspective. It is a history trip.

NOTES

1. Ray Oldenburg, *The Great Good Place: Cafes, Coffee Shops, Community Centers, Beauty Parlors, General Stores, Bars, Hangouts and How They Get You Through the Day.* (New York: Marlowe, 1989, 1997), 288–9.
2. Peter Calthorpe, *The Next American Metropolis: Ecology, Communities, and the American Dream.* (New York: Princeton Architectural Press, 1993), 23.
3. Transportation Redefined, 17
4. Where We Stand, 55, 57
5. Gregory Freeman, "Scattered Neighbors Find Solace In Reunions," *St. Louis Post-Dispatch,* September 6, 1996.
6. David Ashley, *History Without a Subject: The Postmodern Condition.* (Boulder, CO: Westview Press, 1997).
7. Gregory Freeman, "Memories of Opera House Are Too Precious To Lose," *St. Louis Post-Dispatch,* February 22, 1998.

PART V

POLICY ANALYSIS

STATE OF NATURE AND NATURE OF THE STATE: HISTORIANS AND FEDERAL ENVIRONMENTAL POLICY

Martin Reuss

Public historians provide context and insight to discussions of contemporary problems, and few issues generate more interest and activity than the environment. It would, therefore, appear that public and environmental historians have something in common. Yet, their relationship has evolved slowly. Environmental historians have often shunned detailed analyses of environmental policy development, preferring a broader perspective that deals more generally with the forces and institutions at work.[1] Consequently, their interpretations have better illuminated the impact of policy on the environment than the evolution of the policy itself. Frequently lost, too, is an appreciation of the professional culture of the engineers and scientists who manipulate the environment and whose expertise is necessary to both exploit and protect natural resources.

For their part, public historians do not always appear knowledgeable about the latest historiographic discussions or the broad range of secondary literature. There may be good reasons for this—lack of supervisory encouragement to read beyond the archival record or bureaucratic imperatives that require constant attention to agency, legislative, and public demands. Still, policy analysis that lacks broader context loses rhetorical power and diminishes the historian's ability to influence major issues in environmental history. It also prevents readers, including policy makers, from appreciating the full range of questions, constraints, and opportunities that provide the backdrop for a policy decision.

The strength of public historians—especially those employed in government— is their dissection of the bureaucratic dynamics leading to important environmental policy decisions. Usually based on extensive research in agency files and the federal archives, their detailed case studies of controversial projects and programs illuminate agency planning, engineering design process, and the administration of natural resources and regulatory programs. Their subjects are diverse and occasionally overlapping, reaching from military installations to Native American communities, from international trade to domestic infrastructure construction, from public health to environmental protection. Perhaps somewhat unexpectedly, contract historians and permanent employees of developmental agencies, such as the Nuclear Regulatory Commission and the Army Corps of Engineers, have provided some of the best analyses. The National Park Service and the Bureau of Land

Management have also contributed important studies.[2] All of these "official" monographs provide important insights into the ways in which environmental policy is actually formulated, but many never enter into environmental history bibliographies for college classes.

In fact, public and environmental historians do not engage each other's audiences particularly well. Public historians working in environmental history publish environmental articles in the proceedings and journals of various engineering, legal, and scientific associations. Their work also appears in books and pamphlets distributed by the Government Printing Office (GPO). Unfortunately, convention proceedings, journal articles, and GPO produced publications infrequently find their way into academic bibliographies. Equally unfortunate, many academic historians do not communicate with nonhistory audiences. Partially because their tenure and promotion chances depend on professional peer recognition, they receive little encouragement to publish in other than historical journals.

This chapter attempts to bridge the gap between environmental and public historians, suggesting common—and necessary—ways for academic and nonacademic historians to approach environmental policy history. There is work enough for both. Too often analyses of environmental decision making have been left to political scientists, economists, geographers, and even engineers. Almost invariably, these analyses lack historical depth. The skills, perspective, and methodologies of the trained historian are necessary to understand the evolution of environmental policy in the United States.

FEDERAL ENVIRONMENTAL POLICY MAKING— CHANGING VALUES AND OBJECTIVES

Perspective comes from the long view. The nation's environmental policy is not just an accumulation of laws and regulations. Beginning soon after the nation's birth, the federal government developed particular programs and objectives which reflected and reinforced prevalent attitudes about human domination of the natural world—an environmental policy of sorts, albeit one with different values than we currently practice.[3] Perhaps, federal land management best reflected the attitude; the objective generally was to encourage settlement. A more restricted view of land management, embracing only those lands that the government determined to keep in the public domain, still takes us back over a century to the creation of the first national parks. Eventually, it included everything from grazing lands to wildlife refuges. The federal government attempted to leave public health problems to local authorities, but became involved here as well, partly the result of intergovernmental, cross-boundary pollution problems. National authorities began to alter the nation's rivers beginning in the early nineteenth century. Their more or less continuous efforts since then changed landscape and habitat throughout the country. Although the term "environmental policy" is of relatively recent vintage, its roots are deeply embedded in the nation's political development.

Certainly, environmental policy has changed dramatically over the years. The policies of one generation may contradict those of another. Nineteenth-century rhetoric stressed domination: "pushing back the wilderness" and "conquering nature." Early twentieth-century conservation policy emphasized consumption—the maximum human use of a resource consistent with its replenishment. Post-midcentury environmental policy focused on standard of living. "Waste" no longer meant inefficient use of the resource but endangerment of public health or of the environment itself.[4] Environmental policy reflected postindustrial values; physical fitness, diet, and clean water and air became important concerns. Science not only gave the public the capability to measure the danger, but also the ecological perspective that permeated the environmental movement.

In most cases, the new perspective modified, but did not replace—with the possible exception of the 1973 Endangered Species Act—decidedly anthropocentric legislation. Even the landmark National Environmental Policy Act of 1969 (NEPA) did not subordinate human aspirations to environmental requirements. It sought only "to create the conditions under which man and nature can exist in productive harmony . . . "[5] Preoccupied with public health and standard of living concerns, lawmakers divided environmental problems by media (air, land, water, fish and wildlife, etc.) and by class (such as pesticides and hazardous materials) and commonly set standards and target dates to reach objectives. This was a "command and control" approach, in which the federal government determined the objectives and then prescribed the manner in which they were to be met.[6]

In recent years, another generation of policy makers and environmental leaders has concluded that the panoply of environmental laws is fragmented. No one vision informs environmental policy; rather special interests and professional expertise pushed forward narrowly focused legislation. Resulting laws ignore or underestimate the interdependence of habitats; the relationship between air, land, and water; and the interactive effects of various pollutants—historical analysis of these problems is sorely lacking and very much needed. New appreciation for the interdependence of environmental concerns draws attention to issues that generally transcend any one class of problems. Obvious examples are global warming and genetic modification, but there are many others. Nonpoint source pollution (for example, fertilizer runoff) imperils water supply, fish and wildlife, and the land itself. Population growth threatens both economic and environmental havoc. Many citizens also decry the apparent inequitable application of environmental policy. Some populations have suffered so that others might gain. Environmental justice has emerged as an issue.

Faced with competing visions, often overwhelming amounts of data, and political vacillation, the current generation of environmental policy makers displays a new appreciation for flexibility and less inclination to engage in the confrontational style of a generation ago. A key change is the willingness to concede that the market and the environment are not inherent enemies. Indeed, many environmentalists now agree with resource economists who argue that private initiatives and market incentives will be necessary to preserve the environment. Government, whether local, state, or federal, cannot do it alone.[7]

FEDERAL ENVIRONMENTAL POLICY HISTORY—THE CHALLENGES

Policy development in a democratic country is at best a complicated affair. Policy scientists—a discipline dating back to the mid-twentieth century—refer to the policy process and develop normative goals for the process. The fundamental goal in the western democratic tradition is achieving or enhancing human dignity. Two well-known policy scientists, Garry D. Brewer and Peter deLeon, argue that this process can be divided into six stages: initiation, estimation, selection, implementation, evaluation, and termination.[8] Although these stages may help the historian visualize what is happening at particular times, there is the danger of oversimplification, of trivializing the moral and ethical concerns that frame many environmental policy debates.

The very term "process" confers on policy development an organization and logic that appear problematical; the process is hardly sequential but composed of extraordinarily complicated feedback loops. Moreover, Brewer and deLeon's position that a problem begins only when it is recognized ignores slowly simmering underlying causes. Simply put, policy development begins imprecisely, may take years to evolve, and its stages, as described by Brewer and deLeon, generally overlap and even conflict as new players emerge and unanticipated issues arise. The research and methodological issues awaiting a historian are daunting—no more so than in the area of environmental policy. Although there are many ways of characterizing these issues, three generic problems seem to dominate at the national level.

The Cast of Thousands

In the United States, enough agencies, organizations, and individuals influence federal policy to populate a small town. Both houses of Congress and dozens of congressional committees and subcommittees are involved. The Office of Management and Budget, eleven Executive Branch departments, and numerous independent agencies, including the Environmental Protection Agency and the Nuclear Regulatory Commission, oversee or review programs and projects and write regulations and guidelines. Over one hundred federal trial and appellate courts interpret legislation and adjudicate disputes, often fundamentally reformulating policy in the process.[9]

Moreover, while this country's democratic institutions and history allow and even encourage citizen participation in policy formation, environmental legislation, especially NEPA, invites citizen participation in an unprecedented fashion. NEPA requires federal agencies to write an environmental impact statement (EIS) for every federal proposal "significantly affecting the quality of the human environment" (Sec. 102(C)), and to make the statement—often embracing several volumes—available to government agencies and the general public. The resulting public input into environmental decision making has occasionally overwhelmed the agencies; it also challenges the historian wishing to analyze the roots of policy decisions.

The Paper Chase

In the early summer of 1998, the National Park Service distributed 20,000 copies of its fifty-seven-page executive summary for the "Draft Environmental Impact Statement for the Interagency Bison Management Plan for the State of Montana and Yellowstone National Park." Additionally, it sent 2,000 copies of the complete draft to selected individuals and various public and private organizations; scheduled a dozen public hearings; and put the executive summary, including a public comment form, on its web site.[10] The impact statement addressed concerns that brucellosis-infected bison roaming outside of Yellowstone Park would infect and kill cattle.[11] However, many people questioned whether the disease could actually be transmitted from bison to cattle and repeatedly pointed out that not one documented case existed. Within weeks of circulating the EIS, the Service had already received about 200 comments.[12] By the end of August, the National Wildlife Federation had mounted a national campaign to oppose the Park Service's proposals. It circulated a letter in which the executive director of the Montana Wildlife Federation accused the Park Service of writing "a prescription for continued slaughter" of the bison. The letter encouraged recipients to protest directly to the Park Service and to receive updates from the National Wildlife Federation's own web site.[13]

What awaits the historian wishing to write about this issue? The National Park Service constructed a computer database to organize comments into various categories, but whether the database will be retained and for how long is not clear. Based on my own experience working with the files of several federal agencies, I would encourage interested historians to get to the database quickly or risk losing it as well as the original comments. The problem reflects another aspect of dealing with so many participants in the policy-making process. It is easy to lose track of documents, and the historian must make difficult decisions about what sources to pursue and what to ignore.

Clearly, the mountain of paper private citizens and public bureaucrats raise on just one policy issue can defeat unsuspecting researchers. Some historians may decide life is too short for such research; they go home. Others resort to what one frustrated soul called the "smash and grab" approach to archival research—a little bit here, a little bit there, hoping nothing of importance is missed. Poor agency record keeping makes the chore even more onerous. Agencies and congressional committees inadequately document important actions, lose or misplace files, or destroy records simply because destruction is less time-consuming and costly than preservation. Many judicial records are sealed and unavailable. Some historians may forsake the archives for published primary sources such as memoirs, diaries, and collections of letters, or they may try to cobble policy history from whatever biographies and newspaper accounts might be available. The result is rarely satisfactory. Biographers do not usually go into detail about the evolution of policy. If they do, they use personal paper collections, not official files squirreled away in federal records centers and archives. The protagonists themselves are not the best source, as valuable as their testimony might be. As historian Samuel P. Hays

observed, policy makers generally do not make very good historians when looking back on their own careers. Rather, they "transfer the way they saw the world
as administrators into retrospective reflection" which "must be modified drastically in the light of a larger perspective beyond the decision maker and divorced
from the imperatives of decision making."[14] Anyone who has read the memoirs
of Richard Nixon or Henry Kissinger knows what Hays is talking about. There is
really no way of getting around it: policy historians, including those tracking environmental policy, require access to the archives and the files. There is no other
way to obtain the complete record. Be prepared for the long haul.

The job may be challenging, but it is not impossible. Training, proper preparation, and a realistic assessment of the research challenge can ease the work.
Historians need to understand the institutions and agencies with which they deal.
Such awareness not only enables one to appreciate the policy-making dynamics
within the organizations, but also generally provides useful hints on where the
most important files are and which individuals may have served in key positions—which are not necessarily only the senior level ones. Historians also need
to define their topics to accommodate reasonable time and funding constraints.
Much insight can be gained from focusing on parts of the story. Let common
sense prevail.

Another absolutely critical skill is the ability to use the records under the control of the National Archives and Records Administration (NARA). These records
include both those in the possession of the National Archives and those still technically in agency possession but stored in NARA records centers. These latter
records are generally of more recent vintage and therefore contain much material
relating to the development of environmental policy in the last few decades.
Agency records retirement schedules, worked out between agency records managers and NARA officials, will tell historians where the records are located—in
the archives or records centers—and whether they are scheduled for eventual destruction or permanent retention in the archives. In addition, NARA (and, in some
cases, the agencies themselves) have produced guides to select archival holdings.
Historians should always check with agency historical offices to see what is available.

Federal records, it should be emphasized, not only are necessary to trace policymaking but also provide important information on environmental changes in
this country. An obvious case would be Weather Bureau precipitation records. Geological Survey records show changes in surface and groundwater quantity and
quality. The Army Corps of Engineers also has records tracing hydrographic
changes over more than a century. Department of Agriculture records show
changes in salinity in California and other western states. Forest Service records
will show changes in forest cover. Of course, the Environmental Protection
Agency possesses much data on levels of ground, air, and water contamination
throughout the country. Public historians who study environmental impacts, including everything from toxic wastes to cultural resources, will find these infor-
mational records a major aid to their research.

Learning the Lingo

Archival research is necessary, but not sufficient, for policy analysis. Historians should be at least moderately acquainted with the language, fundamental concepts, and cultural perspectives of the disciplines that frame particular policy issues. Although lawyers may draft much of the legislative language, the law and subsequent agency policy rests in no small part upon expert knowledge. Water quality issues require familiarity with hydrology and chemistry. Decisions on where and when to build levees and dams are not only political, but mirror engineering technical training as well. Ecology and biology inform many decisions dealing with fish and wildlife. In almost all policy cases, economics is involved and is often determinative. The examples are endless, but the fundamental point is that historians who must assess professional judgment—and this includes all environmental policy historians—should know something about the relevant professions.

In learning about other professions, public historians have advantages. Those working in environmental and natural resource agencies have far easier access to both the documents and the practitioners. It is almost impossible *not* to learn about the engineering profession in the Corps of Engineers, the nuclear industry in the Nuclear Regulatory Commission, about ecology and chemistry in the Environmental Protection Agency, biology in the Fish and Wildlife Service, forestry in the Forest Service, or about the bureaucratic culture in general. Also, more easily than academic historians, agency historians can integrate documentary evidence with the first-hand knowledge and oral interviews gained from working in the organization. Most, too, are used to working in teams, and this skill may be important in cases when appropriate technical interpretation simply exceeds the historian's capability. Rather than guessing, the historian may form an ad-hoc advisory team of appropriate experts, possibly from within the organization, but preferably from the outside.[15] The ability and opportunity to work with the professionals one is studying carries a potential liability: the public historian must vigilantly guard historical judgment; it is all too easy to be captured by organizational culture. Put another way, the historian's accountability to the client or employer must be subordinated to professional accountability to society.

There is another kind of lingo that environmental policy historians will meet. This is the vocabulary of laws and regulations. The jargon becomes central to agency life. Anyone working on environmental policy and biological diversity needs to understand the difference between endangered and threatened species. Those examining water quality should know what point and nonpoint source pollutants are or the difference between ambient and emission standards. In short, there is a "shorthand" to describe legal and policy requirements. Two good and frequently overlooked guides to this legal and agency jargon are the annual reports of the Council on Environmental Quality and the EPA web site, which has an environmental glossary of the many terms used within that particular agency.[16]

THE EIGHT KEY QUESTIONS—THE "ENVIRONMENT" OF ENVIRONMENTAL POLICY

Generally, any comprehensive effort to describe the context of environmental policy making raises eight key questions. The questions overlap occasionally and carry different weights according to the particular policy question at hand. They are rarely easy to answer or to assign a priority.

1. What Is the Institutional Context?

Professional and bureaucratic context may profoundly affect policy and deserves careful analysis. Most government bureaucracies, especially those charged with the public safety, prize uniformity and reliability. They also tend to have a rather whiggish approach to history, a perspective shared with almost any developmental organization, public or private. Consciously or not, their decisions reflect a belief in progress, the ability and right of individuals to mold the environment (within certain moral and ideological parameters) and a faith that large-scale systems can, indeed, improve the lot of humankind. Bureaucrats of whatever professional stripe may occasionally decry the evils of technology, but they rarely share the apocalyptic consciousness of some environmentalists.

Analyses of organizational culture sometimes make historians uncomfortable. Some would argue that such analysis is beyond the historian's authority because it invariably borrows methodologies and insights from other professions. However, history is by nature an integrative discipline, and historians do a disservice to their profession if they abandon the field to others. I once wrote an essay on the influence of army engineer officer culture on the Corps of Engineers and identified five historical characteristics of that culture. I maintained that army engineer officers were nation-builders, big spenders, adaptive managers, West Point educated and acculturated, and class conscious. The essay amplified each point. Both in thinking about the essay and engaging in subsequent stimulating discussions, I (and I hope others) developed some very useful ideas about bureaucratic constraints and opportunities in the Army Corps of Engineers.

However, the term "culture" tempts historians to do very unhistorical things. As historian Patricia Nelson Limerick has warned, too often the term has provided a simplistic explanation of both behavior and values.[17] We indulge in reification, making culture into something palpable when it is only an abstraction. Hence, "culture" explains the Corps of Engineers' purported institutional arrogance, the Marine Corps' "macho" image, NASA's risk-taking, the Air Force's fascination with technology, or the Internal Revenue Service's easy resort to intimidation. Upon further investigation, the historian invariably discovers that "culture" hardly conveys the complexity of the situation, and agencies rarely are as homogenous as they appear from the outside. "Culture" is useful to capture certain traits and patterns of an agency, but it must be used with caution as an explanatory tool.

2. What Public Values Does the Policy Reflect?

As indicated earlier in this chapter, environmental values change. For much of human history, they were cast largely in economic and military terms. Words like "dominate," "subject," "exploit," "conquer," and "consume" prevailed. No doubt, many people still embrace these terms. Former Secretary of the Interior James Watt called environmentalists "the greatest threat to the ecology of the West" and possessed little doubt that God favored natural resources development.[18] Others have been outraged by Watt's ethic.

In the United States, the question of humankind's relationship to land is particularly sensitive, for one deeply entrenched value in American culture is the presumed right to possess land and to enjoy what one owns. Historically, this attitude deterred state and local governments from establishing land-use and flood-plain regulations. Where such regulations were passed, incessant attempts to modify them in favor of developers occur. Nevertheless, as a result of new scientific evidence, emphasis on "quality of life" issues, and new and effective environmental leadership, Americans successfully transformed anxiety and outrage into political action, articulating a new ecological consciousness and a concern for both short- and long-term environmental impacts. Historians need to be wary, however. It remains to be seen whether this consciousness is temporary or permanent or whether attempts to employ market-based approaches and private initiatives to improve the environment might bridge the gap between environmentalist and developer.

3. What is the State of Scientific Knowledge?

Environmental regulations are presumably science based. They are intended to protect public health, endangered species, natural resources, and, more abstractly, "quality of life." Yet, the science is illusory. There is not even adequate consensus as to what exactly clean air and water are, nor what constitutes a source of pollution. The latter is particularly controversial in regard to clean air standards. The Environmental Protection Agency issued air quality standards for seven air pollutants in the 1970s—ozone, airborne lead, hydocarbons, carbon monoxide, sulfur dioxide, nitrogen dioxide, and total suspended particulates. Every one of these standards generated controversy about their medical and scientific justification. By the late 1980s, EPA's initial assumption that particulate size was inconsequential had been proven to be erroneous; generally, the smaller the particulate the more hazardous it is to humans.[19]

Our ability to measure pollution levels has dramatically improved over the last few decades. Yet, we still debate what levels actually harm humans or the environment. EPA's own conservatism may add to the confusion since the agency's estimates of health risks are routinely worst-case.[20] Politicians throw out enormous sums of money to come up with good answers—or require private citizens and companies to do so—and hope science can subsequently provide a convincing rationale for the expense. For instance, the Clean Water Act of 1972 required the use of the best practicable technology (BPT) or best available technology (BAT) to reduce pollution going into streams, but without agreement about the definition or necessity of such technology. Streams naturally break down certain kinds of bacteria and different streams can handle varying amounts of pollution depending on water temperature, flow, and other conditions. Rather than allowing some flexibility in the system, however, Congress responded to public concerns by requiring efforts that may put unnecessary burdens on polluters.[21]

Science, of course, can confuse as well as clarify. My own research on the Atchafalaya Basin in Louisiana—the largest river swamp in the United States— exemplifies the point. In the late 1970s, a vitriolic debate centered on the amount of water to be retained in the basin at various times. Timber interests desired that the basin be "dewatered" during the summer. Fish and Wildlife personnel feared that draining the basin of water too early would harm crawfish and adversely affect the fishing industry. The Environmental Protection Agency emphasized maintaining sufficient water for aquatic growth. The Corps of Engineers expressed concern over the impact on the federally authorized flood control system. Concerns about balancing economic and environmental requirements infused the debates. Participants, including experts in numerous fields, argued over how much fish and wildlife degradation actually resulted from "dewatering," whether flooding hurt or helped tree growth, and whether sufficient scientific data—particularly, forestry data—had been obtained. Clearly, no amount of scientific data would have resolved all the issues, which were as much political as scientific. In an example of "the politicizing of science,"[22] agency representatives used scientific arguments to advance their own objectives. In the end, the professional experts became politicians and resolved the problems through political compromise, not scientific rationalization.[23]

4. In What Ways May the Market Affect the Resolution of Environmental Issues?

The two keys to environmental restoration and preservation are human behavior modification and the appropriate application of technology. Command and control methods influence both. For instance, tax incentives, financial penalties, and water use restrictions encourage water conservation. Quality standards may result in the installation of new technology to reduce pollution.

Another way to modify human behavior and encourage the use of appropriate technology involves market-based methods.[24] This approach may be relatively simple, such as imposing pollution fees to make polluters pay for their environmentally destructive activities. Economists and environmental regulators are also investigating more imaginative methods. For example, after determining the allowable amount of various pollutants in a watershed, a government could issue pollution permits to waste dischargers that would allow them to emit certain pollutants up to a set limit. The aggregate amount allowed for each pollutant would be kept at or below the established level. These permits could be bought and sold, with the market establishing the monetary value. Another way of accomplishing much the same objective would allow polluters to pay for pollution reduction elsewhere in the region. The level of pollution reduction at one source would have to equal the level of continuing discharge at the other source. A controversial market approach, presently being tried in parts of the country, is mitigation banking. The developer receives credit for purchasing and preserving wetlands that would otherwise be lost to development. The credits are then drawn upon as the developer destroys wetlands elsewhere. A variation is to require wetlands development permits. The permit agency could use the funds it obtains to preserve wetlands within the same watershed.

The market-based approach forces people to think seriously about costs and benefits. Environmental decisions involve transactions and tradeoffs. The metaphor is the auction house. What is the value of a painting by Van Gogh or of Elvis Presley's ring? The answer is determined by individual preference. Similarly, in the market-based approach, preferences determine value. Without often consciously considering it, government bureaucrats may act as brokers in the environmental marketplace, bringing together buyers and sellers—often in the guise of developers and environmentalists—to reach agreements that affect both ecology and economics.

Figure 12-1. This drawing by Charles Graham of a wrecked passenger steamer in the Louisiana bayous is based on a wood engraving by W. Redding. It appeared first in *Harper's Weekly*. The picture vividly portrays the confrontation between technology and nature. Such conflicts often result in governmental intervention—either to assist the technology (in this case, perhaps, through snagging and clearing operations) or, in a later generation, to protect the environment. *Library of Congress.*

Figure 12-2. Determining the amount of effluent that a river can take without endangering public health and fish and wildlife taxes both science and politics. It also raises fundamental issues about the appropriate level of federal intervention in problems that may be resolvable only at a local level. *U.S. Army Corps of Engineers.*

5. What is the Relationship of Technology to the Environment?

Nothing, including the constraints of environmental laws, affects the relationship between the human and natural world more than the application of technology. While environmental historians have examined how technology abuses the environment, sometimes with disastrous effects, they have less often studied how technology may protect or restore the environment.[25] Public historians in environmental and natural resource organizations tell a more ambiguous story. Large developmental bureaucracies manipulate the environment through the construction and operation of complex

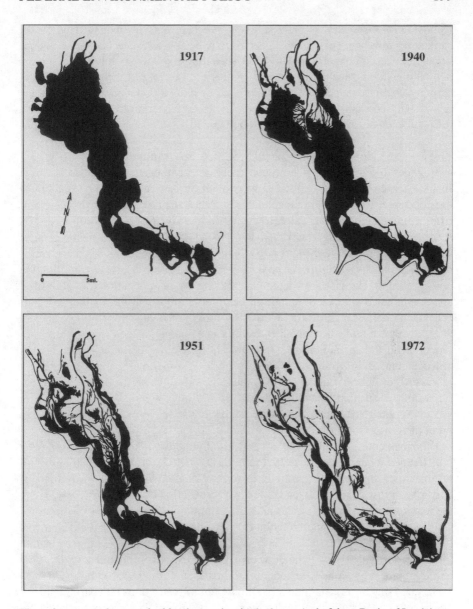

These four maps show gradual land accretion in the lower Atchafalaya Basin of Louisiana. Corps of Engineer structures now do much to regulate the amount of soil and water entering the basin, but the problem of finding the correct water level to meet various and conflicting needs, such as flood reduction, fish and wildlife enhancement, and recreation, remains both a political and technological challenge. *Office of History, Headquarters, U.S. Army Corps of Engineers.*

technological systems. They unquestionably put their footprint upon the land. At the same time, however, government agencies may be able to use technology to reduce human impacts on the natural world and even to restore the environment to a more natural condition. Much environmental policy focuses on just these activities, prescribing appropriate technology to eliminate or reduce pollution and encouraging new, environmentally congenial, technology. Historians must treat technology as a distinguishing human activity for both good and ill.

6. How Have the Courts Modified Environmental Law?

In general, federal courts are remarkably deferential toward the bureaucracy. In the period from 1970 to 1982, government bureaucracies won 62 percent of the court decisions in environmental cases. When the government was the plaintiff, bringing a violator to justice, it won an impressive 67 percent of its cases. Its record was as a defendant, whether sued by industries or environmental groups, was only marginally less impressive. There are many reasons for the government's success. As plaintiff, the government tends to be conservative in litigation and carefully picks cases. As defendant, the government benefits from plaintiffs' attacks on narrow issues of definition or appropriate scientific standards.[26] This is true whether the plaintiffs are industries, looking for vague or ambiguous legal wording that might allow them to escape environmental controls, or environmental groups, insisting on strict interpretation—as they define it—and rigorous enforcement. Both groups attack interpretation, sometimes focusing on only a few words or figures, but they rarely attack the substance of the policy. Their tactic results in an uphill battle. Regulations and laws are rarely so inflexible or loosely worded that courts will lightly throw out agency guidelines and enforcement provisions.

But when courts do throw out or substantially modify a law or regulation, what a difference it can make! In 1975, the U.S. District Court for the District of Columbia ruled in *Natural Resources Defense Council, Inc. v. Callaway* that the Clean Water Act of 1972 extended federal jurisdiction over navigable waters "to the maximum extent permissible under the Commerce Clause of the Constitution." This was a far different interpretation from the limited one the Corps of Engineers had published in its regulations. Ever since, its enforcement has led the Corps into vitriolic confrontations with landowners over the Corps' enforcement of dredging and dumping provisions.[27] In another landmark case, the U.S. Supreme Court in 1992 ruled that South Carolina's establishment of restrictions on coastal land development was a "taking" in that it essentially destroyed the value of the land (*Lucas v. South Carolina Coastal Council*). Although the Court carefully framed its decision, and did not question the necessity of coastal management, its decision encouraged landowners around the country to challenge land and water use restrictions.[28] The first case involved interpreting legislative intent and expanded environmental regulations. The second revolved around fundamental constitutional issues and potentially threatened environmental gains. Both profoundly influenced the dialogue on environmental policy.

7. In What Ways Does the Legislative Process Affect the Making of Environmental Law?

This question is not about constitutional process, although it does raise issues debated in *The Federalist*. Rather, it is intended to alert historians to those aspects of law making that often turn rational, coherent bills into a legislative bouillabaisse. Although no doubt a more complete list of caveats could be developed, I believe that four themes often determine the fate of environmental policy:

a. The influence of congressional staff is pervasive. Modern legislatures, including the United States Congress, are at a disadvantage. Simply put, the world is too complicated, and members depend on staff specialists for much of their information. The influence of congressional staff on the policy-making process cannot be overestimated. In many cases, they write the legislation, develop the compromises, and insert language reflecting parochial interests.

b. The nongermane is often relevant. For example, Secretary of the Interior William Clark proposed to President Reagan in 1985 that Reagan should sign a water resources bill in exchange for congressional support for the administration's Nicaraguan policy, thereby linking two policies that had nothing to do with one another. In another example, Illinois Congressman Dan Rostenkowski, Chairman of the House Ways and Means Committee, would not consider an important inland navigation issue until the Senate agreed to approve a new federal building for Chicago, and the Administration accepted a House initiative to require payment of welfare benefits to families with both parents unemployed. In the end, Congress authorized a building lease in Chicago, and Rostenkowski agreed to delay the welfare proposal until next session. Only then did he consider the inland navigation issue, an important part of a pending water bill.[29] The nongermane can untrack almost any kind of legislation.

c. The particular and the peculiar are important. In some ways, this is another way of saying, ala Tip O'Neil, that all politics is local. When powerful minority leader Senator Robert Byrd of West Virginia feared that new cost-sharing provisions in a water bill would apply to a small water project in his state, he threatened the entire legislation. Under pressure, the administration consequently decided that the project was "technically" under construction and therefore not subject to the new cost-sharing provisions. Then Byrd allowed the massive water bill to continue toward passage.[30] The vignette is revealing. The importance of a project does not depend on dollars or local impact, but on the lawmakers supporting it.

d. In Congress, effectiveness is always subordinated to consensus. Policy agreement is important. In fact, it is the major measure of congressional success. The premium placed on agreement, however, undermines attempts to develop rational and effective policy. Agreement usually means compromise, and compromises often end up as laws that offend the least. As an expression of public will, the process has undeniable attractiveness. However, especially in an area such as environmental policy, which utilizes scientific and engineering expertise, it occasionally leaves rational planning in tatters and long-term goals sacrificed to short-term gains. The approach also causes problems for agencies expected to draft implementing regulations. Regulations are meant to be rational, reflecting appropriate expertise. Somehow, agencies must find the way to reconcile political will and scientific methodology. The means is not always apparent.

8. How Well Do Planners Plan?

This might be called the "Gilbert White" question. White, a world renowned geographer and the leading proponent of nonstructural flood control solutions, has noted that few assessments of the intended and unintended consequences of water projects have ever been done. These assessments he calls "post audits."[31] Historians might use the term "retrospective analyses." These post audits could assess all kinds of environmental projects and programs, not just those in water resources. They would not only illuminate the impact of government programs on affected regions, but also suggest how well planners planned. How well did project and program planners anticipate impacts? What did they not consider that they should have? What criteria and methodologies did they use that may have been inappropriate, of insufficient rigor, or just plain wrong? Even when appropriate, were the methodologies used correctly?

White maintains, and I agree, that agencies are reluctant to spend the money to do postaudits. Only after a disaster, or perhaps under threat of a legal suit, will an agency spend the money to understand "how we got to where we are." Certainly, post audits will cost money. They require interdisciplinary teams of social, natural, and physical scientists; engineers; and other experts, as appropriate. Heading a post audit should be a historian who can integrate the material into a coherent, readable narrative. Though the cost is not insignificant, the payoff of a post audit can be substantial. Post audits might challenge certain assumptions that have informed much of modern environmental policy, touching on everything from flood control to forest fire control, from the emphasis on disease detection to care for the elderly and infirm. Policy historians have much to offer in these assessments. Those in public history have a special obligation to promote their skills in evaluating not just policy, but the connected issue—the subsequent planning of programs and projects.

THE IMPORTANCE OF PUBLIC POLICY ANALYSIS TO ENVIRONMENTAL HISTORY—AND VICE VERSA

An understanding of the dynamics of public policy helps reveal much about human (and governmental) attitudes towards land, water, and habitat. It also quite clearly shows the way in which conflicting environmental sensibilities result in policies that are often ineffective and maybe even contradictory. Additionally, a study of environmental policy enlarges our appreciation of how process, organizational cultures, the unanticipated, and personalities decisively affect environmental decisions for good or ill.

Environmental policy analysis requires expanding the definition of environmental history to include all those historical developments that influence public

sector decisions regarding the environment. It involves familiarity with technological, legal, and political issues, with professional cultures and bureaucratic constraints; it requires oral history and archival skills, an understanding of agency organization and dynamics, and an acquaintance with the professions—and
professionals—which influence environmental policy. It almost invariably demands some fundamental grasp of engineering and ecological concepts and offers
many opportunities for interdisciplinary teamwork. Partly because many public
historians are commonly exposed to this unusual set of skills, they should make
good environmental policy historians.

   Like all public policy, environmental policy results from values and processes
that transcend any one issue. Indeed, the most useful lesson policy historians can
provide may be that careful and organized decision making is needed to discipline
the many forces besetting the policy process. The historian's ability to show these
intertwined forces at work over both short and long periods of time illuminates
policy development in ways that no other discipline can match. The challenges of
writing environmental policy history are substantial, but the reward in telling a
story that can say so much about the values and institutions that mold a nation's
destiny are great. There's much work to do.

NOTES

1. Examples of academic histories that exhibit this approach include Arthur F.
   McEvoy, *The Fisherman's Problem: Ecology and Law in the California Fisheries, 1850–1980* (New York: Cambridge University Press 1986), 156–184;
   and Thomas R. Dunlap, *DDT: Scientists, Citizens, and Public Policy* (Princeton, NJ: Princeton University Press, 1981), 17–75. The academic environmental historian who comes closest in approach to that of the government historian may be Donald Pisani. See his *To Reclaim a Divided West: Water, Law,
   and Public Policy, 1848–1902* (Albuquerque, University of New Mexico
   Press 1992), which reflects an extensive and sensitive reading of federal
   archival documents, and *Water, Land, and Law in the West: The Limits of
   Public Policy, 1850—1920* (Lawrence: University Press, of Kansas 1996).
   Both books should be compared with Donald Worster's, *Rivers of Empire:
   Water, Aridity, and the Growth of the American West* (New York: Pantheon
   Books 1985), a much lauded book that displays more passion than archival
   research.
2. For example, J. Samuel Walker, "Nuclear Power and the Environment: The
   Atomic Energy Commission and Thermal Pollution, 1965–1971," *Technology
   and Culture* 30, (October 1989): 964–992; J. Samuel Walker, "Reactor at the
   Fault: The Bodega Bay Nuclear Plant Controversy, 1958–1964—A Case
   Study in the Politics of Technology," *Pacific Historical Review* 59 (August
   1990): 323–348; George T. Mazuzan, "'Very Risky Business': A Power Reactor for New York City," *Technology and Culture* 27, (April 1986): 262–284;
   Martin Reuss, *Designing the Bayous: The Control of Water in the Atchafalaya*

Basin, 1800–1995 (Alexandria, VA, Office of History, U.S. Army Corps of Engineers 1998); Jeffrey K. Stine, *Mixing the Waters: Environment, Politics, and the Building of the Tennessee-Tombigbee Waterway* (Akron, OH, Akron University Press 1993); Terence R. Fehner and F. G. Gosling, "Coming in from the Cold War: Regulating U.S. Department of Energy Nuclear Facilities, 1942–1996," *Environmental History* 1, (April 1996): 5–33; Todd Shallat, ed., *Prospects: Land-use in the Snake River Birds of Prey Area, 1860–1987,* Social Sciences Monograph No. 1 (Boise, ID: Boise State University 1987). Walker and Mazuzan published their work while working as historians for the Nuclear Regulatory Commission; Fehner and Gosling are with the Department of Energy historical office. Reuss is a historian with the U.S. Army Corps of Engineers. Stine's work began as a contract with the Corps of Engineers, and Shallat's monograph was prepared for the Bureau of Land Management. David Billington, Donald Jackson, and Martin Melosi have prepared a National Park Service theme study on the the the development of large federal dams which includes environmental ramifications.

3. The best overview of the evolution of national environmental policy from colonial days to the present is Richard N.L. Andrews, *Managing the Environment, Managing Ourselves: A History of American Environmental Policy* (New Haven, CT: Yale University Press 1999). However, many of the policies discussed in the book have not been thoroughly studied using available archival and oral history sources. Until these analyses are done, important questions regarding the development of specific environmental policies will remain unanswered. Andrews is a professor of environmental sciences and engineering with a Ph.D. in environmental planning and policy.

4. Samuel P. Hays, *Beauty, Health, and Permanence: Environmental Politics in the United States, 1955–1985* (New York: Cambridge University Press 1987), 13–39; Reuss, *Designing the Bayous,* 294.

5. National Environmental Policy Act, Public Law 91–190, Section 101.

6. Marian R. Chertow and Daniel C. Esty, "Environmental Policy: The Next Generation," *Issues in Science and Technology* (Fall 1997): 74.

7. Ibid., 77–79; "Environmental Policy is the Public's to Make—and the Market's to Shape," (interview with Darius W. Gaskins, Jr., Resources for the Future Chairman of the Board), *Resources* 129 (Fall 1997): 18–19.

8. Garry D. Brewer and Peter deLeon, *The Foundations of Policy Analysis* (Homewood, IL: Dorsey Press 1983), 5, 18. A book that specifically discusses the evolution of federal environmental policy, principally in the Environmental Protection Agency, is Daniel J. Fiorino, *Making Environmental Policy* (Berkeley: University of California Press 1995). He frames the process in terms of models (institutional, systems, group process, or net-benefits model), an approach which offers a template that helps explain the policy process but never actually mirrors complicated reality.

9. Michael E. Kraft and Norman J. Vig, "Environmental Policy from the Seventies to the Nineties: Continuity and Change," in Norman J. Vig and Michael

E. Kraft, *Environmental Policy in the 1990s,* (Washington, D.C.: CQ Press 1990), 5; Fiorino, *Making Environmental Policy,* 61–99.

10. Telephone interview with Sarah Bransom, National Park Service, 10 July 1998.

11. U.S. Department of the Interior, National Park Service, *Summary: Draft Environmental Impact Statement for the Interagency Bison Management Plan for the State of Montana and Yellowstone National Park* (Denver, CO: National Park Service 1998), 2–3.

12. Bransom interview. For background on the bison problem, see Andrew C. Isenberg, "The Return of the Bison: Nostalgia, Profit, and Preservation," *Environmental History* 1, (April 1997): 179–196.

13. Tony Jewett, Executive Director, Montana Wildlife Federation to "Dear Friend," August 1998, with an enclosure from Mark Van Putten, President and CEO, National Wildlife Federation, 28 August 1998. Documents in author's possession.

14. Hays, *Beauty, Health, and Permanence,* x.

15. The importance of teamwork is also emphasized in the editor's introduction in David B. Mock, ed., *History and Public Policy* (Malabar, FL: Krieger 1991), 4.

16. See *www.epa.gov/OCEPAterms/.*

17. Patricia Nelson Limerick, "The Startling Ability of Culture to Bring Critical Inquiry to a Halt," *The Chronicle of Higher Education* (24 October 1997): 39–40.

18. See Tim Palmer, *Endangered Rivers and the Conservation Movement* (Berkeley: University of California Press 1986), 206–207.

19. Richard J. Tobin, "Revising the Clean Air Act: Legislative Failure and Administrative Success," in Norman J. Vig and Michael E. Kraft, *Environmental Policy in the 1980s: Reagan's New Agenda* (Washington, D.C: CQ Press 1984), 228; Walter A Rosenbaum, *Environmental Politics and Policy,* 2nd ed. (Washington, D.C: CQ Press 1991), 192–195.

20. Fiorino, *Making Environmental Policy,* 112.

21. Helen M. Ingram and Dean E. Mann, "Preserving the Clean Water Act: The Appearance of Environmental Victory," in Vig and Kraft, *Environmental Policy in the 1980s,* 254; Rosenbaum, *Environmental Politics,* 195–196.

22. Rosenbaum uses this phrase in *Environmental Politics,* 161.

23. For more on this controversy, see Reuss, *Designing the Bayous,* 297–299.

24. For more on market-based methods, see Fiorino, *Making Environmental Policy,* 177–188.

25. A comprehensive bibliographical essay that discusses the connections between technology and the environment is Jeffrey K. Stine and Joel A. Tarr, "At the Intersection of Histories: Technology and the Environment," *Technology and Culture* 39, (October, 1998): 601–640.

26. Lettie M. Wenner, "Judicial Oversight of Environmental Deregulation," in Vig and Kraft, *Environmental Policy in the 1980s,* 185.

27. On the Corps' early implementation of wetland regulations, see Jeffrey K. Stine, "Regulating Wetlands in the 1970s: U.S. Army Corps of Engineers and the Environmental Organizations," *Journal of Forest History* 27, (April 1983): 60–72.

28. Rutherford H. Platt, "Life after Lucas: The Supreme Court and the Down-trodden Coastal Developer," *Natural Hazards Observer* 17, (September 1992): 8–9.

29. For more on these issues, see Martin Reuss, *Reshaping National Water Politics: The Emergence of the Water Resources Development Act of 1986,* U.S. Army Corps of Engineers Institute for Water Resources Policy Study 91-PS-1 (October 1991), 136, 194.

30. Ibid., 181–182.

31. Gilbert F. White, "When May a Post-Audit Teach Lessons?" in Howard Rosen and Martin Reuss, eds., *The Flood Control Challenge: Past, Present, and Future* (Chicago: Public Works Historical Society 1988), 53–65.

URBAN AREAS, ENVIRONMENTAL DECISION MAKING, AND USES OF HISTORY TO INFORM PUBLIC CHOICES

Hugh Gorman

The notion of "sustainable development" has supplanted "economic growth" as the high-level goal guiding many policy choices. But what does it mean for an urban area to develop in a sustainable manner?[1] Sustainable for whom and for how long? Sustainable for what kind of lifestyle? And how does one translate the notion of "sustainability" into public policy? Like the notion of "progress," the notion of "sustainability" can suggest that there is an optimal direction in which to proceed. Political choices, though, still have to be made.

What sustainable development does imply is that important ecological relationships and significant human uses of the environment should be taken into account when public decisions are made. It also suggests that as many stakeholders as possible, including members of the general public, be represented in decision-making processes.[2] Hence, if policy debates framed in terms of sustainability are to be fruitful, especially in urban areas where many different uses of the environment interact, participants first must reach consensus on their objectives.

Historians, by linking environmental change to human choices, can provide the context that participants need to ask informed questions, identify trends, and make connections that might not be obvious. Urban environments have complex histories, and they continue to evolve as citizens, businesses, and governmental agencies make decisions associated with issues such as the siting and permitting of industrial facilities, recycling practices, waste disposal programs, resource- and land-use strategies, and transportation policies. History—and historians—can raise the quality of these decision-making processes by helping people make sense of the complex interaction between human choices and environmental change, especially at the local level.

USING HISTORY IN URBAN ENVIRONMENTAL DECISION MAKING

Everybody agrees that the air we breathe and the water we drink should be clean, but what other uses of the urban environment should be sustained? And what indicators should be used to monitor and manage changes in those areas?

What standards should be maintained and what should be done when those standards are not met? Civic leaders must address such questions if they seriously hope to manage the environmental quality of a metropolitan area.

A host of factors complicates any effort to address such questions. The lack of history is one such factor. Decision-making processes that ignore past environmental change are likely to be shortsighted in regard to future changes as well. Indeed, understanding how past policies and choices have influenced use of the shared environment is essential. In untangling the causes of environmental change and examining the consequences of human choices, historians not only help make sense of the issues at hand but can also help people reach consensus on what uses of the environment are important to sustain, as well as which indicators are important to monitor.

The Lack of History As a Barrier

In 1993, the Howard Heinz Endowment funded a pilot study to identify significant changes in the environmental quality of Pittsburgh and to highlight any specific points of concern. The advisory committee responsible for defining the general approach consisted of faculty from Carnegie Mellon University: a historian, Joel Tarr; an economist, Lester Lave; and two faculty members associated with the Engineering and Public Policy Program, Cliff Davison and Francis McMichael. The effort was meant to be more exploratory than exhaustive, with the advisory committee simply pointing the person executing the assessment in a wise direction. Therefore, the group spent most of its time discussing what to evaluate.[3]

The most obvious criteria to assess, especially in Pittsburgh, were changes in air and water quality. After all, Pittsburgh had long been associated with pollution-causing heavy industry. However, by the 1990s, with federal pollution control regulations in place and relatively little heavy industry operating in the metropolitan area, the quality of the region's air and water had improved significantly. Indeed, at some point in the 1980s, local television news programs had stopped reporting on air quality in their weather segments. Apparently, that indicator of environmental quality no longer seemed necessary to monitor, at least not at the level of television news. The concentration of pollutants in Pittsburgh's rivers and streams had also decreased over time. If nothing else, then, this study could document those changes and identify whether any pollution concerns remained.

At the same time, most members of the advisory group hoped to move beyond the focus on air and water quality. Tarr, for example, asked about progress made in local rails-to-trails efforts and changes in the accessibility of the city to bikers and pedestrians. He also asked about changes in public transportation and increases in the recreational uses of the Monongahela, Allegheny, and Ohio rivers. Would assessing changes in these areas be useful? Others focused on more technical indicators, such as the ratio of paved to unpaved surfaces, which some researchers have identified as a useful indicator of urban environmental quality.[4]

For the project to move beyond pollution concerns, the advisory group would have had to reach consensus on the specific list of environmental uses they saw as valuable. However, doing so clearly meant devoting far more time and effort than they had available. Even if they reached consensus on what to examine, no guarantee existed that enough data would be available to assess changes in these uses of the environment. Little, if any, previous research had been performed in many of the areas discussed. Indeed, moving beyond pollution concerns probably would have required devoting the entire project to simply defining what to assess.

Given the schedule, the advisory committee agreed that examining trends associated with recent pollution control efforts would represent a useful first step. The assessment—and the report—eventually focused on changes in (1) air quality; (2) waste water discharges; (3) drinking water quality; (4) surface water quality; (5) soil and groundwater contamination; and (6) recycling efforts.[5] Toward this end, the person who executed the project, Eugene Monaco, collected significant amounts of data from agencies and organizations and compiled that data in numerous plots and tables. Each section of the report described the federal regulations applicable to that area of pollution control and listed the criteria used by regulatory agencies to determine compliance. Graphs and plots then showed how the quality of Pittsburgh's air and water compared with standards set by regulatory agencies. For example, the plot of ambient sulfur dioxide over time showed that concentrations in one neighborhood, far above the federal standard in the mid-1970s, dropped rapidly over the next ten years, stabilizing at just below the federal standard by the mid-1980s.

In many ways, the final report served as a high-level compliance document. However, it generated no significant surprises nor suggested any compelling direction in which to invest more serious effort. In retrospect, this result is not surprising. After all, one would not necessarily expect data heavily monitored by other agencies and organizations to yield significant surprises. In the end, the plots and graphs supported the general conclusion that regulatory agencies were doing their job and that the flight of heavy industry had been good for Pittsburgh's air and water quality.

Indirectly, the effort also demonstrated how the absence of historical analysis can be a barrier to serious decision making. The decision by the advisory group not to go beyond pollution-related issues certainly reflected this barrier. In part, members of the advisory group made their decision to focus on pollution because no serious discussion—much less assessment—of other environmental uses was possible without some historical research first being performed. For example, the group had no good starting point for any assessment of the city's pedestrian-friendliness. How accessible was the city to pedestrians fifty years ago? What changes had since improved or degraded pedestrian access? Had there ever been any debates on how specific projects might affect pedestrians? One could also raise such questions for most of the other environmental uses not considered.

Finally, the project also highlighted the lack of any institutional mechanism for monitoring larger patterns of change even in the area of pollution control. Contacts at most agencies and organizations could not point to any reports assessing historical trends or long-term patterns within their area of responsibility. Individuals could answer almost any question asked, but their tacit knowledge could not be captured easily. Therefore, in most cases, Monaco was left with reams of paper—and numerous computer files—full of raw data. Surely, other high-level assessments must have been performed, but the results simply had not entered the institutional memory of the agencies visited.[6]

Integrating History into Environmental Decision Making

How might history be used to inform public choices about urban uses of the environment? Here, I point to three ways. The first involves establishing general patterns associated with an urban area's interactions with the physical environment, with recent histories of St. Louis and New Orleans being good examples. The second involves examining patterns associated with a specific issue, such as the redevelopment of brownfields or problems associated with urban sprawl. Third, one can examine the history of a specific environmental use, especially one directly linked to a current decision-making process.

Two recently published edited volumes, *Transforming New Orleans and Its Environs* (2000) and *Common Fields: An Environmental History of St. Louis* (1997), provide good models for how broad patterns associated with a city's environmental history might be examined.[7] Both volumes contain papers from conferences held on the environmental histories of the two metropolitan regions, with *Common Fields* being about interactions between St. Louis and its environment. A recent conference on the environmental history of Pittsburgh led to a similar edited volume.[8]

A fundamental premise of *Transforming New Orleans* is that one cannot separate the environmental history of New Orleans from either the history of its hinterlands or from ongoing efforts to control and manage the Mississippi River. Hence, the twelve chapters in the volume focus on changes and conflicts throughout the lower Mississippi Valley, a stretch of land that runs approximately from Baton Rouge to the delta. The first set of chapters cover human-induced changes before urbanization, which includes chapters on Native American modifications to the land and French efforts to adapt to the land. Next, the book turns to nineteenth-century efforts to place the Mississippi at the service of the city and, then, to twentieth-century efforts to displace hazards associated with those changes. The last set of chapters focuses on industrial pollution, its effect on human health and the river, and the responses of various actors to pollution-related concerns.

A major part of the story told by *Transforming New Orleans* involves the effort to isolate valuable land along the river from potential floods. Various chapters examine the role of steamboats in the transformation of the river, gradual developments in the use of levees, a debate over whether to preserve outlets to floodplains, and the increasing priority of protecting New Orleans at the expense of rural areas. Essentially, in using levees to cut the river off from its floodplain, engineers confined the river to a single channel. High flows then placed the land behind the weakest and lowest levees at risk. Indeed, throughout the nineteenth and twentieth centuries, the ability of a community to defend itself from floods seems to have been a reflection of both its economic strength and political power.

Channeling the river also had other effects, such as cutting off much of the delta from its needed supply of sediment and encouraging human development into riskier and riskier areas. By the end of the twentieth century, serious "natural" disasters caused by hurricanes and massive erosion, had become less and less natural. Instead, argues Todd Shallat, human actions had magnified dangers associated with natural events, transforming them into disasters.[9] Indirectly, the volume also raises questions about whether ongoing efforts to manage the river represent technological fixes that merely delay and transform problems or whether they encourage changes that gradually make human uses of the environment more compatible with natural ecosystems.

There are also several chapters on the use of the river as a sink for industrial pollution. One, for example, focuses on the consequences of poor land-use planning. Another has to do with the gradual realization that even the Mississippi had limits in its ability to absorb contaminants. A third considers the dramatic growth of the petrochemical industry in the 1960s and points to the importance of community-situated science in responding to health concerns from such industrial clusters. The final chapter examines the effect of industrial pollution and the channeling of the river on fish populations.

The general approach, though, is one that can be modified and fruitfully applied to other urban regions as well, providing decision makers in each city a better understanding of how urban and industrial development in that region have interacted with natural systems and competing human uses of the environment. But there is no set formula as to what patterns should be drawn out. Different metropolitan regions not only have different environmental features, they also have different interactions with that environment. The interactions, changes, and patterns that make sense to draw out vary from city to city. The content of *Transforming New Orleans,* for example, is quite different from *Common Fields.*

Historians can also contribute to policy decisions by examining general trends associated with a particular environmental concern. For example, in the 1990s, officials in many cities started asking about what to do with brownfields, abandoned industrial sites that often place a burden on the communities in which they are located. Past waste disposal practices and a general accumulation of leaks and spills had contaminated many of these sites, causing liability-weary developers to shy away from such properties. The possibility of acquiring a building loaded with asbestos or PCB-containing equipment also dampened interest in these sites. Historians contributed by examining the development of various industrial clusters and providing insight into the decisions that led to their creation and, in many cases, contamination. These histories served as a starting point for informed discussion, allowing stakeholders interested in these sites to raise more sophisticated questions than they would have otherwise. Comparing differences between various sites provided additional perspective.[10]

For example, when buried wastes were discovered on Neville Island, a heavily industrialized island-town in the Ohio River near Pittsburgh, people living on the island generally expressed less concern over possible contamination than people in neighboring communities.[11] In this case, residents tended to be frustrated with policies designed to protect their health because those same policies discouraged redevelopment. But in other cases, such as the infamous Love Canal incident, residents living near the affected site pushed officials to take even stronger action than was initially planned.[12] Given that both sites involved the same class of chemicals and the same poor disposal practices, what accounts for the difference in the reaction of residents? Histories of the two sites provide the necessary context.

Some of the difference can be explained in terms of potential exposure. On Neville Island, the most heavily contaminated site lies at the downstream end of the island. Hence, any release of contaminates from the site flows into the river and away from the island and toward the water intake plants of other communities. At Love Canal, the chemicals were leaching into the basements of homes immediately adjacent to the site. Other differences in perception can be explained in terms of familiarity. In the 1950s, residents of Neville Island watched as trucks carried wastes from one end of the island to the other. A few residents even drove some of those trucks. In addition, many residents of Neville Island had worked in the industrial facilities that generated those wastes, possibly making them seem less dangerous. At the Love Canal site, on the other hand, wastes had been buried before any homes were constructed in the area.

Economic interests also accounted for some of the differences in perception. Taxes from industrial facilities on Neville Island contributed directly to the well-being of residents. Undoubtedly, the desire to protect this tax base encouraged residents to be less vocal in expressing whatever concerns they had. At Love Canal, the community surrounding the waste site was part of a larger political entity — Niagara Falls — and residents had less concern about their effect on the larger tax base. Would residents of Neville Township have been more vocal if their island had been part of Pittsburgh rather than a separate political entity? In addition, residents of Neville Island desired to protect the market value of their real estate. There was little hope of anybody purchasing their homes as long as newpapers continued to smear the island with the brush of toxic contamination. At Love Canal, on the other hand, governmental agencies proved willing to purchase homes near the waste site, encouraging residents with concerns to be as vocal as possible.

Such studies can inform a variety of discussions, including those focused on issues of environmental justice, the assignment of Superfund-related liability, and the interests of stakeholders.[13] However, researchers can also help participants in urban environmental decision-making processes by examining the specific environmental conflict or decision being considered. As Richard Neustadt and Ernest May point out in *Thinking in Time: Uses of History for Decision Makers*, most people find that placing a decision in the flow of time helps them to appreciate the issue more fully. Among other things, they suggest using basic devices such as combining timelines with the "who," "what," 'when," and "where" questions that journalists ask.[14]

Having a basic narrative available not only allows participants in the decision-making process come up to speed fairly quickly, but may also help reveal points on which people disagree. An example of this can be seen in the decision-making processes associated with watersheds designated by the U.S.-Canadian International Joint Commission (IJC) as "areas of concern."[15] Metropolitan regions home to at least one area of concern include Buffalo, Chicago, Cleveland, Detroit, and Duluth.

After identifying the impaired watersheds, the IJC encouraged cities and towns in each watershed to prepare an action plan for restoring and maintaining the waterway's beneficial uses. To develop these plans, the IJC—through the U.S. EPA and state environmental agencies—facilitated the creation of public advisory councils, one council for each watershed. Each council consists of various stakeholders from the watershed, such as shore owners, business owners, environmental activists, health officials, and representatives of local governments. To guide their discussion and planning, councils are supposed to review a list of fourteen "beneficial uses" established by the IJC.

Specifically, the 1987 protocol requires each council to consider any "change in the chemical, physical, or biological integrity of the Great Lakes System sufficient to cause any of the following:[16]

1. restrictions on fish and wildlife consumption;
2. tainting of fish and wildlife flavor;
3. degradation of fish or wildlife populations;
4. fish tumors or other deformities;
5. bird or animal deformities or reproduction problems;
6. degradation of benthos;
7. restrictions on dredging activities;
8. eutrophication or undesirable algae;
9. restrictions on drinking water consumption or taste and odor problems;
10. beach closings;
11. degradation of aesthetics;
12. added costs to agriculture or industry;
13. degradation of phytoplankton and zooplankton populations; and
14. loss of fish and wildlife habitat."

There are no precise thresholds associated with these indicators of degradation. Rather, they represent degraded uses of the watershed the IJC has identified as worth sustaining. Many of the indicators are coupled to one other, and untangling the connections and tradeoffs for a specific watershed requires some discussion and debate. Indeed, reviewing this collection of "beneficial uses" forces a group to think about isolated pieces of data in relation to a larger system.[17] In addition, given that the focus is on monitoring how the beneficial uses identified by the IJC change over time, past changes are also important to understand. Such councils also represent a forum in which environment-centered history is valuable in informing decision making.

For example, the members of one advisory council faced the question of why industrial pollution had caused a certain type of fish—sauger—to disappear from a local lake. In the 1970s, a graduate student in biology discovered that sauger sampled from Torch Lake near Houghton, Michigan, had liver tumors, giving rise to a concern that some toxic substance had contaminated the lake. In a subsequent sample, all the sauger had liver tumors. This finding brought the site to the attention of both the U.S. EPA and the IJC. In the 1980s, the lake was designated as both a Superfund site and an "area of concern." Soon after, though, the sauger disappeared from the lake, and no cause for the tumors was ever found.[18]

A decade later, many residents were still unsure of how serious the problem was or whether a problem existed at all. Indeed, the tension that existed in the community over the issue initially prevented the formation of a public advisory council, with the main divide being between those interested in facilitating development along the lake and those desiring to control development. Hence, in 1997, when the public advisory council for this area of concern was finally created, that tension remained. To facilitate discussion at meetings of the advisory council, students in an environmental decision-making class from Michigan Technological University volunteered to make brief presentations on each of the fourteen "beneficial uses" that the advisory council was supposed to consider. Although none of the students were trained in historical research—disciplines represented were forestry, microbiology, environmental engineering, and environmental policy—they ended up spending much of their time learning the local history of each "beneficial use."

That history suggested a possible explanation for the tumors and the disappearance of the sauger from the waterway. For roughly a century, the area had been a center of copper mining. Until World War I, companies crushed the rock they mined into sand-sized pieces so as to free small pieces of elemental copper embedded in the rock. Companies deposited their waste sand along the shores of local waterways, including Torch Lake. During World War I, these companies began dredging the sand back up to remove any copper that remained behind. To extract the residual copper, mills along Torch Lake first ground the tailings into even finer particles. Then, after removing the copper by leaching or flotation, they discharged the waste particles back into the lake. Those particles—a slurry by this point—turned the water cloudy brown.[19]

In this period, the sauger population increased because young sauger flourish in turbid water. After the copper mills ceased operations in the 1960s, the lake cleared. Young sauger then lost their ecological advantage to other species, and the sauger population that remained ceased to renew itself. Indeed, the sauger sampled in the 1970s were all old, and one assumes, more susceptible to diseases and viruses. Although the mining wastes had made the bottom of the lake sterile, unable to support the benthic organisms found in the sediment of healthy lakes, those wastes probably did not cause the tumors.

Examining the history of the fourteen beneficial uses of the watershed also proved useful in other ways as well. Among other things, discussing the history of each beneficial use provided the two groups with some common ground for dialogue. Although the discussions did not overcome the tensions that existed, they did help members—and, indirectly, the community—to reach consensus on issues associated with the site.[20]

SPRAWL AND BEYOND

Decision-making processes associated with most urban environmental concerns do not fit neatly into boxes that correspond perfectly with political boundaries. Environmental consequences inevitably cross political boundaries. The urban demand for water, efforts to protect watersheds supplying that water, efforts to preserve greenfields by making better use of brownfields, and debates over how to expand a city's infrastructure without destroying an area's character all highlight the need to treat cities and their suburbs as a single interconnected entity. Furthermore, each of these concerns is intimately connected with a problem faced by many cities in the United States: urban sprawl. These and other topics related to urban sprawl represent an important focus of inquiry for historians.

It is not that these topics represent a new area of historical research. Studies focusing on changes in transportation have certainly provided numerous insights into the interactions between policies, public choices, and uses of the land. Historians have long connected changes in transportation systems—from canals and railroads to electric traction systems and highways—to new patterns of urban development.[21] Historian Kenneth Jackson, for example, shows how federal policies encouraging new construction over the rehabilitation of older housing stock contributed to the decline of the central city.[22] Other historians, examining the development of the interstate highway system, point to an institutional culture that discouraged public participation in decision making, resulting in a highway system that did not always serve urban populations well.[23] Still others, such as Samuel Hays, have examined changes in how people value the environment and the consequences of those new values.[24]

Historians studying urban sanitation have also focused on debates over uses of the shared environment. And they have demonstrated that, long before the language of sustainable development, civic leaders had to identify uses of the environment they wished to sustain and then formulate policies to meet those objectives. Were urban rivers to be maintained only as navigation channels and sewers? Or should they also be maintained as sources of drinking water, places of recreation, and habitat for fish? The contours of the associated debates—as well as the consequences of choices made—are well studied.[25] Similarly, much work has been done on the importance of securing and protecting water supplies, with the story of water in New York, Chicago, and Los Angeles being particularly well researched.[26]

Much of this research has also been transformed into documentaries and popular history, making it more accessible to a wider audience. For example, Marc Reisner's popular examination of western water policy—*Cadillac Desert,* which

PBS eventually transformed into a four-part video series—effectively links urban growth to the availability of water. Reisner's book opens with a narrative of Los Angeles's early grab for water. Only by seeking out and transporting water from Owens Valley—an area over two hundred miles away—did boosters free Los Angeles from the shackles of drought and allow the city to grow, grow, and grow. In focusing on a constraint to growth—the lack of water—rather than on the reasons for development, Reisner encouraged people to think in terms sustainable development.[27]

But one cannot explain urban development—even in semi-arid areas—in terms of a single resource, however critical that resource might be. Furthermore, urban growth typically does not depend on a two hundred-mile leap across a desert. Most cities sprawl rather than leap, and managing that sprawl is at the heart of many current policy debates. Indeed, policy debates associated with sprawl bring to the surface complex interactions between environmental quality and choices associated with transportation, water supplies, and sanitation. Historians can contribute to these debates by providing a better framework for asking questions about a particular city's pattern of development.

Urban sprawl generally refers to low-density development on the fringes of populated areas. Such development often gives rise to an automobile-dominated landscape that slights other modes of transportation. The needs of pedestrians and cyclists, for example, generally get short shrift. In addition, residential areas, malls, and office parks tend to be constructed along a few high-traffic corridors, overwhelming small towns along those corridors. Rapid development with little attention to aesthetics also results in long stretches of road being lined with poorly landscaped gasoline stations, fast food franchises, and strip malls. In many cases, this development overwhelms the available infrastructure—from sewers and sanitation facilities to water pipes and traffic control devices—and efforts to develop the necessary infrastructure gives rise to more sophisticated forms of local governance. Eventually, people seeking out the relative isolation and open land that initially proved so attractive move on, and another the cycle of development emerges elsewhere.[28]

The question of how to prevent urban sprawl from compromising uses of the environment that people value is a major concern. However, generalizing about the dynamics of sprawl is difficult. The specifics depend on myriad human choices and actions, as well as on climate and geography. Chicago is not New York and New York is not Los Angeles, and none of these metropolitan areas is like Boston, San Francisco, or Miami. Development patterns for urban areas outside the United States vary even more widely. Even in the same metropolitan area, development in one direction can occur differently from development in another. The location of geological features such as aquifers, wetlands, hills, and lakes affects the choices people make, as do government-enforced regulations and historical settlement patterns. For example, local health codes can discourage development into areas where soil conditions prevent the practical use of septic systems. Local conditions—and local histories—matter.[29]

Sprawl into critical watersheds is an especially important issue. In all cases, complications abound. While civic leaders in urban areas can certainly learn from the experience of other cities, they also must also account for issues unique to their area. For example, in places such as New York and San Antonio, discussions about controlling development into their watersheds have already come to the fore. To use the experience of these metropolitan areas in informing the debates of another city, one must also understand the environmental history of that other city.

Not surpisingly, the New York and San Antonio cases are quite different. In San Antonio, everybody gets their water, directly or indirectly, from the same aquifer. When the region north of the city goes long periods without much rain, the water level in that aquifer drops as San Antonio and the surrounding communities continue to pump water. Newspapers routinely report the height of the water in the aquifer, and this number has meaning because certain events happen as the level falls. Various natural springs stop flowing at specific levels, and the city imposes mandatory conservation measures that get increasingly severe as the water level continues to fall. Maintaining a certain level of water in the aquifer is also important because several springs feed habitats that support species federally listed as being endangered. Indeed, when one set of springs ceased to flow in the mid-1950s, a certain species of fish—fountain darters—disappeared from that particular ecosystem.[30]

Efforts to protect the Edwards Aquifer have also focused attention on development in the aquifer's catchment and recharge zones, which together are roughly the area of New Jersey. In this area, surface streams fed by precipitation flow into the fissures and sinkholes of a unique limestone formation. This porous formation dips underground as it extends to the south and east, where it becomes the aquifer that supplies San Antonio and the surrounding area. Given the importance of the catchment and recharge zone, civic leaders in the San Antonio region cannot help but to be concerned about residential and industrial development in the area. With growth comes not only greater demand for water but also a degradation of the recharge and catchment zones.

New York, on the other hand, has been discouraging development in its watershed for years. The city laid the foundation for its water collection system in the 1840s by damming the Croton River and creating a reservoir thirty miles north of the city.[31] Over the next century, officials steadily expanded the system, eventually reaching out to the Catskills and the headwaters of the Delaware River. Currently, the city maintains eighteen reservoirs in three water collection basins, complete with interconnections to take advantage of excess water in any one basin. Gravity carries the water to New York via hundreds of miles of aqueducts and into Manhattan through two aging tunnels.[32]

But the supply of clean water available to New York is not infinite. As towns in the watershed have grown, so has the amount of sewage and contaminated runoff entering the water that eventually reaches New York. Indeed, when the quality of water reaching New York fell below standards set by the U.S. EPA, authorities in New York had two alternatives. Either they could treat the 1.4 billion gallons of water collected each day, which EPA regulations required, or take immediate steps to protect the watershed. According to Robert Kennedy, Jr., prosecuting attorney for the environmental group Riverkeepers, choosing the first option would have been disastrous. Not only would the cost of treatment be astronomical but the commitment to treatment would have doomed the Catskills to steady development, something the group he represented did not wish to see.[33]

In both cities, significant policy decisions had to be made. In San Antonio, the decision was to manage the aquifer by allocating water rights, a strategy not typically used for groundwater. In the New York case, the main stakeholders involved—New York City, the watershed communities, the U.S. EPA, and New York State—signed an agreement that committed New York City and the upstate communities to work together in limiting development in the watershed.[34] Urban areas that have not faced similar questions already, eventually will. Understanding how use of watersheds have evolved over time and how policies have influenced that evolution is an important component of any discussion leading to efforts to protect watersheds from urban sprawl.

Beyond the City

Policy choices associated with improving the quality of urban life do not necessarily place less stress on the shared environment. One can certainly imagine a prosperous city becoming more comfortable for business travelers, tourists, and most residents but doing so in a manner that is also energy intensive, capable of generating sizable waste streams, and highly dependent on inexpensive agricultural, timber, and mineral products. In such cases, distant ecosystems often bear much of the associated environmental stress.

Indeed, markets carry the consequences of urban choices worldwide. Therefore, to capture the full interaction between cities and ecosystems, one must also examine the effect of urban activity on places well beyond metropolitan boundaries. And as markets become more complex, those effects become increasingly fragmented and difficult to comprehend. Historians can provide the context necessary to examine interactions as this level as well.

In *Nature's Metropolis: Chicago and the Great West,* historian William Cronon explicitly connects cities to distant ecosystems.[35] Specifically, he examines the ecological changes that took place in the Midwest as nineteenth-century entrepreneurs turned to the land for grain, lumber, and meat in quantities sufficient to meet the demands of a rapidly expanding urban population. When viewed from this perspective, Chicago emerges not as an isolated metropolitan district on the edge of a prairie but as an entity that connected urban populations to the forests of Michigan, the farms of Iowa, and the ranches of the high plains.

Starting with Chicago's development in the first half of the nineteenth century, Cronon allows readers to watch as entrepreneurs and innovators add layer upon layer of infrastructure—what he calls "second nature"—over the land they came to occupy. By the 1850s, railroads and telegraphs connected Chicago to urban areas on the East Coast. Railroad lines, radiating outward from the city, snaked into the high plains and northern woods and carried an endless stream of grain and meat and wood to and through Chicago. Cattle that nibbled on grass in Colorado one week ended up as beef in New York the next. Trees that had stood for centuries in northern Michigan ended their days as houses and fences in Illinois, Indiana, and Iowa. The resources of the Midwest were transformed into commodities that could be transported and sold with a minimum of fuss.

In addition to railroads, warehouses, and mills, Cronon includes Chicago's futures market as part of second nature. This institution, in coordinating the flow of commodities, placed one more layer of abstraction between human choices and their ecological consequences. Indeed, Cronon emphasizes that markets, more than any other aspect of second nature, link cities to the ecosystems that support them. From this perspective, one cannot describe the ecology of either a city or its hinterlands without considering market interactions. All urban activity—every banking transaction, grocery purchase, and work of construction—comes to be seen part of a larger ecology in which choices made in one place affects ecosystems in another. In making this connection, Cronon encourages us to think more critically about the consequences of urban activity on areas far from the buildings and streets that give cities their definition.

Asking questions about the effect of urban lifestyles on distant ecosystems is more important than ever. Global markets, inexpensive fossil fuels, and complex technology now carry urban demands throughout the world. A decrease in the popularity of coffee in New York City affects land use not in the Hudson River Valley or rural Connecticut but in Costa Rica and Columbia. An increase in the consumption of beef by the residents of Tokyo or Taipei has as much of an effect on the ecology of Australia and New Zealand as it does Japan or Taiwan.

As connections between urban populations and the ecosystems on which they depend becomes even more distant and fragmented, environment-centered histories will prove valuable in making those connections less abstract. Some geographers encourage individuals to think of their lifestyle choices in terms of an "ecological footprint," which represents the amount of land and resources required to support one's lifestyle. According to Mathis Wackernagel and William Rees, the average sustainable ecological footprint in a world with five billion people is about 2.3 hectares. They assert, however, that citizens of industrialized nations have footprints larger than this, and they emphasize the importance of lowering the size of each society's collective ecological footprint to a sustainable level.[36] If such notions are to be discussed seriously, environment-centered histories that examine the relationship between urban areas and distant ecosystems will prove valuable.

CONCLUSION

At metropolitan and regional levels, new mechanisms to guide public choices affecting urban uses of the shared environment are evolving, with the salient features being (1) the organization of decision-making processes around ecosystems and issues of sustainability; (2) the use of indicators linked to measures of environmental quality worth sustaining; and (3) more public involvement in these decision-making processes. As these decision-making mechanisms evolve, the challenge to historians will be to help participants understand the connection between past environmental changes and human choices and activities.

Given that numerous different choices can affect the same physical environment, managing use of that environment becomes difficult without some understanding of how all the choices interact. For example, numerous policies, social trends, and market decisions interact in complex ways to produce the pattern of development we recognize as sprawl. An environment-centered approach to urban history can help as elected officials, policy analysts, activists, and other decision-makers attempt to make sense of these complex changes. Environment-centered history can also raise the quality of local decision making by helping participants make connections and identify trends that might not be obvious. It can also provide the context that other participants need to understand these connections and trends, ultimately allowing a broader segment of the public to ask informed questions and to participate more fully into the decision-making processes.[37]

To be useful in local decision-making processes, though, such history must be local. Many issues are dependent on the specifics of place. Patterns of land and resource use that apply to cities in the industrial Northeast do not necessarily apply to cities in the arid Southwest or the Pacific Northwest. What are the changing patterns of land and resource use in Phoenix and how do they differ from those in Seattle or Boston? In which ways are they the same? In which ways do they differ? Issues related to waste disposal, habitat protection, siting, recreation, and other uses of the environment also vary from place to place.

In the end, of course, environmental histories do not necessarily show that one policy choice is better than another.[38] However, in making connections, identifying trends, and providing context, historians raise the quality of decision making. And in cases where there is no way to test whether a decision is good or bad, such as when diverse groups value the same environment in different ways, one can only judge the quality of a decision by the decision-making process.

NOTES

1. See Molly O'Meara, "Exploring a New Vision for Cities" in Linda Starke, ed., *State of the World 1999: A Worldwatch Institute Report on Progress Toward a Sustainable* (New York: W. W. Norton, 1999), 132–150.
2. Michael E. Kraft, "Making Decisions About Environmental Quality" in Ken Sexton, Alfred A. Marcus, K. William Easter, and Timothy D. Burkhardt, eds., *Better Environmental Decisions: Strategies for Governments, Businesses, and Communities* (Washington, D.C.: Island Press, 1999), 15–35.
3. I served as Joel Tarr's research assistant in this study while in Carnegie Mellon University's Ph.D. program in History and Policy.
4. Chester L. Arnold, Jr. and James C. Gibbons, "Impervious Surface Coverage:

The Emergence of a Key Environmental Indicator," *Journal of the American Planning Association,* 62 (Spring 1996): 243.

5. Eugene V. Monaco, "Pittsburgh's Environmental Profile," prepared for the Howard Heinz Endowment, 1994.

6. Historical studies of earlier pollution control efforts in Pittsburgh have been made, such as Joel A. Tarr and Bill C. Lamperes, "Changing Fuel-Use Behavior and Energy Transitions: The Pittsburgh Smoke-Control Movement: A Case Study in Historical Analogy," *Journal of Social History* 14 (Summer 1981): 561–588; Joel A. Tarr, "The Pittsburgh Survey as an Environmental Statement" in Joel A. Tarr, *The Search for the Ultimate Sink* (Akron, OH: The University of Akron Press, 1996), 77–102.

7. Craig E. Colten, ed., *Transforming New Orleans and Its Environs: Centuries of Change* (Pittsburgh: University of Pittsburgh Press, 2001); Andrew Hurley, ed., *Common Fields: An Environmental History of St. Louis,* (Missouri Historical Society Press, 1997).

8. The Environmental History of Pittsburgh Conference, Historical Society of Western Pennsylvania (September 16 and 17, 2000). Joel A. Tarr, ed., *Devastation and Renewal: An Environmental History of Pittsburgh and Its Region,* (Pittsburgh: University of Pittsburgh Press, 2003).

9. Todd Shallat, "In the Wake of Hurricane Betsy" in *Transforming New Orleans,* 121–137.

10. Craig E. Colten, *Industrial Wastes in the Calumet Area: An Historical Geography, 1869–1970* (Champain, IL: 1985); Andrew Hurley, "Fiasco at Wagner Electric: Environmental Justice and Urban Geography in St. Louis," *Environmental History* 2 (1997): 460–481; and Eileen Maura McGurty, "The Construction of Environmental Justice: Warren County, North Carolina" (Ph.D. Dissertation: University of Illinois at Urbana-Champaign, 1995).

11. Hugh Gorman, "Manufacturing Brownfields: The Case of Neville Township, Pennsylvania, 1899–1989," *Technology and Culture* 38 (July 1997): 539–574.

12. Allan Mazur, *A Hazardous Inquiry: The Rashomon Effect at Love Canal.* (Cambridge, MA: Harvard University Press, 1998).

13. John R. Finnegan, Jr. and Ken Sexton, "Community-Based Environmental Decisions: Analyzing Power and Leadership" in Sexton, Marcus, Easter, and Burkhardt, eds., *Better Environmental Decisions,* 331–351.

14. Richard E. Neustadt and Ernest R. May, *Thinking in Time: The Uses of History for Decision Makers* (New York: Macmillan, 1986), 232–246.

15. The IJC was originally created to facilitate the Boundary Waters Treaty of 1909. In 1987, the governments of Canada and the United States officially recognized these forty-three watersheds as "areas of concern" having the potential to adversely affect the integrity of the larger Great Lakes aquatic ecosystem. Each area of concern is a watershed that crosses municipal boundaries and was impaired by some form of industrial pollution. For a map showing the location of areas of concerns, see the Environment Canada website http://www.cciw.ca/glimr/raps/.

16. International Joint Commission, United States and Canada, *Great Lakes Water Quality Agreement of 1978, as revised by 1987 Protocol* (IJC: 1987).
17. For the guiding philosophy behind this process, see: Great Lakes Water Quality Board of the International Joint Commission, et al, *If You Don't Measure It, You Won't Manage It,* based on a Public Meeting on Oct. 22, 1997 in Thunder Bay, Ontario.
18. Torch Lake is in the Upper Peninsula of Michigan and is part of the Torch Lake Area of Concern and the Torch Lake Superfund Site. Though not an urban area by today's standards, the region supported a population of about 70,000 people when copper mining was at its peak. The depository for the Superfund site is Portage Library, Houghton, Michigan.
19. A summary of their review can be found at http://www.ss.mtu.edu/EP/Torchlake/.
20. The website maintained the EPA for the "Torch Lake" site is http://www.epa.gov/glnpo/aoc/trchlke/.
21. Sam Bass Warner, *Streetcar Suburbs: The Process of Growth in Boston, 1870–1900* (Cambridge, MA: Harvard University Press, 1962). Also see Mark Foster, *From Streetcar to Superhighway: American City Planners and Urban Transportation, 1900–1940* (Philadelphia: Temple University Press, 1981).
22. Kenneth T. Jackson, *Crabgrass Frontier: The Suburbanization of the United States* (New York: Oxford University Press, 1985).
23. Mark H Rose and Bruce E. Seely, "Getting the Interstate System Built: Road Engineers and the Implementation of Policy, 1955–1985" *Journal of Policy History* 2 (1990), 23–55. For a synthesis of the many trends shaping urban land-use patterns, see Eric H. Monkkonen, *America Becomes Urban: The Development of Cities & Towns, 1780–1980* (Berkeley: University of California Press, 1988).
24. Samuel P. Hays, *Beauty, Health, and Permanence: Environmental Politics in the United States, 1955–1985* (New York: Cambridge University Press, 1987).
25. See Joel A. Tarr, *The Search for the Ultimate Sink* (Akron, OH: The University of Akron Press, 1996), 77–102; Martin V. Melosi, *Garbage in the Cities: Refuse, Reform, and the Environment* (Chicago: Dorsey Press, 1981); Martin V. Melosi, *The Sanitary City: Urban Infrastructure in America from Colonial Times to the Present* (Baltimore: Johns Hopkins University Press, 2001).
26. See Melosi, *The Sanitary City, 117–148* for a brief history of municipal water supplies and the associated references.
27. Marc Reisner, *Cadillac Desert: The American West and Its Disappearing Water* (New York: Penguin Books, 1987); Video, KTEH/San Jose and Trans Pacific Television, *Cadillac Desert: Mulholland's Dream,* distributed by PBS Video, 1997. Also see William L. Kahrl, *Water and Power: The Conflict over Los Angeles' Water Supply in the Owens Valley* (Berkeley: University of California Press, 1982).

28. For an example of the patterns associated with California, see Stephanie S. Pincetl, *Transforming California: A Political History of Land Use and Development* (Baltimore: Johns Hopkins University Press, 1999).

29. For a series of short articles on sprawl in different metropolitan areas of the United States, including Phoenix, Minneapolis-St. Paul, Seattle, and Sacramento, see *The Economist* 352 no. 128 (July 17, 1999) through 352 no. 133 (August 21, 1999).

30. Todd H. Votteler, "The Little Fish That Roared: The Endangered Species Act, State Groundwater Law, and Private Property Rights Collide over the Texas Edwards Aquifer," *Environmental Law* 28 (1998): 845. For a web site that summarizes the issues well, see http://www.edwardsaquifer.net/.

31. Stuart Galishoff, "Triumph and Failure: The American Response to the Urban Water Supply Problem, 1860–1923" in Martin V. Melosi, ed., *Pollution and Reform in American Cities,* (Austin: University of Texas Press, 1980), pp. 35–57.

32. For maps of the NYC water system and a chronology of its development, see http://www.ci.nyc.ny.us/html/dep/html/watersup.html.

33. Arthur Ashendorff, et al, "Watershed Protection for New York City's Supply," *Journal of the American Water Works Association* 89 (March 1997): 75–88. Comments of Robert Kennedy, Jr. are from a lecture given at Michigan Technological University in 1998.

34. A copy of the "Final Rules And Regulations For The Protection From Contamination, Degradation And Pollution Of The New York City Water Supply And Its Sources," can be found at http://www.ci.nyc.ny.us/html/dep/html/agreement.html.

35. William Cronon, *Nature's Metropolis: Chicago and the Great West* (New York: W.W. Norton, 1991).

36. Mathis Wackernagel and William Rees, *Our Ecological Footprint: Reducing Human Impact on the Earth* (Gabriola Island, BC: New Society Publishers, 1996).

37. Peter N. Stearns, "History and Policy Analysis," *Public Historian* 4 (1982): 5–29.

38. For examples of both effective and ineffective uses of history in decision making, see Otis L. Graham, *Losing Time: The Industrial Policy Debate* (Cambridge, MA: Harvard University Press, 1992); and Richard E. Neustadt and Ernest R. May, *Thinking in Time: The Uses of History for Decision Makers* (New York: Macmillan, 1986).

PART VI

ENVIRONMENT AT THE GRASS ROOTS

ENVIRONMENTAL JUSTICE: POLICY CHALLENGES AND PUBLIC HISTORY

Christopher H. Foreman, Jr. and
Martin V. Melosi

Since World War II progressive political advocacy in the United States has generated at least three great sacred causes for domestic policy: the crusade for civil rights, protection of the physical environment, and gender equality. The first two—relevant to the focus of this chapter—were once quite distinct. They now overlap in ways few would have guessed a generation ago.[1] The blend has yielded a challenging and contentious hybrid, known most often today as "environmental justice." Related terms include "environmental equity" and the more incendiary "environmental racism."

Definitions vary. Taken in reverse order, "environmental racism" is regarded as an extension of traditional racism, can be intentional or unintentional, and suggests discrimination in policy making, enforcement of laws, and in targeting certain communities for polluting industries and waste disposal sites. "Environmental equity" incorporates the idea of equal treatment and protection for all people under statutes, regulations, and practices without variation in the impacts relative to the majority population. "Environmental justice," broader in scope, emphasizes the *right* to safe and healthy living and working spaces for all people, and defines "environment" to include social, political, economic, and physical features. The last term is preferred among advocates and has been picked up by analysts, policy makers, and the press.[2]

All of these terms elude precise definition. That is a primary source of the policy challenge spawned by the rise of these rubrics within the national environmental discourse. Environmental justice proponent Bunyan Bryant concedes that "the literature is conspicuously without definitions."[3] Nevertheless, all three terms propel the same general line of criticism: that minority and low-income communities have been disproportionately victimized by, and inadequately represented within, our regime of environmental policy.

Environmental justice claims vary widely because they are anchored in a diverse tapestry of local grievances, empirical studies, and improvisational advocacy spawned by a loosely knit national coalition. Many commentators and analysts focus on facility siting, in large measure because such activity is both visible to ordinary citizens (and thus relatively easy to mobilize around) and amenable to quantitative assessment (albeit with many pitfalls). For example, one much-cited (and disputed) study argues that federal hazardous waste policy is racially biased, taking longer to clean up minority areas and imposing generally lower dollar penalties in such areas than elsewhere for violations of environmental rules.[4] A growing case study literature highlights grassroots activities undertaken in defense of local environments. These case studies are often cited as evidence of the validity of advocacy claims.[5] Recent comprehensive analyses verify significant racial disparity in environmental hazards while suggesting that equitable policy response cannot be race driven.[6]

The emergence of, and subsequent debate over, environmental justice claims and aspirations has produced a highly polemical literature pitting advocates against skeptics or outright critics. In this atmosphere it has been difficult to adequately assess the place of the environmental justice movement in modern environmentalism, examine somewhat dispassionately its claims of environmental racism as a legitimate critique of past and present practices, and weigh the value of its goals.

This chapter attempts to place the environmental justice movement and its major claims and objectives in perspective and to suggest how historical methods and research might be employed-or have been employed-to help move the debate away from its polemical quagmire. Ten policy questions are discussed in order to focus most directly on key claims and objectives. In so doing, we might be able to clarify some policy options that will help to integrate issues of race and class into decision making over future environmental policy. However, it should be noted from the outset that while historical methodology and research can be useful in understanding the origins, evolution, and goals of the environmental justice movement, historians are not in the business of confirming or refuting the movement's political objectives. However, historical analysis can be a powerful tool in helping to understand public policy. By taking a decidedly historical approach in addressing the policy issues underlying environmental justice, public historians can contribute to a political discourse in which historical analysis has been largely excluded.

THE EMERGENCE OF THE ENVIRONMENTAL JUSTICE MOVEMENT

The appearance of the environmental justice issue in the 1980s stimulated intense debate over the degree to which race and class should be central concerns of modern environmentalism.[7] Leaders in the environmental justice movement charged that mainstream environmental organizations and, in turn, environmental policy have demonstrated a greater concern for preserving wilderness and animal habitats than addressing health hazards of humans, especially those living in cities. Some advocates of environmental justice have gone so far as to disassociate their movement from American environmentalism altogether, identifying instead with a social justice heritage as embedded in civil rights activities of the 1950s and 1960s.[8]

Some observers look back to the 1970s for the start of the environmental justice movement, when black residents of Northwood Manor subdivision in Houston filed the first class action lawsuit challenging the siting of a waste facility in their neighborhood as a violation of civil rights, resulting in *Bean v. Southwestern Waste Management Corp.* (1979).[9] But the event that succeeded in "racializing the antitoxics agenda" was the Warren County, North Carolina protest in 1982.[10]

Rev. Benjamin F. Chavis, Jr. is credited with coining the term "environmental racism" while serving as executive director of the United Church of Christ's Commission for Racial Justice (CRJ).[11] He became interested in the connection between race and pollution in 1982 when residents of Warren County, North Carolina—predominantly African American—asked the CRJ for help in resisting the siting of a PCB (polychlorinated biphenyl) dump in their community. The protest proved unsuccessful, resulting in the arrest of more than 500 people, including Chavis. But the Warren County battle galvanized environmental justice advocates into a "movement," especially because the strategy of resisting the construction of the landfill shifted from a more passive protest to "disruptive collective action." The event transcended typical NIMBY (Not in My Backyard) advocacy in the sense that protesters would not have been satisfied merely with relocation of the dump to another community. Moreover, as one historian noted, the protest also helped "to blur the distinction between environmentalism and social justice causes."[12]

In October, 1991, a multiracial group of more than 600 met in Washington, D.C. for the first National People of Color Environmental Leadership Summit. In its *Principles of Environmental Justice,* conference participants asserted the hope "to begin to build a national and international movement of all peoples of color to fight the destruction and taking of our lands and communities . . . "[13] Dramatic charges of environmental racism, such as in the Warren County case, and the call for a new program of environmental justice took center stage. As one observer noted, "The conference put environmental racism on the political map."[14]

For the most part, the movement found strength at the grassroots, especially among low-income people of color who perceived serious environmental threats from toxic and hazardous wastes.[15] What emerged, according to sociologist Andrew Szasz, was a radical environmental populism within the larger tradition of American radicalism, rather than an outgrowth of the modern environmental movement.[16]

Grassroots protest and the NIMBY phenomenon are not inherently bounded by race or class. One study noted that, "local citizens have resisted the siting of [hazardous waste] facilities in their midst because they are being asked unfairly to shoulder the hazardous waste burdens of others."[17] The battles over siting have taken place across the nation, involving thousands of citizens, some through existing environmental and health groups, and others through informal and makeshift organizations. In some respects, the division between mainstream groups and local grassroots protesters became further intensified by issues of race, class, and gender, rather than necessarily initiated by them.[18]

For those pursuing environmental justice, however, grassroots resistance to environmental threats is simply the reaction to more fundamental injustices brought on by long-term economic and social trends. As movement leader and environmental sociologist Robert D. Bullard argued, struggles against environmental injustice are ". . . not unlike the civil rights battles waged to dismantle the legacy of Jim Crow in Selma, Montgomery, Birmingham, and some of the 'Up South' communities in New York, Boston, Philadelphia, Chicago, and Los Angeles."[19] Bunyan Bryant and Paul Mohai at the University of Michigan's School of Natural Resources took the argument a step further, contending that the civil rights movement which faltered in the late 1970s and 1980s may have seen its resurgence in the area of environmental justice.[20] Dumps and smokestacks are, to a degree, convenient proxies for inadequate health care, deindustrialization, and the uneven bounty of modern capitalism.

Efforts to characterize the environmental justice movement as having historical roots in civil rights activism (but neither in traditional conservation nor in the modern environmentalism) stemmed from a sense that the movement's political goals necessitated a distinct identity.[21] "Political agenda-setting" is a prime objective of the activist literature of the movement.[22] In a larger sense, this agenda setting attempts to shift priorities away from what is perceived as a traditional ecocentrism (e.g., global warming, ozone depletion, nature protection) toward homocentrism, or human-centered concerns for individual health, pesticide control, community protection, and various forms of pollution directed at inner-city life.

Despite falling short in gaining congressional support for an Environmental Justice Act, advocates nevertheless placed their issue on the national policy agenda and have played a major role in getting environmental justice themes incorporated into the Washington bureaucracy. In November 1992, an Office of Environmental Justice (originally called the Office of Environmental Equity) was established within the Environmental Protection Agency. Its purpose was to ensure that communities including large numbers of low-income families and people of color received protection under environmental laws.[23] EPA administrator Carol Browner designated environmental justice as one of the agency's top priorities in 1993. In September of that year, the National Environmental Justice Advisory Council (NEJAC) was created as a forum through which activists and communities could bring their concerns to EPA. President Clinton's Executive Order 12898, issued in February 1994, was meant to "focus Federal attention on the environmental and human health conditions in minority communities and low-income communities with the goal of achieving environmental justice." Both the Office of Solid Waste and Emergency Response (OSWER, responsible for implementing the Superfund program) and the agency's Office of Enforcement and Compliance Assurance (OECA) became centers of environmental justice activity. Pursuant to the executive order, several other departments and agencies drafted environmental justice strategy documents, and some (such as Interior and Energy) assigned staff to handle inquiries and policy development.

Activist response to government action on environmental justice has been predictably lukewarm because the official focus consisted largely of public information campaigns, media outreach, economic redevelopment pilot projects, and modest organizational changes. EPA's office of environmental justice ultimately became part of OECA under assistant administrator Steve Herman, a move undertaken to give the environmental justice unit greater stability and clout but aggressive litigation against polluters and congressional support for more stringent environmental protections were slow to materialize. Whether the existing government programs can be effective in setting new precedents for action or a way to placate activists and head off protest remains to be seen.

RACE AND CLASS AS ENVIRONMENTAL ISSUES

The environmental justice movement has generated considerable debate about the role that race and class play in the allocation of environmental amenities. The quantitative and case study literature asserting pervasive environmental inequality is large and expanding. Though much-criticized and never peer-reviewed, United Church of Christ, Commission for Racial Justice, *Toxic Wastes and Race in the United States* (1987) is the seminal quantitative study asserting that the racial composition of a community was the single variable best able to predict the siting of commercial hazardous waste treatment facilities. The report concluded that African Americans and Latinos especially were over represented in targeted communities, and it was "virtually impossible" that these facilities were distributed by chance. Supporters of the report argued that other, less comprehensive studies conducted as far back as the 1970s generally corroborated the findings.[24]

The CRJ report gave powerful ammunition to its supporters, but also set off a controversy over the charge of deliberate racial targeting. Opponents suggested that the role of race has been overstated and that the report suffered from shoddy research and faulty logic.[25] Vicki Bean, associate professor of Law at New York University, has been one of those leading the charge against the blanket claim of race as the key variable in siting toxic facilities. She has argued that studies showing a disproportionate number of waste facilities being sited in minority and poor communities tend to be based on the current socioeconomic makeup of those neighborhoods. This leaves open the possibility that "market forces drove down property values in these communities *after* the waste facilities were sited here, thereby attracting the poor and minorities, who are relegated to less desirable neighborhoods through housing discrimination and economic restraints."[26] Historian Andrew Hurley also has noted that in St. Louis "real estate dynamics" rather than discriminatory siting decisions were primarily responsible for bringing minority populations "into communities that already harbored hazardous waste."[27] Environmental justice advocates regularly reject these criticisms of the racial targeting thesis as unpersuasive.

As the recent development of the environmental justice movement suggests, claims of environmental racism are not going to be easily resolved, nor are demands for establishing new national environmental priorities simply going to fade away. Can historical perspective and methods clarify relevant policy issues and help to provide future directions? The following policy questions-and the brief historical analysis accompanying them-suggest ways in which public historians can play a more active role in the controversies surrounding the environmental racism and environmental justice questions.

TEN POLICY QUESTIONS

The following ten policy questions, which stem from a recent overview of environmental justice written by Christopher Foreman, suggest areas where historical research, inference, and methods may be most useful (and least useful) in evaluating and implementing environmental policy that incorporates-or at least takes into account—environmental justice issues.

1. To what extent do we confront environmental inequities? If such inequities exist, to what degree might they be explicitly "racial" in nature? Few things are equally distributed and, clearly, pollution is not among them. Indeed, planetary gravity may be the only environmental amenity that is equally distributed. It is no surprise that some citizens live and work closer to noxious or otherwise disagreeable surroundings than others. Moreover, wealthier and better-educated citizens enjoy greater flexibility than poorer, less-educated ones. They can be more selective in their residential and occupational choices, a latitude that facilitates avoidance of less desirable, and perhaps riskier, locations and jobs. The poor, in particular, simply have a more restricted menu of life's amenities, some of them environmental. Of course, not all inequities need be tolerated, and government is often expected to play a role in ameliorating them. Racial inequity is particularly "suspect" (to use the language of civil rights jurisprudence). America's peculiar history predisposes many to accepting the likelihood that where a collective inequity arises, an awareness of race will prove essential to comprehending and addressing it. But the precise causal role of race (or racism) cannot be assumed without concrete evidence.

Although not strictly historical in nature, too little has been made of the substantial body of research conducted by social scientists in the 1970s and 1980s focusing on the distribution of environmental risk. Such research can help test charges of environmental racism in a number of contexts, and may suggest areas and topics that public historians can further develop with their own research. A small body of literature, for example, began to appear on the equity of municipal service provision in the 1970s. The so-called "underclass" hypothesis attracted attention among scholars. It postulated that the quantity and quality of service delivery was directly related to the socioeconomic status of the area receiving the service. Thus, poorer neighborhoods received service that was inferior because they were not politically strong enough to resist or to voice their demands. However, research testing the "underclass" hypothesis did not lead to conclusive findings about the connection between class and environmental concerns, and needs deeper historical research through the development of case studies.[28] Despite the lack of certainty of the social science research, the 1968 Kerner Commission Report on urban riots stated that one of the most serious complaints by ghetto residents was the inadequacy of municipal services. During the 1970s, several lawsuits by civil rights lawyers challenged cities to justify their inequitable service delivery patterns.[29]

However, inequity in service delivery was but a part of the larger issue of environmental equity. Of major consequence was the impact of distribution of risk by various forms of pollution. Questions of the distribution of environmental risk and environmental quality led to numerous case study analyses, but with very mixed results, little agreement on the correlation between class and pollution exposure, and insignificant development of historic trend lines in a variety of communities.[30]

Economists Leonard P. Gianessi, Henry M. Peskin, and Edward Wolff produced the first study examining the distribution of air pollution on a nationwide basis. They were concerned with government efforts in the 1970s to apply uniform regulations over the entire nation.[31] While producing incomplete and inconsistent results, they tentatively concluded that when the distribution of policy benefits are considered with the distribution of costs of pollution abatement, the results are not uniform. The study indicated that lower income groups gain the most in this instance, with nonwhites (except those in the highest income group) leading the way.[32] If the study had examined more than air pollution—especially types of land pollution—the conclusions may have been more concrete, and had the starting date been pushed back into the 1950s, for example, the distinction between class and race experiences might have been even more persuasive. Yet, by moving beyond anecdotal evidence and intuitive conclusions, Gianessi, Peskin, and Wolff demonstrated the difficulty in determining a definitive pattern that linked race to incidence of pollution. Other studies also pointed to the complexity of the issue of race, class, and environment, especially when different forms of pollution are measured. Air pollution is particularly difficult to evaluate because of its ubiquitous nature—especially ambient sources such as auto emissions—which fails to discriminate between rich or poor, black or white. Several forms of water pollution are equally ubiquitous.[33]

The policy implications of these studies also were unclear. As economist Peter Nijkamp rightly suggested, " . . . distributional conflicts in economic environmental policy analysis are very hard to solve."[34] Social cost-benefit analysis could not readily encompass environmental equity issues, furthermore, because they could not be easily reduced to economic terms. Without compelling scientific—or social scientific—evidence in support of the theory that race and/or class were key variables in at least some categories of pollution exposure, new laws were not likely to be promulgated or even hotly debated. As Freeman also concluded, " . . . it must be realized that efficiency and equity objectives may be competitive in that to achieve greater equity in the distribution of benefits (costs) it may be necessary to incur lower total benefits or higher costs."[35] The studies conducted in the 1970s and early 1980s, therefore, did not tip the balance in favor of greater attention to environmental equity or convince policy makers that seeking greater equity was worth the costs. Nevertheless, despite the limited domain in which the re-

search circulated, a foundation for inquiry into this subject was established, waiting to be rediscovered and reconsidered by future researchers and environmentalists. Further social science analysis may help determine what factors influence environmental inequity. Historical case studies (as discussed in more detail under
question 2), can help demonstrate how and the extent to which such inequities
have arisen at specific times and in particular places in the past, complementing
the social science research on equity. The limited time lines of the social science
research also seems to skew results. For example, examining a relatively long period when automobile emissions became an environmental concern, beginning
possibly in the 1940s and extending into recent years, might produce clearer sam-
ples for specific neighborhood studies. Public historians interested in policy issues
could help to clarify and expand upon the more limited, but nonetheless intrigu-
ing, studies attempted in the 1970s and early 1980s.

**2. To what extent do we possess policy tools appropriate for mitigating
environmental inequity?** The central and continuing political project of environmental justice advocacy has been the elevation of grassroots voices and
community perspectives. Environmental justice advocates understandably
highlight the vastly greater financial and technical resources controlled by corporate and governmental players, as compared with citizens and communities,
in the environmental policy arena. On the other hand, the history of grassroots
environmentalism makes clear that citizens are not necessarily helpless pawns
of the establishment. The NIMBY phenomenon has effectively challenged
countless incinerators, landfills, and waste treatment facilities. Indeed, so determined and effective has such advocacy proven to be that scholars and policy
makers have struggled to devise political and economic formulas capable of
overcoming it.[36]

In recent years, minority communities have likewise proven remarkably adept
at blocking or negotiating changes in facilities that stir local anxiety and opposition.[37] In 1998, for example, the State of Louisiana witnessed the demise of a proposed uranium enrichment facility and a plastics plant. The proposals succumbed
to intense local opposition amidst charges of "environmental racism." In both instances, local opposition was substantially aided by public advocacy law and by
sympathetic federal environmental officials. Nevertheless, the belief that minority
and low-income communities receive short shrift from environmentalism and environmental policy is widespread.

No one doubts that many minority neighborhoods are relatively undesirable
places to live, largely because their inhabitants are poor and amenities inadequate.
The question is whether environmental advocacy and policy can work a more fundamental kind of social transformation than the far more modest ecology-protection
goals that have remained the foundation of traditional environmentalism. The record
of the relatively limited tools available (community involvement and outreach, environmental job training, Title VI of the Civil Rights Act) do not inspire confidence
on this front. Enterprise-minded critics of environmental justice advocacy also suggest that if the empowerment of minority communities is the goal, restricting job-

producing development with a cry of "environmental racism" is of doubtful usefulness in the long run.[38]

History offers little, in a direct way, in mitigating environmental inequity. But
recent historical scholarship helps to identify cases where environmental inequities may have existed, in what form, and how people responded to them. As
historian Andrew Hurley has noted:

> Thus far, the environmental justice discourse has lacked a historical di-
> mension. Because most studies have relied on current demographic and en-
> vironmental data, we know very little about the conditions that produced
> environmental inequities in the first place. Statistical studies suggesting a
> racial bias on the part of government agencies reach conclusions that can
> only be substantiated through the careful analysis of individual sites.[39]

In an article published in April, 2000, Dolores Greenberg examined the "forgotten struggles against injustices by inner-city people of color."[40] Using New
York City as her case, Greenberg asserted that traditional historical scholarship on
environmental reform going back to the nineteenth century tended to overlook or
ignore many cases of "people-centered" local reform carried out by African Americans well before the advent of the environmental justice movement in the 1980s.
As she argued, "Long before their knowledge of place and humans' place in nature became integrated into the contemporary environmental consciousness, people of color have been speaking out for an alternative social vision. To overlook
this past distorts a continuum of protest and its consequences for the future."[41]

Hurley describes the complicated story of steel mill pollution in Gary, Indiana,
between 1945 and 1980, how environmental risk was distributed among its citizens, and the nature and extent of environmental protest against air, water, and
land pollution. By and large, however, protests against pollution remained fragmented in Gary—factory workers urging management to improve health and
safety conditions, white suburbanites looking for pollution reform measures,
African Americans seeking redress of environmental grievances through the civil
rights movement. And despite periods of citizen cooperation across lines of race
and class, industrial capitalists ultimately used the "socially fragmented landscape" to their advantage.[42]

These historical studies and others explore the theme of environmental injustice
sincerely, through substantial primary research, and with no apology for their own
sympathies. Yet, the stories they tell are messy and complex, and sometimes ambiguous. They do not fit neatly into a mold that either proponents or opponents of
the environmental justice movement might prefer. Murky lines of causation between race versus class as determinates of environmental injustice, or the potential value of government regulatory policy in settling environmental disputes, are
more typical in historical research than in the polemical literature that has dominated the field of environmental justice. Ironically, murkiness and ambiguity may
be necessary to broaden and deepen the discussion of the origins, impact, and future of the environmental justice movement.

Historical case studies are but one way to document environmental inequities. Public historians, through myriad community history projects, have utilized oral interviewing techniques to bring life and attention to grassroots reactions and responses to a variety of issues. Research on environmental justice is in desperate need of making more neighborhood and community voices heard, and in helping to increase understanding of how and when grassroots organizations emerged to challenge pollution risks. There are many other voices to be heard as well—not all of them in the neighborhood, but also in the boardroom and in government offices. A deeper historical dialog among a variety of participants in the toxics debate will go a long way in broadening and deepening the literature of environmental justice, and may even influence policy formation.

3. What contribution can the environmental justice movement make to raising and resolving the issue of inequity? The environmental justice movement's great political success has come on two related fronts: mobilizing individual communities against localized sites, and placing environmental justice on the agenda of policy makers at every level of government. It is quite probable that future administrations will find equity an unavoidable issue within the environmental policy discourse. Producing this state of affairs remains the signal achievement of the environmental justice movement. But successfully addressing the many concerns raised under the environmental justice rubric will not be easy. To the extent that environmental justice advocacy poses questions to which environmental policy alone (and especially its federal component) cannot offer reliable answers, disappointing results may be inevitable. Environmental justice is about a great deal beyond alleged unfairness in siting and emissions exposure. Indeed, activists appear inclined to view these matters largely as convenient launching pads for much broader forays into the social equity terrain. If the environmental justice movement's rhetorical and protest tools have proven useful for agenda-setting, they may be blunt (and perhaps even counterproductive) instruments for realistically and precisely defining targets for the official policy response apparatus.

The use of history in this case has been and is likely to remain muted. Environmental justice advocates, if anything, have perpetuated some historical myths— quite unintentionally it seems—in defense of their cause. Critics of the environmental movement in general—from the right as well as the left—have presented it as monolithic and out of touch with the realities of everyday life. The variety of views and objectives within the broad environmental community cannot be so easily characterized, nor can its values be distilled into a homogenous belief system. To suggest, for example, that urban issues have been ignored, is to fail to take into account the historical origins of the movement in its fullest sense.

For the urban environmentalists of the late-nineteenth and early-twentieth centuries, for example, problems of epidemic disease, lead poisoning, malnutrition, and air, water, and noise pollution were the most immediate and severe issues that required attention. The effort to build more urban parks and to plan for city growth were reminiscent of concerns of resource conservationists and preservationists, but fundamentally the environmental problems that mattered the most to urban reformers were those affecting human beings.[43]

In this sense, a powerful bond in time should exist between turn-of-the-century urban reformers and modern environmental justice activists. However, that bond was never made. Part of the reason is that the typical comparison between the conservation movement and the modern environmental movement omits almost entirely the urban struggles over health and pollution.[44] The aura of John Muir and Gifford Pinchot, the bombast of Teddy Roosevelt, and the legacies of John Perkins Marsh and John Wesley Powell drew attention westward to the Hetch Hetchy in California and to the National Parks. The national attention given to conservation through its celebrated battles and its landmark legislation overshadowed the essentially local concerns over urban environmental problems.

Unfortunately contemporary obscurity has led to historical oblivion. Environmental justice advocates looking back at the traditional historical interpretation on the conservation movement saw only the John Muirs and the Gifford Pinchots— if they looked that far back at all. Second, the urban environmental activities of the turn-of-the-century focused on human-centered and urban-oriented environmental issues—like those addressed by environmental justice advocates. But the earliest urban environmentalists gave little or no attention to race and class, nor to the issue of equity (insofar as that implies equal protection from environmental threats or equal exposure).[45]

Even if environmental justice advocates had access to the history of urban environmentalism of the Progressive Era, they certainly would be displeased by the neglect of race and class, and repelled by the sometimes open hostility to ethnic groups and people of color. Typical of the Progressive Era, urban environmentalists could show compassion for new immigrants as did the settlement house reformers, but that compassion was often wrapped in noblesse oblige, paternalism, and efforts at encouraging cultural and social assimilation. Some reformers and city leaders blamed the occupants of the ethnic and racial ghettoes for causing disease and sanitation problems. Still others ignored the fact that sanitary services were rarely distributed equitably and were unlikely to be so even after a successful reform campaign. The reactions of urban environmentalists to issues of class and race mirrored the views of most citizens at the time, ranging from hostility to the underclass to the invisibility of their problems.

The fairest assessment to make about the history of turn-of-the-century urban environmentalism is that it provides a partial legacy for modern environmental justice advocates, rather than no legacy at all. Unfortunately, it has been common to see no continuity with environmental reformers of the past and thus assume a greater aura of originality for environmental justice precepts and interests.

Furthermore, many observers give the impression that the modern environmental movement has demonstrated little interest in urban issues. A deeper examination reveals more diversity than popular perceptions suggest. Indeed, modern environmentalism is even more diverse than its turn-of-the-century predecessor. Concern over urban pollution and quality of life issues broadened, and questions of environmental equity became a growing topic of interest among at least a small circle of social scientists. In the political arena, battles fought over environmental issues from the 1960s through the early 1980s tended to highlight saving nature and ending pollution, while often ignoring environmental equity (an idea that appeared to be more esoteric than policy driven). Battles over saving wildlife, preserving wetlands, and cutting back on air pollution were promoted as having universal value and thus worthy of national support. Nevertheless, questions of personal health and well-being—problems where inequities were great—still remained local and necessarily redirected toward other problem-solvers, namely social workers and public health officials.[46]

In quantitative terms, the Johnson administration's "New Conservation" of the 1960s significantly confronted national environmental issues. The New Conservation also ventured into the urban environment in imaginative and innovative ways. While individual components of the urban program stressed well-known concerns—air and water pollution, recreational space, land use, waste disposal, and historic preservation—taken as a whole, they reflected a fresh recognition of the urban environment. By elevating local urban issues to national prominence, cities no longer had to take a back seat to the wilderness as vital environmental challenges. The natural environment and the built environment were being fused in the national consciousness, possibly for the first time.[47] Curiously, however, a president and an administration that would pride itself on its civil rights accomplishments never made the connection between its civil rights and environmental goals. The Johnson years, therefore, helped to fuse urban environmental issues with traditional nature concerns, but did not create the environmental justice issue as we think of it today.

The role of the historian in presenting a more balanced view of the environmental movement over its history would serve many interests well. This is not simply a debunking role, but an opportunity to help identify some possible common ground between environmental justice advocates and traditional environmentalists in such organizations as the Sierra Club, the Wilderness Society, and so forth. Public historians, in particular, can play a role in devising public forums where shared views could be discussed, and common (and divergent) historical paths could be explored.

4. Do we need stronger priority-setting in environmental justice? If the environmental justice movement does not set priorities, who will? As a diverse "bottom-up" coalition of local groups and their allies, the environmental justice movement conspicuously lacks the capacity for, or inclination toward, prioritization among its concerns. Coalitions are built and sustained by addition, not by subtraction. Overt de-emphasis or removal of any issue or claim would prompt the offended coalition partners to depart. Real priority setting also runs contrary to radical egalitarian value premises. No one covets the title of "victimizer," least of all the intensely democratic activists associated with environmental justice. Therefore, movement rhetoric argues that *no* community should be harmed, and that *all* community concerns and grievances deserve redress. The trouble with this vision is that, while a superb tactic for unifying diverse interests long enough to place environmental justice on the policy agenda, it simply cannot be realized in real-world policy implementation.

Pragmatic choices about what to remediate, when, and to what extent—these are the very essence of environmental policy as workaday enterprise. Rhetoric and activism may camouflage or delay such choices, but cannot evade them altogether. To the extent that the environmental justice movement eschews prioritization, does this not mean that environmental policy makers are left with little choice but to do the dirty job themselves, albeit behind their own rhetorical smokescreen of "full protection?" In this situation, historical cases studies might be quite useful. But getting them in the hands of policy makers appears quite difficult. This is a case where format may be as important as substance. The traditional historical monograph or academic essay can be off-putting or just too cumbersome for policy makers and the public to digest. Experimenting with a variety of forms of media—articles in popular magazines, op-ed pieces in newspapers, museum exhibits, film and video all need to be explored. In other words, emphasis has to be placed on audience as well as message. This is intuitive for public historians, and is an approach they can spearhead within the historical profession.

5. How can the benefits of new facilities be balanced against the burdens they impose? What is the role for environmental justice in this process? If priorities are generally alien to environmental justice advocacy, the concept of a tradeoff is likewise troublesome. That is because political mobilization is least painful when those doing the mobilizing can keep their arguments simple and compelling. A moralistic message of opposition to a facility siting allows activists to play a relatively uncomplicated game: build citizen outrage toward stopping the facility. But what is to be done when a proposed facility offers perceived benefits (i.e., local employment and tax revenue) as well as perceived costs (i.e., nuisances or perceived health risks)? That was the bind activists found themselves in as they strenuously opposed construction of the Shintech plastics plant in Louisiana.[48] African American residents of Saint James Parish took both sides of the issue in a polarizing struggle that ended only when Shintech elected to jump to another parish where it could collaborate on building a smaller plant without all the fuss. What did the residents of Saint James Parish lose thereby? For Greenpeace and other facility opponents this was a victory for public health and for accountability, while others perceived a missed economic opportunity. Lacking a sophisticated and broadly accepted set of integrated criteria for assessing such locales, we currently make do with a varying combination of crude proximity analysis and raw politics. The development of historical cases has great value here, especially to indicate the range of interests at stake before decisions about policy are etched in stone.

6. Does race complicate the tension between "expert" and "popular" conceptions of risk? Nobody wants to poison anyone or to be poisoned. But while experts rely on the maxim that "the dose makes the poison" and on technical assessments, laypersons are often primed to reject the results of analyses conducted in terms they may not comprehend by persons they do not trust. Grassroots environmentalism is inclined to judge expertise by criteria of its accessibility, inclusiveness, and the leverage it provides in battles over a terrain where uncertainty looms. Among citizens facing sensitive toxics issues, intuitive or "common sense" judgment may seem far more persuasive than any opposing technical analysis ever could.

Generally speaking, industrial pollution is more compelling to citizens than to technical experts as a risk to human health, an oft-noted divergence of perspectives.[49] And when the citizens in question share a collective history of adverse treatment, it may be especially easy to incline them to the view that they are being singled out for environmental discrimination, even when that is not the case.[50] It is at least plausible to suggest that the racial identity of many African Americans, Latinos, Asian Americans and Native Americans may, given an appropriate stimulus, strongly inform their intuitions about many things (including perceived health risks and the intention of persons associated with their dissemination).[51] If this is so, then "good" science, or "the best" analysis—historical analysis included—may be hopelessly overmatched when pitted against such intuitions.

7. To the extent that environmental inequity is not racial in origin, can race be appropriately de-emphasized? Although the available empirical literature assessing the extent of environmental inequity offers no consensus on the role of race, it is nevertheless clear that race (and racism) do not always play the causal role assigned to it by environmental justice advocates. Among others, Vicki Been's analyses of siting history suggests—as stated above—that ethnic communities may develop near previously constructed facilities. When that is the case it would, be inaccurate to describe a facility as having been imposed on the community in question.[52]

Whatever empirical analysis may suggest about the dynamics of facility siting, it is clear that the image of minority communities bearing up under a deliberate toxic siege is politically compelling. The impression of racially motivated targeting offers rhetorical firepower that activists will be reluctant to surrender in their campaign to pressure the establishment for attention and procedural concessions. This is a key obstacle to putting race and racism in their proper perspective from a purely empirical point of view. This is not to suggest that race has never been a factor in any locational decision, but that it will be difficult for political reasons to disentangle race from other factors and to discard it entirely, even when it ought to play no role.

This is where historical research may be particularly effective. That is, historical analysis can help place race within an understandable context—as opposed to contributing to polarized debate—in disputes over environmental inequity. *Environmental Inequalities* and other historical studies discussed earlier do a particularly good job in placing the issue of race within the larger environmental context. Another good example, is Ellen Stroud's article "Troubled Waters in Ecotopia: Environmental Racism in Portland, Oregon," which examines problems related to the pollution of Columbia Slough in north Portland, contaminated by the city's raw sewage and more than 200 industries. Beginning in the early twentieth century, the slough was clearly "sacrificed to industry." In more recent times, a local environmental group charged that the slough became and remained polluted because the areas most affected were communities where African Americans and new immigrants resided.

Stroud accepts the view that there is a direct connection between toxic pollution and poor and nonwhite communities. However, the thrust of the article was not to revisit the race/class debate of environmental injustice, but to explore what she called the shaping of "a landscape of inequity" in post-World War II north Portland. As she stated:

> The pollution and industrial development which have kept property values lower on the peninsula, which were in turn encouraged by assumptions about the types of people who did and should live in these neighborhoods, meant that relatively inexpensive housing was available here for African Americans looking for better housing, and for working-class white Portlanders, and for recent immigrants from Vietnam, Cambodia, Laos, Eastern Europe, Mexico, and Central America.[53]

Such a trend, coupled with chronic discriminatory housing practices and zoning and development decision in Portland, reinforced the emergence of this landscape of inequality. Stroud's scenario provides a substantially different characterization of environmental racism than the notion of a community "targeted" with the building of a toxics facility, but one that is equally disturbing. In a larger sense, the study of north Portland over an extended period of time allows for examination of land-use decision making that grows out of the convergence of several trends—concessions to industrial polluters, indifference to low-income housing, and choices made as to what to improve and what to ignore.

Angela Gugliotta in "Class, Gender, and Coal Smoke," broadens the discourse over race, class, and environmental injustice by adding the variable of gender. In her study of the anticoal smoke battles in Pittsburgh in the late-nineteenth and early-twentieth centuries, Gugliotta explains how elites in the 1910s focused their criticism of the smoke problem on the serious health effects facing poor women and children, rather than on working men confronting severe risks inside the mills. There definitely was enough environmental danger to go around in the Smoky City, but the delineation of risk and suffering by gender adds another layer to the assessment of environmental justice that is missing from many of the more recent confrontations.[54] Certainly, the central role of women in grassroots protests is indisputable, and claims of environmental threats to families as expressed by leaders such as Lois Gibbs during the Love Canal uproar are well known. But a more general discussion of the relationship among race, class, and gender in the debate over environmental justice needs to be taken deeper.[55] The more confounding problem, however, is how to get this information—and in what format—in the hands of policy makers. Public policy historians, and public historians in general, need to focus substantial attention on the method of delivery as much as on the message. The pipeline of information to policy makers that applied social science has achieved over the years still remains undeveloped by historians.

8. How do we assess and cope with the wide array of grievances and aspirations raised under the rubric of environmental justice? Clearly a primary use of the term "environmental justice" is that it provides convenient rhetorical shelter for aspirations and grievances that actually have little to do with "the environment" as understood by the framers of traditional environmentalism. Indeed, this is one reason for the sometimes hostile relations between traditional and grassroots environmentalists.[56] "Environmental justice" provides a convenient rubric under which to reiterate redistributive claims to which the American regime has generally exhibited only very limited responsiveness. At the community level, redistributive aims are most clearly apparent in the larger agendas, and even the names of grassroots organizations such as the Southwest Network for Environmental and Economic Justice or the Environmental Justice Project of the Southern Organizing Committee for Economic and Social Justice. Moreover, a striking characteristic of citizen testimony offered when environmental justice concerns are at issue is the wide range of themes on display in that testimony. These include: wellness, fairness, community empowerment, solidarity, diversity, impatience with technical expertise, economic prosperity, and overall quality of life. Environmental justice proponents also hope to inject inadequacies in housing, health care access, education and so on into debate on "the environment" experienced by low-income and minority communities.[57] In a context created to evoke and amplify the undistilled voices of citizens who confront a variety of challenges, how do we decide on a reasonable course of action? By and large, however, this is a political issue. History can be used as a justification for inclusiveness, but in so doing it may be more of a weapon than a tool if used too casually.

9. Can environmental justice policy disentangle "risk and racism" from the "quality of life" issues that may not fall under the prior heading? The political usefulness of a rhetoric of "risk and racism" is by now clear. But to some extent this may involve a rhetorical bait-and-switch game. Much of what animates environmental justice advocacy are grievances best described in quality-of-life terms: odors, noise, dust, rubbish, dilapidated buildings, traffic congestion. Although such concerns are the real heart of much environmental justice advocacy, they lack the galvanizing power of appeals grounded in perceptions of risk and racism. But can an advocacy so reliant on the latter effectively propel a policy discourse, much less a substantive policy response, that engages the real underlying issues?

Grievances that make their way into the courts, one might assume, depend on history to reveal a community's basis for complaint. Some scholars disagree, and argue that the legal system "has perpetuated environmental injustice" by misreading or disregarding a community's history. Charles P. Lord and William A. Shuntkin have argued that "an awareness of the uses of history is critical to a community's fight for environmental justice."[58] Rather than to map out discrete instances of environmental inequities, they suggest seeking patterns that document past injustices and current community aspirations. "To approach history casually and complacently," they contend, "is to evade history's inevitably multiplicitous facts and to mask the many meanings the facts could support."[59]

They do not deny that history has been and continues to be used in court cases, but often used too rigidly: "History is subjective and cannot be cast as monolithic." Utilizing the critical historical method as a persuasive tool for unraveling past events is hardly new to historians, but the spirit of Lord and Shuntkin's argument is worth heeding. Communities need to state their cases as effectively as they can by showing patterns of injustice, not simply pointing to specific instances of injustice. For their part, courts and public officials need to view historical inquiry in a more flexible manner, with an eye toward "an understanding that their interpretation is necessarily provisional."[60] This may be too much to ask of those not trained or not aware of the subtleties of historical inquiry, but the rigidity in the application of historical truisms suggests the degree to which a good understanding of historical method and its application to environmental laws remains unfulfilled. Conversely, the identification of problems such as environmental injustice needs to be understood in a substantially more intricate way than it has been presented by both advocates and detractors of the environmental justice movement.

10. To what extent can we (and ought we) further democratize environmental policy as it affects racial and ethnic constituencies? Environmental justice is integral to a broader debate about the appropriate character of environmental policy reform.[61] This larger contest pits alternative *rationalizing* and *democratizing* reform perspectives against one another, prompting a search for ways to straddle, if nor reconcile, the two. Environmental justice is a version of the democratizing critique that gives voice to a range of minority and low-income community concerns, many of which are not fundamentally "environmental" in the traditional sense.

The rationalizing emphasis is both economic and scientific. The strictly economic version holds that environmental policy has been too often wasteful because program ends and means have displayed insufficient regard for the social costs imposed by regulation. From this perspective, cost-benefit and cost-effectiveness analysis, as well as market-like alternative to command-and-control regulation, have been too seldom used or have been accorded insufficient weight.[62] A different sort of rationalizing critique, while respectful of the need to address cost and benefits formally when possible, encompasses broader concerns: the discordant, meandering, and sometimes panic-stricken aspect of regulatory politics and policymaking.

In this view, according to Justice Stephen Breyer for instance, regulation too often fails to: (1) set priorities grounded in the severity or pervasiveness of problems; (2) define and adhere to consistent approaches among issues and agencies; and (3) remediate risk only to a degree deemed reasonable in light of the relevant costs and benefits.[63] Widespread appreciation of the uncertainty pervading environmental regulation has also generated regular calls for access by policy makers, and by EPA in particular, to better scientific analysis, especially in epidemiology and toxicology. Advocates of a National Institute for the Environment, which is intended to improve the scientific basis for environmental decision making, are animated by a rationalizing spirit similar to Justice Breyer's.[64]

Grass-roots environmentalism in general, and environmental justice in particular, are guided by an alternative democratizing ethos. They are undergirded by several factors: a general suspicion of elites; an unease with industrial capitalism (especially as pursued by multinational corporations that evade accountability); a conviction that citizen perspectives are inadequately mobilized and represented in policy processes; and awareness of profound racial and economic inequality. The democratizing orientation in environmental policy reform assesses progress not by the conventional expertise brought to bear, nor by the extent to which decisions are harmonized, nor by the promotion of efficiency (in any sense). Rather, grassroots environmental populism gauges success largely by standards of inclusiveness, community comfort and legitimacy, and fidelity to democratic practice. Thoughtful commentators on environmentalism are aware that the rationalizing and democratizing orientations must be bridged somehow, but the fit is proving awkward. Environmental officials avidly embrace varieties of "stakeholder outreach"—environmental justice has been, if nothing else, the focus of a seemingly endless parade of ad hoc meetings, advisory committees and task forces—partly because procedural inclusion is the easiest card for officials to play. But an effective synthesis of expert and popular energies remains perhaps the most serious political challenge facing environmentalism (and environmental justice) in the new millennium.

In such a confounding setting, it appears that the ability of the environmental justice movement to achieve its goals of equal rights and fair treatment under the law is indeed beyond the scope and power of historians—or any group of scholars or researchers for that matter. But if such goals are to be clearly articulated as well as to be understood by the variety of stakeholders—not simply launched as political salvos—history has a place. The role of historical inquiry in this instance, however, is not reconciling environmental justice goals with traditional environmentalist ones. It is, more logically, to be employed as a useful tool in sorting out the ways and means that race and class (and possibly gender) have intertwined with myriad environmental issues and concerns in the past. The correlations and relationships of these key elements in the environmental history of community living at once will make more complex what appears simple, and at the same time— we hope—will lead us to ask some new questions about the relationship between race, class and the environment. To its credit, the environmental justice movement has gone a long way in bringing these issues to the forefront. It is now imperative that we understand them in a more complete way.

But traditional historical inquiry is only part of the role of history in dealing with this knotty and controversial issue. Communicating the complexity and texture of environmental justice—its past and present—to policy makers and to the public in general is a challenge to be met by, among others, public historians. All the books and articles in the world are insufficient to become party to the discourse. The challenge for public historians is to help devise ways of bringing history to the table. The melding of expertise in environmental history and the track record of public historians to present history in a variety of venues offers real possibilities in the debate over environmental justice.

NOTES

1. Some unusual early writings that anticipate the modern concern with environmental equity include Nathan Hare, "Black Ecology," *The Black Scholar* 2 (April 1970): 2–8, and Norman J. Faramelli, "Perilous Links Between Economic Growth, Justice and Ecology: A Challenge for Economic Planners," *Environmental Affairs* 1 (April 1971): 218–227.
2. The Environmental Protection Agency (EPA) defines 'environmental justice' as the "fair treatment for people of all races, cultures, and incomes, regarding the development of environmental laws, regulations, and policies." See "About Environmental Justice" on the Internet at *www.epa.gov/ swerosps/ej/aboutej.htm.* See also definitions discussed in a course offered at the School of Natural Resources, University of Michigan, on the Internet, *www.personal.umich.edu/jtajzer/nre/defintions.htm;* Bunyan Bryant, ed., *Environmental Justice: Issues, Policies, and Solutions* (Washington, D.C.: Island Press, 1995), pp. 5–6.
3. Bunyan Bryant, "Introduction," in Bryant, ed., *Environmental Justice*, p. 5.
4. Marianne Lavelle and Marcia Coyle, "Unequal Protection: The Racial Divide in Environmental Law," *National Law Journal* 15 (September 21, 1992): S1-S6.
5. See Robert D. Bullard, ed., *Unequal Protetcion: Environmental Justice and Communities of Color* (San Francisco: Sierra Club Books, 1994); Bullard, ed., *Confronting Environmental Racism: Voices from the Grassroots* (Boston: South End Press, 1993); Richard Hofrichter, ed., *Toxic Struggles: The Theory and Practice of Environmental Justice* (Philadelphia: New Society Publishers, 1993); Vernice D. Miller, "Planning, Power and Politics: A Case Study of the Land and Siting History of the North River Water Pollution Control Plant," *Fordham Urban Law Journal* 21 (Spring, 1994): 707–722.
6. See James P. Lester, David W. Allen, and Kelly M. Hill, *Environmental Injustice in the United States: Myths and Realities* (Boulder, CO: Westview Press, 2000).
7. The Internet lists a wide array of environmental justice groups. See the Eco-Justice Network on EcoNet, *www.igc.apc.org/envjustice.* See also the Center for Health, Environment and Justice, *www.essential.org/cchw/ cchwinf.html;* Environmental Justice Resource Center, *www.ejrc.cau.edu;* and Environmental Justice Links, www-personal.umich.edu/jrajzer/nre/ links.html.
8. A substantial portion of the historical background of the environmental justice movement was drawn from Martin V. Melosi, "Environmental Justice,

Political Agenda Setting, and the Myths of History," *Journal of Policy History* 12 (2000): 43–71, and Melosi, "Equity, Eco-racism, and Environmental History," in Char Miller and Hal Rothman, eds., *Out of the Woods: Essays in Environmental History* (Pittsburgh: University of Pittsburgh Press, 1997), pp. 194–211.

9. See Andrew Dobson, *Justice and the Environment: Conceptions of Environmental Sustainability and Theories of Distributive Justice* (New York: Oxford University Press, 1998), p. 18; Robert D. Bullard, "Race and Environmental Justice in the United States," *Yale Journal of International Law* 18 (1993):325; Bullard, ed., *Confronting Environmental Racism,* p. 9.

10. Giovanna Di Chiro, "Nature as Community: The Convergence of Environmental and Social Justice," in William Cronon, ed., *Uncommon Ground: Rethinking the Human Place in Nature* (New York: W.W. Norton, 1996), p. 303.

11. The CRJ was founded in 1963 after the assassination of black activist Medgar Evers, church bombings in Birmingham, Alabama, and other anti-civil rights activities.

12. Eileen Maura McGurty, "From Nimby to Civil Rights: The Origins of the Environmental Justice Movement," *Environmental History* 2 (July, 1997): 318. See also pp. 301–02, 305–07, 309–14.

13. Quoted in Karl Grossman, "The People of Color Environmental Summit," Bullard, ed., *Unequal Protection,* p. 272.

14. Marc Mowrey and Tim Redmond, *Not in Our Backyard: The People and Events that Shaped America's Modern Environment Movement* (New York: William Morrow, 1993), pp. 435–36.

15. Andrew Szasz, *Ecopopulism: Toxic Waste and the Movement for Environmental Justice* (Minneapolis: University of Minnesota Press, 1994), p. 5.

16. Ibid., pp. 6, 69–72. See also "The Grassroots Movement for Environmental Justice," *Everyone's Backyard* 11 (February, 1993):3.

17. Daniel Mazmanian and David Morell, *Beyond Superfailure: America's Toxics Policy for the 1990s* (Boulder, CO: Westview Press, 1992), p. 181.

18. Robert Gottlieb, "Beyond NEPA and Earth Day: Reconstructing the Past and Envisioning a Future for Environmentalism," *Environmental History Review* 19 (Winter, 1995): 10. See also Barry G. Rabe, *Beyond NIMBY: Hazardous Waste Siting in Canada and the United States* (Washington, D.C.: Brookings Institution Press, 1994), pp. 2–3; Tom Arrandale, "When the Poor Cry NIMBY," *Governing* 6 (September, 1993):36–41.

19. Robert D. Bullard, *Dumping in Dixie: Race, Class, and Environmental Quality* (Boulder, CO: Westview Press, 1994; second ed.), p. xiii.

20. Bunyan Bryant and Paul Mohai, eds., *Race and the Incidence of Environmental Hazards: A Time for Discourse* (Boulder, CO: Westview Press, 1992), pp. 1–2.

21. For example, civil rights law was used in 1993 as a basis for filing the first environmental justice complaints with EPA. It also was used in other litigation on the state level as early as 1979 in Houston, Texas. Courts have hesitated to

overturn locally undesirable land uses on the basis of environmental justice concepts, however. See Daniel Kevin, " 'Environmental Racism' and Locally Undesirable Land Uses: A Critique of Environmental Justice Theories and Remedies," *Villanova Environmental Law Journal* 8 (1997):145; Kathlyn Gay, *Pollution and the Powerless; The Environmental Justice Movement* (New York: Franklin Watts, 1994), p. 106.

22. Christopher H. Foreman, Jr., *The Promise and Peril of Environmental Justice* (Washington, D.C.: Brookings Institution Press, 1998), p. 2.

23. U.S. Environmental Protection Agency, *Environmental Justice Initiatives, 1993* (Washington, D.C.: EPA, February, 1994). See also "A Skeptic Scrutinizes Environmental Justice," *Brookings* 8 (Winter, 1998):5.

24. See United Church of Christ, Commission for Racial Justice, *Toxic Wastes and Race in the United States: A National Report on the Racial and Socioeconomic Characteristics of Communities with Hazardous Waste Sites* (New York: United Church of Christ, 1987). See also Charles Lee, "Toxic Waste and Race in the United States," in Bryant and Mohai, eds., *Race and the Incidence of Environmental Hazards,* pp. 10–16, 22–27; Rosemari Mealy, "Charles Lee on Environmental Racism," in Dana A. Alston, ed., *We Speak for Ourselves: Social Justice, Race, and Environment* (Washington, D.C.: Panos Institute, 1990), pp. 8; Paul Mohai and Bunyan Bryant, "Environmental Racism: Reviewing the Evidence," ibid., pp. 163–69; Grossman, "Environmental Racism," pp. 16–17; Grossman, "From Toxic Racism to Environmental Justice," *E: The Environmental Magazine* 3 (May/June, 1992):30–32; Dick Russell, "Environmental Racism," *Amicus Journal* 11 (Spring, 1989): 22–25; Bryant, "Toxics and Racial Justice," pp. 49–50.

25. For arguments making race the core issue in siting toxic facilities, see Rachel D. Godsil, "Remedying Environmental Racism," *Michigan Law Review* 90 (November, 1991): 397–98; Bullard, *Confronting Environmental Racism,* pp. 10–13, 18, 21. For a listing of empirical studies of environmental disparities by income and race in the United States, see Benjamin A. Goldman, *Not Just Prosperity: Achieving Sustainability with Environmental Justice* (Washington, D.C.: National Wildlife Federation, 1993), pp. 5–6.

26. See Vicki Been, "Market Forces, Not Racist Practices, May Affect the Siting of Locally Undesirable Land Uses," in Jonathan S. Petrikin, ed., *Environmental Justice* (San Diego, 1995), p. 38. See also "What's Fairness Got to Do with It? Environmental Justice and the Siting of Locally Undesirable Land Uses," *Cornell Law Review* 78 (September, 1993): 1014–15, 1018–24; Been, "Locally Undesirable Land Uses in Minority Neighborhoods: Disproportionate Siting or Marketing Dynamics?" *Yale Law Journal* (April, 1994): 1386, 1406. See also Richard J. Lazarus, "Pursuing 'Environmental Justice:' The Distributional Effects of Environmental Protection," *Northwestern University Law Review* 87 (1993): 796; Douglas L. Anderton, et al., "Environmental Equiry: The Demographics of Dumping," *Demography* 31 (May, 1994):

229; Kevin, "'Environmental Racism' and Locally Undesirable Land Uses," pp. 133–38, 145–50.

27. Andrew Hurley, "Fiasco at Wagner Electric: Environmental Justice and Urban Geography in St. Louis," *Environmental History* 2 (October, 1997): 474.

28. See Robert L. Lineberry, *Equality and Urban Policy: The Distribution of Municipal Public Services* (Beverly Hills, CA: Sage, 1977).

29. M.C. Ircha, "Municipal Service Distribution: Equity Concerns," in Paul N. Cheremisinoff et al., eds., *Civil Engineering Practice* (Lancaster, PA: Technomic Pub. Co. 1988), pp. 590–93.

30. A. Myrick Freeman III, "Distribution of Environmental Quality," in Allen V. Kneese and Blair T. Bower, eds., *Environmental Quality Analysis: Theory and Method in the Social Sciences* (Baltimore: Johns Hopkins University Press, 1972), p. 264.

31. Leonard P. Gianessi, Henry M. Peskin, Edward Wolff, "The Distributional Effects of Uniform Air Pollution Policy in the United States,"*Quarterly Journal of Economics* 93 (May, 1979):281.

32. Ibid., pp. 281-96.

33. Michel Gelobter, "Toward a Model of 'Environmental Discrimination,'" Bryant and Mohai, eds., *Race and the Incidence of Environmental Hazards,* pp. 64–73. For a contrary view, see Mohai and Bryant, "Environmental Racism: Reviewing the Evidence," p. 164.

34. Peter Nijkamp, "Equity and Efficiency in Environmental Policy Analysis: Separability Versus Inseprability," in Allan Schnaiberg, Nicholas Watts, and Klaus Zimmerman, eds., *Distributional Conflicts in Environmental-Resource Policy* (New York: St. Martin's Press, 1986), p. 61. See also Miley W. Merkhofer, *Decision Science and Social Risk Management* (Boston: D. Reidel, 1987), pp. 181–82.

35. Freeman, "Distribution of Environmental Quality," p. 274.

36. Rabe, *Beyond NIMBY,* and Herbert Inhaber, *Slaying the NIMBY Dragon* (New Brunswick, NJ: Transaction Publishers, 1998). Like several of the grassroots organizations of the past, women have played a major role in the toxics campaigns—possibly a greater role than in any previous environmental protest activity. See David E. Newton, *Environmental Justice: A Reference Handbook* (Santa Barbara, CA: ABC-Clio, 1996), p. 25; Celene Krauss, "Blue-Collar Women and Toxic-Waste Protests: The Process of Politicization," in Hofrichter, ed. *Toxic Struggles,* pp. 110–12; Barbara Epstein, "Ecofeminism and Grass-roots Environmentalism in the United States," in Hofrichter, ed. *Toxic Struggles,* pp. 144–52; Carolyn Merchant, *Radical Ecology: The Search for a Livable World* (New York: Routledge, 1992), pp. 181ff; Di Chiro, "Nature as Community: The Convergence of Environmental and Social Justice," pp. 299–301.

37. Foreman, *The Promise and Peril of Environmental Justice,* pp. 41–44.

38. See for example Henry Payne, "Green Redlining," *Reason* (October 1998):26–33.

39. Hurley, "Fiasco at Wagner Electric," p. 462.

40. Dolores Greenberg, "Reconstructing Race and Protest: Environmental Justice in New York City," *Environmental History* 5 (April, 2000):225.

41. Ibid., p. 243.

42. Andrew Hurley, *Environmental Inequalities: Class, Race, and Industrial Pollution in Gary, Indiana, 1945–1980* (Chapel Hill: University of North Carolina Press, 1995), pp. 180–181.

43. See, for example, the essays in Martin V. Melosi, ed., *Pollution and Reform in American Cities, 1870–1930* (Austin: University of Texas Press, 1980).

44. See, for example, Samuel P. Hays, *Beauty, Health, and Permanence: Environmental Politics in the United States, 1955–1985* (Cambridge: Cambridge University Press, 1987).

45. In "Efficiency, Equity, Esthetics: Shifting Themes in American Conservation," Donald Worster, ed., *The Ends of the Earth: Perspectives on Modern Environmental History* (New York, Cambridge University Press 1988), pp. 233–34, Clayton Koppes argues persuasively that three ideas dominated the rising conservation movement: efficiency (management of natural resources); equity (distribution of the development of resources rather than control by the few); and esthetics (the preservation of nature free from development). Of the three, efficiency held the greatest sway in the Progressive Era. However, Koppes makes little provision for an urban equivalent of the conservation movement in his argument, and equity is defined in substantially different terms than in the more recent environmental justice context.

46. See Robert Gottlieb, *Forcing the Spring: The Transformation of the American Environmental Movement* (Washington, D.C.: Island Press, 1993), p. 6.

47. Martin V. Melosi, "Lyndon Johnson and Environmental Policy," in Robert A. Divine, ed., *The Johnson Years, Volume Two: Vietnam, the Environment, and Science* (Lawrence: University Press of Kansas, 1987), p. 140.

48. Payne, "Green Redlining," 26–33.

49. Howard Margolis, *Dealing with Risk: Why the Public and the Experts Disagree on Environmental Issues* (Chicago: University of Chicago Press, 1996).

50. Foreman, *The Promise and Peril of Environmental Justice*, pp. 86–87.

51. See ibid., chapter 4. See also Margolis, *Dealing with Risk*.

52. See Been, "Market Forces, Not Racist Practices, May Affect the Siting of Locally Undesirable Land Uses," p. 38; Been, "Locally Undesirable Land Uses in Minority Neighborhoods: Disproportionate Siting or Marketing Dynamics?" pp. 1386, 1406.

53. Ellen Stroud, "Troubled Waters in Ecotopia: Environmental Racism in Portland, Oregon," *Radical History Review* 74 (Spring, 1999):87.

54. Angel Gugliotta, "Class, Gender, and Coal Smoke: Gender Ideology and Environmental Injustice in Pittsburgh, 1868–1914," *Environmental History* 5 (April, 2000):183–184.

55. For more on women and environmental activism, see Elizabeth D. Blum, "Pink and Green: A Comparative Study of Black and White Women's Envi-

ronmental Activism in the Twentieth Century" (Ph.D. dissertation, University of Houston, 2000).

56. Helen M. Ingram, David H. Colnic, and Dean E. Mann, "Interest Groups and Environmental Policy," in James P. Lester, ed., *Environmental Politics and Policy: Theories and Evidence* 2nd ed., (Durham, NC and London: Duke University Press, 1995), p. 120.

57. See for example the testimony of Pat Bryant, executive director of the Gulf Coast Tenants Association in U.S. Congress, House of Representatives, Committee on the Judiciary, *Environmental Justice* (hearings before the subcommittee on civil and constitutional rights), 103d Congress, 1st sess., March 3 and 4, 1993, pp. 10–15.

58. Charles P. Lord and William A. Shuntkin, "Environmental Justice and the Use of History," *Boston College Environmental Affairs Law Review* 22 (March, 1994):4.

59. Ibid., 5.

60. Ibid., 24.

61. Foreman, *The Promise and Peril of Environmental Justice,* chapter 6.

62. See for example Robert E. Litan and William D. Nordhaus, *Reforming Federal Regulation* (New Haven, CT: Yale University Press, 1983), and Richard D. Morgenstern, ed., *Economic Analyses at EPA: Assessing Regulatory Impact* (Washington, D.C.: Resources for the Future, 1997).

63. Stephen G. Breyer, *Breaking the Vicious Circle: Toward Effective Risk Regulation* (Cambridge, MA: Harvard University Press, 1993).

64. Committee for a National Institute for the Environment, *A Proposal for a National Institute for the Environment: Need, Rationale, and Structure* (Washington, D.C.: Committee for a National Institute for the Environment, 1993).

ENVIRONMENTAL HISTORY AT THE GRASSROOTS: THE MISSOURI STATE PARKS EXPERIENCE

Susan Flader

Like other academics seeking professional credibility, including many in the field of environmental history, I had sought to keep my academic research and teaching quite separate from my avocations of hiking and canoeing and my periodic bouts of participation in environmental issues. If I had thought about it, it was my scholarly contributions that had won me positions on national boards of conservation organizations where I had frequently drawn on my historical understanding and perspective, in turn enriching my teaching and research. But these efforts had been more along the lines of institution building than of advocacy, and they were focused at the federal rather than the state or local level. True, I had taught historic preservation, which inevitably drew me to consider state and local issues; but again, like many, I had tended to keep my involvements in historic preservation and in environmental issues quite rigidly compartmentalized, however much I may have sensed—and even taught—that such issues could not logically be separated.

Though I had been fairly active in environmental issues in Wisconsin, I had avoided entanglement in local issues when I moved to Missouri in 1973, not only because of the drain on time but also because I felt a bit embarrassed to become too identified with Missouri, a state that seemed somewhat backward and wary of both academics and outsiders. One could be a Missourian only if one had been born there. Missouri seemed to have nothing like the progressive Wisconsin Idea uniting academics and public officials in service to the state, in which I had so reveled back home. And I did not think I would stay long in any case. That is, until I became involved in state parks and historic sites.[1]

This new preoccupation would demand an increasing amount of my time and energy for the next two decades. It would lead me to tie academic research to institution building and advocacy to an extent I would never have imagined, and it would compel me to appreciate more of the commonalities between natural and cultural resources and between environmental issues and historic preservation. My efforts to help build a citizen constituency for these linked values would draw me inevitably to involvement at the grassroots. In spite of myself, I would come to identify with Missouri and Missourians and to take pride in what we as citizens could accomplish. In the process I even came to think of myself as a Missourian and, as I shall illustrate through a recent case study, to appreciate more of the potential of environmental history at the grassroots.

It all began at a statewide Audubon meeting I attended as an onlooker in the spring of 1982, when the young and passionately idealistic director of state parks, John Karel, who had been a student in my first environmental history class at the University of Missouri nearly a decade earlier, rose to tell of a crisis in the park system. Federal funding from the Land and Water Conservation Fund had been zeroed out by the Reagan administration and recession and inflation had forced a series of recisions in state support, leaving parks with a budget only half what it had been in the late '70s. To many legislators an obvious solution was to transfer parks from the Department of Natural Resources (DNR) to the Conservation Department (MDC), which was handsomely funded with a dedicated one-eighth-cent sales tax resulting from a successful initiative petition campaign in 1976. The conservation department was buying hundreds of thousands of acres of forest and wildlife lands, and some members of its commission and staff apparently saw the park crisis as an opportunity to gain control of another hundred thousand acres of prime public lands simply for the taking. To Karel this solution was anathema. He worried about dilution of the preservationist mission and land management philosophy of the parks within the more utilitarian MDC, and about what would happen to historic sites and other cultural resources in an agency that had no experience with or mandate to protect them; the historic sites could even have been split off from the parks and left hanging out to dry. Karel pleaded with the assembled environmentalists instead to support an alternative bill that would transfer funds from the MDC sales tax to the DNR to support parks.

The confusion and tension in the room were palpable. Undoubtedly some did not even realize that the state had two different natural resource agencies that tended to compete with each other. Survey after survey showed that most Missourians thought parks were part of MDC, a venerable and powerful agency with a well-oiled public relations apparatus that did little to dispel the confusion. Of those who did distinguish between parks and conservation lands, most tended to view the park division in the relatively new DNR (1974) as a poor cousin of MDC concerned primarily with providing for camping, swimming, picnicking and other mass recreation; they had little comprehension of the array and quality of resources preserved in the park system as a whole or of the values at stake in the current crisis. If they thought at all about historic sites, they tended to view them as entirely separate from parks, with little consciousness of any shared values or management concerns. I was in this group, aware that there were two agencies but familiar with only a few parks and historic sites and with no consciousness whatever of a statewide system or of the range and quality of resources it contained. Many people in the room had worked actively in the mid-1970s circulating petitions for the conservation sales tax—or, like me, cheered from the sidelines—and they were understandably reluctant to see part of the hard-won tax diverted by the legislature to unintended uses. But many were also friends and admirers of John Karel, more as a fellow environmentalist than in his role as park director. In short, we had never thought much about parks and felt torn and utterly confused in the current crisis.

In truth, as I came to realize later, it could fairly be said that Missouri had scant constituency for either parks or historic sites and certainly no public appreciation for the two as part of an integrated system.[2] Several historic sites had small but devoted "friends" groups, but there was no statewide organization that focused attention on the sites as a collectivity. The only statewide constituencies that had been cultivated by the park division were a vestige of an earlier time, more oriented to recreational interests than to resource values—groups of campers, hikers, off-road vehicle interests, or equestrians. There was also a professional society, the Missouri Park and Recreation Association (MPRA). But the user groups promoted only their particular uses, and even MPRA, to which many park staff belonged, did not pay much attention to the state park system because the vast majority of its members were employed by city and county park departments, which were more facility than resource driven. In the flush times of the '70s, the park division had hired a number of young naturalists and historians, but these resource-minded professionals had not yet begun to develop statewide constituencies for the natural and cultural resource values in state parks. Many of the naturalists had personal links to Sierra Club and Audubon chapters, but leaders of those groups, like the national organizations of which they were a part, tended to focus on the U.S. Congress and federal land management agencies rather than on state government, which they considered largely ineffective if not benighted. On state legislative issues they usually followed the lead of the Conservation Federation of Missouri, an affiliate of the National Wildlife Federation, which dealt with a wide range of issues but, when the chips were down, almost always sided with MDC.

The painful uncertainty and even contention among environmental leaders being lobbied to side with one agency or the other was finally alleviated when Charles Callison rose to speak. Callison had been head of the Conservation Federation back in the 1940s and then longtime executive vice president of the National Audubon Society in New York, but he had recently retired and moved back to Jefferson City. He was so unassuming that it is likely that many people in the room did not even know who he was, though I had formed an enduring friendship with him when he had warmly welcomed me, a recent transplant from Wisconsin, as a fellow Missourian when I joined the National Audubon board back in 1974. Addressing Karel he said forthrightly, "John, you are doing a good job with the parks and you need help; we will see that you get it, but we are NOT going to raid the conservation sales tax."

Several months later, after the legislative session ended with no action on parks, Callison invited Karel and a number of environmental leaders to his home to lay the groundwork for a new citizen group devoted solely to state parks, the Missouri Parks Association (MPA). As the person who had led the establishment of the Audubon regional structure and encouraged the formation of hundreds of new local chapters nationwide, he was a great believer in the power of an alert, active citizen; and he understood also the importance of a focused mission. I was not at all sure that Missouri needed yet another conservation organization, but I had too much respect for Callison and Karel to decline to participate. The new non-profit organization, independent and non-partisan, would be dedicated to the protection, enhancement, and interpretation of Missouri state parks and historic sites. Though we all assumed Callison would head the new organization, he prevailed on me to be president, saying "I'll be your Boy Friday."

Although the impetus for the new organization had come from the environmental community, MPA was determined from the outset to address historical and cultural as well as natural values of the system, however little precedent there had been for history advocates to work with environmental groups on statewide issues. Callison himself had profound historical consciousness; he had written a history of *Man and Wildlife in Missouri* (1953) and regularly placed environmental issues in historical context in his columns and articles. As volunteer editor of MPA's newsletter, *Heritage*, he continued to do so. Karel had been an undergraduate history major before switching to wildlife ecology for his master's degree. As the first park director with a background in history, he had already been making efforts within the park bureaucracy to bring cultural and natural resource professionals into closer working relationship and to stimulate appreciation for cultural values in natural parks and natural values in historic sites. Among others on the first board of the new MPA were Dorothy Heinze, who had led efforts to save a number of historic sites; Erle Lionberger, a leader of the Missouri Trust for Historic Preservation; Leonard Hall, author of *Stars Upstream*, an historical memoir of the Ozarks; and Roger Pryor, a St. Louis environmental leader with a decidedly historical bent.[3]

As leaders of the association we saw our initial challenges as twofold—to develop a constituency for parks by educating Missouri citizens and public officials about the nature and mission of the park system and to establish a consistent base of financial support. Fortunately, park officials had devoted considerable attention during the darkest days of the funding crisis to articulating and developing a clear understanding among park staff of the three-fold mission of the Missouri system— to preserve and interpret the finest examples of Missouri's natural landscapes; to preserve and interpret outstanding examples of Missouri's cultural heritage; and to provide healthy and enjoyable outdoor recreation opportunities consistent with its mission—and they had undertaken conceptual planning to lay the groundwork for a prioritized program of improvements should funds become available. But they had barely begun to communicate these efforts to the general public.

In a rush of enthusiasm MPA began laying plans with park administrators for an ambitious color-illustrated book about the nature and mission of the system with essays on each of the seventy-five parks and historic sites, somewhat on the model of the early national park portfolios that had created the mystique of national parks as inviolable places back in the 1920s. We had to develop a critical mass of Missourians who believed that the parks were worth protecting and supporting, and we would create this constituency by awakening their interest in both history and natural history. We were determined to impart an understanding of the cultural and natural values at stake in every unit of the system, both parks and historic sites, and to present the system as an integrated whole. At the time there were few models at the state level to go by, other than Freeman Tilden's classic *The State Parks: Their Meaning in American Life* (1962) and a history of *State Parks of California* (1980) by Joseph Engbeck and Philip Hyde.[4] But both were highly selective. We wanted to highlight and explore linkages of cultural and natural resource values in both parks and historic sites throughout the system, in order to make separation of historic sites from parks unthinkable in the future. And of course we also wanted to enhance understanding and commitment within the agency regarding the implications of that linkage for management and interpretation.

Because there had been no previous history of the park system amounting to more than a few pages, much of which turned out to be inaccurate, and no histories of individual parks or sites beyond the limited copy in brochures, MPA and the park division teamed with the Missouri Cultural Heritage Center at the university, which I had helped establish, in a successful effort to seek funding through the university's research board for original archival research by a history graduate student. We contracted with Roger Pryor to begin visiting and writing essays on each of the parks, drawing on our archival research as well as on his own vast knowledge of the state's natural and cultural history, and with Oliver Schuchard, an art professor who had studied photography with Ansel Adams, to make large-format 'signature' images of each park. We all met frequently as a planning team to discuss appropriate images and themes for the various units.

MPA also began that first year to lobby legislators, especially with regard to a promising proposal for a one-tenth-cent sales tax to be split evenly between parks and soil conservation, two programs administered by DNR. The plan was obviously modeled on the state's conservation sales tax, but it was more modest and combined an appeal to urbanites (parks) with a program for rural areas (soil); at the time Missouri was second in the nation in the severity of its cropland erosion problem. In tax-averse Missouri, there would be no chance to secure enactment of such a measure by the general assembly, but in the throes of the park and soil crises legislators might be willing to approve a resolution placing the measure on a statewide ballot as a referendum for Missouri citizens to decide. With the Missouri Parks Association in strong support and other citizen organizations following its lead, the measure won legislative approval literally in the final hour of the 1983 session, after a regrettable amendment to change a ten-year sunset clause to only five years.

In an effort to establish the leadership role of our fledgling organization, MPA hosted a series of meetings in my living room that summer with conservation, agriculture, and agency leaders to plan strategy for a major public campaign for citizen enactment of the tax. We eventually formed a new umbrella organization, the Citizens Committee for Soil, Water, and State Parks, with several of us from MPA among the directors, to spearhead the effort. It should be noted that historical societies and other cultural organizations were conspicuously absent from the coalition, presumably believing (erroneously) that their 501-C-3 status prevented them from any such political action.

While the campaign for the parks and soils tax was underway, the Missouri Parks Association, by now aware that our proposed book on the parks would be a long time in coming, sought to focus more public and media attention on the park system by hosting, in concert with a wide array of other environmental, cultural, and recreational cosponsoring organizations, what we billed as the "First Missouri Conference on State Parks." It was a three-day event funded in part by the Missouri Committee for the Humanities, complete with field trips to nearby parks and workshops on park resources and issues. Realizing the importance of a broader perspective on the values at stake in the Missouri system, MPA invited two nationally known experts on state parks—historian Robin Winks of Yale University and Ney Landrum, Florida park director and past president of the National Association of State Park Directors—to keynote the conference, taking them on a whirlwind tour of ten representative parks and historic sites with park officials prior to the conference. They came through by explaining how park systems represent the heritage and values of a state and lauding the quality and cohesiveness of the Missouri system, which they rated one of the best in the country, if only it were adequately funded.[5]

After months of substantial public education and media spotlight on the parks, Missouri citizens in August 1984 voted by the narrowest of margins—only 1699

Figure 15-1. MPA President Susan Flader with Yale historian Robin Winks (center), who keynoted the First Missouri Conference on State Parks in spring 1984, and State Representative LeRoy Braumgardt, who introduced the resolution for the Parks and Soils Sales Tax approved by Missouri voters a few months later. *Photo contributed by author.*

votes out of nearly a million cast—to approve the tax. We went to bed election night fearing we had lost and awoke to victory. Money for the new tax would not even begin to flow for nearly a year, and only a few years after that it would be necessary to return to the voters for reauthorization, so it was critical for the park division to show quick results and for MPA to be vigilant in defending use of the tax for its intended purposes. These purposes, in true Missouri conservative spirit, were primarily "to take care of what we have," rather than substantially to expand the system. In the years to come, MPA would spend far more time and energy fighting *against* inappropriate, money-draining proposals than *for* new parks.

As it happened, there would be more new funds in the ensuing years than any of us had contemplated. A state bond issue for capital improvements that had been kicked around in the legislature for years at last became reality in 1985, after a change in administration, and parks—because of shrewd decisions by DNR officials in the depths of the funding crisis in the early '80s—would ultimately reap nearly $60 million for upgrades of water and sewer systems and roads and campgrounds, restoration of ecosystems and historic structures, and construction of visitor centers and museums, especially at historic sites. The emphasis on historic sites and cultural resources was a direct consequence of Karel's leadership of the system, but MPA was especially vigilant in defense of the funds, realizing that visitor centers and restorations might be the first to be lopped by the legislature if funds ran short. Combined with more than $13 million a year in additional funds from the sales tax, mostly for operations, the Missouri system was poised for a renaissance akin to that in the CCC days of the 1930s.

The aura of sudden wealth attracted an enormous array of proposals for what some treated as a "park barrel," a trough of riches at which it was supposed anyone could feed. Proposals surfaced for urban storm sewers and for local golf courses, swimming pools, zoos, and other projects that could not possibly meet the test of statewide natural or cultural significance. But each was in the district of some legislator who wanted his or her share, and MPA was kept busy in the halls of the capitol explaining the mission of the system and the need to resist diversions and use funds as the voters intended. MPA found itself increasingly defending the concept of cultural and natural resources of statewide significance against a legion of interests arguing for local recreational facilities.

Some proposals were more difficult to fight than others because of the array of political forces lined up on their behalf. MPA failed to turn back a $2 million diversion for a new African-American community center in Kansas City, despite arguing that the site itself had no intrinsic cultural value, the facility would not be operated by the state, and the cost would preclude investment in other African-American sites worthy of preservation. But the constellation of interests that wanted this particular facility had more sway with the state political leadership at the time than other African-American groups advocating truly significant sites. It would be fourteen years, under continual prodding by MPA, before an agreement could finally be negotiated with the city for the park division to share in operating the center as a bona fide state park facility by developing a state civil rights museum.

On another high profile issue MPA was more immediately successful. When the governor himself proposed use of $1.4 million in park funds to repair the exterior stonework of the state capitol, park officials—situated as they were within a cabinet agency—had no choice but to acquiesce. It remained for MPA to issue press releases and rally other organizations in opposition to the diversion, carefully explaining that while the capitol might indeed be the state's most important historic building, within which the park division administered the state museum, maintenance of the building itself was not a state park responsibility. Each victory in defense of the park system and its dedicated tax added to the credibility of the organization and made the next battle a bit easier.

The positive influence of a citizen organization such as MPA on strategic decisions *within* the agency it supports and on staff understanding of the agency's mission is also worthy of note. On numerous occasions over the years MPA spoke up, in board meetings or through its quarterly newsletter or quietly in conversations with key park administrators or, if necessary, through public news releases and lobbying with other organizations and state officials, on behalf of resource values that might otherwise have been given short shrift by certain park officials. As often as not, it was cultural resources—such as the extraordinary vertical-log houses and common field landscape in Ste. Genevieve—that needed defending in an agency that, in spite of its best efforts, was still weighted toward the natural and the recreational. Often too there were natural resources—such as the integrity of dedicated wild areas—that could best be defended with a historical or cultural line of argument.

During the course of these unremitting struggles I came to a far deeper understanding and even appreciation of Missouri political culture. Long discussions with my colleague David Thelen, who was working on a history of Missouri from the Civil War to World War I, led me to appreciate that Missouri had a progressive tradition, but it was different than that in Wisconsin and at the federal level. As a legacy of unpopular government and massive indebtedness after the Civil War, Missourians had developed a strong skepticism of government and antipathy to taxes that left it by the 1980s as what the *St. Louis Post-Dispatch* called "the forty-something state," perennially near the bottom in expenditures on most public services when its population and wealth should have placed it middling or above among the states. Missouri had resisted institutionalization of new governmental functions in the Progressive Era. Despite a stunning resource base, it did not begin to develop a park system until the mid-1920s and even then did so on a shoestring, and it did not authorize national forests or begin a state forest system until the 1930s. Missouri progressives instead had insisted on respect for law throughout the political and corporate as well as civic realms, so that the government, however weak and impecunious, was essentially honest and public spirited. The state had also been one of only three east of the Great Plains to enact the initiative petition advocated by progressives as a way to give more direct democratic control to the voters.[6] Missourians had used the initiative in 1936 to "take fish and game out of politics" by establishing a non-partisan conservation commission;

they used it again in 1976 to better fund their conservation programs, and they would resort to it repeatedly to reenact the soils and parks tax. In short, though they held the reins tightly on government, they would exert themselves as citizens to protect and support what they valued. The upshot was a more vibrant tradition of citizen action in Missouri than I had experienced even in Wisconsin with its vaunted progressive tradition.

When the sales tax came up for renewal in the late 1980s, proponents of sundry worthy causes came out in force, seeking to gain a ride on the bandwagon. After two years of unsuccessful struggle to secure a referendum on simple renewal from the state legislature, MPA and a few other groups, including soil conservation interests, decided to mount an arduous initiative petition campaign for renewal of the tax. It would require gathering well over 200,000 signatures of registered voters properly distributed across congressional districts in order to place such a measure on the ballot. Laborious as the process is for the hundreds, even thousands, of volunteers involved in organizing the campaign and circulating petitions, such an effort in direct democracy engages people in defense of values about which they care and infuses understanding and a sense of ownership among substantial segments of the public. The petition drive was successful, and the voters in November 1988 approved renewal of the tax by more than two to one. However parsimonious Missourians might have been with their state government, they were proud of their parks and willing to support them.

A year after reauthorization of the parks and soils tax, it was the featured case example of park funding in a major national study of state parks funded by the Conservation Foundation. Generalizing from experience with special funds in a number of states, the study concluded: "Perhaps the most important lesson is that an earmarked fund does not put a park system outside the political arena. . . . It is rather a fresh point of entry to raise the visibility of state parks, air information about their condition and future prospects, and build new alliances."[7] Indeed, the Missouri experience suggests that parks are inevitably political because virtually every citizen and public official feels some sort of personal stake in at least certain parks or certain uses of parks. And this is doubly true of historic sites, which after all represent the people's history, on which they believe they are the experts. The challenge is to create a vision for the system as a whole guided by a clearly articulated mission that can provide a basis for assessing the myriad issues and proposals that arise, and to develop a constituency committed to defending that mission and advancing the vision. In Missouri, a vital aspect of that mission and vision was the integration of cultural and natural heritage values.

In 1992, a full decade after laying the initial groundwork for a color-illustrated book about the system, the ambitious project finally came to fruition with the publication of a handsome, large-format volume, *Exploring Missouri's Legacy: State Parks and Historic Sites*. In the end, the project had proved too ambitious for one writer and one photographer to complete by themselves, so John Karel (no longer park director but now on the MPA board), Charlie Callison, and I also assumed major roles in the writing. We also combed park division and other sources for

missing images, and several park staff volunteered to take particular shots we still
needed. In the final year we undertook a massive review process—the entire 750-
page manuscript was reviewed by five cultural and natural resource specialists and
each individual essay was read by eight to ten others—a process that had the effect of investing virtually the entire professional staff of the agency in the book. I
then devoted months to what I called "getting the gremlins out"—excising literally hundreds of apochrypha that get repeated in book after book but cannot be
substantiated or are contradicted by original sources. Having decided not to identify authors of individual essays in order to write insofar as possible in a single
voice, we also engaged in several running battles over interpretation, refighting the
Civil War and the battle of the eastern red cedar (to eradicate or to revere?) in every
conceivable essay. As the book grew ever larger and more elaborate, MPA un-

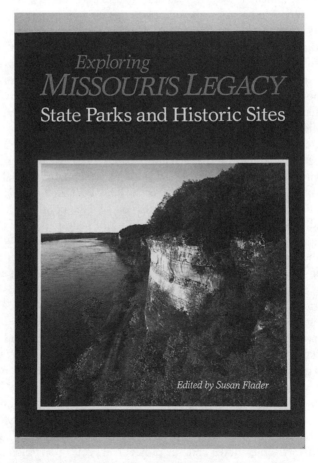

Figure 15-2. The cover of Missouri's state park book, showing the Katy Trail State Park
that links natural and cultural heritage along some 200 miles of the Missouri River. *University of Missouri Press, photo by Frank Oberle.*

dertook a campaign to raise funds from our members to keep the price within reach of ordinary citizens and to provide complimentary copies for legislators and other public officials—thus fortuitously further spreading ownership of the enterprise.[8]

The new book—coupled with the presentation of the parks themselves through new visitor centers and museums, superb natural and cultural interpretation, and upgraded facilities and stewardship as a result of the bond issue and park sales tax—left little doubt about the quality and integrity of mission of the Missouri system. And the system, though only middling in size at 138,000 acres in some eighty units, won recognition nationally, being selected three years in a row by the late '90s as a finalist for the National Gold Medal for state park systems. Because MPA had been so closely involved in shepherding the book project from its inception, the organization gained additional credibility from the book to augment that gained from the passage, renewal, and defense of the sales tax, credibility on which we would draw frequently in subsequent years in defense of the natural and cultural values of the parks and in making the case for yet another renewal of the sales tax. There is no question that Missourians now realize they have something special in their state park system and that they are willing to defend as well as to enjoy it.

The remainder of this essay offers a detailed case study of a recently successful historical-cultural argument in defense of a prime natural park, Taum Sauk Mountain at the geologic core of the Ozarks, together with the argument itself as published in MPA's newsletter, *Heritage*. The case also demonstrates how quickly and effectively MPA members and other Missourians will respond to defend what they value, illustrating the power of an active, alert citizenry.

The issue began to materialize in spring 2001, when MPA heard rumors from park staff that the state's biggest electric utility, Ameren (formerly Union Electric Power of St. Louis), was trying to purchase private property along Taum Sauk Creek that it would need in order to build a second pumped storage hydroelectric plant on Church Mountain similar to its existing Taum Sauk Plant on nearby Proffit Mountain. Union Electric already owned much of Church Mountain, immediately adjacent to Taum Sauk Mountain State Park, and had leased it to DNR for park trail development. Park naturalists considered the area equal in quality to adjacent public lands, 7000 acres of which constituted the St. Francois Mountains Natural Area, the state's largest. Obviously, this would be a threat of major proportions to the integrity of the park and the natural area, and MPA reported the issue briefly in its April newsletter as something to watch.

In late June we learned that Ameren had quietly issued a news release, not picked up by the press, that it had filed a request with the Federal Energy Regulatory Commission (FERC) for a preliminary permit to further evaluate the project, though there were still no specifics available. I was in my second stint as president of MPA and was also interim editor of the newsletter, so I visited the park to visualize the situation in preparation for an article and any action we might need. While there I ran into the park superintendent who told me that he had just that day

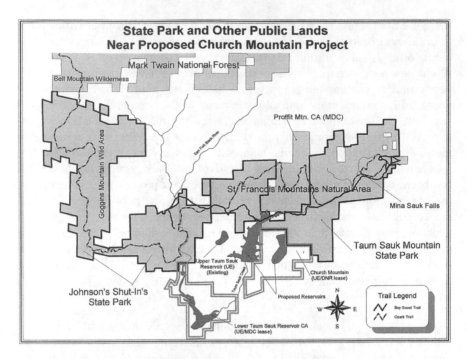

Figure 15-3. Map of Taum Sauk area prepared by Kris Dolle and Susam Flader for *Heritage,* August 2001.

encountered surveyors on park land who were working for Ameren. They showed him a map with the proposed elevation of the lower reservoir along the creek, indicating that it would indeed flood some park land and a popular Boy Scout trail. But not until mid-July did park officials learn, apparently from a staffer who had been surfing the internet, that Ameren's application for a FERC permit was now available on-line and that a sixty-day period for filing comments or motions to intervene had already begun July 5—meaning it would effectively end the week before Labor Day, following a period when many people are away on vacation. On checking the byzantine FERC regulations with legal help, we also discovered that it would be virtually impossible to intervene after the initial deadline. The timing seemed to some of us a deliberate effort to slip the permit through with minimal public interference.

MPA leaders realized that this project was probably the greatest threat to the integrity of a state park in the two decades of the association's existence, and that MPA would obviously have to take the lead in shaping a strategy for dealing with the issue. It would be complicated not only by the short time frame—only six weeks—but also by the fact that the country was still reeling from an energy crisis and many Missourians did not regard the existing Taum Sauk reservoirs as much of a problem; hence they might not appreciate the threat posed by the new ones, which only people intimately familiar with the area would realize were in much more exposed and sensitive locations. There was thus an urgent need to educate our own board, and our members, and public officials, and leaders and members of other potentially supportive organizations—all in time for them to express themselves within six weeks.

On checking Ameren's website, I noted that despite a recent corporate restructuring the top executives were long-time Union Electric employees with deep involvement in various community efforts. This observation—together with the persistent question, "How could they possibly think they could get away with this?"—led to an hypothesis that perhaps the executives themselves did not fully understand the values at stake in the area. And it led to a corollary, that if MPA could somehow find a way to sit down with them in a non-polarized atmosphere and explain the situation, the firm might yet decide to withdraw the project.

This line of thinking was premised on a fundamentally historical argument: Perhaps Ameren executives actually thought they were thinking historically, in that they were following a plan they had developed forty years earlier when they had acquired the land for two pumped storage plants but built only one; now that the economics were favorable, especially in the wake of the California energy crisis, they might simply be following through on the original plan. What they had probably not considered, however, was the extent to which the larger historical context of their decision making had changed in the meantime—e.g., public investment in nearby lands, an established pattern of recreational use, new citizen environmental attitudes, greater scientific appreciation of biodiversity values.

The task at hand was to flesh out the argument in an article for the newsletter, an article that could simultaneously address *all* the different audiences we had to reach (our members, members of other groups, Ameren executives, public officials, the media) because there would be no time to tailor it. We also began immediately to seek through various channels to arrange a meeting with Ameren executives at which the issues might be discussed and the article shown to them, if possible even before it would be mailed to others. Through the grapevine, we learned that other organizations were also gearing up to oppose the project, including the St. Louis-based Missouri Coalition for the Environment, the Ozark Chapter of the Sierra Club, and several Audubon groups. This made it imperative for us to call an early meeting of environmental leaders in order to discuss the issue and seek consensus, if possible, on MPA's strategy.

In the few days prior to our July 25 meeting of environmental leaders, I redoubled my efforts to find answers to myriad questions (most of them historical) and draft the article, a task that might have been insurmountable in the short time available had it not been for earlier research on the Taum Sauk area for the state park book and more recent research for an article on Missouri's forest history that could provide a context for understanding the issues.[9] A visit to the state archives and library turned up precious little on Union Electric or its existing Taum Sauk plant, except for an obscure reference to an old master's thesis on the company. But there was no copy of the thesis available anywhere except at Truman State University a hundred miles north, and they would not send it on interlibrary loan. Fortunately, a former graduate student now on the Truman faculty agreed to copy the thesis and meet me at a highway interchange the next morning en route to a soccer match in St. Louis. The thesis, though quite unreliable, led me to several key references. An MU student interning with the park division agreed to help generate a map of the proposed reservoirs in relation to other public lands in the area, a surprisingly complex process, and numerous conservationists, Boy Scout leaders, and public officials responded openly to questions during telephone interviews.

With the draft article and map available in time for the July 25 meeting, environmental leaders agreed with MPA's interpretation and adopted our strategy to seek a meeting with Ameren executives and to refrain from "going public"—to the media—until the more conciliatory approach had had an opportunity to work. But with the deadline for FERC comments now only five weeks away, it was

Figure 15-4. Missouri's new Taum Sauk State Park, which graced the cover of DNR's 1992 study of threats to the parks, ironically became the most threatened park in the system in 2001 when Ameren announced plans for a hydroelectric plant on Church Mountain (in the distance under the pine bough). *Missoula Department of Natural Resources.*

agreed that the newsletter would include instructions for commenting to FERC and encourage writers to send copies of their comments also to the CEO of Ameren and to the governor, who would presumably be determining the state's official position and deciding whether the DNR would intervene in the proceeding (the new governor was a friend of parks but we knew he had received significant contributions from Ameren, one of the state's most powerful corporations). The MPA article would be made available electronically for use by other organizations as soon as it was in final form, but we all agreed we would encourage personal, respectful expressions of involvement in and concern about the Taum Sauk area rather than to rally any massive "canned" statements of opposition, in keeping with our conciliatory strategy. It was also agreed that we would reach out to some of the more politically conservative organizations such as the Nature Conservancy, the Conservation Federation of Missouri, and the Boy Scouts in an effort to demonstrate essential unanimity along the entire spectrum of the conservation community in the state. We reluctantly concluded that, though our argument was essentially historical-cultural, there was scant hope of getting historical and cultural organizations in Missouri to take a position on such an issue, especially on short notice during the summer.

As it happened, the unfortunate summer-vacation timing of the FERC comment period had more detrimental impact on our efforts to secure a meeting with Ameren than on our efforts to secure expressions of citizen concern. Virtually all of the people we knew who could have served as "go-betweens" to help set up such a meeting were on vacation themselves. When one finally returned and attempted to reach a friend on the Ameren board his calls were not returned, perhaps because the Ameren official was on vacation. Instead, it became necessary for me to *write* to the Ameren CEO to request a meeting, enclosing a copy of the newsletter article. But there was no response. In the meantime, the MPA newsletter reached those of our 1,800 members who were not away on vacation and stimulated dozens of them to write heartfelt expressions of their experiences and concerns. The letters began appearing on the FERC website by the second week of August; several came from Boy Scout leaders or former scouts who had had formative experiences hiking the historic Taum Sauk Trail that would be flooded by the lower reservoir. We knew the personal testimonials would not make much difference in the pro forma FERC proceeding, but we hoped they would be read with more effect in the offices of Ameren and the governor.

MPA developed a board resolution on the issue, stating our concerns and our intent to consider formal intervention in the FERC proceeding, then sent copies of the resolution and the newsletter to all state elected and appointed officials who might be expected to have an eventual role in the approval process for the plant, including the governor, attorney general, legislators, conservation commission, public service commission, and numerous DNR divisions and boards. (MPA has no staff, so the writing, organizing and secretarial efforts obliterated my research agenda for a time.) Other organizations used MPA's resolution as the basis for similar resolutions from their own boards. The mailings were followed by personal phone calls with key officials to alert them to citizen concern about the issue and discuss possible avenues for their involvement; we especially encouraged DNR, the attorney general, and the public service commission to intervene formally in the FERC proceeding. When we learned that Ameren had applied to DNR for a routine Land Disturbance Stormwater Permit in order to clear access roads and drill sites on Church Mountain, MPA and several other groups petitioned DNR to require more extensive review and opportunity for public comment. It seemed clear to us that Ameren was in earnest about this project, with bulldozers ready to roll.

In the meantime, assuming from our lack of response from Ameren that we were in for a long struggle, we began laying the groundwork for a more formal network of cooperating organizations, the Taum Sauk Coalition, that would span the conservation spectrum in the state; and MPA, along with the Coalition for the Environment and the Sierra Club, began seeking legal advice concerning intervention. The legal process was complicated by the need to file a formal motion containing all relevant evidence by the end of August, when no conservation groups or attorneys in Missouri—or state agencies, for that matter—had had previous experience with hydroelectric projects in the FERC era. And it was frustrated by our inability to reach knowledgeable attorneys elsewhere in the country, many of whom were on vacation. Eventually, with the help of an attorney I had fortuitously met in Alaska earlier in the summer, I located an attorney in Berkeley, California, who was immediately intrigued by historical aspects of the case—its relationship to the significant Taum Sauk and Storm King Supreme Court decisions in the 1960s— and was willing to help. The board approved legal action, for the first time in MPA's history. I began working with our partners to gather material for the brief, which would then be put in final form and submitted by our attorney in California as a joint motion of MPA, CFE, and Sierra Club.

On Sunday, August 19, the *St. Louis Post-Dispatch,* which had carried one brief article about the project earlier, ran a lead editorial, "Desecrating a Mountain." It began, "If Godzilla went on a bender through the heart of the Ozarks, it's doubtful he could do much worse than what Ameren has in mind for Church Mountain." Though coalition members had not sought the editorial—we were still continuing efforts to secure a meeting with Ameren—and newspapers elsewhere in the state did not follow up on it with coverage of their own, the editorial had the effect of galvanizing Ameren, who apparently assumed it had been instigated by MPA. Several days earlier I had had a cordial phone call from the manager of Ameren's existing Taum Sauk plant, who had seen the *Heritage* article, of which he was quite complimentary, and thought it would be useful to sit down with us. He indicated he was unaware of our efforts to seek a meeting with the CEO of Ameren but said he doubted that someone at that level would meet with us anyway. But after the editorial appeared, communications to set up the lower-level meeting slowed appreciably, and a week later, following an obviously intense period of reassessment at Ameren, the plant manager emailed that he had been directed to withdraw the proposed meeting.

That same night I received a call from a friend in the attorney general's office alerting me that Church Mountain had just appeared on the Public Service Commission agenda for the next morning. The hearing included a background presentation by DNR, following essentially the historical argument in the MPA article, and discussion about the potential roles of DNR and PSC in reviewing the project, including implications if the plant were to be constructed by an unregulated affiliate of Ameren that would sell the electricity outside the state. It was obvious that at least one commissioner thought PSC should itself intervene in the FERC proceeding—DNR had indicated it was working on a draft motion, though the governor had not yet decided what the state's position would be—and the commission agreed to seek more information and take the matter up again two days later, which would still allow for a last-minute intervention.

Following the hearing, I was approached by a woman I recognized from dealings years earlier with the DNR director's office who asked if I had time to meet with several people to be briefed on recent developments. Only after saying yes did I realize that she had passed through the revolving door and now worked for Ameren. Though I felt distinctly alone and unprepared, the meeting was a low-key, informative exchange with four Ameren officials, including the lead engineer and attorney for the project, about the realities of competition during the uncertain transition to deregulation. They spoke specifically about how the energy field was being reshaped by Ken Lay at Enron (who was unknown to me at the time), and we also discussed the values at stake and possibilities for mitigating environmental concerns in the Taum Sauk area. They said they appreciated our concern about the area, having seen both my *Heritage* article and our park book. On my return to Columbia, John Karel phoned to say there had been a forceful letter to the editor in the *Post-Dispatch* that morning by the senior vice-president of Ameren, Paul Agathen, refuting the paper's earlier editorial. Having had a high school classmate in St. Louis by the name of Agathen, Karel had phoned his friend to see if he might be Paul Agathen's brother. He was, and he volunteered to tell his brother of our desire for a meeting. At long last it seemed we had a channel to the top.

The next afternoon, August 29, a flurry of last-minute work on our joint citizen motion to intervene was repeatedly punctuated by phone calls about breaking developments in Jefferson City—the attorney general that morning had filed a motion with FERC on behalf of DNR *in strong opposition* to the project, the governor had also indicated his opposition, and DNR had turned down Ameren's application for a general land disturbance permit. Then another phone call. It was from the Ameren attorney I had met the day before informing me that Ameren had decided to withdraw its application for the FERC permit and would not proceed with the plant on Church Mountain. "We've heard loud and clear from the people of Missouri," he told me, congratulating us on the victory and on the tenor of the campaign. As I hung up the phone in utter shock, it rang again, and John Karel reported a similar call from Paul Agathen.

It was a stunning denouement—a realization of the goal toward which MPA and our allies had been working but which had seemed beyond reach, at least in the

short run. No state official with whom any of us talked after the fact would acknowledge that the incredible end-game had been choreographed in any way.
MPA, CFE, and Sierra Club decided not to submit our joint motion to intervene,
and on behalf of the Taum Sauk Coalition I issued our first and only news release,
lauding Ameren for its decision. We also invited Ameren and state officials who
had been involved in the issue to a celebratory picnic and hike on Church Mountain several weeks hence, which the local plant manager graciously attended. And
in October John Karel and I finally had a meeting with Paul Agathen for a cordial
and highly positive discussion of a range of options for preservation of natural and
cultural values as Ameren planned for the future of its Church Mountain property.

Discussions with Ameren officials and various state policy makers after the fact
seemed to confirm that MPA's historical-cultural argument and the upwelling of
its grassroots constituency had indeed made a difference. The local plant manager
had deep family roots in the area and acknowledged being fascinated to learn history he had not known, and several others from Ameren admitted that in reading
the *Heritage* article and essays about the area in the park book they had begun to
realize how much resonance the values articulated there had with the general public. The depth of feeling in the letters sent to FERC, the governor and Ameren and
the immediacy with which virtually the entire spectrum of the conservation community in Missouri joined the cause offered ample evidence of how much Missourians cared about the area. More than seventy comments were posted on the
FERC website and there would surely have been more if Ameren had not with-
drawn before the deadline—*and every one of them was in opposition to the project.* One burly hiker encountered months later on a park trail admitted he had cried
when he read the *Heritage* article because he had felt so hopeless about the situation until he saw the nature of the argument that could be made.

As one Ameren official explained, "We are engineers and economists who were
just following a plan made years ago." When the economic situation appeared favorable they began engineering studies, assuming they would be able to take care
of any environmental problems along the way. They simply had not considered
how many thousands of Boy Scouts had taken the measure of themselves on the
historic Taum Sauk Trail or how much public investment had gone into land in the
area or how much more willing citizens were to rise to the defense of heritage and
biodiversity values in the years since the first plant had been built. In short, they
did not appreciate the change over time in their decisionmaking environment or
the extent to which Taum Sauk had become a cultural icon. The governor and
many state officials had undoubtedly also thought first about the need for energy
at a time of national energy crisis; though they were concerned about the state
park, they were waiting to see a compelling argument for saving the mountain and
a demonstration that citizen organizations and ordinary citizens cared enough to
make their voices heard.

The experience of Missouri suggests that there is a vital role for history and historians in citizen organizations concerned with what most people would regard as
environmental matters. Historical arguments resonate with ordinary people be-

cause it is their history on which we draw. Our challenge is to broaden our concept of the environment to include people and their values and to deepen the nexus of cultural and natural resources in public understanding. Only by developing a strong foundation at the grassroots can we create an environment in which agency staff will sensitively manage and interpret both cultural and natural heritage and citizens will rise to the challenge of protecting what they value.

NOTES

1. Parts of this essay are adapted from "Building a Constituency for State Parks: The Missouri Experience," *The George Wright Forum,* 17:3 (2000): 31–39.
2. In Missouri, state historic sites are legally state parks. Missouri in this respect is similar to the federal model, unlike many states in which parks, historic sites, and historic preservation are in separate agencies.
3. Charles Callison, *Man and Wildlife in Missouri: The History of One State's Treatment of its Natural Resources* (Harrisburg, PA: The Stackpole Company), pp. 134; Leonard Hall, *Stars Upstream: Life Along an Ozark River* (Chicago: University of Chicago Press, 1958), pp. 252.
4. Freeman Tilden, *The State Parks: Their Meaning in American Life* (New York: Alfred A. Knopf, 1962); Joseph H. Engbeck, Jr., and Philip Hyde, *State Parks of California from 1864 to the Present* (Portland, OR: C.H. Belding, 1980). Among other books on state park systems that have appeared since 1982 are Thomas Cox, *The Park Builders: A History of State Parks in the Pacific Northwest* (Seattle: University of Washington Press, 1988); Roy W. Meyer, *Everyone's Country Estate: A History of Minnesota's State Parks* (St. Paul: Minnesota Historical Society Press, 1991); Dan Cupper, *Our Priceless Heritage: Pennsylvania's State Parks,* 1893–1993 (Harrisburg: Pennsylvania Historical and Museum Commission, 1993); Rebecca Conard, *Places of Quiet Beauty: Parks, Preserves, and Environmentalism* (Iowa City: University of Iowa Press, 1997); and James Wright Steely, *Parks for Texas: Enduring Landscapes of the New Deal* (Austin: University of Texas Press, 1999).
5. Susan Flader, ed., *First Missouri Conference on State Parks, June 15–17, 1984: Proceedings* (Columbia, MO: Missouri Parks Association, Missouri Department of Natural Resources, and Missouri Cultural Heritage Center, 1984), p. 40.
6. David Thelen, *Paths of Resistance: Tradition and Dignity in Industrializing Missouri* (New York: Oxford University Press, 1986); Peter Hernon et al, "Missouri: The Forty-Something State," *St. Louis Post-Dispatch,* November 25–30, 1990.
7. Phyllis Myers, *State Parks in a New Era; Volume 2—Future Directions in Funding* (Washington, D.C.: The Conservation Foundation, 1989), p. 21.
8. Susan Flader, ed., *Exploring Missouri's Legacy: State Parks and Historic Sites* (Columbia: University of Missouri Press, 1992), p. 352.
9. "History of Missouri Forests and Forest Conservation," in Susan Flader, ed.,

Toward Sustainability for Missouri Forests (St. Paul: USFS North Central Research Station), forthcoming.

APPENDIX

(Article in *Heritage,* Newsletter of the Missouri Parks Association, August 2001, by Susan Flader)

Taum Sauk Area Threatened By Hydro Plant

When state park officials selected a cover photo to illustrate their first-ever assessment of "threats to the parks" nearly a decade ago, they chose not a scene of despoliation but a symbolic representation of the best of what they were seeking to protect. It was a vista at the core of the Ozarks, looking from the state's grandest waterfall near its tallest peak across its deepest valley into the heart of Taum Sauk Mountain State Park, Missouri's then-newest public park but also its geologically oldest, wildest, most intact, and most ecologically diverse landscape.

Scarcely could one imagine that the very symbol of what they were seeking to protect through their threats study, titled "Challenge of the '90s," would itself become the most seriously threatened landscape in Missouri at the dawn of the new millennium. The photo showed two forest-blanketed, time-gentled igneous knobs in the heart of the St. Francois Mountains, on the left Smoke Hill, recently acquired by the state, and on the right Church Mountain, leased to the Department of Natural Resources for park trail development by Union Electric Company of St. Louis (now AmerenUE). But on June 8, the Ameren Development Company, a subsidiary of Ameren Corporation, filed an application for a preliminary permit with the Federal Energy Regulatory Commission (FERC) for the Church Mountain Pumped Storage Project. It would consist of a 130-acre reservoir ringed by a 12,350-foot-long, 90-foot-high dam on the top of Church Mountain, a lower reservoir of 400 acres formed by a 1,900-foot-long, 100-foot high dam flooding several miles of Taum Sauk Creek, which has been designated a State Outstanding Resource Water, and associated tunnels, powerhouse, transmission lines, roads, and related facilities.

Leaders of the Missouri Parks Association, who have examined the proposal in the context of the resource values within the potentially impacted lands, consider this project the greatest threat to any unit of the park system in the nearly two decades of MPA's existence. The proposed project strikes at the heart of what MPA and the Missouri state park system stand for: preservation and interpretation of the state's most outstanding natural and cultural features and provision of outstanding recreational opportunities in keeping with the system's mission.

To be sure, the Ameren application seeks a *preliminary* permit—not one to authorize construction but a 36-month permit to proceed with economic and environmental studies and prepare engineering plans, including the drilling of boreholes and construction of access for drilling equipment. FERC has issued a notice dated July 5 allowing 60 days from that date for comments, protests, and motions to intervene. The Ameren application and instructions for commenting are available on line at ferc.gov, using the "RIMS" link and selecting docket # P-12049.

The Missouri Parks Association, in addition to filing comments and perhaps a motion to intervene in the FERC proceeding, aims to persuade Ameren executives, most of whom are longtime Missourians with extensive civic involvement, that the environment of decisionmaking and public consciousness of the values at stake in this area have changed dramatically since the late 1950s, when Union Electric first began to acquire land to build their their initial—and, at the time, highly innovative and widely hailed—Taum Sauk pumped-storage plant on Proffit Mountain just to the west of Church Mountain. In short, we aim to persuade them that this project at this time in this place is decidedly not in the public interest.

The Taum Sauk area in the heart of the St. Francois Mountains at the geologic core of the Ozarks is wildness incarnate. Indeed, at a time when Americans have come to value wild lands and are determined to protect what remnants remain, the wild character of these lands, with their remarkable biodiversity, unspoiled vistas, and outstanding recreational opportunities, has taken on surpassing cultural as well as natural value.

The region near the forks of Black River, including Taum Sauk and Church Mountains, was once part of the largest land grant ever made by French or Spanish authorities in Colonial Missouri. The Catholic priest at Ste. Genevieve, Father James Maxwell, was awarded four leagues square—150 square miles—in 1799 for the purpose of settling destitute Irish Catholics that he would rescue from "British tyranny" in order to help populate the interior of the territory. This was Missouri's original "Irish Wilderness," six decades before Father Hogan's Irish settlement in Oregon County. But the area was too inaccessible. Though Maxwell's heirs continued to litigate the unconfirmed grant as late as 1875, it remained remote and largely unproductive, sparsely settled by hardscrabble hunters and farmers who ran their stock on open range until the state finally outlawed the practice in 1967. The bottomlands along Black River were tillable and hence more heavily degraded by settlers and their stock, but the interior from Proffit and Church Mountains to Taum Sauk, including its principal drainage, Taum Sauk Creek, retained much of its biotic integrity.

When conservation sentiment began to sweep the country in the first decades of the twentieth century, this area at the heart of the St. Francois Mountains was recommended for acquisition as national forest in a 1914 federal reconnaissance. In the same year, a state senatorial committee investigating potential sites for state parks recommended two tracts totaling more than 15,000 acres in this area, in addition to Onondaga Cave and Ha Ha Tonka. Missouri lagged behind many other states in acquiring public conservation lands, however; it was not until 1924 that it began to purchase its first state parks—mostly big Ozarks springs—and it was the depression '30s before the state authorized purchase of national forest land, which nearly surrounded but did not include the Taum Sauk area.

In the 1940s, Leonard Hall proposed a 60,000-acre roadless wilderness preserve in the St. Francois Mountains, in a grand arc from Bell and Lindsey mountains in the north through Goggins on the west to Proffit, Church, Taum Sauk and on, but the plan faltered owing to multiple ownerships. Meanwhile, Joseph Desloge of St. Louis had persistently over the course of seventeen years assembled more than 2,300 acres and two miles of river frontage on the east fork of Black River that the Desloge Foundation donated to the State Park Board in 1955 as Johnson's Shut-Ins State Park, the first substantial tract in the Taum Sauk region in public ownership. That same year, the Conservation Department acquired Ketcherside Mountain State Forest east of Taum Sauk, and the park board continued its efforts to secure at least a portion of the 1.5 billion-year-old pink granite Elephant Rocks to the north, which had been suggested as a state park as early as 1924. A 135-acre remnant of the site would finally enter public ownership in 1966 as a gift from St. Joe Lead Company geologist John Stafford Brown.

Some time in the mid-1950s, Boy Scouts from Pilot Knob and Festus and their leaders began laying out a 28-mile trail through this rugged terrain from Elephant Rocks to Fort Davidson in Pilot Knob (which would become a state historic site in 1967), over Shepherd and Russell Mountains to Taum Sauk, then down to the base of Mina Sauk Falls, through the Devil's Toll Gate and west along Taum Sauk Creek for three miles, fording the creek some twenty times before ascending the south flank of Proffit Mountain, then down Sugar Camp Hollow to the East Fork Black River and Johnson's Shut-Ins State Park. The "Taum Sauk Trail" was dedicated in April 1958, and since then the "wildest walk in Missouri" has been a seminal experience in the lives of well over 25,000 Boy Scouts and countless others who have here taken the measure of the Ozarks and of themselves.

In the midst of this rediscovery of the wilderness and recreational values of the Taum Sauk region and the beginnings of public commitment to the area's preservation, the Union Electric Company became interested in the possibilities of storing excess power for periods of peak demand through a pumped storage hydroelectric plant. The technology, which had been used in Europe and Japan but seldom in the United States, resulted in a net energy drain, requiring about 3 kilowats to pump the water uphill for every 2 kilowats of hydroelectricity produced, but it could be profitable owing to the difference between peak and non-peak rates. UE did not initially focus on the St. Francois Mountains, however; rather it began its search for sites at Lake of the Ozarks, where it already had a ready-made lower reservoir. But for various reasons, including the distance from the St. Louis load center, they turned their attention to sites nearer St. Louis, settling by 1956 on Establishment Creek near the Mississippi River in Ste. Genevieve County. When that proved infeasible owing to geological deficiencies and the routing of the new Interstate 55, it occurred to them that they could get by with smaller reservoirs if they had the greatest possible head of water. That led them inevitably to the St. Francois Mountains.

Taum Sauk Mountain at 1772 feet is the highest point in Missouri, and Taum Sauk Creek flows through the deepest valley (in terms of elevation differential). We don't know why UE avoided Taum Sauk, but we can imagine that they appreciated the extent of public interest in this spectacular area. Instead they settled on nearby Proffit Mountain, which would accommodate a 55-acre upper reservoir, and, for a 395-acre lower reservoir, the East Fork Black River just below the new Johnson's Shut-Ins State Park. In December 1959 they awarded a construction contract and began quietly but quickly to purchase land—some 3,600 acres in 38 different tracts. Even before completing land acquisition they began construction of road access and leveling the mountain top, blasting and quarrying rock to the floor level of the reservoir and using the quarried granite for the reservoir walls.

In the late '50s and early '60s, UE operated in a relatively benign political environment. There was apparently no significant opposition to the project from conservation organizations or anyone else, but that is hardly surprising. This was the greatest era of water development project construction in U.S. history and most people regarded such projects as virtually unstoppable. Moreover, what organizational capacity there was in Missouri at the time was engaged in trying to find an alternative to proposed dams on the Current River, an effort that led by 1964 to establishment of the Ozark National Scenic Riverways. As further indication of the decisionmaking environment at the time, we may note that Union Electric completed construction of the project and dedicated it in October 1963 before hundreds of dignitaries who arrived on a special train from St. Louis—all while still arguing in the courts with the Federal Power Commission (FPC) over whether a federal license was required for the project. It was, the U.S. Supreme Court decided in 1965, but by then the plant was a fait accompli.

Even as the Taum Sauk plant was being brought on line, however, a controversy began over licensing of another, even larger pumped storage project at Storm King Mountain on the Hudson River that would permanently alter the decisionmaking environment for such proposals nationwide. Scenic Hudson Preservation Conference, a coalition of conservation groups, intervened in FPC licensing proceedings against the Consolidated Edison application and, when FPC granted the license, took the case to court, winning a landmark decision in 1965 that required the FPC to consider scenic and historic values equally with economic values. Though hearings and litigation would drone on for fifteen more years before Con Ed finally abandoned the project and donated the land for a park in an out-of-court settlement, the 1965 precedent clarified the public interest in natural and cultural resources, guaranteed citizen groups the right to argue for protection of environmental interests in court, and led in 1969 to passage of the National Environmental Policy Act.

In Missouri it would require several decades for conservationists, biologists and government officials to begin to appreciate the magnitude of wildland and ecological values at stake in the Taum Sauk area. Realization began to dawn as a result of roadless area surveys and natural area inventories initiated throughout the state in the 1970s. The former, which led to the designation of the 9,000-acre Bell Mountain Wilderness in 1980, impressed on conservationists the extent to which wild land had become a finite resource in Missouri. And the latter, which involved especially intensive study of state parks, revealed that Johnson's Shut-Ins had a more diverse array of plant species than any other park in the state, with over nine hundred recorded species of trees, shrubs, vines, grasses, wildflowers and ferns. A new emphasis on ecosystem management, supported by increased interest in conservation biology and restoration ecology, began to penetrate most federal and state land-managing agencies by the late 1980s, and with it came a heightened interest in and concern about biodiversity and the negative consequences of landscape fragmention on neotropical migrant songbirds and other species of plants and animals. By this time it was becoming understood that the Ozarks, especially at its core in the St. Francois Mountains, was a major center of endemism and biodiversity of national and even global significance.

With the new appreciation of the need to preserve and restore biodiversity on a landscape scale, in contrast to the earlier focus on protecting individual species in tiny natural areas, state park officials with the support and encouragement of DNR Director G. Tracy Mehan and the approval of Governor John Ashcroft initiated efforts in the late '80s to acquire substantial additional parkland in the Taum Sauk region. With legislative appropriations from the parks and soils tax at a time of highly constrained state budgets, DNR in 1990 alone acquired more than 3,000 acres in 35 separate parcels, and by the time the new park was dedicated in 1993 it was nearly 6,900 acres stretching from Taum Sauk Mountain all the way to Johnson's Shut-Ins. The new park was a tribute to more than twenty local landowners who willingly agreed to part with their property so that the land could be preserved intact for future generations, as well as to the citizens of Missouri who funded it to the tune of nearly $1.2 million. Union Electric cooperated by granting the state a 25-year lease on 1300 acres of Church Mountain for the development of hiking and backpacking trails.

Later in 1993, the park division acquired nearly 5,000 acres of wild land immediately west of Johnson's Shut-Ins, including all of Goggins Mountain and part of Bell Mountain, funded by a $1 million gift from the Richard King Mellon Foundation's American Land Conservation Program. The new tract was contiguous with the Bell Mountain Wilderness on the Mark Twain National Forest and it already contained twelve miles of the Ozark Trail, which had been developed in the mid-1980s from Bell Mountain all the way to Taum Sauk. Virtually the entire Goggins addition to Johnson's Shut-Ins was designated a State Wild Area (Missouri's largest) in 1995. By this time, Missouri had gone a long way toward realizing the vision of early park enthusiasts dating back to 1914 and even key parts of Leonard Hall's audacious wilderness proposal in the '40s, with more than 15,000 acres in the region now in state parks, more than 5,000 acres in the Conservation Department's Ketcherside and Proffit Mountain areas (the latter acquired in 1969), another 1340 acres surrounding the Lower Taum Sauk Reservoir leased by UE to the Conservation Department for management in 1967, 9,000 acres in Bell Mountain Wilderness, and other Mark Twain National Forest lands.

In 1996 the interagency Missouri Natural Areas Committee designated 7,028 acres at the core of this area with the greatest concentration of significant and exceptional features, including nearly all of Taum Sauk Mountain State Park and the Proffit Mountain Conservation Area, as the St. Francois Mountains Natural

Area. It included more than four miles of Taum Sauk Creek, the upper 5.5 miles of which had previously been designated by the Missouri Clean Water Commission as a State Outstanding Resource Water. The new natural area was by far the largest of more than 160 such areas officially designated in Missouri since 1971, in recognition of the exceptional quality of the Taum Sauk region and the new scientific emphasis on maintaining biodiversity through landscape-scale preservation. Ecologists had hoped to include also the 1300 acres of Church Mountain leased by UE to DNR, which was fully equal in quality to the rest, but Union Electric declined.

In recent years DNR has sought to acquire additional private lands in the vicinity, including two tracts along Taum Sauk Creek for which they were negotiating when it was rumored, in spring 2001, that AmerenUE had acquired them under threat of condemnation and was studying the feasibility of constructing a second pumped storage reservoir on Church Mountain. Not until the application for preliminary permit became available in mid-July could the dimensions of the proposed project be confirmed by DNR, MPA, or other concerned parties, even though it is now clear that some park land on Church Mountain would be directly impacted by the dam for the upper reservoir and other park land along Taum Sauk Creek would be flooded.

Since the Governor and DNR have not yet taken an official position on the Church Mountain Project, it remains for concerned citizens to express their views on the project's potential impact on public interest values in the area to state and federal officials as well as to Ameren.

Some who are aware that there is already one UE hydro plant in the area wonder whether a second one nearby would make much difference. The existing upper reservoir—named Taum Sauk even though it is on Proffit Mountain—is 55 acres, compared with 130 acres and more than double the generating capacity for the Church Mountain project. Moreover, the existing reservoir is on a secondary summit of Proffit Mountain and it is hidden from many vantage points by Church Mountain and by the higher dome of Proffit to the north. By contrast, Church Mountain has only one dome and it is directly in the line of sight from virtually everywhere, especially from Taum Sauk Mountain and Mina Sauk Falls, visited by thousands of people every year who seek "the wildest vista in the Ozarks." It is also visible from nearly everywhere along the Ozark and Boy Scout trails, from both the valley and the high country.

The existing lower reservoir on East Fork Black River south of Proffit is not visible from anywhere in the interior of the Taum Sauk area, while the new reservoir on Taum Sauk Creek would be visible from virtually everywhere. Moreover, it would flood out more than a mile of the historic Boy Scout trail in the valley, making it impossible to use a route that most scouts and many other hikers prefer to the higher Ozark Trail, because of the beauty of the creek and access to water, shade, less rugged terrain, and a three-mile shorter route from Taum Sauk to Johnson's Shut-Ins. If the new reservoir fluctuates as much as the existing one, up to fifteen feet twice daily in hot weather, it could also be a hazard to recreationists.

Even more destructive to the public interest than the massive impact on esthetic, cultural and recreational values would be the ecological impact of major fragmentation in the highest quality area that could be identified in Missouri in which to preserve a landscape-scale mosaic of the natural communities that make this part of the Ozarks one of the greatest centers of biodiversity on the continent. The impact on the aquatic and riparian communities in Taum Sauk Creek valley would be devastating—and this is a stream that retains a more natural riparian zone than practically any stream in the Ozarks, including the East Fork Black River, which was always more accessible to settlement and livestock. The St. Francois Mountains Natural Area and Church Mountain itself, which ecologists believe is of equal quality, is thought to be more important for the preservation of biodiversity even than Johnson's Shut-Ins, with its more than 900 plant species, because it has suffered less disturbance and has been much less fragmented. Although the area has yet to be studied as intensively as Johnson's Shut-Ins, it is known to harbor at least seven state-listed species of conservation concern, including the federally listed Mead's Milkweed.

There can be no question of the vast importance of the central "high peaks" region of the St. Francois Mountains, of which Church Mountain and Taum Sauk Creek are so integral a part. These ancient rounded mountains are so critical for their inherent natural history value, but they also have played an historical role of great importance; they are a time honored scenic treasure, and an enduring resource of wholesome recreation and spiritual inspiration. They are for many Missourians and visitors to Missouri the core of what remains of the oldest, wildest Ozark landscape. All of this has been reinforced through the latter twentieth century by a massive investment from the state of Missouri in the acquisition and protection of these lands.

The current proposal by Ameren to decapitate Church Mountain and drown the valley of Taum Sauk Creek would violate not just a pleasant Ozark ridge and hollow—it would gut a key visual and natural heritage resource of all Missourians. This situation might seem to doom Missourians to an inevitable and disastrous confrontation between one of the most powerful and respected utility companies in the state, on the one hand, and the united voices of civic and conservation responsibility on the other.

We dare to hope that it need not be so. Whatever planning considerations led Ameren to broach this preliminary proposal, it is only reasonable to assume that it was done without a full and acute awareness of the enormity of the heritage values that would be destroyed. The responsibility now lies with all of us to bring these factors to their attention, forcefully but respectfully. Only preliminary plans have been drawn up. There is plenty of time for Ameren to withdraw this plan and find alternatives. Ameren can in fact emerge from this issue with a heroic act of public citizenship to its credit. That is our hope. That is our goal.

What You Can Do?

To make the case for widespread citizen concern about the threats posed to the Taum Sauk area by Ameren's proposed Church Mountain Project, MPA encourages its members and other friends of state parks to express their views in a letter to FERC by August 27 (comments must be **received** on or before September 3, which is Labor Day), with copies to Governor Holden, Ameren CEO Charles W. Mueller, and the Missouri Parks Association (for our information). **Please include the title "COMMENTS" (in caps) and Project Number P-12049-000 on your comments to FERC.**

• David P. Boergers, Secretary, Federal Energy Regulatory Commission, 888 First Street NE, Washington, DC 20426 (send **original and eight copies** to Boergers and **one additional copy** to Director, Division of Hydropower Administration and Compliance, Federal Energy Regulatory Commission, at the above address). Comments may be filed electronically—see instructions at *www.ferc.gov* under the "e-filing" link—but this may be difficult.

• Governor Bob Holden, Missouri State Capitol Building Room 216, P.O. Box 720, Jefferson City, MO 65102-0720 (**one copy**). Electronic communications may be sent through *www.gov.state.mo.us/contact.htm* under "Express Your Opinion."

• Charles W. Mueller, Chairman, President and CEO, Ameren Corporation, One Ameren Plaza, 1901 Chouteau Avenue, P.O. Box 66149, St. Louis, MO 63166-6149 (**one copy**).

• Missouri Parks Association, c/o Susan Flader, 917 Edgewood Ave., Columbia, MO 65203 (**one copy**).

Personal letters expressing your interest in the area, including experiences you may have had there, are best, but mention also the threat to Taum Sauk and Johnson's Shut-Ins state parks and to the St. Francois Mountains Natural Area. And tell your friends about the problem, encouraging them to write. If you a member of an organization that might be interested, encourage the organization also to write.

If you receive this information too late to meet the FERC deadline of September 3, please write anyway, as the deadline may be extended and the copies (or original letters) to the governor and the Ameren CEO will still be valuable evidence of citizen concern. An expression of views from a wide range of citizens and organizations will help to turn the tide.

INDEX